THE CHURCH UNDER ATTACK

A Closer Look At Revelation

I dedicate this book to my kind friend Tim H
Whose ongoing help and suggestions
Have been a godsend for me
As I wrote this book

THE CHURCH UNDER ATTACK

In the midst of the lampstands I saw one like the Son of Man, clothed with a long robe and with a golden sash across his chest. His head and his hair were white as white wool, white as snow; his eyes were like a flame of fire, his feet were like burnished bronze, refined as in a furnace, and his voice was like the sound of many waters. In his right hand he held seven stars, and from his mouth came a sharp, two-edged sword, and his face was like the sun shining with full force.

When I saw him, I fell at his feet as though dead. But he placed his right hand on me, saying, "Do not be afraid; I am the first and the last, and the living one. I was dead, and see, I am alive forever and ever; and I have the keys of Death and of Hades. Now write what you have seen, what is, and what is to take place after this. As for the mystery of the seven stars that you saw in my right hand, and the seven golden lampstands: the seven stars are the angels of the seven churches, and the seven lampstands are the seven churches".

Revelation 1:12-20

A catalogue record for this book is available from the British Library.

First published winter 2023-2024.

ISBN 978-1-916722-09-5

Designed by Tim Underwood   timund@hotmail.com
Printed by Sarsen Press   22 Hyde Street, Winchester, SO23 7DR

CONTENTS

AUTHOR'S PREFACE

Many Christians today are frightened at the very thought of studying the book of Revelation. It is such a strange book, with its symbolical language and bizarre visions. There is a Lamb that appears on several occasions, and he has seven eyes and seven horns. There is a great red dragon with ten horns and seven heads, each with a diadem on it, and he has two accomplices. One is a beast akin to the dragon, with seven heads and ten horns, each with a diadem on it. The other has two horns like a lamb, but speaks like a dragon. What good could possibly come to anyone who reads a book like this? The answer is a great deal, because Revelation paints a realistic picture of the world in which we live.

Near the start there are thoughtful pen portraits of seven churches, and later on there are further indications that during the Christian era there will be attempts made by the forces of evil to infiltrate and lead astray the worldwide church. It is sadly the case that many Christians, who congregate to worship God the Father and his Son Jesus Christ, and who study his word and pray for the needs of the suffering world, are increasingly realising that they are being persecuted by anti-Christian forces and sidelined in their own congregations. It is as if the true church is being fiercely attacked by giant many-headed monsters of evil. And the book of Revelation was written precisely to encourage the persecuted people of God.

The main decision anyone writing a commentary on this book has to make is how to interpret it. Did its author write it primarily for people of his own time, or for anyone throughout the Christian era, or for those who will live just prior to the end of the world? I believe it was for all three classes of people. And how do you interpret the timespans mentioned, like the three and a half years or forty-two months or 1,260 days? Or, for that matter, the thousand years or 'millennium' that has caused such controversy? In this commentary all of these are considered to refer to the entire Christian era. This view is not held by all Christians, but it suggests that the book of Revelation is not a weird one-off book. It provides the same theology and teaching as the rest of the Bible.

This has seemed to me the paramount principle to follow in interpreting such a visionary book. It fits in well with all of the Old Testament and the rest of the New, and it bears the same God-centred message as the rest of scripture. Its style is unusual because it belongs to a genre which we call apocalyptic literature. Its author wrote an apocalypse because this would conceal his extremely subversive message from the persecuting authorities, and bring much needed encouragement to his readers, many of whom were undergoing severe persecution.

May the book of Revelation continue to sustain those who are weary, and bring fresh hope to many bruised reeds and dimly burning wicks within the church.

HOW TO READ THIS BOOK

The purpose of this book is to help the reader to understand the meaning of the text of the New Testament book of Revelation. Christians believe that this book was written to help the church during times of affliction and persecution. The book claims to be a series of reflections, songs and visions communicated by angelic messengers and inspired by God himself, and it is therefore best read in a prayerful frame of mind, with an ardent desire to be visited and helped by God. You may or may not find the following approach helpful:

Begin with a short, simple prayer. Ask God to help you to learn about himself, about Jesus Christ the Lamb of God, and about yourself from your reading of this amazing visionary book that was written some 2,000 years ago. Ask God's Son, Jesus our Saviour and Lord, to make himself real to you as you read the inspired words which point to him. The Holy Spirit of God will delight to answer these prayers. He will teach you about God and make Christ real to you.

Then thoughtfully read the section which you have reached (there are 52 in all). If possible, use a good translation of the Bible such as the New Revised Standard Version, the New International Version or the English Standard Version. In this book, all the quotations from the Bible are taken from the New Revised Standard Version, and the commentary is based on the English text of this translation.

Begin by reading the Biblical text. As you do so, remember that you are reading a book that millions of people down the ages have regarded as the word of God. If anything strikes you, make a mental note of it (or even better, a written one). If something does not seem to make sense, think about it. Then read the verse-by-verse commentary. Go through each verse of the section once more, comparing your thoughts with those in the commentary. It may be that the commentary will clear up some of the difficulties you may have. Then read the meditation at the end of the section. Finally, try to think of one thought or idea that you would like to remember during that day. Maybe at some convenient moment later on, think about it and apply it to your own life.

These are just suggestions. What is important is to read the book of Revelation and understand what God was saying through it to the Christians who first read it and, in the light of this, what its meaning will be for us today. Hopefully this book may help you to do this – and if it does, then it will then have succeeded in its main purpose.

INTRODUCTION

The Purpose of the Book of Revelation

The book of Revelation brings both the New Testament and the Bible as a whole to a close. It is the climax of God's revelation of himself to us. Like the rest of the Bible, it points us to Jesus Christ, and in particular it spells out in pictorial images his final triumph over evil. It was probably written towards the end of the first century so as to encourage the seven churches in the Roman Province of Asia (now Western Turkey), and indeed Christians everywhere, with the certain hope that Christ's victory would also be theirs, provided that they remained faithful to him in spite of all the forces that were massed together to fight against them.

Those forces were mighty indeed. Until around the year AD 60 those who were spreading the good news of Jesus Christ abroad could count on a neutral if not a benevolent or protective stance from the Roman Empire. But after AD 60 the new Christian faith ceased to be a *religio licita*, and followers of Christ had no right to exist until the time of the Emperor Constantine some 250 years later. In AD 64 Nero attacked the Christians, perhaps out of personal motives of malice, or in order to use them as scapegoats, and subsequent emperors were officially hostile towards this sect which had acquired a subversive and anti-social reputation. The Jews out of whose ranks the Christians had grown and spread were also opposed to a group who laid such stress on a crucified Messiah and Saviour. But perhaps the most dangerous threat to Christianity would come from false teachers who were inveigling their way into the church. Their teaching would pervert the grace of God into licentiousness, and they would ultimately deny that Jesus Christ was the only Saviour and Lord.

During the terrible years of persecution and of being forced to be a largely silent and underground church, the book of Revelation proclaimed words of reassurance and hope to suffering Christians, but after AD 312 the persecutions died down, and there were some prolonged seasons of comfort and ease for the church, in which the book of Revelation was downgraded to being merely a book of cyphers and puzzles. In our own time it has become the object of disputes between various schools of interpretation, and many church leaders in effect dismiss it because of its uncomfortable background, declaring it to be unworthy of study by modern Christians. This very downgrading of it is, of course, an example of trouble or persecution arising on account of the word (Mk 4:17), and it is precisely when this happens that Revelation again becomes what it really is, a living word from God, full of encouragement and strength for those who are finding that "all who want to live a godly life in Christ Jesus will be persecuted" (2 Tim 3:12).

This pattern is being replicated in our own day. The church flourishes in places where "the rulers take counsel together against the Lord and his Anointed One" (Ps 2:2). This brings suffering and even martyrdom to many Christians, who are steadfast in their obedience to the word of God and the testimony of Jesus Christ. But in the affluent west the godly remnant in the church is also suffering because of the increasing pressure to conform to the relativism and the tolerance of evil that are pervasive features of 21st century life. Many western countries today are marked by an increasing intolerance of any belief in absolute truth. Without such truth there can be no absolute moral standards, and it becomes more and more difficult to believe in a God who is absolutely holy as well as wonderfully loving.

The church is on the whole capitulating to current trends, and the result is that any believers who wish to take the standards of the Bible seriously are sidelined or even completely marginalised. It is a curious paradox that the same religious leaders who seek to tolerate every group under the sun are themselves intolerant of those who do not tolerate what is unholy. For the despised remnant who pursue holy living, the message of Revelation is that although the spiritual warfare that the followers of Christ must engage in may be long-lasting, the decisive battle has already been won, so the final victory is assured. The followers of the One who was crucified and risen are called to persevere in good works and in a faithful confession of Christ, and to count it a privilege when they face suffering or even death. It is not unreasonable for God to place this yoke on their shoulders, for by it they are united to Christ, who won the decisive battle at the cost of his own life blood. We are assured that all power has been given to the risen Christ, and not to national or church leaders. It is Jesus who is the Lord of history, and he will ensure that those who live and die for him will receive their reward at his coming.

The New Testament apocalypse

The book of Revelation is the principal Christian apocalypse. An apocalypse is a special genre of religious writing in which a supernatural being reveals cosmic mysteries or the future to a human intermediary. There are a few apocalypses in the Old Testament, the main ones being Isaiah chapters 24-27 and Daniel chapters 7-12. In the New Testament each of the first three gospels contains an apocalyptic section (Mt 24, Mk 13, Lk 21:5-36), but there is only one full-length apocalypse, the book of Revelation, with numerous visions of Christ that are presented to us as having been revealed by God to a servant of his whose name was John.

John Stott wrote that these visions of Christ make the book of Revelation like a picture gallery with many portraits of him. We see him as the first and the last, as the one who was dead and is alive forever, as the overseer of his church, as both the lion and the lamb, as the one who shares the heavenly throne with God, as the one who controls history, as the one who calls all people to repent, as the one who triumphs over evil, as the thief in the night, as the King of kings and Lord of lords, as the judge who will officiate at the last judgement, and as the heavenly host and bridegroom. We who are the humble followers of this incomparable Christ will want to do justice to his portrait gallery, studying each depiction carefully in order to appreciate all of Christ's excellences, and thus get to know him better. We shall catch many glimpses of his glory, and this will inspire us in our worship of him and in our efforts to live lives that are fully pleasing to him.

How should this book be interpreted?

Many books have been written claiming to possess the code or cipher that will unravel the complicated visions in the book of Revelation and thereby bring to light the date and details of the end of the world. They have proved to be fruitless undertakings, which is hardly surprising in view of the fact that Jesus himself, speaking of the end of the world, said to his disciples, "But about that day and hour no one knows, neither the angels of heaven, nor the Son, but only the Father. Keep awake therefore, for you do not know on what day your Lord is coming" (Mt 24:36, 42). So Revelation is not a book that is written with a secret code that we are challenged to discover, and which will reveal every secret under the sun.

Instead, its purpose is to encourage us to stay awake and to keep on renouncing impiety and worldly passions, and in the present evil age to continue to lead lives that are self-controlled, upright and godly, while we wait for the blessed hope and the manifestation of the glory of our great God and Saviour Jesus Christ (see Titus 2:12-13). It is as we read Revelation that we shall receive new and fresh visions of Christ, which will inspire us to continue to be his militant warriors in this fallen and desperately needy world. But how are we to read it? What are the principles that we might follow in order to discover its message for us today?

(a) **This book's literary genre should be borne in mind.** It is not a historical book, although some history may be discerned in its pages. It is not a prophetic book, although some of its declarations are prophetic. It is not a book of psalms, although it contains some wonderful psalms of praise. It is not a wisdom book, although we shall be wise if we read it and do what it says. It is an *apocalypse*, and as such it is full of visions and unveilings, many of which are symbolic.

We may well ask, why did John use so much strange symbolism in this book? There are two obvious reasons. The first is that John is dealing with truths about God that are so powerful and transcendent that they would fall flat if he had used straightforward prose. The second is that John's writing is of a seditious nature. He commends any Christians who refuse to worship the Emperor, and he outlines the overthrow of the worldly Empire. Such statements needed to be veiled.

The symbolism used by John is best understood by comparing it to the teaching in the rest of the Bible, which is consistent in the way it humbles sinners and exalts God who is our Creator, Saviour and Strengthener. It is confusing and even grotesque at times to take the symbolism literally. For example, the blood of the Lamb is a symbol of Christ's death by which he bore away our sins, so for us to wear clothing that has been made white in the blood of the Lamb simply means that we are made righteous in God's sight by trusting in the one who died for our sins on the cross.

(b) **This book speaks about the past, the present and the future**. It would be a mistake to concentrate its focus on just one or two of these three. The *preterist* interpretation regards the book as referring to the past, to the rise of the Christian movement, the opposition it encountered, and the eventual defeat of the Roman Empire. Most modern commentators adopt some variant of this interpretation. The *historicist* interpretation is to see in the book the story of the establishment and expansion of the Christian church, and to point out its good and bad aspects in our own time. And the *futurist* interpretation looks for the book's fulfilment in the years leading up to the return of Christ. But the Bible as a whole speaks of all three – past, present and future. Our understanding of the book of Revelation will likewise be impoverished if we limit its scope to only one or two of them.

It has been said by someone who may have been a mathematician that the lives we live in the present are like an ellipse that has not one centre but two foci, the past and the future. And the last book of the Bible brings the Bible to a natural climax by making it clear that it is our faith in the finished work of Christ in the past, and our sure hope of the final consummation that God is preparing for us in the future, that are the two great stimuli for us to lead a life of love in the present. We may therefore combine the preterist, historicist and futurist views by adopting a parallelist interpretation. Each successive section of Revelation recapitulates the whole period between Christ's first and second advents, and each concludes with scenes of judgement and salvation. John sees the sections as if they happened one after the other, but in fact they are not successive. They are repetitions of the same pattern, but their depictions become more intense and powerful as we move forward. As soon as John ends one section he goes back on his tracks and covers the same ground all over again, but now he views it from another angle. And after we have read all of the sections we shall, like John, have a clear overview of the complete picture. We shall know all that God wishes us to know.

(c) **This book celebrates God's glorious victory.** It describes the familiar and intense conflict that is going on throughout our lives. It is the war between God and Satan, between the Lamb and the dragon, between the church and the world, between the holy city of Jerusalem and the proud city of Babylon, between the pure bride of Christ and the great harlot, and between those who are marked with the name of Christ and those who are marked with the number of the beast. This war is unremitting, and it is a recurring temptation to try and escape to a secret hideaway, but we who follow Christ are called to be like our Lord and to engage fully in it. The book of Revelation discloses the final result of the war. Christ has already won the decisive battle, and we are asked to help him in the remaining skirmishes that will culminate in the final victory. D-Day has already happened, complete victory is now certain, and V-Day is imminent but still in the future.

(d) **This book focuses on Jesus Christ and exalts him.** Of course every book of the Bible does this in its own way, but there is a real sense in which Revelation is one of the most Christian books, just as Christ-centred as the four gospels. As we have seen, it offers us a number of portraits of Christ, giving us a rounded picture of him as our Creator, Saviour and Lord. The book begins with the words "The revelation of Jesus Christ". Here *revelation* is the English translation of the Greek word *apokalupsis* which means an *unveiling*. Previously the greatness and glory of Christ were partially hidden away, as if they were covered with a veil. But now the veil has been removed and anyone who cares to do so may see for him or herself how wonderful and great Christ is, our Teacher, Saviour, Lord, and God. Apocalyptic writing takes us behind the scenes and discloses unseen truths that interpret history and determine the future. It brings hope in times of despair and gives us a complete worldview that makes sense of everything.

This is precisely what the persecuted church needs more than anything else. Not further prophecies about the present or the future, not a coded presentation of church history, but a revelation of our one and only God and Saviour Jesus Christ, the hope and the focus of anyone who by the grace of God forms part of God's holy remnant. The real Christ, the Christ of the Bible, the gospels and the book of Revelation, is the Christ who emptied himself of all his divine privileges and came down to be one of us, living a human life with no sin or selfishness or deceit. He suffered the opposition and rejection of evil people, and was crucified for us. On the third day he was raised from the dead by God the Father, with whom he now reigns in heaven. From there he keeps watch over us and intercedes for us. One day he will return in power and great glory to consummate his victory over death and evil, and to bring to completion the work he has begun in our lives.

Who was John?

We know that the writer of Revelation was called John (1:4, 9; 22:8), and that he endured widespread persecution. He had been banished to the island of Patmos just off the coast of what is now Western Turkey (1:9). The way he refers to himself as John without any qualification points to him being John the Apostle and Gospel-writer. Only one John was distinguished enough to call himself by this name and not give further details of who he was. The general air of authority which marks the book of Revelation accords with an apostolic authorship.

In early Christian literature the references to the authorship of Revelation are unanimous in ascribing the book to John the Apostle. As early as AD 145 Justin Martyr wrote this in one of his *Dialogues*, and he was soon followed by Irenaeus, Clement of Alexandria, Tertullian, and by the author of the Muratorian Fragment. The early church fathers accepted this ascription. The solid historical tradition that John lived to a ripe old age in the city of Ephesus fits in with the likeliest date of writing the book of Revelation, which is during the persecution of Christians promoted by the Emperor Domitian in AD 90-96.

The main objections to John the Apostle being the author of Revelation are ones of style. The style of Revelation is quite different from that of John's Gospel and the first epistle of John. The latter two do seem to come from the same hand and are written in simple but faultless Greek. They display considerable literary skill in their diction, their reasoning, and the constructions in which they are expressed. The book of Revelation, on the other hand, contains many linguistic irregularities, some barbarous idioms and a few downright solecisms. These differences may, of course, have arisen on account of the special genre of Revelation. To describe visions one makes use of poetic language which employs uncommon words. The writer of Revelation was "in the spirit" (1:10), in an excited state. We would not have expected calm detachment and polished prose from him when he described his terrifying and tremendous visions. Furthermore, we should not rule out the influence of an amanuensis or secretary. We know that the Apostle Paul dictated some of his letters to a friendly scribe, and it is not impossible that a cultured disciple of the Apostle John wrote the fourth Gospel in polished Greek at John's dictation, while John himself wrote the book of Revelation in his rough Hebraic Greek. It is possible to account for the differences in style while holding that the Apostle John is the author of the fourth Gospel, three epistles and Revelation.

Apart from the differences in style between John's Gospel and Revelation, there are also several similarities, notably in the designation of Jesus Christ as the *Logos* or Word of God. Also, the predilection for using heptads (i.e. groupings of seven) in Revelation continues a trend that was set in the Gospel.

Why does the Bible end with this book?

The book of Revelation is the most appropriate ending for the library which we call the Bible and regard as God's word. God inspired some forty people during a period of around 1,500 years to write the books of the Bible. They are there to reveal to us what we could never find out for ourselves – who made the universe and why, what the one true God is like, what his good purposes are for us, how greatly we have fallen from his grace, and his wonderful plan to save us from our selfishness and sins, along with their terrible consequences. It is therefore right that the Bible should end with a book that presents Christ as the special envoy sent by God to accomplish our salvation, to be the Lord of history, and finally to wind up the present evil age and inaugurate a new one in which there will be no evil. For Christ has triumphed over the evil one, and his victory is described in the book of Revelation in all its glory and wonder and wisdom.

How else could the Bible have ended? If the book of Revelation had never been written, the Bible might have ended uncomfortably with the book of Jude. Our final inspired book would have left us with, on the one hand, the unresolved chaos of multitudes of wickedly-minded people who have committed many ungodly deeds in an appallingly ungodly way, and also spoken many harsh things against God; and on the other hand, the unending dilemma of saints who must continually contend for the faith that was once for all entrusted to them. With such an ending the ultimate issue would have seemed to be in doubt. But thanks to the book of Revelation the Bible closes with the clear-cut triumph of good over evil.

Through the victory of the Lamb God has defeated evil once and for all, and his redemptive purposes have attained their fulfilment.

The importance of the book of Revelation

Leon Morris began his superb commentary on Revelation by observing that it is one of the most difficult books of the Bible. It is full of strange symbolism. There are curious beasts with unusual numbers of heads. There are some extraordinary events like the turning of one third of the sea into blood, which are impossible to envisage. Modern readers find it strange. They are moreover turned away by the fantastic schemes of prophecy which some exegetes profess to find in it, and whose ingenuity is only matched by their improbability.

The result is that for most modern people Revelation remains a closed book. Apart from one or two passages like the messages to the seven churches (chapters 2 and 3), or the description of the heavenly Jerusalem (chapters 21 and 22), it remains largely unread. We know where it is in the Bible. We recognise that it is part of the Canon of Scripture and therefore we accord it formal recognition. But we remain uneasy and fail to make use of it. We turn our backs on its mysteries and luxuriate in John's Gospel or the Epistle to the Romans.

This is a great pity. The book of Revelation has much to teach us in the 21st century. Its theology of power is of the utmost importance to an age as concerned with the problems of power as is our own. J.B. Phillips, who translated all of the New Testament into modern English, described what a thrill it was for him to translate Revelation in particular: "In this book the translator is carried into another dimension – he has but the slightest foothold in the time-and-space world with which he is familiar. He is carried, not into some never-never land of fancy, but into the ever-ever land of God's eternal values and judgements".

It is of the utmost importance for modern people that we do not lose touch with the eternal realities that are presented to us in Revelation. Perhaps in no other age has its essential teaching been so important. We are distressed by the problems of power and by our own powerlessness to respond to them. The book of Revelation was written to an enfeebled minority who were being oppressed by people who were much more powerful than they were. It has been subtitled, not unjustly, "A theology of power". Nothing will settle us and calm our nerves, nothing will lift us up and renew our vision, and nothing will speak to our deeply troubled age as profoundly as the truth that the risen and triumphant Christ holds the keys of death and Hades.

The structure of Revelation

The 22 chapters of the book may be divided up as follows:

(**a**) Chapter 1. John introduces himself and his great theme:
Christ the faithful witness and the firstborn from the dead.

(**b**) Chapters 2 and 3. The seven churches:
Christ measures and assesses his church here on earth.

(**c**) Chapters 4 and 5. The throne, the scroll and the Lamb:
Christ shares God's throne in heaven.

(**d**) Chapters 6 and 7. The seven seals, the servants and worshippers:
Christ controls the course of history.

(**e**) Chapters 8-11. The seven trumpets and the two witnesses:
Christ calls for repentance through the suffering church.

(**f**) Chapters 12-14. The seven significant signs:
Christ stands by his people as they overcome the devil.

(**g**) Chapters 15-18, 19:1-10. The call to stay awake and be ready:
Christ will come suddenly and unexpectedly.

(**h**) Chapters 19:11-21 and 20. The final defeat of evil:
Christ comes riding victoriously on a white horse.

(**i**) Chapters 21 and 22. The new earth, city and garden:
Christ the bridegroom comes to claim his bride.

ACKNOWLEDGEMENTS

I would like to thank Andrew, Tim H and Robert for reading through the text of my book. They made comments that resulted in numerous changes for the better. Andrew came up with some amazing insights that I had not come across in any commentary, one of which I have cited with his permission. Tim H read the early drafts during a period of illness and frailty, and he checked the cross-references. Robert was happy to collaborate at a particularly busy time in his career. I am very greatly indebted to all three of them. I am also grateful to Robert's father Donald, whom I have not met, but who some years ago suggested via Robert that I should write a commentary on Revelation. At first I dismissed the idea, but as the months went by and as I mulled it over, it became ever more firmly lodged in my mind, until the adventure that this work would entail captured my imagination. Thank you, Donald, for sowing that tiny seed.

On a similar note, Elizabeth devoted many hours of her time to hearing me read out every word I had written, and at the end of each session she would make the hesitant offer, "Well, I could say two or three things if you like" – and of course further improvements resulted. Andrew, Tim H, Robert and Elizabeth should not be blamed for flaws that remain on account of my ineptitude or stubbornness.

In my writing, I have been influenced by several books I have read and by some sermons I have heard. There are some which I must acknowledge openly.

First of all I must declare my huge debt to Leon Morris for his magnificent commentary on Revelation, from which I have gleaned literally hundreds of small but important insights into the text. I have made many my own and included them in my verse-by-verse commentary in this book. I have also quoted him directly on several occasions. I consider his commentary to be easily the most helpful ever written on the last book of the Bible, and it is the one which I would recommend to anyone who wishes to make a careful study of this difficult book.

Two other commentaries that I found very helpful were those by F.F. Bruce (in *A New Testament Commentary* published by Pickering & Inglis) and John Stott (included in his superb book *The Incomparable Christ*). I also learnt a great deal from studying the scholarly commentaries by George Beasley-Murray, George Eldon Ladd and Robert Mounce. The popular commentaries by Richard Bewes and Phil Moore provided further wonderful insights, and the one by Tom Wright was an exciting and interesting view by a distinguished modern theologian. I have also included a few quotations from certain other commentaries cited in my text but not included in the Bibliography that follows this section. Two superb books which are not full commentaries on Revelation are John Stott's unparalleled *What Christ thinks of the Church* (on chapters 1-3), and Robert Coleman's *Singing with the Angels* (on the songs of worship in Revelation).

For the writing of certain of my "meditations" I acknowledge the invaluable help from certain talks or sermons preached by John Stott and from some of the books in the Bibliography, as follows:

III to XI – my work on the seven churches of Revelation 2 and 3 would have been greatly impoverished without the invaluable help of John Stott's great little book *What Christ thinks of the Church*. He wrote it back in 1958, and it has never been superseded.

IX – from a sermon by John Stott on Rev 3:7-8, "*Open doors of opportunity*".

XI – from a sermon by John Stott on Lk 4:14-30, "*The local boy*".

XII – from a sermon by John Stott on Rev 4, "*God the Creator and Sustainer*".

XIII – from a sermon by John Stott on Rev 5, "*The closed scroll*".

XIV – from *The Incomparable Christ*, pp. 185-187.

XVIII – from a talk by John Stott given at the Keswick Convention in 1972, "*The Spirit in the believer*".

XIX – from a sermon by John Stott on Rev 7, "*Who survives the tribulation?*"

XLIII – from a sermon by John Stott on Lk 12:13-21, "*Rich man, poor man*".

XXVIII – from a sermon by John Stott on Rev 12, "*War in Heaven*".

XLV – from a sermon by John Stott on Rev 19:11-16, "*God's word of judgment*".

Appendix 3 – from J. Oswald Sanders' book, "*The best that I can be*".

Finally, I am once again hugely grateful to Tim U who did such a marvellous job of the typesetting, enlivening the text with his patient use of two distinct typefaces, and to Tony the owner and manager of Sarsen Press, who guided me with great kindness through the final steps of the process of getting this book into print. Not only did they both do a superlative job, but they did so in a way that enhanced the sense of adventure that I felt throughout the adventure. If the result is pleasing and attractive, it is thanks to the delightful way in which they brought the project to its consummation.

FOR FURTHER READING

Beasley-Murray, G. R., *The Revelation* (The New Bible Commentary Revised, IVP, 1970)

Bewes, R. T., *The Church Overcomes* (Mowbray, 1984)

Bruce, A. B., *The Training of the Twelve* (T & T Clark, 1877)

Bruce, F. F., *The Gospel of John (Eerdmans, 2018)*

Bruce, F. F., *The Real Jesus* (Hodder & Stoughton, 1985)

Bruce, F. F., *The Revelation to John* (A New Testament Commentary, Pickering & Inglis, 1969).

Coleman, R. E., *Singing with the Angels* (Fleming H. Revell Co., 1998)

Edersheim, A., *The Life and Times of Jesus the Messiah* (Eerdmans, 1971)

Eldon Ladd, G., *A Commentary on the Revelation of John* (Eerdmans, 1972)

France, R. T., *Matthew* (TNTC, 1985)

France, R. T., *The Gospel of Mark* (NIGTC, Eerdmans, 2002)

Gordon, S. D., *Quiet Talks on Power* (Fleming H. Revell Co., undated)

Gordon, S. D., *Quiet Talks on Service* (Fleming H. Revell Co., undated)

Griffith Thomas, W. H., *Christianity is Christ* (Longmans, 1916)

Lane, W. L., *The Gospel of Mark* (Eerdmans, 1974)

Meyer, F. B., *Elijah* (Lakeland, 1972)

Moore, P., *Straight to the Heart of Revelation* (Monarch Books 2010)

Morris, L., *Luke* (TNTC, 1974)

Morris, L., *The Cross in the New Testament* (Eerdmans, 1965)

Morris, L., *The Gospel according to Matthew* (Eerdmans, 1992)

Morris, L., *The Gospel according to John* (Eerdmans, 1971)

Morris, L., *Revelation* (IVP, 1969)

Mounce, R. H., *The Book of Revelation* (Eerdmans, 1977)

Naismith, A., *1200 Notes, Quotes and Anecdotes* (Pickering & Inglis, 1963)

Naismith, A., *1200 More Notes, Quotes and Anecdotes* (Pickering & Inglis, 1975)

Sanders, J. O., *Satan no Myth* (Lakeland, 1974)

Sanders, J. O., *The best that I can be* (OMF Books, 1976)
Packer, J. I., *Knowing God* (Hodder & Stoughton, 1973)
Skinner, J., *Prophecy and Religion* (CUP, 1948)
Stalker, J., *Imago Christi* (Hodder & Stoughton, 1901)
Stalker, J., *The Life of Jesus Christ* (T & T Clark, undated)
Stott, J. R. W., *Basic Christianity* (IVP, 1958)
Stott, J. R. W., *Epistles of John* (TNTC, 1964)
Stott, J. R. W., *The Cross of Christ* (IVP, 1986)
Stott, J. R. W., *The Incomparable Christ* (IVP, 2001)
Stott, J. R. W., *What Christ thinks of the Church* (Lutterworth Press, 1958)
Wright, N. T., *Revelation for Everyone* (SPCK, 2011)

COMMENTARY

I

1:1-8 Prologue to the Book of Revelation

The book of Revelation begins with an introduction and blessing, the customary greetings from the writer, a humble invocation, a challenge to look forward to the return of Christ, and a divine authentication. The concise and rapid-fire nature of these initial statements prepares the mind of the reader for the vision that follows, and sets the scene for the rest of the book.

1. The very first word, *apokalupsis*, is translated as *the revelation*. It means an uncovering of something that was hidden. Because people could never find it out for themselves, God had to remove the veil and reveal it (Isa 25:7). What exactly was hidden away? Important matters concerning the future and the last things. *God gave the revelation* initially to *Jesus* who was the *Christ* or Anointed One of God. One of the themes of John's Gospel is that the Son receives what he has and what he says from the Father, and then reveals to us both the Father's will and the Father's heart (Jn 1:18, 3:35, 5:19-27, 7:16, 8:28, 12:49, 17:8). Having received the revelation, *Christ passed it on to his servants, to show them what must soon take place*. There are predictions of the future in the book of Revelation. The word *soon* may refer to *imminent* events in the first century, or to later events that would happen *suddenly* or *without delay*. It may also imply that the events were *certain* to take place. This revelation about Jesus Christ *was passed on to John by an angelic messenger* (22:6, 16). Throughout the book references appear to angels who pass on information or visions from Christ to John.

2. This John was not only *a servant of God and of other people* but also someone *who testified to the word of God.* The word of God is active and dynamic (Heb 4:12). It possesses a creative power of its own, which will do the job God assigns for it (Ps 33:9, Isa 55:10-11). If, as seems likely, John was the Apostle, he had already testified when he wrote the fourth gospel, and now he was about to pick up his quill once more and write the book of Revelation. He would bear witness to *the testimony of Jesus Christ.* Here *testimony* translates the Greek *marturia*, from which we get the English word *martyr*. This reminds us that there have been and continue to be times when bearing witness to Christ costs people their lives. This was certainly the case for Jesus. For him, being the pioneer of our faith meant being handed up to his enemies, being tried unjustly for sedition, and dying on a Roman cross. John will remind us of Christ's death by testifying to *all the visions that he saw.* Revelation is a visionary book, and we too shall see its vivid images.

3. There is *a blessing* at the beginning of Revelation, and a corresponding curse at the end of it (22:18-19). The blessing is *for anyone who either reads aloud in church the words of this prophecy,* or who *hears them* (or reads them in private) – provided that the reader or hearer *keeps what is written in it* (Lk 11:28). John calls this book a *prophecy,* so it is clear that he regarded it as belonging to Holy Scripture. A prophet is someone who speaks from God and proclaims, "Thus says the Lord". John reminds us that *the time is near* (22:10). Jesus likewise warned us to be ready, "for the Son of Man is coming at an unexpected hour" (Lk 12:40). The first of seven blessings in the book of Revelation comes in this verse (the other six will follow in 14:13, 16:15, 19:9, 20:6, 22:7 and 22:14). Here we have the first of the heptads or groups of seven that are a feature of this book, and two more will follow shortly in the next verse.

4. *John* proceeds to clarify the nature of his writing. Revelation is a circular letter, written initially *to seven churches* (1:11) in Western Turkey, a part of the world known today as Asia Minor and which was called *Asia* in the first century. Letters used to begin with a greeting that included good wishes, and this is no exception. John wishes his readers *grace* and *peace*. Grace means undeserved favour and strength from God, and peace means both peace *with* God (Rom 5:1) and the deep inner peace *of* God that guards our hearts and minds (Phil 4:7). Grace and peace come to us from God, who is described as *the one who is and who was and who is to come* (see also 1:8, 4:8, 11:17 and 16:5). This is a vivid description of the eternity and the changelessness of God (Mal 3:6, Heb 13:8). It was John's way of writing God's ineffable name *Yahweh*, which was a participle meaning *I am who I am* or *I will be what I will be* (Ex 3:13-14). Grace and peace also come from *the seven spirits who are before God's throne*, in his very presence.

This is an unusual plural reference to the Holy Spirit. Isaiah prophesied that the Spirit would rest on the Messiah and equip him for service with a sevenfold endowment (Isa 11:2). We should make a mental note of the two important heptads that receive their first mention in this verse – the seven churches and the seven spirits.

5. We have seen that grace and peace come from God the Father and God the Holy Spirit. John now adds that they also come from God the Son, *Jesus Christ*, who is described as *the faithful witness*, underlining what John has already hinted at in verse 2, namely that Jesus was faithful unto death. Jesus Christ is also *the firstborn of the dead*, for God raised him up on the third day in accordance with the scriptures (1 Cor 15:4), and *the ruler of the kings of the earth*, for he is the King of kings and Lord of lords (19:16). John clearly has the highest opinion of Jesus Christ, mentioning him in the same breath as God and the Holy Spirit. He is inspired to embark on a doxology or short hymn of praise, invoking Christ as *the one who loves us and has freed us from our sins by his blood*. John is delighted to remember that Christ loves us and that he gave himself for us, delivering us from our sins at the cost of his own life blood (Gal 2:20).

6. As a consequence of what Christ achieved on our behalf, *he has made us to be a kingdom*. In his teaching, Christ highlighted the kingdom of God. It is not a geographical place, but rather a gathering of people who own Christ as their king. Because Christ the King has freed all of his people from the burden of their sins, he has also given them the dignity of being *priests who serve his God and Father* (Ex 19:6). In the New Testament, all ordinary Christians are priests. A priest is someone who prays and witnesses. He or she presents others to God in prayer, and also presents God to others by talking to them about Jesus Christ.

And it is *to Jesus Christ*, our King, that *glory and dominion belong forever and ever. Amen.*

7. John now urges his readers to *look ahead* to the return of Christ. *He will come with the clouds*, as the one like a person in the prophecy of Daniel (Dan 7:13). In the Bible clouds are sometimes mentioned in connection with the actions of God (e.g. Ps 104:3, Isa 19:1). There will be a universal burst of visible divine majesty when Christ returns triumphantly to earth in the clouds of heaven, with power and great glory (Mt 24:30). *Every eye will see him, all who* disdained him, rejected his lordship and by their hostility *participated in piercing him*. In his first advent his sovereignty was challenged, but in the second it will no longer be open to doubt, but will be evident to all.

Those who loved darkness rather than light, and hated the light because their deeds were evil (Jn 3:19), will *wail on his account irrespective of the ethnic group they were part of* (Zech 12:10, Jn 19:37). John declares his approval of this both in Greek – *So it is to be*, and in Hebrew – *Amen*. He is not being vindictive. When persecution comes to Christians, Christ's name is abused and his cause despised, but that is not the last word on the matter. John is relieved by the reassurance that in the end evil will be defeated, and is encouraged because Christ and his holy followers will be vindicated. The godly need have no qualms about the coming judgement, and the book of Revelation will go on to spell out forthrightly the full implications of it.

8. The God who inspired the writing of the book now authenticates it by declaring in clear terms exactly who he is. *I am the Alpha and the Omega, he says*, referring to the first and last letters of the Greek alphabet. He could equally have said what Christ would say, that he was the first and the last (1:17, 22:13). *He is and he was and he is to come* (see v 4), for he is the one eternal Being who created all others. He is *the Almighty*, whose sovereign power cannot be resisted. From beginning to end, and at every moment in between, history is *his story*. He rules over every eventuality, and through all of them he is working out his purposes.

Meditation: A bracing but encouraging Start

The prologue of Revelation leaves us breathless. There is so much to take in. We are about to be shown visions about matters that are kept hidden from the majority of people. God has uncovered them and revealed them to the man, Jesus Christ, whom he chose to be the sole intermediary between himself and humankind (1 Tim 2:5). Christ then sent these visions by means of an angel to John, who in his turn wrote them down in order that they might reach us. What John wrote down is the very word of God, a prophetic and trustworthy testimony about Jesus Christ, who in his turn is the faithful witness *par excellence*. We may therefore take it for granted that the message of Revelation is altogether true and reliable.

It is a matter of the utmost importance that we should read or hear the words of this book. Nothing is more important than our reaction to them. Because the time is near, there is a special blessing promised to the readers and hearers of these words *provided that they keep them*.

John does not speak much on his own accord in this book, but in the first eight verses he greets his readers wishing them grace and peace from the one true and living God, who is a Trinitarian God, for he is one being but also three persons. It follows that we may get to know him in three different ways:

(a) As God the Father. John tells us twice in the first eight verses that God is the one *who is and who was and who is to come*. He is the one true and eternal God, whose vision embraces the past, the present and the future. He describes himself as *the Alpha and the Omega* and as *the Almighty*. It is of interest that God is called the Almighty nine times in the book of Revelation and only once elsewhere in the New Testament (2 Cor 6:18). The last book of the Bible underlines the fact that he is irresistible. History is the account of how God works out his purposes, and we are promised that in the end the victory and triumph will go to Jesus Christ.

(b) As God the Holy Spirit. John describes him as *the seven spirits who are before God's throne*. He will go on to use this same appellation, *the seven spirits*, on three further occasions in this book (3:1, 4:5, 5:6). Later we will study the very important Old Testament background of this phrase, but at present we should note that the Holy Spirit of God appears in God's presence, before his very throne.

(c) As God the Son, Jesus Christ. He is on a par with God (Jn 1:1, Titus 2:13) and is included in the godhead together with God the Father and the Holy Spirit. He bore witness to God and did so faithfully, unto death. But those who put him to death did not succeed in getting rid of him. Death was unable to hold him in its power (Acts 2:22-24), and he became the firstborn of the dead. He is the Christ, God's Anointed One, against whom the kings of the earth and the rulers take counsel together, but God laughs in derision at the conspiring rebels and will one day terrify them in his fury (Ps 2:2-6), for God has appointed Jesus Christ to be *the* King, who rules over all earthly kings.

As he thinks of Jesus Christ, John pauses and remembers what Christ has done for him and for all who put their trust in him. Christ loves his people. He loves us so much that he has freed us from our sins by his blood. "He died that we might be forgiven, he died to make us good, that we might go at last to heaven, saved by his precious blood". Christ also made us to be a kingdom, priests serving his God and Father, thereby filling our lives with adventure and purpose. We are to be his ambassadors, since God is making his appeal to other people through us. He has entrusted us with the message of reconciliation between God and sinners.

John goes on to express his prayerful longing that all glory and dominion should belong to Christ forever and ever. This is more than a prayer, it is an assured hope and an expectation that will certainly be fulfilled. For the Day will come when all the aspirations of Christians will be realised, and Jesus Christ will return in power and great glory. On that day everyone will see him. It will be the Day of days for all who loved and followed him. But for any who rejected him and disdained him, it will be a terrible day – a Day that John will describe with tears in his eyes.

That Day will loom large in our studies later on. But at present some wonderful thoughts about Jesus Christ are at the forefront of John's thinking. God is going to bless John on account of his Christ-centred focus. He is about to grant him a vision of the majesty of Christ that will change him forever.

II

1:9-20 The Vision that is Life-changing

The writer of Revelation informs us that he was called John (1:4, 9). If he was the author of the fourth gospel, he might have been longing to write another inspired book all about Jesus Christ, but he would have known that the special inspiration required for this could only come from God. One day it arrived, and he describes where, when and how this happened (v 9-11). He saw an overpowering vision of the risen and glorified Christ, and life would never be the same again – for him to whom the vision was given, and for us who read or hear about it. We too may see in our mind's eye what John saw on that unforgettable day (v 12-20).

9. It was a day like any other in the refugee camp (or rather the prison camp) in *the island called Patmos* off the coast of western Turkey. Patmos is shaped like a sea-horse and has an area of 34 square kilometres. *John* had been banished there. He shared with most of the Christians of his time *the persecution and the kingdom and the patient endurance* (Jn 16:33, Acts 14:22, Mk 13:13). Times of affliction had come because of their faithfulness to *the word of God* and *the testimony to Jesus*. John, who says that he is *their brother*, was a prophet. His fellow Christians would have longed to hear any "word from the Lord" that he might receive. Days of drudgery passed, then a word of the Lord did come to him (Jer 37:17, 42:4, 7).

10. It was a Sunday, *the Lord's day*. This is the earliest reference by this name to the Christian Sunday. John was caught up in a trance. He described it as *being in the Spirit*. This would happen periodically to him (4:2, 17:3, 21:10), and would be accompanied by visions or words granted to him by the glorified Christ. This time the vision was preceded by *a loud voice* that sounded *like a trumpet*. In the book of Revelation trumpets are heard on several occasions. They are loud and are often associated with the return of Christ and other "last things".

11. The loud voice told John to *write in a book what he saw*, and to *send it to the seven churches, to Ephesus, to Smyrna, to Pergamum, to Thyatira, to Sardis, to Philadelphia and to Laodicea*. These seven towns lay on a trade route that formed a loop around Western Turkey. Why seven? Why all these various heptads in the book of Revelation? Seven came to be the number that denoted completeness or perfection. It is one of the numbers associated with God. It keeps recurring in this book, sometimes implicitly as in the case of the seven blessings (see the note on 1:3), but more often explicitly as with the seven churches and the associated seven lampstands (v 13) and seven stars (v 16).

12. After the instruction to write what he saw, *John turned around to see whose voice it was that spoke to him, and he saw seven golden lampstands*. A lampstand holds up a light so that people who would otherwise walk in darkness may see, and here they represent the seven churches (v 20). The function of any church is so to present Jesus Christ that people may see what he is like (Mt 5:14-16).

13. *In the midst of the lampstands*, made visible by their light, was a divine figure. John calls him *one like the Son of Man*. He was referring to Daniel 7:13-14, where a "Son of Man" came with the clouds of heaven to God, the Ancient of Days, and received from him dominion and glory and kingship. Jesus often applied this title to himself, and the Son of Man whom John saw was the glorified Christ, *clothed with a long robe and with a golden sash across his chest*. The robe and sash were part of the attire of the High Priest (Ex 28:4), and the golden sash befitted a royal priest. In the first chapter of Revelation, Christ is presented as Prophet, Priest and King. He receives and passes on God's revelation (v 1), he wears the vestments of the High Priest (v 13), and he is the ruler of earthly kings (v 5).

14. What did the glorified Christ look like? He was perfectly pure, immeasurably wise and frighteningly sharp. His purity and wisdom are symbolised by *his head and his hair*, respectively, being *white as white wool and white as snow* (Isa 1:18), just like the hair of the Ancient of Days himself (Dan 7:9). Pure and wise Christ certainly was, but he was neither placid nor inward-looking. *His eyes were like a flame of fire* (19:12), full of energy and flashing spiritedly and penetratingly.

15. *His feet were like burnished bronze, refined as in a furnace.* Those feet would take him anywhere and everywhere, and there would be no escaping his presence (Ps 139:7-10). *His voice was like the sound of many waters*, like the voice of God according to the Prophet Ezekiel (Ezek 43:2). To John it might have sounded like the ongoing, dependable waves of sea-water that broke on the cliffs of Patmos.

16. *In his right hand he held seven stars.* The heptad of stars represents the angels of the seven churches (v 20). We shall shortly consider what this might mean, but it is clear that in some sense the risen Christ holds the church in his hand, and that his preference is to favour and protect it. But there is also a stern side to his nature, since *from his mouth comes a sharp, two-edged sword* (19:15, Isa 49:2). The short Roman sword was shaped like a tongue, which prompted the picture of a sword emerging from a mouth that was ready to speak decisively against any opponent. In the New Testament the sword is the word of God (Eph 6:17,

Heb 4:12), which proclaims grace to those who repent and believe in Christ, but conversely brings irresistible judgement to the disobedient and impenitent (Jn 3:36). Furthermore, *his face was like the sun shining with full force* (Mt 17:2). In a future day Christ's followers will reflect his glory (Dan 12:3, Mt 13:43). Christ's glorious appearance might have dazzled John, but his opponents would have been blinded by it.

17. *When he saw him,* John could not bear his radiance, and *he fell at his feet as though dead* (Ezek 1:28). Christ comforted him, *placing his right hand on him.* The one who holds the whole church in his hand can use that same hand to revive needy individuals who belong to the church. He then spoke to John. What would such an august and hallowed figure say? He began with a word of reassurance, *do not be afraid,* words attributed to God in the Old Testament and to Jesus in the gospels (e.g. Isa 41:10, Lk 12:32). Then he continued, *I am the first and the last* (2:8, 22:13; Isa 44:6), similar in meaning to "I am the Alpha and the Omega", used by God (v 8). Divine terms keep on being applied to Christ in Revelation.

18. Christ used exalted language: *I am the living one. I was dead, and see, I am alive forever and ever.* God lives forever and ever (4:10, 10:6; Dan 12:7), and so does his Anointed One. Christ's death had appeared to be the triumph of evil over good, but his resurrection had transformed everything. Having been raised from the dead, Christ will never die again (Rom 6:9). He is pre-eminently "the living one", and death has now lost its sting thanks to him (1 Cor 15:51-57, 2 Tim 1:10). Revelation will leave us in no doubt about the extent of Christ's victory. Consider his next words: *I have the keys of Death and Hades.* The keys symbolise authority. God has the power to destroy both soul and body in hell (Mt 10:28), and he has given to Christ the authority to carry out this unpleasant task for him (Isa 63:1-6, fulfilled in Rev 19:11-16). Christ has the keys of Death and Hell. This is such an extraordinary power that earthly tyrants do not even dream of it.

19. John is again told to *write down what he has seen* (v 11). The vision concerns *what is now* as well as *what is to take place after this.* The present, particularly the state of the church, is about to be revealed in chapters 2 and 3. Some aspects of what is to happen in the future will follow later, for the comfort and reassurance of those who at present have to suffer for the sake of Christ's name.

20. Christ explains *a mystery*. It concerns *the seven stars* that John saw in his right hand, and *the seven golden lampstands.* A mystery is something that we cannot work out for ourselves, so God has to reveal it to us. *The seven lampstands are the seven churches.* Churches are gatherings of Christian believers whose purpose is to reveal the light of Christ (Jn 5:35, Phil 2:15-16), so they are well symbolised by lampstands. *The seven stars are the angels of the seven churches.* "The angel of a church" probably denotes the essential character or nature of that particular church, or what God recognised as its prevailing spirit. Churches differ: some are better, some worse, and nearly all have both good and bad points. We are about to study what churches are like, and what Christ thinks of them. This will prove to be both a challenge and an encouragement.

Meditation: The Glory and the Majesty of the risen Lord

This mind-blowing vision of Jesus Christ comes straight after the prologue, since the whole book is a revelation or unveiling of Christ's person and his victory. The Christians were a small and insignificant remnant who were being perse-cuted by very strong enemies. In human terms their plight was hopeless, but the reality was otherwise. God had won a mighty victory. Evil had been deci-sively defeated by Jesus Christ on the cross, and God had declared him to be his Son with power by raising him from the dead (Rom 1:4). It was important that afflicted Christians should see Jesus as the victorious conqueror he really was, so John does this using words and concepts from the Old Testament which referred to God. Only divine terms are adequate to describe the majesty and splendour of Jesus, and John will use the same terms again in chapters 2 and 3, in the letters to the seven churches.

What would it be like if the curtain between heaven and earth was suddenly to be pulled aside? Something truly amazing would be revealed – or rather *someone* truly amazing, namely Jesus Christ. We may have cut him down to our own size, but seeing him as he really is will come as a shock to us. This could happen at any time. We might catch this vision of him on a Sunday, as John did, at a time when we were painfully conscious of the world's opposition to Christ, and when our lives were marked by humdrum drudgery. We might even sense the duty to write a book about this vision, and to send it to the churches.

The first thing we notice in the vision is the churches of the world. Their remit is to shed light on Jesus. He stands in their midst, holding them in his hand. Next we would see Jesus himself, and he is utterly dazzling. Full-power sunlight is a danger to the eyes, and John had to turn his eyes aside when he saw Jesus in his glory. Jesus Christ is not a cosy person whom we may regard as *my mate*. He is someone we may get to know, yes, but to know him will be the supreme privilege of our lives. It will involve loving and revering him, and even fearing him.

He speaks to us about what he has heard from God, because he is a Prophet. His robe and sash mark him out as our great High Priest. He has been given universal rule as King in the kingdom of God. He possesses divine and eternal wisdom, and the look in his eyes as he searches our hearts is both fiery and penetrating. There can be no escape from him, for his feet never get tired, as they are made of refined metal. Like the hound of heaven, he never gives up chasing us. His voice is like the waves of the sea, unceasingly crashing down. His message is the word of God. His sayings are living and active like a sharp, two-edged sword. They cut through our cover, and slash in ribbons all our presuppositions.

Did John recognise this Son of Man whom he saw? Had he read about him in the book of Daniel? Daniel had written about "One like a Son of Man coming in the clouds of heaven", who met God, the Ancient of Days, "and to him was given dominion and glory and kingship". It was "an everlasting dominion that shall not pass away", and a kingship "that shall never be destroyed" (Dan 7: 13-14). Daniel later had a close-up view of the Son of Man, very similar to the vision John saw: "A man clothed in linen, with a belt of gold round his waist. His body was like beryl, his face like lightning, his eyes like flaming torches, his arms and legs like the gleam of burnished bronze, and the sound of his words like the roar of a multitude" (Dan 10:5-6). On seeing this figure, Daniel's strength left him and he fell to the ground – as did John, who wrote, "When I saw him, I fell at his feet as though dead". How would we react if we saw Jesus? If we were to see him as he really is, our reaction would not be to snuggle up to him, but to fall at his feet as if our life had drained away. But surely John recognised him! He had seen, heard and touched one who called himself the Son of Man. On one occasion he saw him with his face shining like the sun, and his clothing dazzling white (Mt 17:1-2).

It is a fearful thing to see the Son of Man. Let his eyes of flame search you and read your thoughts. Imagine you are beside a rushing waterfall hearing the crash of the water. And then see him as he stretches out his hand to touch you. What does he say to you? *Do not be afraid*. He died but is now alive forever and ever. All power now belongs to him, and he holds the keys of Death and Hades.

See him and obey him. A vision without a task makes a visionary; a task without a vision makes drudgery; but a task with a vision makes a missionary.

III

2 and 3 The Letters to the Seven Churches

Before we study chapters 2 and 3 in detail, we shall take a look at their contents. Nowhere else in the New Testament are such challenging details provided of how Christ scrutinises and assesses the state of his church. Each of the seven churches referred to had its own particular character, personified by its angel, to whom the letters are directed. It is no accident that *seven* churches are the subject of God's scrutiny. The number seven represents completeness in Revelation, so the seven churches represent the worldwide church in all its diversity. John was to send to each of the churches a copy of the entire book of Revelation, including all seven letters. Although these letters are directed to real churches late in the first century, they also speak to the universal church throughout the ages. The strengths and weaknesses of the seven churches reflect the state of all churches at all times.

The seven letters follow a general pattern, as follows:

(**a**) There is an identification of the immediate recipient of the letter: "To the angel of the church in ____, write". The greeting is addressed to the *angel* of the church, which probably means what God regarded as its prevailing spirit or its essential character and nature. But it is clear that the message of each letter was for all the members of that church. Moreover, it would be read by the members of the other six churches, and studied carefully by the worldwide church thereafter.

(**b**) This is followed by an identification of the author, who is of course the risen Christ. He describes himself in different ways in each letter, quoting some phrases used about him in chapter 1, either from the salutation in verses 4-7, or from the vision in verses 12-18. This would get that church thinking about some aspect of Christ's being that it would be particularly helpful for them to meditate on.

(**c**) Then comes a section headed "I know", describing the character of the church and/or the difficulties it was facing. Christ knows his church intimately, for he walks among the seven golden lampstands (2:1). His eyes are like a flame of fire (2:18). He searches minds and hearts (2:23). He therefore knows all their deeds, and is generous with praise for all the good aspects of each church – except in the one case of Laodicea. Here was a church that receives no praise from Christ.

(**d**) Words of criticism come next, describing serious faults in the church – except in the cases of Smyrna and Philadelphia. Here were two churches that Christ did not criticise. However, life was far from easy for their members. They faced some very challenging problems and it was a struggle to keep going.

(**e**) The main message follows. It might be an admonition about the present, or a warning about what could happen (or was certain to happen) in the future. Each church deserves praise or blame, and receives commendation or condemnation accordingly. Most of them are called to repent, and are given a serious rebuke or exhortation. The glorified Christ is not offering wise advice or making various suggestions that these churches might consider at their pleasure. As their risen Lord, he is telling his people what he expects of them and how they could put right certain things that were wrong. He expects his warnings to be heeded, and makes clear the inevitable consequences that will follow if they are not.

(**f**) Then comes an appeal, always in the same words, "Let anyone who has an ear hear what the Spirit is saying to the churches". John is the writer and the churches receive the letters, but their words are carried home to each church member by the Holy Spirit. The saying would remind them of words that Jesus often spoke during his earthly ministry, "Let anyone with ears to hear listen!" (Mk 4:9, etc).

(**g**) Each letter ends with a promise, beginning with the words "to everyone who conquers, I will give. . .", or a variation of them. The promise is of eternal life, but it uses different phrases to describe the ultimate gift. This time the phrases are taken from the climax of the book, in chapters 21 and 22. The order of (f) and (g) varies, being (f) then (g) in the first three letters, but (g) then (f) in the last four.

There is a chiastic structure in the order of the letters, of the form ABCCCBA. The first and seventh churches, Ephesus and Laodicea, are *cold-hearted* towards God, and their future hangs in the balance. The second and sixth, Smyrna and Philadelphia, seem weak but they are *commended* by Christ. The third, fourth and fifth, Pergamum, Thyatira and Sardis, are *corrupted* – by false teachers, by immoral behaviour, or by hypocrisy. They have grieved the Holy Spirit.

John Stott has observed that each letter highlights a good quality that churches may or may not have. Because of this, we may regard these seven qualities as the marks of an ideal church. They are, in the order of the letters: love, suffering, truth, holiness, reality, mission and wholeheartedness.

The risen Lord makes himself known to his people as the chief pastor and good shepherd of his flock. He patrols his churches, inspecting and supervising them, and possesses an intimate knowledge of them. He is able to pinpoint seven marks that he would like them to display: love for him and the willingness to suffer for him, balanced Biblical truth in their beliefs and holiness in their everyday lives, transparent sincerity, engagement in mission and wholehearted commitment. He knows about the inner pressures of sin, error and lethargy, and the outward ones of affliction and persecution. Chief among these was the temptation to forsake Christ for Caesar. Some decades had passed since the evangelisation of the region by Paul and others in the years AD 52-55. Much pressure was now being put on Christians to be less intransigent concerning the socially-approved worship of the Emperor, and more open towards ideas that differed diametrically from their own, which were perceived as outdated. This pressure might involve the real possibility of martyrdom, as in Smyrna or Pergamum, if they remained faithful to Christ. It also offered the alluring prospect of realising how their lives would be much more comfortable if only they conformed to a few pagan customs and rituals.

Meditation: Why is the Church so imperfect?

The risen and glorified Christ chose to send letters to seven churches in western Turkey. He could have chosen other churches in the region, such as the ones in Troas, Colossae and Hierapolis, but he chose these seven because between them they provide an identikit picture of all the churches in every age throughout the world. Their descriptions are not a pleasant read. Two of the churches received Christ's unqualified approval, but even in these we read of severe persecution or pressure from "the synagogue of Satan", who deceitfully declared themselves to be true believers when they were not. And the other five churches were all in a poor state, the details being both disgraceful and embarrassing.

Why did Christ arrange to make public the sinful shortcomings of his people and so allow their filthy linen to be exposed in full view of the whole world?

The answer is that part of Christ's purpose for the church is that it should be like a hospital for the rehabilitation of repentant sinners. All sorts of people seek help in the church. Many are extremely damaged people. Some of them are not yet followers of Christ, but they act out their role in order to find in the church the acceptance they so desperately need. These damaged people are like "birds of the air" who "come and make nests" in the branches of an institution that has now become the greatest of shrubs (Mt 13:31-32). It is part of Christ's wish that this should be so. There can be no better place for damaged people than the church, where they can meet regularly with true believers, learn from the Bible and begin to worship the one true and living God.

But surely this is dangerous, I hear you say. It may lead to some who have never repented or trusted in Christ becoming established in the church. A few will turn into false teachers, who will corrupt true believers. Some may go on and become church leaders. But God foresaw these possibilities, so he arranged for the New Testament epistles to be written, with their strong condemnation of every sort of false teaching. We also see why Christ commissioned John to write the letters to the seven churches. But the fact remains that false church leaders can discourage their congregations from reading the Bible, or urge them to be selective about the parts of it they read. In this way they try to ensure that their falsity is not exposed by God's word, but their ministry may lead to their churches dying a slow death. Sometimes whole groups of churches become spiritual graveyards. The presence of the Holy Spirit is no longer noted in their church buildings. He is not welcome in them anymore, so he has departed (Ezek 10:1-22). In fact it is the false leaders, those who persistently teach error and twist the plain meaning of scripture, who should have been made unwelcome. They can do great harm.

Would it be a good thing if churches made it an absolute priority to ensure that all of their members were sound in doctrine and that they read and studied their Bibles regularly? You might think so, but such a course of action might not work out in the way you hope. Outsiders would not necessarily be attracted to such a church. Some insiders might be made to feel so uncomfortable that they would end up going somewhere else. Of course, every church should encourage regular Bible reading, and it should be common practice that most of the preaching will consist of edifying expositions of scripture. But compelling the members to be sound and scriptural might prove as unhelpful and offensive to some of them, as compelling them to be unsound and unscriptural would be to others.

This is why Jesus gave us the parable of the wheat and the weeds (Mt 13:24-30 and 36-43). The church is like a field in which a variety of seeds have been sown. Some seeds are good wheat: they have been sown by the Son of Man and they are the children of the kingdom. But there are also bad seeds in the field – who has done this? The answer is that the devil has sown them, they are his children. Should the weeds be separated from the wheat? It is difficult to do this, because the plants look the same and in the early stages it is impossible to tell them apart. You can only distinguish the wheat from the weeds at harvest time. It is then that the weeds are collected and bound in bundles to be burned, but the wheat is taken into the barn. Jesus said that the harvest is the end of the age, and "the Son of Man will send his angels, and they will collect out of his kingdom all causes of sin and all evildoers, and they will throw them into the furnace of fire, where there will be weeping and gnashing of teeth. Then the righteous will shine like the sun in the kingdom of their Father. Let anyone with ears listen!" We should be glad if outsiders mix with God's people in the church. We should not try to be rid of those who are not true believers. We cannot tell the true from the false, and we might throw out the baby with the bathwater. Besides, a surprise may occur, and some of the faithless may find faith. What better place to do so than in church!

The same lesson is taught in the parable of the ten bridesmaids (Mt 25:1-13). Five were wise and five were foolish, and yet all ten were invited to meet the bridegroom. The five wise bridesmaids were made welcome at the great wedding banquet, but the five foolish ones arrived late and the door was shut. Then the bridegroom said to them, "Truly, I tell you, I do not know you". Here the church is compared to people who are preparing for a banquet. Some keep their light shining. Others neglect this, and they will be rejected on the last day.

We see that weeds grow alongside the wheat, and foolish bridesmaids who do not let their light shine mix with wise ones who do. The church will always have false disciples as well as true ones. God is at work in both. The risen Christ says to the church, "I reprove and discipline those whom I love. Be earnest, therefore, and repent" (3:19). True disciples will welcome the divine discipline, knowing that it is a sign that God loves them and is persevering with them (Heb 12:5-11). Bit by bit, a step at a time, their repentance deepens. They are learning to trust and obey. But false disciples will remain rebellious and unbending towards God. They usually resent his discipline, and in due course react against it.

Suppose I am a church member. Is there a way of knowing whether I am a true disciple as opposed to a false one? Here are some questions I may ask myself:

(i) Do I love God? (Mt 22:36-37, Jn 21:15-17).
(ii) Do I love God's people? (Jn 13:34-35, 1 Thess 4:9-10).
(iii) Do I love God's word? (Ps 119:97, Mt 4:4).
(iv) Do I long for others to be saved? (Ps 67:1-7, Mt 9:37-38).
(v) Do I help the poor and needy? (Isa 1:16-17, Jas 1:27).

If my answer to all these questions is a resounding yes, this is a very good sign, no matter how good or bad my church might be.

IV

2:1-7 The Letter to Ephesus, who lacked Love

Ephesus was the most important city in the province of Asia. It was situated at the mouth of the River Cayster. Although its harbour had a tendency to silt up, it was a great commercial centre. The great road to the Euphrates terminated there. It was also a very important religious centre, the chief cult being that of Artemis. The Apostle Paul spent three years of his life in Ephesus establishing the church (Acts 19:1-16, 20:31). He provoked a riot there when his preaching led to so many people turning to Christ that the trade in silver shrines of the goddess Artemis was affected (Acts 19:23-41).

Ephesus was famous for being the home of one of the seven wonders of the ancient world, the great Temple of Artemis, which was extraordinarily ornate and measured around 425 x 220 x 60 feet in size, four times the area of the Parthenon. Magical arts were widely practised in the city, and on one remarkable occasion the Christian converts gathered their magic books and publicly burned them, even though their value was more than fifty thousand silver coins (Acts 19:17-20). Later, reflecting on his varied experiences there, Paul sent one of his greatest epistles to the Ephesian church. Timothy lived there for several years (1 Tim 1:3), and according to early tradition, so did the Apostle John in his old age, both before and after he wrote the book of Revelation.

1. The letter from the risen Christ was written down and sent by John (1:11). It is addressed *to the angel of the church*, probably a personification of the character and outlook of the church. It claims to be *the very words of Jesus Christ*, described as *the one who holds the seven stars in his right hand* (1:16) and *walks among the seven lampstands* (1:13). Christ is alongside his church (Mt 18:20). He holds it firmly in his right hand. He cares for it and is deeply concerned for its welfare.

2. *Christ knows their good works*, their *hard toil* to the point of weariness, and their *patient endurance*. These are excellent qualities in any church. Furthermore, he knows about their *intolerance of evildoers*. In the Ephesian church they could pray, "Hallowed be your name". They knew that God had said, "You shall be holy, for I am holy" (Lev 11:44, 1 Pet 1:16). They had *tested certain people who claimed to be apostles* or pioneer missionaries, and *found them to be false*. Having sifted them, they openly declared their falsehood, and had no further fellowship with them. This was absolutely right. It was the way taught by Christ himself and his apostles (Mt 7:15-20, 2 Tim 3:1-9). Moreover, the Apostle Paul foresaw that the problem of false teachers would afflict them (Acts 20:28-31).

3. Christ knew why *they were enduring patiently* (v 2) and *bearing up* in spite of the dangers posed by wolves in sheep's clothing. It was *for the sake of his name* (Mt 10:22; Acts 5:41, 9:16; Rom 1:5; 3 Jn 7). And *they had not become weary* in doing what was right (1 Cor 15:58, Gal 6:9). It cannot escape our notice that the church at Ephesus received more praise from Christ than any other church. They were an excellent congregation with faithful leaders, and an admirable work of grace was taking place there. How could anything possibly be badly wrong?

4. Something was wrong, however, and it was very serious. It was a fault that met with one of Christ's most memorable rebukes, and provoked one of his sternest warnings. The rebuke begins with the word *But*. In the Bible this adversative may preface a dreadful problem (as in 2 Sam 11:27b) or a wonderful encouragement (as in Ps 130:4 or Eph 2:4). Here it is the former: *But I have this against you, that you have abandoned the love you had at first*. Was it their love for Christ, or for each other, or for outsiders in general? It could have been all three. These faithful Christians had somehow contrived to lose that love-filled sense of

God's grace and presence that so often characterises the early stages of a Christian life. They had allowed their own selfishness and pride to quench that "love divine, all loves excelling", and their own love had grown cold (Mt 24:12). While Robert Mounce may be unduly pessimistic in believing that "Every virtue carries within itself the seeds of its own destruction", this was certainly the case concerning the doctrinal purity of the Ephesian church. Leon Morris wrote that "They had yielded to the temptation, ever present to Christians, to put all their emphasis on sound teaching. In the process they lost love, without which all else is nothing". William Barclay put it like this: "the eagerness to root out all mistaken people had ended in a sour and rigid orthodoxy". And so Christ spoke to this church by his servant John just as God spoke to Israel by the prophet Jeremiah, "I remember the devotion of your youth, your love as a bride, how you followed me in the wilderness, in a land not sown" (Jer 2:2). Those were such good early days. But that first love was gone.

5. There was only one route back to their previous felicity, and Christ now sternly points them to three steps they had to take: remember the past, repent now in the present, and return to the good habits of old in the future. First, *remember from what they had fallen*. They needed to do what the prodigal son did in the parable. They had probably slipped away gradually, hardly realising what was happening. It would help them to return in thought to the halcyon days of old. *Remember* is in the present imperative: they had to *keep on remembering*. They were to let their minds dwell in the past for a little while. Then they were to *repent*. They were to do an about turn. They had wandered into paths of pride by patting themselves on the back, feeling smugly self-right-eous, and judging others censoriously. They had to get back on the right track. Finally, they were to *do the works they did at first*. They was no other way to bring back that first joy. They needed to return to the good actions and habits that had resulted from their first love. That way, they would once again be loving God, their fellow Christians and outsiders, and their old joy would be restored (Ps 51:12, Jn 14:21). The alternative was too terrible to contemplate. If they did not remember, repent and return, then *Christ would come to them and remove their lampstand from its place*. This means that the Ephesian church would

pass away. A loveless church is a contradiction in terms, so it can only die, no matter how great its knowledge and its hard work may be.

6. Lest they misunderstand him, Christ once again commends the members of the Ephesian church for their intolerance of evil. *Yet this is to your credit*, he says, *you hate the works of the Nicolaitans, which I also hate.* Love is one of God's two principal characteristics, and the other is holiness. We are to love God always, and to seek what is good in and for other people. But in order to be, like God, both loving and holy, our love for what is good must be accompanied by a hatred for what is evil (Ps 97:10). God said, "You shall be holy, for I am holy". To put it differently, *God's love is a holy love*, so our love is not to be undiscerning but holy, like his. Who were these Nicolaitans that John mentions? We simply do not know. They were certainly false teachers of some sort (v 15), probably the same group who claimed to be apostles, but were not (v 2). They offered an improved, modernised version of Christianity, which effectively contradicted the teaching of Christ. They were insidious fifth columnists, who had stolen into the church and now sought to discourage Christians from reading God's word (Acts 17:11) and from building their lives upon it (Mt 7:24-27).

7. Christ is about to bring this letter to an end. *Let anyone who has an ear listen to what the Spirit is saying to the churches.* This letter is a warning not only for the Ephesian church, but also for every subsequent church that enjoys the blessing of good teaching and perseveres in good works. The Holy Spirit will praise God's people for what is good, rebuke them if they have lost their first love, and urge them to recover it – if they have an ear. It is the Spirit who is saying something to the churches, yet the words are Christ's. This is because the Holy Spirit is the Spirit of Christ and of God (Rom 8:9-11). The bond between them is so close that Paul could write that the Lord is the Spirit (2 Cor 3:17). As in all the seven letters, a promise is given for *everyone who conquers*. In this case, victorious Christians *will have Christ's permission to eat from the tree of life that is in the paradise of God* (22:2, 14, 19; the imagery is taken from Genesis 2:8-9, 3:22). As a result they would enjoy eternal life. What is eternal life? It is to know God and his Son Jesus Christ (Jn 17:3). The reward of loving God now will be the freedom to love him perfectly forever. Those who conquer will

see God and exult in his presence. The new earth will be paradise, and to reside there will be pure bliss.

Meditation: The Indispensable Nature of Love

The church members at Ephesus had done extremely well. They had been highly commended by no less than Jesus Christ on three of the most important aspects of the Christian life. As regards *service*, they had worked hard in every way. They had fed the poor, visited the lonely, taught the young and cared for the elderly. They were famous for their good works. As regards *endurance*, they had kept the faith in spite of living in an oppressively pagan city. They knew what it was to be despised and hated for their belief in a crucified Saviour. This was foolishness for the pagan citizens, who socially ostracised them and discriminated against them in business affairs. But they had persevered. And as regards *belief*, they had learnt their faith well from the Apostles Paul and John. When wandering teachers came to their church, they gave them a fair hearing. They "tested the spirits" to see if they came from God (1 Jn 4:1), and then held fast to whatever was good (1 Thess 5:21), while rejecting absolutely any false teaching and confounding anyone who tried to propagate it. In all this, they had pleased Christ. They had done what was good and hated what was evil, and had thereby followed in his footsteps.

It must have come as a huge shock to them to hear that Christ was displeased with them, and that he might even have to "remove their lampstand" – in other words, allow their church to die. How could anything mar the correctness and the all-round strength of their witness and worship? But their lack of love did mar it. If left unchecked, it would spell the end of their witness as a church.

Jesus had taught that love was to characterise Christian life – love for God and for other people, especially for their fellow believers (Mk 12:28-34, Jn 13:35). The Ephesian Christians had known this love earlier on, but their struggle against false teachers and their detestation of heretical teaching had led them to espouse such hard feelings and such harsh attitudes that as a result they had effectively forsaken their first love. Doctrinal purity and loyalty can never be a substitute for love, and when they are unaccompanied by love they will inevitably be perceived as an off-putting and unacceptable rejection of outsiders.

All good works done in the name of Christ are empty if they are not motivated by love. The Apostle Paul spelt this out with utter clarity (1 Cor 13:1-3). Here are some wonderful words about Jesus Christ, which are easy to write out:

Jesus is patient; Jesus is kind; Jesus is not envious, or boastful, or arrogant, or rude. Jesus does not insist on his own way; he is not irritable or resentful; he does not rejoice in wrongdoing, but rejoices in the truth. He bears all things, believes all things, hopes all things, and endures all things.

As you will have noticed, this is just part of Paul's hymn to love (1 Cor 13:4-7) with the words *love, its* and *it* altered to *Jesus, his* and *he.* The point is that God is love, and so is his Son Jesus Christ. To say, as perhaps we do, that *Christianity is Christ,* is to say that *Christianity is love.* Again and again the New Testament emphasises the pre-eminence of love. Henry Drummond said that "Love is the greatest thing in the world". Knowledge is important, and the church in Ephesus possessed correct knowledge in abundance. But love is greater than knowledge. As the Apostle Paul put it, "Knowledge puffs up, but love builds up" (1 Cor 8:1). While knowledge fills clever people with wind, love produces real character in them. It is much better to be real than to be a windbag. Love is the indispensable ingredient of Christian faith. If the love of a church cools off, this will show in all its activities: in its worship, its relationships, and the impact of its outreach. Any outsiders will sense this as soon as they enter that church. William Temple wrote, "It is not virtue that can save the world or anyone in it, but love". Love is the only quality that is indispensable in God's people. With love, all other good qualities are enhanced and have divine life. Without love, they are lifeless and sterile.

It is not a coincidence that the Apostle Paul ended his epistle to the Ephesian church with the following benediction: "Peace be to the whole community, and *love with faith,* from God the Father and the Lord Jesus Christ. Grace be with all who have *an undying love* for our Lord Jesus Christ" (Eph 6:23-24). We all need love. So much so, that we could almost say that "all you need is love".

V

2:8-11 The Letter to Smyrna, who endured Suffering

Smyrna was a great city that rivalled Ephesus for the title *the first city of Asia.* It remains a great city today – modern Izmir has a population of nearly 4.4 million. After being destroyed by the Lydians in 627 BC, Smyrna was rebuilt around 290 BC to a comprehensive plan, so it was one of the few planned cities of antiquity, and many writers commented on its beauty.

It had a good harbour at the head of a well-protected gulf, and was an important trade centre. Early on it jumped on the bandwagon of emperor worship. In AD 26, just before the start of the public ministry of Jesus, it secured the honour of building a temple to Tiberius Caesar. This letter informs us that in Smyrna there was a colony of Jews, some of whom were hostile to Christians, and who incited the civil authorities against them.

8. *The message is, as for all the churches, from Christ.* Here he describes himself as *the first and the last, who was dead and came to life* (1:17-18). This is a most appropriate greeting. Several centuries earlier the city of Smyrna had perished, but it had later been rebuilt as a city and come back to life. Now Christians there faced the fearful possibility of martyrdom, so they needed reassurance that their Lord had conquered death. After death they would, like him, spring back to life.

9. *Christ knows* about the grievous troubles that befall the Christians at Smyrna. The word for *affliction* is sometimes translated *tribulation*, and means a crushing burden. The word for *poverty* means more than a lack of the superfluous; rather it implies utter *destitution*. Yet in spite of this, *Christ describes them as rich.* Leon Morris commented that "There is a richness in spiritual things which has nothing to do with this world's wealth", so it is vastly preferable to be materially poor and spiritually rich than the other way round (3:17).

The poverty of the Christians in Smyrna may have arisen because their goods were being plundered (Heb 10:34). To follow Christ as they did constituted a *religio illicita*, and this made it easy for their enemies to take legal action against them. Those who opposed them included *some Jews who slandered them. They said that they were true Jews, but were not.* While the church at Ephesus was troubled by self-styled apostles, the church at Smyrna was troubled by self-styled Jews. But there is more to being a Jew than merely possessing the outward signs of Judaism (Rom 2:28-29). Christ declared that these particular Jews formed *a synagogue of Satan.* They were deceitful and therefore not true Israelites (Jn 1:47). Physically they may have been descendants of Abraham, but this did not imply that they were automatically his spiritual descendants as well (Jn 8:37-59; see also Rom 4:9-12, Phil 3:3).

10. Although suffering was certain, Christ urged his followers at Smyrna *not to fear what they were about to suffer.* God would see them through

the big test that they were about to face. Its originator was not a human anti-Christian agitator but *the devil* himself, who *would arrange for some of God's people to be thrown into prison*. This might be an incarceration of limited duration but more probably, in the light of the exhortation that follows, a confinement that would result in their execution.

Christ says that this would go on for *ten days*. This could be the exact time they would have to endure, or else an assurance that their suffering would be for a limited time only, even though *they would be tested to the limit*. But it would be God, not Satan, who would have the last word. The encouragement Christ gives to his suffering servants is *be faithful until death, and I will give you the crown of life*. There is an article with *life* – it is *the* life, eternal life, the life that is truly life (1 Tim 6:18-19). As for the *crown*, the word used here for it meant a victory wreath, and this would have been a powerful image for the people of Smyrna, which was famous for its Games. If a believer remained faithful to Christ even to death, he would conquer Satan (Rev 12:11) and receive from the Lord the ultimate trophy, which consisted of abundant and everlasting life (1 Cor 9:25).

11. No further words of command or exhortation are needed. Christ simply says, *Let anyone who has an ear listen to what the Spirit is saying to the churches*. The words have come from God and they have been heard, but have they been listened to? Have they been weighed? Have they sunk in? There is a wonderful promise for those who have taken them to heart and who persevere to the end. *Whoever conquers will not be harmed by the second death*. There are two types of death. The first is physical death, which affects all human beings with a few exceptions, namely Enoch (Gen 5:24), Elijah (2 Ki 2:11), and those who are alive when Jesus returns to wind up this age (1 Thess 4:15-17). The *second death* is described in Revelation in terms of the lake of fire (20:6, 14; 21:8). It is the awful destruction of body and soul in hell (Mt 10:28) which is reserved for any person whose heart remains hardened and who persists in rebellious unbelief. It is the only alternative to the life that is truly life, but no one who overcomes will be harmed by it.

Meditation: The inevitable Necessity of Suffering

Smyrna's strong allegiance with Rome led them to espouse the cult of emperor worship. Most businesses there would have been connected to guilds, and they would have required this cult to be observed, making it impossible for Christians to belong to them. There was also a large colony of Jews in Smyrna, some of whom were actively hostile towards the new Christian religion. All this made life extremely difficult for those who followed Christ. They could not make a living, and they might be occasional victims of looting or mob violence.

This letter gives us some idea of the remarkable courage and inner strength of many of the early Christians. Christ's words to the church in Smyrna assume that their attitude to physical suffering was similar to his own when he faced the cross. He speaks about it to them as one would speak about familiar troubles that all of us must face. Such a brief message, sent to people who might at any time die for their faith in him, implies a heroism on their part that ought to stir our hearts.

One of the best-known Christian martyrs was a young member of the church in Smyrna when the book of Revelation was written. His name was Polycarp. He may already have been the leader of the church in Smyrna when he read John's letter, since Irenaeus wrote, around AD 180, that Polycarp had been consecrated Bishop of Smyrna by John himself. Irenaeus was born in Smyrna in AD 130, and he had heard Polycarp's preaching. As leader of the church in Smyrna, Polycarp would have meditated long hours on the letter to the church there, and this could well have been a source of strength to him when his hour of testing came. There are no contemporary accounts of his death, but it is possible to reconstruct what happened by studying *The Martyrdom of Polycarp*, written a few years later.

It took place on the 22nd of February, probably in the year AD 156. The elderly bishop had fled from Smyrna at the pleas of the church members. He was tracked down to his hiding place because someone betrayed him to the authorities. He did not attempt to escape, but instead offered food and drink to his captors, who in turn gave him permission to retire alone for prayer, and he prayed for two hours. After this they arrested him, and as they drove him back into Smyrna, the senior arresting officer urged him to recant: "What harm can it do, to sacrifice to the emperor?" Polycarp refused. When they arrived, he was roughly taken out of the carriage and brought before the proconsul in the amphitheatre, who spoke to him in the presence of numerous hostile pagans and Jews: "Show respect, as befits your old age, and swear by the genius of

Caesar. Swear, and you will be released. Revile the Christ". It was then that Polycarp replied with the immortal words, "I have served him for eighty-six years, and he has never done me any wrong. How then can I blaspheme my King who saved me?" The proconsul then threatened to throw Polycarp to the wild beasts, but this had no effect on the old man.

At this stage the hostility of certain Jews against the Christian faith was evident by their zeal to speed up the execution. They joined the pagans in clamouring for the death of Polycarp on the ground of his opposition to the state religion – even though they did not subscribe to it. The angry anti-Christian mob cried out loudly, "This is the teacher of Asia, the father of the Christians, the destroyer of our gods, who teaches many neither to offer sacrifice nor to worship". The proconsul then spoke again to his elderly prisoner, "I see that you despise the beasts, so unless you change your mind and swear by the genius of Caesar, you shall be destroyed by fire". Polycarp did not change his mind. Although it was the Sabbath, the Jews helped the pagans gather wood for the fire in which the martyr would be burnt.

Polycarp asked not to be tied to the stake, but stood by it. The fire was kindled, and the old saint was heard praying, "O Lord, Almighty God, Father of your beloved Son Jesus Christ, through whom we have received our knowledge of you, I thank you that you have thought me worthy on this day and at this hour, to share in the cup which your Christ drank, and to be numbered among your witnesses". A wind arose, which drove the flames away from Polycarp, prolonging his agony. The exasperated executioner, frustrated by how long it was taking the old man to die, could endure the process no longer, so he took out his sword and killed him.

It was inevitable that the church at Smyrna should suffer for the faithfulness of its members. Nowadays church members in the affluent West do not suffer in this way. This is because we have learnt how to avoid suffering by compromise. Our moral standards are not perceived as being higher than those of the world, because we no longer dare discourage divorce or sexual promiscuity, or refuse to join in business malpractice. In certain churches the good news of forgiveness for the repentant is no longer announced, because we dare not tell others that they need to repent. Our lives are no longer radiant with God's holy love. We have so little purity, integrity and love that we find ourselves unable to rebuke the ungodly. We are respectable but ineffectual, and quite incapable of cutting any ice.

We live in an age where there is an unparalleled ignorance of the saving truths of the Christian gospel. It is not that very many have rejected these truths. A few have, but the vast majority of people have not heard any of the basic facts of the Biblical revelation, such as the universal sin of men and women, the holy anger of God against our sin, the death of Jesus Christ which saves us from judgement, our need to repent and believe in Christ, and the subsequent process of growing in holiness thanks to the work of the Holy Spirit in our hearts.

Have we forgotten that part of the *raison d'être* of the church is to pass on to unbelievers the good news of God's love for them in Christ? Some churchgoers would reply that the Christian gospel is unpopular nowadays. People want to get right with God in their own way. But this has always been the case! Nobody likes to be told that they cannot save themselves in their own way by their good works. From the earliest days the message has been unpopular that God loves us so much that he devised his own master plan to save us through Christ. People would so much rather get to heaven by their own steam. It is a humbling killer blow to their pride when they are told that this is altogether impossible.

To be effective and powerful, any presentation of the Christian gospel or good news should always be preceded by the bad news. The bad news is that we cannot save ourselves. Our selfishness and our pride are so ingrained that apart from the grace of God, we can do nothing from completely altruistic motives. And when we dare confront others with this unhappy truth about themselves, they will often hate us for it. The New Testament makes it quite clear that suffering is one of the indispensable marks of every true Christian and of every true church, and that if we are true to Christ, persecution will inevitably be our lot.

If we look up Jesus Christ's eight beatitudes at the beginning of the Sermon on the Mount, the one he laid the greatest stress on was the last, for he repeated it. "Blessed are those who are persecuted for righteousness' sake". "Blessed are you when people revile you and persecute you and utter all kinds of evil against you falsely on my account" (Mt 5:10-11). He also added a complementary woe to any of his followers who shirked their duty to fulfil his great commission, "Woe to you when all speak well of you" (Lk 6:26). If our outreach consists of giving posies to passers-by, they will all speak well of us, but we shall be under a curse. This theme often recurred in Christ's teaching (e.g. Jn 15:18-25, 16:33). It was echoed by the apostles (2 Cor 11:23-27, Phil 1:29, 2 Tim 3:12, 1 Pet 4:12-14).

Christ loved us and faithfully bore witness on our behalf (1:5, 3:14). The reason why the church rarely suffers nowadays is because it does not bear witness to him. A willingness to suffer for Christ proves the genuineness of our love for him.

VI

2:12-17 The Letter to Pergamum, who watered down the Truth

Pergamum became the capital of the kingdom of the Attalids after Alexander the Great. Later it was incorporated into the Roman Empire in 133 BC, and was made the capital of the province of Asia. Apart from its administrative importance, it housed one of the great libraries of antiquity, with perhaps as many as 200,000 parchment scrolls. Indeed, Pergamum gave its name to parchment (which in Latin is *pergaminum*). Its library was second only to the great library at Alexandria, and many people would have consulted its writings in their search for truth.

But Pergamum was also a centre for many religions. People went there searching for physical healing by the god Asclepius, whose shrine was like an Asian Lourdes. Behind the city was a conical hill covered with numerous heathen shrines. The prevalence of paganism made Pergamum an oppressive city for Christians to live in. Temples had been built there in honour of Zeus, Dionysos and Athene, and in 29 BC another was added, dedicated to Rome and Augustus Caesar. Later two further temples were built for emperor-worship. On designated holidays, citizens were supposed to sprinkle incense on the fire beside the Emperor's statue, and to confess that Caesar was Lord. For Christians to do this would constitute a denial of Christ. What message did the risen Christ have for them?

12. *Christ greets them*, describing himself as *the one who has the sharp two-edged sword*. In 1:16 John saw this sword coming out of Christ's mouth. It represents *Christ's words*, which are truthful and have a sharp cutting edge. God is looking for people who value his truthful word, recognise it, and respond to it with awe and fear (Isa 66:2). Those who disobey or disdain the truth of God will find that Christ will wage war against them with the sword of his mouth (v 16).

13. As always, Christ knows all about their lives. *He knows where they are living*. He describes Pergamum as *the place where Satan's throne is*. Satan

exercised a domineering authority there. Some commentators have suggested that this is a reference to the symbol of Asclepius, which was a serpent. It represented healing for some residents of Pergamum, but evil for Christians (12:9, 20:2). Others think it is a reference to the great altar of Zeus, to be seen in the acropolis which was on a hill dominating the city. The most likely suggestion, however, is that Satan's throne being in Pergamum was a reference to the city's pre-eminence in emperor-worship. This would have presented a threat to the Christians there, more than it did at Smyrna. *Yet they were holding fast to Christ's name and did not deny their faith in him.*

When believers are bold for Christ and for his word they always earn his approval, but if they are ashamed of him or of his words in an adulterous and sinful generation, he in his turn will be ashamed of them when he returns on the last day (Mk 8:38). A time of severe testing had come to Pergamum, when faithful Christians were faced with the choice of holding fast to Christ's name or being martyred. One of them, *Antipas, was Christ's witness and was faithful. He was killed among them in the place where Satan lives.* The Greek word for *witness* is *martys*, and here it was coming to mean a martyr. Nothing more is known about Antipas, though several later legends have it that he was placed in a hollow bronze bull, which was then heated until it was red hot.

14. Christ now turns to what was not right in the church at Pergamum. *I have a few things against you*, he says. It seems that they were tolerating and maybe even embracing some false teaching. To begin with, there were in the church *some who were holding to the teaching of Balaam, who taught Balak to put a stumbling block before the people of Israel, so that they would eat food sacrificed to idols and practise fornication.* Balaam was a pagan prophet who was hired by Balak, King of Moab, to curse the Israelites while they were wandering in the wilderness (Numbers chapters 22-24), but the Lord forbade him from cursing them. Balaam then advised Balak to try to lead the Israelites into sin by inducing them to join in idol-worship, eating the food that had been sacrificed to idols and committing fornication with Moabite women (Num 25:1-3; 31:16). Here a *stumbling block* is the English translation of the Greek word *skandalon*, which originally was the bait stick of a trap that triggered off the trapping mechanism when a bird perched on

it. To join in temple dinners where sacrificial meat was served and to have sex with prostitutes who plied their trade at pagan temples were rites associated with idol worship, both in the Old Testament and the New. The worship of idols had always been strictly forbidden for God's people (1 Jn 5:21), and to have sex with prostitutes constituted scandalous behaviour (1 Cor 6:15-17). But what about the eating of meat, purchased in a market, which had earlier been offered to an idol? Might this perhaps be permissible? The Apostle Paul had considered these issues (Romans chapter 14, 1 Corinthians chapters 8-10), and concluded that although Christians should never compromise with pagan or idol worship, there could be some flexibility as regards eating food that had been offered to idols.

15. *Likewise, some of the Christians at Pergamum also held to the teaching of the Nicolaitans* (2:6), who may similarly have permitted or encouraged idol worship and its associated malpractices. The Nicolaitans remain a historical enigma, and we know nothing for certain about them (but see Appendix 4 on pages 314-317). The tendency of their teaching was to cast doubts on the word of God (Gen 3:1b, Lk 4:9) and provoke Christians to disobey the commandments that forbade the worship of idols and restricted sexual relations to marriage only. They encouraged Christians to go beyond the permitted flexibility, and to compromise their beliefs. Why stand out like a sore thumb when you can so easily go with the flow? Whether their inclination was Balaamite or Nicolaitan, Christ's injunction to the compromised Christians in Pergamum was as sharp as a sword.

16. He called them to *repent then and there*, and warned them that the alternative they would face was that *he would soon come to them and wage war against them with the sword of his mouth*. Only some in the church were compromised, but all were tolerant of those who could lead them astray. Because Christ is perfectly holy, he always has zero tolerance against sin. The sword is the word he speaks. That word reassures and strengthens, but it also destroys those who disregard it.

17. Once again *every church* is exhorted *to listen to Christ's word* to *a particular church*. It is a challenging word, and we are free to let it go in one ear and out of the other, but this would not be a prudent response. When Christ speaks, it is best to listen carefully and act according to

what we have heard. If we obey we shall be conquerors, and *everyone who conquers will receive from Christ* a wonderful double reward. First, in this life, *some of the hidden manna.* While the Israelites wandered in the wilderness, God supplied them with special bread, *manna,* which prompted them to ask, *What is it?* (Ex 16:11-18). In his public ministry, Christ described himself as the living bread that came down from heaven (Jn 6:51). Now he was promising the Christians who lived in the spiritual desert of Pergamum that he would feed them with the hidden manna that was himself. In every age many ordinary followers of Christ have found this promise to be true whenever they become spiritually hungry in a hostile environment (12:6, 14).

Secondly, in the life to come *we shall receive a white stone, and on the white stone a new name is written that no one knows except the one who receives it.* Commentators have spent centuries puzzling what this white stone might be. We know that in public trials, the jury members would be given two stones, one white and one black. At the end of the trial they would hand the white stone to the teller if they thought that the accused person was innocent, and the black one if they thought he or she was guilty. In the next life, Christ says, God will make it clear in public that his people are acquitted and justified. But there is a secret element to this. Everyone will see God giving us a white stone, but only we shall be able to read the new name written on it. In the life to come, we shall have a new body and new tasks that will enrich and fulfil us. They will sum us up perfectly, so they are referred to as our *new name* or nature. The new name will not be made public. It will be a little secret between Jesus Christ and ourselves. As we shall see, Christ himself will also have a new name, unknown to the world (19:12). Will he tell *us* what it is? The answer is yes, for he will write his name upon us (3:12 and 22:4).

Meditation: Why the Truth is so important

If the sin of the Ephesian church was intolerance that was marred by harshness, then the sin of the church at Pergamum was tolerance that was marred by laxity. Christ's complaint to his people in Pergamum was that although they had held fast to his name and had not denied their faith in him, they were tolerating some false teachers in their fellowship. This tolerance may have sprung from love, but if so, it was a misguided love. Love can become sentimental and unreal if it is not strengthened by truth, just as truth can come across as sternness and severity if it is not mellowed by love. Truth and love should complement one another, and all Christians should aim to speak the truth in love, to love others in the truth, and to grow in both love and truth (Eph 4:15, 3 Jn 1, Phil 1:9).

Christ is himself very interested in the truth. He called himself *the truth* and *the light of the world*. He promised his followers that if they continued in his word, they would know *the truth* and *the truth* would make them free. He said to Pilate that he had come to testify to *the truth*, and that anyone who belonged to *the truth* would hear his voice (Jn 14:6, 8:12, 8:31-32, 18:37-38).

In 1626 the Lutheran theologian Rupertus Meldenius wrote *Sit in necessariis unitas, in dubiis libertas, in omnibus caritas*. This could be translated as "unity in what is essential, freedom in what is uncertain, and love in everything". This is an apt commentary on the letters to Ephesus and Pergamum. Christians are free to disagree about non-essentials, but they should never compromise with regard to important basic truths. One such truth concerns the person and work of Christ, who is both our Lord and our Saviour. He is the unique Son of God, who died for our sins on the cross. If I am to call myself a Christian, it is because I trust him as *my Saviour* and obey him as *my Lord* (v 13). I worship *him*, not the emperor. Another truth to which Christians must hold fast is the absolute requirement for holiness in God's people (v 14-16). Christ insisted on this, for God himself is holy, and he demands that we likewise should be holy (Mt 5:48, 1 Pet 1:15-16). There were those at Pergamum who were captivated by Baalamite or Nicolaitan teaching which permitted them to worship Caesar, dabble in idolatry and indulge in sexual relations outside marriage, but these activities are unacceptable to God, who forbids his people from doing abominable things that he hates (Jer 44:2-4).

The sharp sword of God's revealed truth in Christ was much needed in a place like Pergamum. When religious pluralism is rife, there is a danger of compromise. Jesus Christ, sent by God to save us, is not one of many ways to God. He stands alone, for he alone is *the way* to God, he alone reveals *the truth* about God's holy love for us, and he alone is *the life* (Jn 14:6) which he gives abundantly (Jn 10:10).

We should take note of Christ's identification of the source of error. It is Satan. Satan lived and made his throne in Pergamum (v 13). Satan is a defeated foe, for Christ overcame him (Gen 3:15, Lk 10:18, Col 2:15). But despite his overthrow,

Satan and his forces of darkness continue to contest every inch of their territory. Retreat they must, but only as God's kingdom advances. In Pergamum Satan held almost undisputed control. In our own day he is visibly at work in the affluent west, recapturing some lost ground. His favourite tactic is to resist the truth, and he loves to beguile humans into error and spiritual brain fog. He lies to us about God and his requirement that we should be holy (Jn 8:44, 2 Cor 4:4).

But in the book of Revelation the curtain is drawn aside, and we are allowed to see Satan's doom. Christ has won the great battle, and he will help his followers to win the war. The truth will triumph. When intruders steal into our fellowships, pervert the grace of God into licentiousness and deny our only Master and Lord, Jesus Christ, we are to realise that they are destined to be condemned as ungodly (Jude 4). Where the church has permitted grievous error to be taught unchecked, Christ calls his people to *repent* (v 16). He indicates the way of conquest – it is through *his word*. Christ's word is like a sharp sword (v 12), as was prophesied by Isaiah (Isa 49:2). One day this sword will change its function, and the word of truth will become the word of judgement (v 16). The same gospel of Christ which saves those who obey it, will one day destroy those who disobey it.

VII

2:18-29 The Letter to Thyatira, who neglected Holiness

The longest of the seven letters is addressed to the church in the least important of the seven towns. Little is known about Thyatira. It was well situated between two valleys and was probably a good commercial centre. It had a number of trade guilds, including ones for wool-workers, linen-workers, leather-workers, tanners, dyers, potters, bakers, slave-dealers and bronze-smiths. In the book of Acts we read of Lydia, a dealer in purple cloth who had been a dyer and a wool-worker in Thyatira. She had travelled on business to Philippi, where she heard the Apostle Paul preach the gospel. The Lord opened her heart and she was baptised (Acts 16:13-15). We do not know if she subsequently returned to Thyatira, but if she did, she may well have planted the Christian church there.

18. *Christ introduces himself to the church in Thyatira*, this time *as the Son of God*, a title that emphasises his majesty. He has *eyes like a flame of fire* *and feet like burnished bronze*, as in 1:14-15. The eyes of Christ gaze pene-tratingly and see everything, and his feet will pursue all that is evil and trample it down.

19. *He knows the good works* of these Thyatiran Christians. They possess *love*, which is the greatest of the graces (1 Cor 13:13); *faith*, which is vital for initial trust in Christ and continuing reliance on him; *service* of God and their neighbour, which God expects all his people to abound in; and *patient endurance*, something we all find difficult and which requires all the strength that comes from God's glorious power (Col 1:11). What is more, they had been growing in each of these qual-ities. *Their last works were greater than their first.* The Christian life is meant to be a life of progress and growth, like a child growing into mature adulthood or a vine that spreads and yields much fruit after being pruned. While Ephesus was backsliding, Thyatira was moving forward, and deserved Christ's commendation.

20. Once again, however, Christ has to use the adversative *But* (as in v 4, 14). He points to certain defects in the church in connection with a woman whom he refers to as *Jezebel*. The name must be symbolic, for no woman would have been called Jezebel in Jewish or Christian circles at that time, because Jezebel, the Sidonian princess who married the Israelite king Ahab, had been notoriously evil. She had introduced and encouraged the cult of Baal into Israel, and was infamous for her whoredoms and sorceries (1 Ki 16:30-32; 18:4, 19; 21:25-26; 2 Ki 9:22). In our own day it is likewise unusual to name a male child Judas or Adolf. This "Jezebel" *called herself a prophet*, and *she was teaching and beguiling the servants of God to indulge in fornication and to eat food sacrificed to idols.* She was a false teacher who sought to seduce God's people into immorality and eating idol meats. She too held to the teaching of Balaam (v 14). It seems that Jezebel and Balaam are symbolic names for the same sinful tendencies, but whereas in Pergamum they orig-inated from the obligation to worship the emperor, in Thyatira they arose from the desire to succeed in commerce and trade.

The trade guilds there provided banquets for their members. These meals were dedicated to a pagan god, and to join in them involved revering the god and engaging with the temple prostitutes. Now what was alarming in Thyatira was that God's people *tolerated that woman*

Jezebel. In our day tolerance is a highly esteemed quality, but its value must surely depend on what is being tolerated. As John Stott wrote, tolerance is not a virtue when what is being tolerated is evil. But immorality and idolatry are intolerable as far as Christ is concerned. He looks at unholy churches like the one in Thyatira with eyes like a flame of fire. It makes him very angry when a church is "tolerant" enough to turn the grace of God into an excuse for taking part in activities that he loathes, and which Christians are called to shun (1 Cor 6:18; Gal 5:19-20; Eph 5:3-5; Col 3:5; 1 Thess 4:3-8; Tit 2:11-14; Jude 4, 7).

21. Christ is patient and slow to anger. *He gives wrongdoers time to repent. But Jezebel did not repent. She persisted in her fornication* and her wrong teaching. What was worse, by claiming to be a prophet she was passing her beliefs to others in God's name. Christ graciously invited her to turn from evil and return to him, but she disdained his warning. She let herself in for a most unpleasant surprise.

22. Her punishment is vividly depicted. Christ captures our attention by asking us to *Beware*. He would proceed to *throw her on a bed.* She had profaned the bed of love, and would therefore find herself in a bed of sickness. Christ would also *throw those who had committed adultery with her into great distress.* This would refer primarily to those who had been foolish enough to accept her teaching, but since it involved sexual laxity some of them would have committed adultery in the literal sense. There was still the possibility of mercy, for Christ added the rider *unless they repented of her doings.* The book of Revelation contains several grim warnings of judgement, but they always come with a promise of forgiveness for those who repent. The enormity of Jezebel's sin is made clear by the fact that they were to repent of *her* doings, and begin to do *Christ's* instead (v 26). She had not only committed serious sins of her own, but had deliberately led others into sin.

23. If *her closest followers* did not return to him, then Christ would *strike them dead.* The Greek means "to kill them with death", which in the Bible often implies a death by plague or some other severe illness (as in 6:8). This judgement would have an effect on *all the churches.* They would know that *Christ searches minds and hearts* (Ps 7:9; Jer 11:20, 17:10, 20:12). He knows both our thoughts and our emotions. Nothing is hidden from him. Even our secrets are well known to him (Ps 139:1-4,

Heb 4:13). *All people will be recompensed as their works deserve* (20:12-13). In the Bible works are never the basis or means of our salvation, but they are the evidence that we have been saved, and because of this they constitute an excellent criterion for judgement. There will be nothing impersonal about the Day of Judgement. Each of us will be judged individually, personally and fairly.

24. Christ was aware that some members of the church in Thyatira *did not hold to this teaching*. They were true believers and had not been led astray into idolatry or immorality. They *had not learnt what some people call "the deep things of Satan"*. It was the false teachers who held to "the deep things of Satan". They believed that in order to defeat Satan, the most important thing was to keep their souls pure. What their bodies did was unimportant. Even though they lapsed into gross sensuality, they believed this was all right because it involved their bodies only, while their minds and souls remained pure. But it is incorrect to differentiate in this way between our behaviour and what our bodies do. If my body sins, then so do I.

   But Christ had guarded *the rest of them*. They had not fallen for the false teachings. He now reassures them by saying that *he lays no other burden on them*. They had willingly assumed all the duties of loving, faithful and patient Christian servants (Acts 15:28-29). Surrounded by laxity in sexual practices, they might think it wise to become ascetic or extremely rigid. But this was as unnecessary as it would have been unhelpful. No further burden would Christ lay on them.

25. Not that they were being promised a life of ease. On the contrary, they were to *hold fast to what they had until Christ came*. His coming was certain – it would either be on the day of their death, or else on the day of his return. What exactly were they to hold on to? It was the balanced and joyful goodness enjoined in the Bible, and the glorious liberty they had as God's children. It was the pure morality that regarded the right use of sex as something beautiful and God-given, and its wrong use as ugly and ungodly. It was the teaching that marriage should be held in honour by everyone, and the marriage bed kept undefiled, for God would judge fornicators and adulterers (Heb 13:4). God's commandments are not burdensome (1 Jn 5:3). Christ's yoke is easy and his burden is light (Mt 11:30).

26. This time Christ's promise is for *those who not only conquer, but continue to do his works to the very end*. There must be no question of dabbling in Jezebel's doings (v 22). A different sort of life is required from Christ's followers, who are to stay holy for the rest of their lives, doing *his* works. Only those who endure to the end will be saved (Mk 13:13). *Christ will give them authority over the nations.* They will be given leadership roles in the life to come (Mt 19:28, Lk 19:15-19).

27. *They shall rule them with an iron rod, as when clay pots are shattered.* It is the Messiah who will shatter all rebellious earthly rulers with an iron rod (12:5, 19:15; Ps 2:9; Jer 51:20-23), but those who overcome will have a part to play in the final decisive victory of Christ over worldly forces that oppose him. In order to consummate it, evil itself will be destroyed on the final day (20:10).

28. This gift of authority by Christ to his victorious people *will echo the gift of authority by God the Father to him* (Mt 28:18, Lk 22:29), so it is an awe-inspiring prospect. *Furthermore, Christ will give them the morning star.* Since he himself is the bright morning star (22:16), the promise is that his presence will forever remain with those who have persevered. The ultimate reward of the true Christian is to be with his Lord always (Mt 28:20). Nothing could be better than that.

29. *Let anyone who has an ear listen to what the Spirit is saying to the churches.* This letter is not only for this particular church, but for all subsequent churches. The need for holiness is paramount for all of God's people. God himself is utterly holy, and they must strive to be holy as well. The Holy Spirit continues to speak to every church as he spoke to the one in Thyatira. We who belong to the church have been given two ears. Let us listen closely to what the Holy Spirit has to say.

Meditation: When the Future is at Stake

The strong trade guilds in the town of Thyatira would have made it difficult for Christians there to earn their living without belonging to one of them. This would involve attending the guild banquets, which entailed eating meat that had earlier been sacrificed to an idol. Anyone who did not conform was out of a job. Jezebel may have taken a seemingly Christian line, arguing that idols were lifeless (1 Cor 8:4), so it was fine for Christians to enter into the spirit of the meals. However, these could easily degenerate into sexual orgies when prostitutes from the pagan temples made their appearance. Some Christians welcomed her teaching, for it enabled them to keep up their Christian profession while indulging in immoral heathen rites. The fact that Jezebel was a prophetess gave their lifestyle some credibility. A similar temptation to conform to worldly standards faces Christians today. How far should we accept or adopt contemporary standards and practices? We form part of society, but we must not deny Christ. So we must find Christian solutions which enable us to maintain high Christian standards while we play our part in everyday life. We must both *remain in the world* and *be distinct from it.*

The church at Thyatira was the opposite of the church at Ephesus in two ways:

(a) The Ephesian church had abandoned the love they had at first, but at Thyatira the most recent works of the church were greater than their first works.

(b) The Ephesian Christians rightly did not tolerate false teachers, but they lacked love. Those at Thyatira had plenty of love, but they tolerated an evil prophetess who was leading many of them away from Christ.

If we go the way of the Ephesian church, our beliefs will be correct but our lack of love will alienate us from the world to such an extent that in the end we shall have no unbelieving friends. We shall be unable to be the salt of the earth because our flavour will no longer be salty but will instead be bitter – and so Christ will remove our lampstand from its place. But if we imitate the laxity of the Thyatiran church, the world will find us engaging although our lives will no longer be godly and pure. Because we put expediency above principle, we shall suffer the fate of all worldly cults and gradually die away. *Holiness without love* is unattractive, and *love without holiness* is unconvincing. It is *holy love* that is Christlike.

The Apostle Paul wrote, "Do you not know that the saints will judge the world?" (1 Cor 6:2). As John Stott memorably put it, those who have learnt to do Christ's works in this life will continue to do them in the next. Those who are able to rule over their own passions here on earth will rule over other people in heaven. Those who welcome Christ as King of their lives now will share in his kingly rule forever. It is those faithful Christians who have spurned the standards of this world, controlled the desires of their flesh, and resisted the alluring appeals of the devil, who will receive the reward of ever-present light from the morning star. They will rule the nations together with the Lord of the nations. Refusing to plunge into the depths of Satan, they will fathom the depths of Christ. However great their renunciations may have been in the battle for holiness, they will go on and remain with Christ, absolutely and eternally content.

VIII

3:1-6 The Letter to Sardis, who lacked Reality

Sardis was located where five important roads met, and was a very wealthy town and an active commercial centre. It was once the capital of Lydia, whose emperor Croesus was famed for his fortune. Wealth came easily to Sardis, and this made its people complacent and lackadaisical. It was captured by Cyrus the Great in 546 BC, and again by Antiochus in 218 BC, each time because the citizens were slack. The town was built on a very steep hill and was said to be impregnable, but on both occasions enemy soldiers scaled the precipice by night and found that the Sardians had not taken the trouble to set a guard. The main religion in Sardis was the cult of the Phrygian nature goddess Cybele, but no mention is made of any persecution of the Christians, nor of any heretical tendencies aimed at unsettling them. The church in Sardis led a relatively sheltered existence, and the problems it encountered may have arisen because of this. When all is going well, Christians are inclined to take it easy, and they become slack. In Sardis the majority of the Christians were nominal and just went through the motions. Spiritually they were lifeless. They professed to be Christians, but their words lacked conviction, their pretensions were unjustified, their rituals lacked reality, and their promise would remain unfulfilled. Only *a few* had not *soiled their clothes* and *were worthy* (v 4).

1. The greeting to *the church in Sardis* emphasises the need for divine endowment and sincere reality in the church. Christ is the one *who has the seven spirits of God and the seven stars* (1:4, 16, 20). From the fact that he "has the seven spirits of God" we may learn that Christ himself had been endowed by God with seven wonderful gifts or graces of the Holy Spirit (Isa 11:2, Jn 3:34-35). The fact that he also has the seven stars implies that we who form part of the worldwide church may also be filled with the Spirit of reality. It must have come as a shock to hear the terrible words, *I know your works; you have a name of being alive, but you are dead.* The Sardian church was renowned as being alive, when in reality it was lifeless. Its members held to the outward forms of godliness, but denied its power (2 Tim 3:5). They had faith and their beliefs were correct, but faith without good works is dead (Jas 2:17). They had a good reputation, but that was all they had.

2. Christ's call to *Wake up* (16:15, Rom 13:11) must have struck some chords in Sardis, where on two occasions the city had been captured while nobody was on the watch. Every Christian needs to cultivate spiritual vigilance, in case they lose everything. Only a little bit of life *remained* in Sardis, and Christ urged the church to *strengthen it*, for even that tiny living remnant was *on the point of death*. If an ember is not fanned into flame, it becomes cold. This church may have pleased some people, but it clearly did not please God. Its good works were incomplete, and Christ *did not esteem them to be perfect in the sight of God* (Dan 5:27).

The believers in Sardis were like the prodigal son about whom the father complained, "This son of mine was dead" (Lk 15:24). They needed to hear the call of Christ (Jn 5:25), wake up and thereby come back to life (Eph 5:14). Why was this church not persecuted by the Jews or the Romans? George Caird suggested that nobody felt threatened by it: "Content with mediocrity, lacking both the enthusiasm to entertain a heresy and the depth of conviction which provokes intolerance, it was too innocuous to be worth persecuting". They were putting on an act, summed up by the Prophet Isaiah as follows: "These people draw near with their mouths and honour me with their lips, while their hearts are far from me, and their worship of me is a human commandment learnt by rote" (Isa 29:13).

3. Here the word *Remember* means "bear in mind" rather than "recall". They were to bear in mind *the good news that they had received and heard*. They might have placed their faith on it, but they had not *obeyed* it, and *their repentance was weak* if it existed at all. They had never really got going on "the obedience of faith" (Rom 1:5). The need for them to *wake up* was now imperative. If they did not do so, *Christ would come like a thief* and *they would not know at what hour he would suddenly appear before them* (Mt 24:43, Lk 12:39, 1 Thess 5:2, 2 Pet 3:10). This does not refer to Christ's return but to a visitation of judgement, whose nature is not spelt out. This makes it all the more ominous. God is to be feared. One of the causes of the malaise of the Sardian Christians was that they did not fear him.

As an aside, it is worth noting the suggestion of some commentators that the verse now in 16:15, which is somewhat startling in its present position, may once have belonged in the middle of verse 3, but later it was somehow displaced.

4. There remained *a few persons in this church who had not soiled their clothes.* If we were slightly old-fashioned we might have said that they had not blotted their copybook. In today's language, they had not spoiled their record or harmed their reputation in God's eyes. In spite of the pernicious and stifling influence of the pagan environment, they had not surrendered to the spiritual lethargy that was clogging up their church. *They would walk with Christ* (Gen 5:22, 24), *dressed in white, for they were worthy.* White clothing is mentioned seven times in the book of Revelation – another implicit heptad (3:4-5, 18; 4:4; 6:11; 7:9, 13; 19:14).

   White is the colour linked with purity and here it suggests being in the right with God, for it is linked to being inscribed in the book of life (v 5). Their worthiness was, initially, *imputed.* They could say that before God they were "just as if I'd never sinned" (or, using the appropriate biblical term, "justified"). But those who are made worthy by God always display this worth in their lives. God then *infuses* godliness in them by forming the fruit of the Holy Spirit in their lives (Gal 5:22-23). In the Bible righteousness is first imputed and then infused (Isa 61:10-11).

5. Having issued a formidable challenge to all the believers in Sardis, Christ now has a wonderful promise for those who have taken his challenge to heart: *If you conquer you will be clothed like them in white robes, and I will not blot your name out of the book of life.* Those who "strengthened what remained and was on the point of death" would be treated like those who had not soiled their clothes: their names would be retained in *the book of life*, which is the register of all the citizens of the eternal kingdom (Ex 32:32-33; Ps 69:28, 139:16; Isa 4:3; Dan 12:1; Mal 3:16; Lk 10:20; Phil 4:3; Heb 12:23). This book of life is mentioned several times in the book of Revelation (3:5, 13:8, 17:8, 20:12, 20:15, 21:27). All those whose names were inscribed in the book were assured of eternal life. They would be seen to be worthy, prepared as a bride adorned for her husband, clothed with garments of salvation and covered with a robe of righteousness (21:2, Isa 61:10). They need have no fears about the next life because, far from blotting out their names, *Christ would confess them before his Father and the holy angels.* He had previously made similar promises in his earthly ministry

(Mt 10:32-33, Lk 12:8). To know that Jesus Christ, the Son of God, is going to vouch for you before God and the heavenly court gives you a cast-iron guarantee of final acceptance.

6. The Holy Spirit features prominently in this letter to the church in Sardis. Its message originates from the one who has the sevenfold endowment of the Spirit upon him, and who wants all the churches to be similarly endowed (v 1). *He is also speaking to us all today. Are we listening to him? What is our reaction to his warnings? Are we heeding his advice? Will we be strengthened by his promises?*

Meditation: The Seven Spirits of God

Who can make a dead church come back to life? The answer is the Holy Spirit! He is the Spirit of God and of Christ (Rom 8:9), and he is described as *the Spirit of life* (Rom 8:2). He can breathe into our formal worship until it becomes alive and is real. He can animate our dead works and make them pulsate with life. He can take a moribund church and make it a living force in the community. He can teach us all to *live* by the Spirit (Gal 5:16, 25), to *pray* in the Spirit (Jude 20), to *testify* in the Spirit (1 Thess 1:5), and to *worship* in the Spirit (Jn 4:24, Phil 3:3).

The book of Isaiah lays great store on the fact that the Messiah would have the Spirit resting upon him (Isa 42:1, 59:21, 61:1). It prophesied that the Spirit would bestow seven divine graces on him: "The Spirit of the Lord shall rest on him, the Spirit of wisdom and understanding, the Spirit of counsel and might, the Spirit of knowledge and the fear of the Lord" (Isa 11:2). The book of Revelation refers to his sevenfold bestowal by calling him "the seven Spirits" (Rev 1:4, 3:1, 4:5, 5:6). God did not give the Spirit "by measure" to Christ, but in fullness (Jn 3:34). Christ in his turn will send the Spirit to his followers (Jn 14:16-17, 15:26, 16:7), so that we may be filled with him (Eph 5:18). But what is the Spirit like? What did he do for Christ, and what can he do for us? The answers are to be found in Isaiah 11:2.

(a) He is the Spirit of the Lord, for the promotion of godliness. God is both loving and holy. That is his nature. God's Spirit is the Holy Spirit, the Spirit of holy love. When Christ began his ministry, he was so filled with the Spirit of God that he radiated the love and holiness of God. He was "full of grace and truth" (Jn 1:14), and Christ wants his church to be loving and holy like himself. With the Spirit's help, our character can be perfectly balanced, just like Christ's was (Jn 1:17).

(b) He is the Spirit of wisdom, for just and discerning government. In his ministry Christ encountered both leaders and servants. Led by the Spirit, he dealt with each one according to their station in life. He encouraged those in power to be kind, and the poor to keep the law. He longed for justice, equity and a fair deal for all. Thanks to the Holy Spirit's wisdom those in the churches will be able to discern the longings and aspirations of all types of people, and in a compassionate way do what they can in order to enable these desires to be fulfilled.

(c) He is the Spirit of understanding, for empathy with other people. With his mind sharpened by the Spirit, Christ knew how to meet every person at his or her point of need. Quoting Isaiah (35:4-6, 61:1), he proclaimed that "the blind receive their sight, the lame walk, the lepers are cleansed, the deaf hear, the dead are raised and the poor have good news brought to them" (Mt 11:4-5). With the Holy Spirit's gift of understanding, the church may also draw alongside the needy.

(d) He is the Spirit of counsel, for the edification of the damaged. The words of the Spirit-filled Christ were wonderfully positive and had an unprecedented moral and edifying persuasiveness. He brought peace to troubled minds by his words of authority (Mk 5:1-15). He helped people who had once been promiscuous to turn their lives around, and instructed them on how to be pure (Jn 4:5-26, 39-42). By using the Word of God, which is the sword of the Spirit, the church can similarly help those who wish to do so to repent and have a new beginning.

(e) He is the Spirit of might, for warfare against evil and deceit. Christ was given heroic energy. After being tempted, he was "filled with the power of the Spirit" (Lk 4:14). Among his many mighty restorative acts, he healed people from their diseases and delivered those who were oppressed by evil spirits. He liberated the captives, and set free those in bondage to evil thoughts. With the Holy Spirit's enabling, the church may likewise engage in a ministry of liberating prisoners.

(f) He is the Spirit of the knowledge of the Lord, for the growth of the church. Knowing God's will, Christ broadcasts the salvation that is available to those who personally trust in him (Jn 3:16). He defined eternal life as being the same thing as knowing God and his Son Jesus Christ (Jn 17:3). People who met him had their lives transformed. The church has been entrusted with the great commission to make disciples of all nations, and to achieve this end they need the Spirit's filling.

(g) He is the Spirit of the fear of the Lord, for the cultivation of humility. Christ always found fulfilment in accomplishing God's will (Jn 4:34). He lived a life of

perfect submission to his Father (Jn 5:19-20, 30, 36). He always waited for God's will to become clear, and then he spoke or acted accordingly. So great was his longing to please his Father at all times, that the very possibility of deviating from his Father's will in any way would have distressed him. He was afraid of causing God grief. Before his Father he was always humble. This is what "the fear of the Lord" means. Someone who fears God does not cower away from him in petrified terror. On the contrary, his fear of God releases him from every other fear, and facilitates his perfect obedience of God. As the hymn-writers Tate and Brady put it, "Fear him, ye saints, and you will then have nothing else to fear".

In today's church believers are being urged to seek all kinds of manifestations of the Spirit of God. In fact, there are seven which are more important and more useful than any of the others, both for the one who has been given them and for those with whom he or she comes into contact. They are the seven that Christ was so wonderfully endowed with. And the last of the seven is the most important and useful of all, for we read of Christ in Isaiah 11:3a that "His *delight* shall be in the fear of the Lord". This was what he prized above all else. He loved his heavenly Father so much that to walk in the fear of him was his ongoing delight.

The letter to the church at Sardis makes it clear that there is a difference between reputation and reality, between what people see and what God sees (1 Sam 16:7b). To be obsessed with appearance and reputation leads to hypocrisy, which Jesus hated. A true and living church is characterised by sincerity and reality. These are qualities that the Holy Spirit produces in the heart and life of any Christian who regularly meets with God and by faith drinks in the Holy Spirit (Jn 7:37-39).

IX

3:7-13 The Letter to Philadelphia, who had an open Door

Philadelphia was founded by Attalus II Philadelphus around 140 BC at a junction of several important trade routes to the East. Its situation and its vineyards made it a prosperous town. It was a centre of worship of Dionysos, also called Bacchus, a Greco-Roman nature god of fruitfulness and vegetation, especially associated with wine and ecstasy. Its church was small (v 8) but good. Its enemies were not within the church but outsiders, since there is no mention of heresy or factions. It had much in common with the church in Smyrna. Both received much praise and no blame from Christ; both suffered at the hands of those who said that they were true Jews but were not; both were also persecuted by the Romans; both were told by Christ that their opposition was satanic; and both were promised a crown.

7. Christ introduces himself to *the church in Philadelphia* as the *one who is holy and true* (6:10). The word *holy* implies that he is dedicated to God and his service, while the word *true* tells us that he is utterly reliable. Christ *has the key of David. He opens and no one will shut, he shuts and no one opens.* This phrase is taken from the Old Testament, where King Hezekiah's chief steward Eliakim was given the keys of the household of David (Isa 22:22). The opening and shutting tell of the power to include or exclude people, which only the king could override. Such a great responsibility was God-given and its purpose was the good of the many. This provides the background for Christ's commission of Peter (Mt 16:19) and of the church (Mt 18:18). God gave ultimate authority to Christ. He has the keys of Death and Hades (1:18). He alone can admit people to the heavenly Jerusalem.

8. *Christ knew their works.* They were many, and he has nothing but good to say about them. *He had given to these Christians at Philadelphia an open door* for effective work (1 Cor 16:9), *which no one else was able to shut.* If Christ decrees that his work will prosper, nobody else may interfere. *He knew* that *this church had little power.* This would not stop them from being mighty and effective in his service (1 Cor 1:26-29). Despite their weakness, *they had kept his word and had not denied his name.* Their lot was to be persecuted and opposed, but these weak and vulnerable believers were standing firm in their faith.

9. Christ goes on to say that *he would deal with those of the synagogue of Satan* (see the comments on 2:9), *who said that they were Jews and were not, but were lying.* Therefore *he would make these false Jews come and bow down before the feet of Christians* (who were now the Israel of God, Rom 2:28-29, Gal 6:16), and *the false Jews would learn that Christ had loved those who were true.* In contrast to the misguided Jewish expectation that the Gentiles would eventually submit to them (based on

a misinterpretation of Isa 60:14), Christ says that all unbelievers, false Jews included, must one day submit to the Christians whom they despised, for it is the latter whom Christ loved so much that he gave them an open door into his kingdom. Nobody else could shut that door, nor open it for themselves.

10. God honours those who honour him (1 Sam 2:30b). *Because the Christians at Philadelphia had kept Christ's word of patient endurance,* he in his turn would *keep them from the hour of trial that was coming on the whole world to test the inhabitants of the earth.* Christ had said, "Be faithful unto death, and I will give you the crown of life" (2:10). This was the way for his people to conquer Satan (12:11). This was Christ's word of patient endurance (Mk 13:13). Because those at Philadelphia had kept it in spite of strong opposition, Christ would keep them from the thoroughgoing test that would come to everyone in the world. This test could prove to be a severe mercy for *the inhabitants of the earth,* who would face the test before being judged and perhaps punished, so that God could assess their reaction to severe affliction. This group does not include those who know Christ, because the latter are citizens of heaven, who would not be led into the test, but would be kept from the visitation of judgement by being "sealed" (7:2-8) and by "fleeing into the wilderness" for refuge (12:6, 14).

11. *Christ promises that he himself will come again.* Of course we want to know exactly when this momentous event will be. Christ does not give a specific answer (Mk 13:32), but he assures us that it will be *soon* (1:1, 22:7, 12, 20). This is in agreement with the well-known saying that Christians should live as if Christ had died yesterday, is sending his Spirit to help them today, and will return tomorrow. Therefore now, in the present, *his people must keep a firm grip on what they already have, so that no one may seize their crown* (2:25). Nobody can steal their crown from them, but they might foolishly forfeit it, just as Esau forfeited his privileged position to Jacob, and Saul to David. To serve God is a high privilege which comes with its corresponding responsibility, which is to persevere and be faithful until the end (2:10). Christ enjoins his people to do just this.

12. If we keep going, we shall be *those who conquer.* Our reward will be to be made *pillars in the temple of my God.* A pillar of the church is

someone who is absolutely stable, and will stand firmly for the truth of the gospel against powerful opposition (Jer 1:18, Gal 2:9, 1 Tim 3:15). Pillars represent permanence, and in Philadelphia, often shaken by earthquakes, they gave a sense of security. To be in the temple of God symbolises the fact that we shall be forever in the presence of God, for *we shall never go out of it.* The words *my God* are repeated four times in this verse, to emphasise the fact that the promises Christ makes are backed up by the one true God with whom Christ is at one (Jn 1:1, 10:30). And what Christ has promised is that *on his people he will write the name of his God, the name of the city of his God, and his own new name.* Each one of us belongs to God, each has citizenship rights in the New Jerusalem (21:9-27, Heb 11:10, 12:22, 13:14), and we shall all relate to Christ in our own individual way.

Leon Morris wrote, "[Christ's] new name possibly refers to the new state of affairs brought about by the consummation of redemption. Then Christ appears in a character in which he could not appear until this consummation was reached". The idea of a new name would have appealed to this church, because the town had already received a new name on two occasions – Neocaesarea, to thank Tiberius for his help in rebuilding the town after an earthquake, and Flavia, in honour of Vespasian's family name. Fortunately the beautiful name Philadelphia persisted. It means "brotherly love".

13. Once again we read the words: *Let anyone who has an ear listen to what the Spirit is saying to the churches.* This refrain provides us with three foundational principles about God's word, the Bible. First, *Scripture has a double authorship*, for although the letters were written by John, the Holy Spirit speaks through them. As we read the Bible, God's word is passed on to us through the Biblical writers.

Secondly, *Scripture has a universal application*, for although each letter was sent to a particular church, through it the Holy Spirit speaks to all the churches. The Bible is for everyone, not just for those to whom it is addressed.

Thirdly, *Scripture is God's word for every age*, for although the letters were written before they were read, the Holy Spirit "is saying" something to the readers, whenever they study them. The Bible speaks with power and immediacy to all who read it down the centuries. We should therefore read it expectantly day by day, and listen carefully to what the Holy Spirit is saying to us. He is our sanctifier and teacher.

Meditation: An open Door for effective Service

The metaphor of an open door is used in the New Testament to denote those who are receptive to the gospel message, but a closed door means that they are resistant to it. In his letter to the Christians at Philadelphia, the risen Christ says that he has the key of David, with which he can open closed doors and close open ones (v 7). He had set before them an open door, which no one was able to shut (v 8). This door was a door of opportunity: a wide door to preach the gospel effectively had been opened for them. They were free to pass on the good news of Christ to other people. True, there were many adversaries, but they could pass on the good news because the door of opportunity was open. They could be witnesses to Christ in a pagan culture. Philadelphia was open to Christian mission. The church was small and weak, but Christ had opened for them a door of fruitful service. What exactly was this door that he had opened? We may think of it as a threefold door:

(a) *It was the door of external opportunity*. The Apostle Paul often referred to the idea of an open door of opportunity (e.g. Acts 14:27, 1 Cor 16:9, 2 Cor 2:12). He could preach the gospel only because Christ had opened this door. There were times when the door was shut and he was impeded in his missionary enterprise. There are doors that can be closed for missionaries today: *legal doors*, closed by the power of hostile governments; *cultural doors*, closed by the power of alien embedded ideas; and *ethnic doors*, closed by the power of national loyalty. The devil wants them to stay closed, because of laws forbidding Christian mission, or a culture that rejects Christian belief as folly or weakness, or by confusing religion with patriotism. The few conversions to Christ that may still happen will then be equated with lawlessness, apostasy or treason. It is completely impossible for us to open closed doors, but the risen, reigning and triumphant Christ has the keys, and *he can open them*. Are we praying to him, asking that he may do so?

(b) *It was the door of the mouths of those who witnessed to Christ*. Paul asked his friends to pray for him that he might be given the gift of communication. He longed to declare the message of Christ *clearly, as he should* (Col 4:3-4), and also to make known the message of the gospel *boldly, as he must* (Eph 6:19-20). We in our turn should also tell forth the gospel *clearly*, i.e. lucidly, intelligibly and relevantly; and also *boldly*, i.e. courageously, without soft-pedalling those aspects of the gospel that are unfashionable, unpopular or politically incorrect. It is clear that in answer to prayer, *God did open the door of Paul's mouth.* His presentation of the good news of Christ was remarkably clear and forthright. May God open our mouths today by speaking to us the word "Ephphatha", as Christ did to a deaf man who could not speak (Mk 7:32-35).

(c) It was the door of the hearts of their listeners. This is the third of the doors that must be opened. Nothing will be achieved if the lives of our listeners remain closed to Christ. People are naturally blind to Christ and cannot see the kingdom of God without being born from above (Jn 3:3). The god of this world has blinded their minds, to keep them from seeing the light of the gospel of the glory of Christ (2 Cor 4:4). Lydia, who went from Thyatira to Philippi as a dealer in purple cloth, was a pagan who found Judaism attractive. She was a God-fearer who attended Jewish services. She went along to them and one day Paul came there and spoke. *The Lord opened her heart* to listen eagerly to what he said. She was converted and baptised. There are many like her today, disillusioned with worldviews such as secularism, communism, hedonism or Islam. They are searching for reality, significance and transcendence. They are slowly realising their need for the living Christ. We need to pray that their hearts and minds will be opened to receive him.

All three of these doors need to be open, and here is a fable to illustrate this: A Christian evangelist was invited to a town hall to preach the gospel to the people of that town. On arriving, he found the town hall locked and he could not enter. Moreover, during the trip he caught a bad cold and completely lost his voice, so that he could only whisper inaudibly or croak unintelligibly. Even worse, he was informed that there was a full house in the town hall, but all of them were deaf. He had a communication problem! He needed all the various doors to be opened: those of the town hall, the one of his mouth, and those of the ears of the crowd.

We need to acknowledge that some doors are shut and some are open. We may pray that Christ will open closed doors, and we may seize the opportunity of those that are open, and speak to people about Christ as clearly and boldly as we can.

X

3:14-22 The Letter to Laodicea, who were not wholehearted

Laodicea was one of the richest commercial centres in the world, so this letter to them gives us a picture of the church in an affluent society. The city was famous for its banking, for its manufacture of clothing from the local black wool, and for its renowned medical school. There was a large Jewish colony, which numbered over 7,000 men as well as women and children. The church at Laodicea may have been established by the preaching of Epaphras (Col 1:7, 4:12-13). We know that the Apostle Paul wrote them a letter (Col 4:16). This has been lost, unless it was a copy of Ephesians. But by the time John wrote the Revelation, the Laodicean church was in a very bad shape, and it received the most severe condemnation.

14. The risen and glorified Christ introduces himself as *the Amen, the faithful and true witness, and the origin of God's creation. The Amen* echoes the title "the God of faithfulness", literally "the God of Amen" in Isaiah 65:16. Just as God is faithful, so is his Christ, who is *the faithful and true witness* (1:5). He remained reliable unto death, in direct contrast to the Christians of Laodicea, who were self-satisfied and faithless. Christ is also *the origin of God's creation*, for all things were made through him and he was God's supreme agent in the creation (Jn 1:3, Col 1:15-16). This exalts the Creator above the puny creatures who boast in their self-sufficiency. Leon Morris points out that there are in this letter several echoes of the epistle to the Colossians, which Paul had asked the Laodiceans to read (Col 4:16), and that John is now appealing to their knowledge of it.

15. *Christ knows their works.* He does not give details, but sums up the members of the church as being *neither cold nor hot. He wishes that they were either cold or hot.* If they were cold, they would be like a chilled refreshing drink on a hot summer's day (1 Cor 16:17-18). If they were hot, they would be fervent in spirit and have a healing effect (Rom 12:11). These comparisons may have arisen from the fact that Laodicea's water supply was drawn from hot springs to the south, at Denizli, and was still tepid after flowing for eight kilometres through stone pipes. It made for an unpleasant drink, unlike the supply of cold water that was welcome refreshment to their neighbours at Colossae, or that of

hot water with healing salts which was a continual blessing to those in Hierapolis.

16. The trouble with the Laodicean Christians was that *they were lukewarm. Not cold, not hot* – just tepid and disgusting. So much so, that *Christ is about to spit them out of his mouth.* The word for *spit* is *emeo*, from which we get our English word *emetic.* Instead of *spit*, it should be translated *spew* or even *vomit.* Christ is warning them that he will utterly repudiate them. If the Ephesians had too much zeal (aggravated by their disagreeable lack of love), then the Laodiceans had no zeal at all. Their lukewarm nature was intolerable.

17. Their proud boasts revealed what they were really like. *They said, "I am rich, I have prospered, and I need nothing".* Laodicea was a city of self-made and self-reliant people. This independence may be admirable in material things, but in the spiritual realm, self-sufficiency brings destitution. The Laodicean Christians were materially rich but spiritually bankrupt. They were the very opposite of those in Smyrna, who were materially poor but spiritually rich (2:9). So Christ sums them up in a devastating sentence: *"you do not realise that you are wretched, pitiable, poor, blind and naked".* There is an article before *wretched*: they had become *the* wretched ones. Of all peoples, they were the ones most to be *pitied.* Spiritually they were *poor, blind and naked* – and that in spite of their Laodicean banks, their medical school and their clothing industry. Their spiritual poverty was like the material poverty of the Christians in Smyrna – it amounted to destitution.

18. The remedy for their spiritual malaise is *Christ himself.* He bids them to come to him and *buy* three life-changing blessings. The word *buy* means *obtain freely,* as in Isaiah 55:1-2. First, they needed true wealth, *gold refined by fire so that you should be rich.* There is a richness to be found in the costly service of Christ that trumps the greatest treasures to be found on earth (1 Pet 1:6-7). Secondly, their spiritual rags had to be replaced by *white robes that would clothe them and keep the shame of their nakedness from being seen.* In antiquity, to be naked was the greatest humiliation (2 Sam 10:4-5, Isa 20:4, Ezek 16:37-39), but to be clothed in fine robes was an honour (16:15, Gen 41:42, Esther 6:6-11, Dan 5:29). The white colour of the robes symbolises the holiness without which nobody is righteous in God's eyes (6:9-11), and it contrasted with the black clothing for which the city was famed. Thirdly, *they had to anoint their eyes with the special salve given by Christ in order to see.* Not far from Laodicea Phrygian stone was mined, which was powdered and mixed with oil so as to produce collyrium, an eye ointment. But it is only from Christ himself that we receive true spiritual vision (Jn 9:39).

19. This strong rebuke is actually a sign that Christ loves them, and so he says, *I reprove and discipline those whom I love* (Prov 3:11-12, Heb 12:5-6, Jn 15:1-2). It is a touching manifestation of the love of God, which extends to those who least deserve it. It is obvious that love must reprove, but perhaps it is less obvious that love must also discipline. In times of old, when a sheep persistently wandered off on its own way, the exasperated shepherd would take hold of it and break one of its legs. He would then splint it and it would soon heal. After that, the sheep would no longer go astray. The injury inflicted was a sign of the shepherd's love. If he had not loved that sheep, he would have allowed it to stray ever further, until one day it would be lost forever. The Laodicean Christians are expected to respond to their great shepherd's love (Heb 13:20-21). Christ urges them, saying, *Be earnest, therefore, and repent.* They should proceed with positive zeal, continually being in earnest, and so prove that they have decisively repented, once and for all. The call to repent goes out to all the churches except Smyrna and Philadelphia.

20. To this undeserving and unsatisfactory church Christ makes one of his most gracious invitations. He captures their attention with the imperative *Listen!* Then he says, *I am standing at the door, knocking; if you hear my voice and open the door, I will come in to you and eat with you, and you with me.* The risen Christ is knocking repeatedly, in the hope of being heard. There is a tone of tender pleading from the one whose nature is love (Song 5:2-5, I Jn 4:8, 16). The pronoun *you* is singular, as if he was addressing each person in the church individually. Christ will enter into the life of anyone who opens the door of the soul to him (Jn 14:23). He also says that he will eat with that person. It will not be a hurried snack, but a leisurely meal. The words *and you with me* imply communion and fellowship.

21. *The one who conquers* is the one who ceases to live selfishly and opens the door of his or her life to Christ, receiving him as their Saviour and

Lord. *They will be given a place with Christ on his throne, just as he himself conquered and sat down with his Father on his throne* (Lk 22:28-30). How did Christ conquer? By the way of the cross. This set the pattern for his followers. By receiving him they would face difficult days. They should remember that what seemed like utter and ignominious defeat for Christ was in fact his victory over evil. If they were called to suffer, that very suffering would be their pathway to glory (2:26-28). As Thomas Kelly put it in his hymn, "The highest place that heaven affords is his, is his by right", *and yet* he allows his people to participate in his sovereignty.

22. Once again the Spirit has been doing his work. He loves to take Christ's words and illuminate them so that they come alive in the hearts and minds of those who hear or read them. *Let anyone who has an ear listen to what the Spirit is saying to the churches.* And if we have two ears, we should listen even more (Mt 11:15).

Meditation: The Door that only we can open

John Stott believed that, of the seven letters, the one which was written for the Laodicean church was the most relevant in our times. "It describes vividly the respectable, sentimental, nominal, skin-deep religiosity which is very wide-spread among us today. Our Christianity is flabby and anaemic. We appear to have taken a lukewarm bath of religion". But Jesus Christ deserves better treatment than this. He wants his followers to be either cold or hot. We may be cold and refreshing, like the river water from the mountains that slaked the thirst of the Colossians on hot summer days. Alternatively we may be fervent in spirit, like the hot mineral water which was prized by the inhabitants of Hierapolis for its healing properties. But the Laodicean Christians were tepid and lacked vigour. Their faith was half-hearted and needed fanning into flame (Acts 18:24-28, 2 Tim 1:6-7).

Christ has always wanted his followers to be enthusiastic and zealous for good works (Titus 2:14). Sadly, this longing of his is not shared by many senior church leaders, who are intent on discrediting and sidelining enthusiasts. John Wesley and his "Methodists", as they were mockingly nicknamed, were at the receiving end of this contemptuous rejection, as have been many others both before and after. God's zealous people, his holy remnant, are regarded as fanatics by those in the church who are nominal and self-satisfied. But there is a difference between wholeheartedness and fanaticism. Fanaticism is an unreasoning and unintelligent commitment. The wholehearted commitment that Christ requires of his followers is born of deep reflection on scripture. It is based on the sum of it (Ps 119:160), and it is attained by comparing one scripture with another. The best commentary on scripture is other parts of scripture. As we persevere in our study of it, we have a growing assurance that God's word is eternal and true (Ps 119:142). Worldly church leaders may despise our enthusiasm, but Christ warmly welcomes it.

But what of those lukewarm church leaders, who feel so threatened by the zeal of God's people? Christ's opinion of them is that they are wretched. They are also pathetic and pitiful. Far from belonging to him, they are poor, blind and naked beggars. Poor, for they have no merits to buy their forgiveness (Eph 2:8-9). Blind, for they have no vision to see either their spiritual destitution or God's provision for it (2 Cor 4:4). And naked, for they have no clothing to make them fit to stand before God (Mt 22:11-13). Far from needing nothing, as they proudly claim, they are in dire need of the grace of the Lord Jesus Christ. Their leaders did not receive him themselves, and by their tacit silence about many life-changing truths of the Christian faith, they also kept other people from finding the eternal life that Christ offers (Mt 23:13). Can there be any hope for such a church? Yes.

It seems that Christ addressed this letter to these self-satisfied people in order to give them a last chance. He had some stern advice to pass on to them, and then he offered them the most gracious invitation of all time. His advice was that these Laodiceans should come to him and receive *his* spiritual gold, refined by fires of suffering (Ps 66:10); *his* white garments, namely a robe of imputed righteousness (Isa 61:10); and *his* eye-salve, to give them vision to see God (Mt 5:8). To put it in more familiar theological language, they were to *respond to his reproof and discipline*, and the way to do this was to *be earnest and repent* (v 18, 19).

Then he issued his loving and gracious invitation. *Listen!* He said, *I am standing at the door, knocking; if you hear my voice and open the door, I will come in to you and eat with you, and you with me.* As in Holman Hunt's three paintings of "The Light of the World", we may think of Christ standing outside the door of the house of a rebellious and recalcitrant human soul. He wears a royal robe and a crown of thorns, and holds a lantern with his left hand, for he is the light of the world who alone can guide us into God's pathways. With his right hand he knocks patiently at a door that is barred and overgrown with weeds, for it has never been opened. It is the house of the life of someone who has always been scared stiff of Christ, has felt very threatened by his approach, and has rejected him. The Christ who died for this person is now risen, ascended, and glorified. All authority and power has been given to him. He will soon return and settle accounts, but before he does so he gives the self-satisfied a final opportunity to avail themselves of the salvation that he has won for them at such a great cost. All they need to do is open the door of their lives and invite him to come in. But is this not the same Christ who opens doors that no one will shut? Yes, but this is not the door of opportunity but that of the human heart. In his painting of this scene, Holman Hunt omitted to paint a handle on the door. When this was pointed out to him, he replied that the door of the human soul only has a handle on the inside. Christ has given each of us free will, which he will never override. Only we may open our soul to him and invite him to come in. He cannot and will not force his way in.

XI

Further Thoughts about the Letters to the seven Churches

(a) The seven aspects of a church that is fully pleasing to Jesus Christ. In each of the seven letters Christ highlights a different quality which should mark every church that is making good progress thanks to the direction and teaching of the Holy Spirit. The Ephesian Christians were encouraged to return to the *love* which they had for him at first, for without it all freshness had departed from their good works. The church at Smyrna was commended for enduring the *suffering* that always comes to those who are faithful to Christ. God's people in Pergamum were to insist on *truth* when faced with the temptation to compromise with emperor worship and its associated idolatrous rites. Because the Christians in Thyatira had to live in a prevailing atmosphere of lax sexual practices, their lives were to shine with the *holiness* without which no one may see God. The church at Sardis needed an inward *reality* to match their outward and hypocritical displays of piety. The Christians at Philadelphia were doing so well that Christ had set before them an open door of opportunity for *mission*, through which he urged them to enter. Finally, the church at Laodicea

was first castigated by Christ because it was self-satisfied and lukewarm, and then gently invited to welcome him into their church life and begin to serve him with *wholeheartedness*.

A church that is marked by each of these seven qualities will be commended by its Lord. We should consider whether the church we attend displays *love*, endures *suffering*, makes a stand for *truth*, preaches *holiness*, exhibits *reality*, engages in costly *mission* and serves God *wholeheartedly*. If the answer is yes in each case, then our church is close to perfection. Perhaps we should be wary of attending it, for we are damaged and imperfect, and our presence at its meetings could well spoil it!

(b) The difficulty churches have is to progress in all seven of these aspects. It is relatively easy to be committed and to succeed in four or five of them, but to press forward in all seven is almost impossible. Think of the following examples:

Church X has managed to get the majority of its members to pray and to read and study the Bible on a daily basis. They can all sniff out a heresy a mile away, and they are good at stamping out wrong teaching. They strive to be holy and on the whole they succeed. But they come across to visitors as being judgemental, and any Christian with doubts or with a sense of failure feels unwelcome in their church. Furthermore, several church leaders find that their devotional times suffer from dry periods, and their faith is beginning to feel hollow and unreal.

Church Y think that they have learnt from the failings of Church X. They know what the secret of success is. They aim to treat everyone with love (except those who take the Bible seriously, whom they disdain and regard with a supercilious smile). They welcome those with heterodox beliefs, and have long discussions with them. They encourage those who, after a failed marriage, have discovered happiness in new relationships. They affirm and welcome those with same-sex partners. They preach about God's love, but do not mention his holiness. But their congregation seem to prefer the church parties and wine-tasting sessions to the rather dull and bland services, with their brief and inconsequential homilies. Their scepticism about the Bible has worn the life and the reality out of them.

Church Z is having a tough time. They are considered to be an over-enthusiastic bunch by other churches. As a result of expository preaching or "words from the Lord" they are seeking to serve God, but they find themselves doing so in a way that runs counter to prevailing trends. Their leaders and other members who join in wholeheartedly are suffering persecution. Their property and belongings are being vandalised, and their children are being falsely accused at school. Some of the worshippers are wondering if their lives are worth living, for the opposition is intense. They ask themselves if this is what the Christian life is really like. *(c) Awkward questions that arise when studying the seven letters.* Here are two, but there are others that may strike you. Read the letters and think them through.

The first is, *how can we express disapproval of untrue views or unholy lifestyles without being unloving and judgemental?* In his ministry, Jesus appears to have stressed the positive side as it is found in scripture, but he did also mention the negative. For example, when asked about divorce, he pointed to God's ordinance on marriage: "From the beginning of creation, 'God made them male and female'. 'For this reason a man shall leave his father and mother and be joined to his wife, and the two shall become one flesh' (Gen 1:27, 2:24). So they are no longer two, but one flesh. Therefore what God has joined together, let no man separate" (Mk 10:6-9). We too may point to scripture, stressing its positive message, but also showing how it applies to related controversial matters. When Christ said to the Ephesian church, "Yet this is to your credit: you hate the works of the Nicolaitans, which I also hate" (2:6), he was praising them. But there may have been a harsh ring in their disapproval of what was untrue or unholy, and it evinced the loss of their first love. Perhaps they could have said what they had said, word for word, in a sad and gentle way instead of harshly. But sometimes it is right to be angry and forthright. There were times when Jesus spoke and acted angrily (Mt 23:1-36, Mk 11:15-17). He was hated and persecuted for his intolerance (Jn 15:18-25). The Christians in Ephesus were rightly intolerant of false and immoral teachers (2:2), but Christ had to warn them that the loss of their first love was very serious.

The second question is, *How can a church live comfortably and feel satisfied with its progress, and yet continue to flourish and grow?* The answer is that it is impossible. Every Christian in the world must have longed to find a church like this! The church at Sardis had attained a comfortable existence, and its members felt at ease – but then their worship and witness began to be unreal. When a church is comfortable, it is sure to end up full of nominal Christians. Likewise Laodicea had settled into a state of self-satisfaction, as a result of which they had become lukewarm. A few centuries earlier they would have been cursed by the prophets (Amos 6:1), but now they faced being severely repudiated by Christ unless they opened their lives to him. Being comfortable and lukewarm has never been good for any church. History has shown that the greatest church growth occurs in times of persecution or of strong disapproval because of the Christian missionary spirit. When any church reaches out to the poor and to unbelievers with the good news, they suffer the same fate as befell Jesus Christ. But if a church elects to keep in the world's good books, it may well attain a state of self-satisfaction and ease, but it will also lose touch with its Saviour and Lord. The message of the cross is integral to the Christian faith, but it is an offence to those who hear it, for it makes it quite clear that we cannot save ourselves. Salvation is an undeserved gift from God, and it is not earned by our own good works (Eph 2:8-9).

Meditation: The Partnership of Word and Spirit

It is notable that in the seven letters, as in other parts of the Bible, God's way of helping us to live godly lives could be summed up under two headings – his word and his Holy Spirit. The seven letters claim to be words of the risen and glorified Christ (1:10-11) who is God the Son, and they were written down by John. They are part of *the word of God*. Moreover, each letter ends with the directive that any person who hears or reads it should listen to what *the Spirit of God* is saying to the churches (2:7, 11, 17, 29; 3:6, 13, 22). The word and the Spirit both play a part in helping us discern God's message to us when we read the letters. The word of God is living and active, and the Spirit of God illumines the word so that we meet Christ as we read it, and are guided in our Christian walk. When we read the Bible and the Holy Spirit is at work, God's word comes alive. It is like a live electric wire. It has the power to change our lives, and to renew entire churches.

We see this same pairing of word and Spirit in the personal manifesto of Jesus Christ. At the start of his public ministry he proclaimed it in Nazareth, where he had been brought up (Lk 4:14-30). After his time of temptation he was filled with the power of the Spirit, and when he came to Nazareth, he went to the synagogue on the Sabbath day, as was his custom. He stood up to read, and the synagogue attendant gave him a scroll. They did not have books then, and the Bible, which was just the Old Testament, was written on scrolls, and

Jesus had asked for the scroll of the Prophet Isaiah. He found what in our Bibles is Isaiah chapter 61, and read out the beginning of it: "The Spirit of the Lord is upon me, because he has anointed me to bring good news to the poor. He has sent me to proclaim release to the captives and recovery of sight to the blind, to proclaim the year of the Lord's favour". He added from memory part of another verse (Isaiah 58:6), which refers to "the oppressed". After the reading, he handed the scroll back to the attendant, and sat down to preach. The eyes of all who were there were fastened upon him. Here was their boy, Jesus of Nazareth. Now a travelling preacher, he was turning the world upside down. What would he say? Luke summarises his sermon: "Today this scripture has been fulfilled in your hearing". This amazing claim must have taken their breath away. He stated that Isaiah was referring to *him*, to Jesus, to what they had just heard him read.

He kept on claiming this throughout his ministry. He said, "The scriptures testify on *my* behalf" (Jn 5:39). He interpreted the things about *himself* in all the scriptures (Lk 24:27). Matthew and Luke recorded some amazing words spoken by him to his disciples on a later occasion: "Blessed are the eyes that see what *you* see! For I tell you that many prophets and kings desired to see what *you* see, but did not see it, and to hear what *you* hear, but did not hear it" (Mt 13:16-17, Lk 10:23-24). The prophets and kings of the Old Testament had lived in an age of expectation, but the disciples of Jesus lived in the age of fulfilment. Their eyes were seeing, and their ears hearing, what many prophets and wise men had written about. It was *in Christ* that the time was fulfilled. The kingdom of God had arrived, and *Jesus Christ was the king*.

Jesus was much, much more than just a prophet. Consider a cart wheel which has lots of spokes. Out on the circumference are the prophets, and their proph-ecies are the spokes. The spokes are not parallel to each other, but they all point towards the centre of the wheel, and at the centre is Jesus Christ. All of the prophets had spoken about *him*. They referred to him as God's Anointed One, which in Hebrew is *Messiah*. When you translate *Anointed One* into Greek, you get *Christos*, which in English is *Christ*. Jesus was God's Christ. He was the special Anointed One of God, who had been promised again and again. All of the ancient promises and prophecies given to the Jewish people found their fulfilment in *him*.

This double emphasis on the word of God and the Spirit of God is evident in Jesus Christ's sermon in Nazareth. The public ministry of Jesus was exercised in the power of the Spirit, as should our outreach be exercised to unbelievers. He was filled with the power of the Spirit, and in Nazareth he read the verse from Isaiah that says, *the Spirit of the Lord is upon me, because he has anointed me to bring good news to the poor.* And the second factor that inspired Jesus was God's word, the Bible, which in Jesus's day was just the Old Testament. It was there that he learnt all he needed to know about God's will for his life and ministry. He spent thirty years reading, marking, learning and inwardly digesting its message, from the age of about two until he died. Even the very fact that he was to study the scriptures was prophesied (Isa 49:1-2, 50:4-5). As far as he was concerned, *what the Bible said, God said.* He built his life on the two foundations of *the word of God* and *the Holy Spirit*, and so should we.

It is a sad fact that much of the western church no longer believes in keeping together the word and the Spirit. There are some who preach and spread the word faithfully, but they neglect the Holy Spirit, who alone can illumine the word and carry it home to the minds, hearts and consciences of the hearers. There are others who seek the power of the Holy Spirit but neglect the word, forgetting that the sword of the Spirit is the word of God. Both are mistaken. If you emphasise the word without the Spirit, you will *dry up.* If you emphasise the Spirit without the word, you will *blow up.* If you do not know either the scriptures or the power of God (Mk 12:24), then you will cause Christ to *throw up* (3:16) – and you will be the vomit. But if you emphasise the word and the Spirit together, then you will *grow up,* and those who hear you will grow up as well. The church today urgently needs growth. We all need to be built up by the careful exposition of God's word in the power of the Holy Spirit. Christ valued both together, and so should we.

XII

4:1-11 The Worship of God in Heaven

It has been an enormous challenge to be confronted with what Christ thinks of his church here on earth. For a fresh and awe-inspiring vision of Christ, we now move on from his scrutiny of the suffering and change-able lampstands to his sharing the sovereign and unchanging throne of God. We Christians are sometimes prone to anxiety as we face the powers of darkness and feel them closing in. We do not need to be afraid, for at the very centre of the universe there is a throne. From it orbiting planets receive their orders. To it the most immense galaxies offer their allegiance. Thanks to it all microscopic living organisms come to life. Before it angels, human beings, living creatures and the inanimate creation bow down and humbly worship. The Lord our God the Almighty reigns (19:6).

1. John says, *After this I looked.* He uses similar words to introduce some of the new visions that will follow (7:1, 9; 15:5, 18:1, 19:1). To his astonishment, *there in heaven a door stood open!* Heaven is the place where God dwells. The door of revelation has been opened by Christ, and no one may block it (3:7-8, Jn 14:6). John is given the first viewing, and all who read his book may share the benefit. *The first voice,* which earlier on John *had heard speaking to him like a trumpet* (1:10-13), was that of the glorified Christ. He called John to *come up to heaven,* where *he would be shown what must take place after this* (1:1, 19).

   In chapters 2 and 3 John had seen what Christ thought of the church in the present time; now he is promised visions of the future, to be revealed in chapter 6 and onwards in the parallel judgements of the seven seals, seven trumpets and seven bowls. Leon Morris underlines the importance of the words *must take place.* It is certain that the divine plan will be fulfilled, for God is in supreme control.

2. *At once John was in the Spirit,* caught up again in a trance (see 1:10, 17:3, and 21:10). He had entered into *heaven,* where *there stood a throne.* John is interested in the throne of God. In the book of Revelation he mentions it 42 times, which is a multiple of 7. The word *throne* appears a total of 62 times in the New Testament, and 49 of the 62 are in Revelation. Clearly this word characterises the last book of the Bible. Leon Morris observed that John's readers were familiar with earthly thrones, and were troubled by the demands made on them by Caesar's throne. John seeks to remind them that there is a throne that dwarfs all the other thrones. This throne is in heaven, and *there is One seated on it!*

3. John proceeds to describe *the One who is enthroned* above all, and he does so very concisely, no doubt conscious that even absolute superlatives would not do justice to God. John simply likens him to *jasper and carnelian.* Here the word for *jasper* may in fact refer to a diamond, since it is said to be clear as crystal (21:11). The *carnelian* was a red stone and

very precious. Because carnelian and jasper are the first and the last in the list of twelve precious stones that were set in the High Priest's breastplate (Ex 28:17-21), this may be another way of saying that God is the Alpha and the Omega (1:8). *Around the throne is a rainbow that looks like an emerald.* This is a symbolic statement, since a rainbow is multi-coloured and emeralds are green. A rainbow is a reminder of God's everlasting covenant (Gen 9:11-17). Therefore the most exalted of all the thrones is a throne of *grace*.

4. *Around God's throne are twenty-four thrones, and seated on the thrones are twenty-four elders.* These elders are a senior order of angels, called "thrones" in Colossians 1:16. They represent all of God's people (twelve patriarchs of the Old Testament and twelve apostles of the New). In the New Jerusalem the names of the patriarchs are on the gates, and those of the apostles are on the foundations (21:12, 14). The elders are enthroned, for they represent those who have followed Christ and who will one day sit on thrones (Mt 19:28, Lk 22:28-30). They are *dressed in white robes*, as befits their perfect purity, and *they have golden crowns on their heads*, to emphasize both their own high estate and the high privileges that will be conferred on the people of God whom they represent.

5. *From the throne come flashes of lightning, and rumblings and peals of thunder.* These are awe-inspiring phenomena. Leon Morris wrote, "We have already noted the reserve with which [John] speaks of God, and there can be no doubt that here *the throne* is a reverent way of referring to him who sat on it. Thunder is the voice of God in several Old Testament passages (e.g. Ex 19:16-19, Ps 29:3-10), and we should understand the term in this sense here". John uses similar descriptions in 8:5, 11:19 and 16:18. *In front of the throne burn seven flaming torches, which are the seven spirits of God.* As in 1:4, *the seven spirits of God* beside the throne is a reference to the Holy Spirit. He would equip the Messiah and his people for service with a sevenfold endowment (Isa 11:2). It is significant that "torches moving to and fro" are also mentioned in Ezekiel's vision of God (Ezek 1:13).

6. *In front of the throne there is something like a sea of glass, like crystal.* There is a mystery as to what this sea of glass signified. Its immensity seems to proclaim God's transcendence, rather like the "unapproachable

light" in the midst of which he dwells (1 Tim 6:16). In one of the stanzas of Reginald Heber's hymn "Holy, holy, holy" we sing, "All the saints adore thee, casting down their golden crowns around the glassy sea" (v 10). *Around the throne, and on each side of the throne, are four living creatures, full of eyes in front and behind.* Ezekiel saw a similar vision of "the appearance of the likeness of the glory of the Lord", seated on a sapphire throne and looking like gleaming amber surrounded by fire (Ezek 1:4-28). Here too, God was surrounded by four creatures with living wheels that were "full of eyes all around", examining all of us with ceaseless vigilance (Ezek 1:18). The living creatures are holy, for they live very close to God. They always praise him (v 8), and are associated with the pouring out of his wrath (6:1-8, 15:7).

7. John proceeds to describe *the four living creatures. The first is like a lion, the second like an ox, the third has a face like a human face, and the fourth is like a flying eagle.* There is a very early Jewish writing that says, "The mightiest among the birds is the eagle, the mightiest among the domesticated animals is the bull, the mightiest among the wild beasts is the lion, and the mightiest among all is the human being". In his commentary, Henry Swete wrote, "The four forms suggest whatever is noblest, strongest, wisest and swiftest in animate nature".

The whole creation is represented by these four living creatures before the throne. They play their part in fulfilling God's will and in worshipping his majesty. Why four? It has been argued that this number symbolises God's creation, since there are four corners of the earth and four winds (7:1). In medieval times it was widely believed that there were four living creatures because there are four gospels, and the human form was linked to Matthew, the lion to Mark, the bull to Luke and the eagle to John. Interesting but implausible reasons were adduced for these particular links.

8. *Each of the living creatures has six wings*, like the seraphim in Isaiah 6:2, and again we are told that *they are full of eyes all around and inside.* John believes their all-encompassing vision is important and worth stressing. It is easy for us to deceive ourselves into thinking that we will get away with sin because nobody is watching. But of course, God sees everything (Ps 139:1-4) and so do these beings. They always praise God, for *day and night without ceasing they sing, "Holy, holy, holy, the*

Lord God the Almighty, who was and is and is to come". The Trisagion or triple repetition of the word *holy* is also reminiscent of the seraphim in Isaiah 6:3. The attribute of God that they consider to be most worthy of praise is not his love but his holiness.

We live in a desperately fallen and twisted world where evil is rampant and seemingly all-powerful, but in John's first vision of heaven he is shown that this is a false picture. God is *holy*. God is good. He is also *almighty*. Real power is not on the side of evil but on the side of *God who is holy*. This is not a temporary state of affairs, for *God was and is and is to come*. Because he is both all-powerful and eternal, his holiness is certain to triumph over evil.

9. We have noted the ceaselessness with which *the living creatures give glory and honour and thanks to the one who is seated on the throne, who lives forever and ever*. The majesty and eternity of God are the subject of their glorifying, their bestowal of honour, and their thanksgiving. At this stage John proceeds to make it clear that the praise of the four living creatures is not unaccompanied.

10. The representatives of the people of God join in with them. *The twenty-four elders fall before the one who lives forever and ever; they cast their crowns before the throne.* And *they sing* a heavenly song whose words are echoed here on earth.

11. The song begins *You are worthy, our Lord and God*. The elders ascribe *worth-ship* to God. They quite literally *worship* him. They declare that he is *worthy of receiving glory and honour and power*. The *glory and honour* echo verse 9, but *power* replaces the *thanks* of that verse, possibly because creation, the theme here, is a work of power. *God created all things*. He is celebrated as Creator in the Old Testament (e.g. in Gen 1, 2 and Ps 104, 139:13-16, 148). Moreover, *by his will all things existed and were created*. He created them by willing them into being.

Meditation: The Revelation of the divine Purpose

There are 25 verses in Revelation chapters 4 and 5, and in them the throne of God is mentioned no less than 17 times. God's throne room is indescribable, and John stretches language to its limit in an attempt to convey what it was like to be taken up in the Spirit to observe the proceedings in the control room of the universe. The amazing truth is that we too are as involved as John was, for we are seated "with God in the heavenly places in Christ Jesus" (Eph 2:6). There is no need for us to be in the Spirit and experience the vision ourselves. John has written down what he saw (1:10-11), and as we read the book of Revelation we will see in our mind's eye what John saw in his visions, and it will capture our imaginations.

What can we learn from the vision of God in chapter 4? We have been given a glimpse of ultimate reality. We have seen the lofty throne in the control room of the universe. We have discerned the figure seated on it, sparkling with dazzling light, as from carnelians and diamonds, and have been encouraged by the emerald rainbow of grace encircling the throne. This will force us to ask whether our view of the future glory is determined only by what will not be there. It is indeed good to know that in eternity there will be no more hunger or thirst, no more tears or pain, and no more sin, falsehood, death or anything accursed, for all these things will have passed away (21:4, 8, 27; 22:2-3, 15). But this coin has another side.

As John Stott wrote, "It would be better and more biblical, however, to focus not so much on these absences as on the cause of their absence, namely the central dominating presence of God's throne. For when God takes his power and reigns without rival, and the kingdom will have come in its fullness, then everything incompatible with his reign will be destroyed and God will be 'all in all' (1 Cor 15:28). Meanwhile, we are called to anticipate on earth the God-centred life of heaven, to live our lives now in conscious relationship to the throne, so that every thought, word and deed comes under God's rule".

What a privilege it is to have been made privy to the future. If we have stood in the throne room, we have entered into the council of the Lord and have perceived and heard his counsel. Like the prophets of the Old Testament, we have seen the fate of the impenitent, and we may proclaim God's word and declare what he will do, and thereby encourage people to turn from their evil ways (Jer 23:18-22). Like Micaiah, we shall be able to tell others what will certainly happen in the future, because we have seen and heard the Lord sitting on his throne (1 Ki 22:19-23). For God is not secretive. Quite the opposite: he does nothing without revealing his secret to his servants the prophets (Amos 3:7). We shall be numbered among the prophets if we read and study the scriptures, including the last book of the Bible. We shall learn about the events of the future and their meaning by being with John as he is caught up to heaven in the Spirit, and will share his visions, first of God (Rev 4) and then of Christ (Rev 5).

Both of them attain their climax with heavenly worship, first of God as eternal Creator (4:8, 11), then of Christ as Redeemer (5:9-10, 12), and finally of both God and Christ together (5:13).

It is both edifying and enlightening to study the hymns of praise in Revelation (4:8, 11; 5:9-10, 12, 13; 7:12, 15-17; 11:17-18; 15:3-4; 19:1-8). If the praise of the church on earth should be an echo of the worship of heaven, there is plenty of inspiration here for those in our day who aspire to write hymns, and the first theme they may like to tackle is that of God the great Creator.

XIII

5:1-5 The Scroll sealed with seven Seals

Following his vision of God as the eternal and holy Creator, John keeps on gazing at him on his throne, and notices that he is holding in his right hand a scroll that is sealed with seven seals. A problem arises because no one in heaven or on earth or under the earth is able to open the scroll and read it. John believes it is vital to know the contents of this scroll. Overcome with sadness, he begins to weep. Then one of the 24 elders informs him that there *is* someone who has conquered evil, and who is therefore worthy to open the scroll and its seven seals.

1. In his scrutiny of the throne and what surrounds it, John focuses again on the One who is seated on it and who looked like jasper and carnelian (4:3). *He saw a scroll lying on the palm of his right hand.* In those days they had scrolls rather than books. A scroll was made up of sheets of papyrus joined up edge to edge. A sheet was made by placing thin strips of papyrus in two layers at 90 degrees to each other. The layers were joined together by a combination of glue, water and pressure. The resulting scroll had two sides: the one with horizontal strips was better for writing on than the one with vertical strips, but occasionally both sides were used. In this case the scroll had writing on both sides, for *it was written on the inside and on the back.* It was *sealed with seven seals*, for it consisted of seven parts, each one a separate scroll, kept rolled up by an individual seal. The seven scrolls together made up one book (also called a scroll), but what John saw was seven small scrolls rolled up like cylinders in God's right hand. At a certain time

they would be opened one by one by first breaking their seals. Why seven seals? This was because in Roman law any will or official document had to be sealed by seven witnesses. The seals could be broken and the document opened only by someone with the appropriate authority to do so. At any rate, we are dealing with another of John's heptads here. The seals will be broken in chapter 6 and in 8:1.

2. The breaking of the seals would not be easy. This particular book was special, and no ordinary person or being could possibly open it up. *John then saw a mighty angel* (others who are mighty like him will appear in 10:1 and 18:21). Here the implication is that only an extremely powerful herald could make his voice carry to every human being and angel (v 3). *With a loud voice he proclaimed, "Who is worthy to open the scroll and break its seals?"* The one who would open the book had to be *worthy*. Worthy of what? Worthy of performing the supreme service of bringing history to its final consummation. In order to aspire to such an honour, the opener of the book must combine perfect holiness and love in his nature, and he must have succeeded in conquering sin and death.

3. No such person or angelic being could be found, *in heaven or on earth or under the earth* (Phil 2:10; this tripartite division of the universe may have originated from the wording of the second commandment in Ex 20:4). Nobody could even draw near to the book, let alone *open it or look into it*. As Leon Morris put it, "No angel in heaven, no saintly man on earth, no prophet in the realm of the departed was sufficient for this". In his book "The Apocalypse Today", Thomas Torrance wrote as follows: "The secrets of the world belong to God, and no one can pry into them. Who knows what a day or a night may bring forth? Who knows what this year holds in its dark unknown future? Even the strong angels of God are unable to open the book. Only God can unseal the seals and read the secrets".

4. *John began to weep bitterly.* He was frustrated because he longed to know what was written in this book, and he feared that this might not be possible *because no one was found worthy to open the scroll or to look into it.* God had promised him that he would be shown what must take place after this (4:1). Must he in spite of this promise be denied this viewing of the Revelation of the future?

5. The answer came from *one of the elders, who spoke to him*. He said, *"Do not weep"*. The seals would be opened after all. There was someone who was worthy, someone who *had conquered and therefore could open the book and its seven seals*. Who was he? He is described in two ways, neither of which can be found in the Old Testament. He was *the Lion of the tribe of Judah*. This expression can only be found here in the Bible. Judah was one of the sons of Jacob, and his father called him a lion's whelp (Gen 49:9), who would in due course crouch and stretch out like a lion, and woe to anyone who might dare to rouse his anger. The worthy one was also *the root of David* (notice "the root and the descendant of David" in 22:16). The root of Jesse is mentioned in Isaiah (Isa 11:1, 10), but the expression *the root of David* is peculiar to Revelation. These two descriptions are Messianic, and they imply that the Messiah would be born a descendant of Judah and he would also be the origin or root of King David, as well as being descended from David. This Lion and Root *had conquered*. When John wrote the Revelation, the conquest had already been accomplished. As we are about to see, the victory was achieved by a sacrificial lamb who had been slain. He alone was marked out to be the Lord of history and the master of the world's future. He and only he was worthy to break the seals and open the book of human destiny.

Meditation: The Book of Destiny is securely sealed up

There has been much speculation about the content of the scroll that was sealed with seven seals. One suggestion is that it refers to the Old Testament. This cannot be right for the simple reason that the Old Testament (and most of the New) had already been revealed and committed to writing. Another suggestion is that it refers to the book of Revelation. The first six seals would then refer to chapter 6, the seventh is about a prayerful interlude (8:1), and the scroll itself is the rest of the book. This seems like a clumsy suggestion. But then, what exactly did the scroll signify? By what title might we refer to it? Leon Morris wrote, "The book surely is the one which contains the world's destiny, and its contents are revealed to us pictorially as the seals are broken". George Eldon Ladd believed that the most natural way to interpret the scroll in God's hand is as "the prophecy of the end events, including both the salvation of God's people and the judgement of the wicked. It is God's redemptive plan for the dénouement of human history, the overthrow of evil, and the ingathering of a redeemed people to enjoy the blessings of God's rule. History will not end until the purposes of God have come to their full consummation; when they are complete, the end will come". The idea that there is a heavenly book that contains the entire course of world history, past, present and future, is foreshadowed in the Old Testament (e.g. Ps 139:16).

This is the book of world history, the sealed record of the unknown future that "must take place after this" (4:1). Only the one who is worthy to open the book and break its seals can disclose the future. The future is safely held by God. There it is, on his right hand. The future is written or inscripturated on a scroll made up of seven smaller scrolls, each written on both sides and each sealed up, waiting to be opened and fulfilled in the lives of ordinary men and women throughout the world. John becomes aware that absolutely no person or angel is worthy to open up the scrolls, and this makes him so sad that he bursts into tears. He feels as we would if we were searching high and low for someone who was suitable to take over as the new leader of our church, and we just could not find the right person. That could rightly make us feel distraught, but eventually we would rewrite the advertisement more simply, specifying that any applicants for the post should be humble and fear God. Eventually we would find our man or woman. But as far as the book of destiny is concerned, the mere fact of being a humble servant of God would not have sufficed as a credential for opening it. It was a necessary condition but not a sufficient one. The one who would do so had to be *worthy*.

The situation was desperate. God's people were in extreme need of God's help. The Christian movement was a tiny minority scattered across the mighty Roman Empire. Most of the Christians, and certainly all of the faithful Christians, found themselves insignificant and powerless, with few if any options open to them in seasons of persecution. The church would have been up against it anyway, but in addition to the political and cultural opposition, false teachers were stealing into some of the churches, and were manipulating the faithful into practices that were idolatrous and unholy. There were times when absolutely everyone seemed to be against God's faithful remnant. What could they do? They knew that there was a throne in heaven, and they could bow down and worship before it. But what about the future? What secrets did the scroll contain? What was the meaning of all their suffering? Was there a divine plan and purpose in all that was happening? Did history have a plot to explain it and if so, what was it? Oh please, where was the right person who could open the book of destiny and present them with the true answers to their agonising questions?

It is a terrible quandary when you simply cannot solve the mystery of life. It happened in the first century, when people despaired about the finality of death. For them the answer could be found in the resurrection of Jesus Christ, for which there was incontrovertible evidence. Christ said, "I was dead, and see, I am alive forever and ever; and I have the keys of Death and of Hades" (1:18). It happened again in the Middle Ages, when a dread-filled fear of guilt gripped the minds of many people. For them the answer was to be found in the message of the Cross, of which we in turn are about to be reminded (5:6). This erased human guilt and led millions to an assurance that their sins were forgiven and that they had been given a new start in life, adopted as God's children.

What about our own day? There is an anxiety, an *angst* that chokes us with its chilly and clammy grip. It is a sense that life is meaningless, and this permeates books, films and the news. The answer to it is to be found in the eternity of God (4:8), which he wishes to share with his human creatures, and in the new quality of life that Christ offers. During his ministry Christ said, "I came that they may have life, and have it abundantly" (Jn 10:10). Now he shares God's throne and says, "See, I am making all things new" (21:5).

There are several perplexing mysteries in life. We sometimes get caught up in the evil and misery of this world, and are unable to break free. It is tempting to become a determinist, and all of us sometimes feel helpless and hopeless, as if we were in the grip of forces stronger than ourselves. This can be agonising. Serious consequences may arise from our inability to break free from the reality of guilt. Those seals that keep the book of destiny closed seem to underline our inability to escape from evil. But the book will not stay sealed forever. The next scene of the drama of Revelation will be entitled, "Enter the Lamb".

The fact is that, apart from the person of Jesus Christ and the redeeming work that he undertook on behalf of the world, history remains an impenetrable enigma. Until the start of the 19th century, the Christian view of history was that it had a divinely ordained goal which was closely linked to the death and resurrection of Christ. Starting with the so-called Enlightenment, most philosophers rejected this view, and history became riddled with purposelessness. The evolutionary view of inevitable progress is untenable today. Many of our greatest minds are profoundly pessimistic and see dark clouds gathering on the horizon. History appears to have neither meaning nor purpose. It is altogether incapable of reaching a goal or even of progressing towards it. This secularist and godless way of thinking has even influenced theologians and parts of the church. They are unable to discern the end or goal of history, and have to conclude that it is meaningless.

There are, however, two facts for the 21st century Christian to note. The first is that the book of destiny rests in God's right hand. The whole of history is under his sovereign control. This is a comforting picture. Our destiny rests on the hand of the reigning and omnipotent Creator who sustains the universe, so we are safe. The second fact is that the book is made up of seven scrolls which are so tightly sealed that no human eye can read its contents. Only Christ, the Lion of the tribe of Judah and the Root of David, can unlock the meaning of human history. He is worthy to open the book and reveal our destiny to us. Without his past death and resurrection and his future return, history is void of hope, meaning and purpose. It is little wonder that modern thinkers have no good news for us. For them, as for their followers, there is so much darkness and gloom. But for those who know and love Christ, there is light. We shall know "what must take place after this". There will be tribulation in the immediate future, and later there will be glory.

XIV

5:6-14 Enter the Lamb

John keeps his eyes open and continues to gaze in wonder. One of the elders has just announced that the Lion of the tribe of Judah, who has conquered, is worthy to break the seals and open the book of human destiny. John expectantly awaits his arrival. But when he does appear, John sees not a lion, but a lamb. John knew perfectly well who this lamb was. It was Christ. The characteristic designation of him in the book of Revelation is as the Lamb of God, who was slain so as to take away the sin of the world once and forever. John continues to look, and hears one chorus of praise after another begin to resound in the throne room of heaven, and also in the rest of heaven, on the earth and under the earth, and even in the sea. Every living creature that exists is joining in the worship of God and of the Lamb.

6. *Then* – after hearing about the Lion of the tribe of Judah – *John saw between the throne and the four living creatures and among the elders a*

Lamb. In the Bible the title *the Lamb* is applied to Christ only in John's Gospel and in the Book of Revelation. A lamb was the most common sacrificial victim. John describes him as *standing as if he had been slaughtered* (Isa 53:7), so there is no doubt that he is thinking of him as a sacrificial lamb. He had the appearance of having been slaughtered, but as a matter of fact he was very much alive. *He had seven horns –* another heptad. The horn was a symbol of strength in ancient Israel (e.g. Deut 33:17). As seven is the number that implies completeness or perfection, the seven horns indicate the perfect power of the Lamb, who is ever strong to save. *He also had seven eyes* (yet another heptad), which means that his vision is perfect. There is nothing whatsoever that can possibly escape his gaze. John describes the seven eyes of the Lamb as *the seven spirits of God* (1:4) *sent out into all the earth.* We are to associate the perfect vision of the Lamb with the ministry of the Holy Spirit here on earth. In the Old Testament the Spirit of God is symbolised by a golden lampstand with seven lamps, of which it was said that "These seven are the eyes of the Lord, which range through the whole earth" (Zech 4:2, 10b). Having seen and assessed our human deeds, words, thoughts and intentions, the Holy Spirit will proceed to convince the world of its guilt, of the possibility of righteousness, and of the inevitable judgement that awaits the impenitent (Jn 16:8-11).

7. As John continued to gaze at the activities around the throne, *he saw the Lamb go and take the book of the seven scrolls from the right hand of the one who was enthroned.* Martin Kiddle suggested that "in his own way, John is expressing the perfect harmony between the will of God and the will of Christ". John is sharing a vision of Christ's session when, after his death, resurrection and ascension he returned to heaven and sat on the throne at the right hand of God (Heb 1:3). All authority in heaven and on earth has rightly been given to him (Mt 28:18). When Christ took possession of the book of destiny, he became *de facto* the controller and director of history. Starting at chapter 6, John will begin to see "what must take place after this" (4:1) as the Lamb begins to break the seals one by one.

8. *When he had taken the book of seven scrolls,* a stirring outburst of praise and worship rang out in heaven in anticipation of its opening. It began when *the four living creatures and the twenty-four elders fell before*

the Lamb. *Each one held a harp*, which in Revelation is an instrument of praise, *and also a golden bowl full of incense*, which John defines as being *the prayers of the saints* (8:3-4). On earth the saints (i.e. God's holy remnant who seek to lead holy lives) are disdained and deemed of no importance by worldly people, including some church leaders, but in heaven their prayers are greatly esteemed, and are brought before the presence of God himself, borne by their heavenly representatives in precious golden bowls. As Leon Morris discerningly pointed out, "John often brings out the reversal of values in heaven from those accepted by his earthly contemporaries".

9. The four living creatures and the twenty-four elders proceed to *sing a new song*. The Greek word *kainos* means "new" in the sense of being altogether fresh and without any precedents. The Lamb's work in winning our salvation has brought about a completely new state of affairs, and it calls for a completely new type of worship song, new in comparison with the ancient song of creation in 4:11. The title of this particular song could be, "Who is the worthy one?" It begins, *You are worthy to take the scroll and to open its seals*. At last John will be allowed to know what must take place after this. Someone has been found who is worthy. He is worthy for three reasons: he was slain (a fact of history), he purchased saints for God (the consequence of the fact), and he made them a kingdom and priests (the final outcome).

The song spells this out clearly: *You were slaughtered and by your blood you ransomed for God saints from every tribe and language and people and nation*. The excellence of Christ the Lamb is due not only to his power or majesty, but to the fact that he died for our sins on the cross. He was slaughtered once and for all (1 Pet 3:18), and by his blood shed in death he ransomed the holy remnant of saints *for God*. This means that God now owns them. They are his; if they are made to fall, then underneath will be his everlasting arms (Deut 33:27, New International Version). The purchase price for the redeemed (1 Cor 6:19-20) is much more than any number of pounds. It is the blood of Christ. As Archbishop William Temple put it, "My *worth* is what *I am worth* to God; and that is a marvellous *great deal*, for Christ died for me". We should not fail to notice the universal scope of the redemption. One day it will be seen that the saints come from *every* tribe and language and people and nation on earth. John stresses that the good news is for everyone. These four categories of people appear five times in Revelation (5:9, 7:9, 11:9, 13:7, 14:6) – always in a different order. This universality has led to costly worldwide mission.

10. But this is not all. The song continues, *you have made them to be a kingdom and priests* (1:6) *serving our God.* The service of self is demeaning bondage, but the service of God is perfect freedom. God's saints *will reign on earth.* They are humble and lowly, but they are given great dignity. This song looks forward to the vindication and final triumph of the despised saints of God, as in the Exodus (Ex 19:4-6). We should notice in passing that in the book of Revelation worship is reserved for God alone (19:10, 22:8-9). The fact that the Lamb is worshipped in several songs is proof that he is fully divine, fully at one with God (Jn 10:30).

11. John continues his gaze at the heavenly throne, and *he hears the voice of many angels surrounding the throne and the living creatures and the elders.* They are in an important place, but not at the centre. There are so many that they cannot be counted. *Myriads of myriads and thousands of thousands* (Dan 7:10) – this was an inconceivably large number in antiquity, and if we were present and tried to count them, we would soon realise the magnitude of the task and desist.

12. The immense concourse is full of these innumerable angels, who *are singing with full voice.* They begin by emphasizing *the worthiness of the Lamb who was slaughtered.* He is *worthy to receive* every kind of reward, and seven qualities are mentioned (another heptad). The first four are qualities he possesses: *power and wealth and wisdom and might.* The last three express the attitude of the saints to him: *honour and glory and blessing.* But this loud burst of singing is not the end.

13. John now *hears every creature in heaven and on earth and under the earth and in the sea, and all that is in them, singing.* John wants to spell out what "every creature" means, and he not only includes every location he can think of, but for good measure adds an unnecessary and redundant *and all that is in them.* He may well have known Psalm 148, which is similarly all-encompassing in listing both animate beings and inanimate objects as rendering due praise to God. But in this particular song they are *singing to the one seated on the throne and to the Lamb,*

to God the Father *and* to God the Son. To them *be blessing and honour and glory and might forever and ever.* Innumerable hearts are full of adoration and praise for all that God has done through the Lamb. The Book of Revelation links God and the Lamb several times (5:13, 6:16, 7:9-10, 17; 14:1, 4; 21:22, 23; 22:1, 3). Leon Morris observed that "there cannot be the slightest doubt that the Lamb is to be reckoned with God and as God" (See also Jn 1:1, where Christ is the Word).

14. *The four living creatures* began the time of worship (4:8, 5:8), and now they *close it by saying, "Amen!"* The *twenty-four elders* had already twice *fallen down in worship* (4:10, 5:8), and now they *do so again* for a third time. The numberless years of eternity will not provide time enough to render to God and to the Lamb all the adoration that is their due. As the hymnwriter John Newton memorably put it, "When we've been there ten thousand years, bright shining as the sun, we've no less days to sing God's praise than when we first begun".

Meditation: The Worthiness of the Lamb

The fifth chapter of Revelation contains a surprise which is always astonishing. John was expecting to see a lion, but instead he saw a lamb. This is a striking and unexpected designation of Christ. In his commentary on Revelation, Julian Love wrote that "None but an inspired composer of heavenly visions would ever have thought of it. When earth-bound men want symbols of power they conjure up mighty beasts and birds of prey. Russia elevates the bear, Britain the lion, France the tiger, the United States the spread eagle – all of them ravenous. It is only the Kingdom of Heaven that would dare to use as its symbol of might, not the lion for which John was looking but the helpless Lamb, and at that, a slain Lamb".

Here is a life-changing truth. The decisive victory of Christ, the Lion of the tribe of Judah, was made possible by his suffering as the Lamb of God, who takes away the sin of the world (Jn 1:29). George Eldon Ladd wrote that, "If he had not come in humility as the suffering Saviour, he could not come as conquering Messiah". Robert Mounce put it like this: "In one brilliant stroke John portrays the central theme of New Testament revelation – victory through sacrifice".

Several of John's heptads focus around the person of Christ. In this passage we have seen that the Lamb has seven horns and seven eyes (v 6), and that only he is worthy to break the seven scrolls (v 9). These heptads are perfectly evident for any reader to see. But there are others which only the studious reader of the Book of Revelation will spot. Consider for a moment the four main names by which the second person of the Trinity is called in this book:

(i) He is called "Christ" seven times. A quick count using a concordance will confirm this statistic and the ones that follow.

(ii) He is called "Jesus" fourteen times. This is a double heptad: 2 x 7 = 14.

(iii) He is called "Lord" seven times. God the Father is called "Lord" fourteen times. In Revelation, the word "Lord" appears a total of twenty-one times. There are several heptads here, since 7 = 1 x 7, 14 = 2 x 7 and 21 = 3 x 7.

(iv) He is called "the Lamb" twenty-eight times. This time we have a quadruple heptad: 4 x 7 = 28. In fact the Greek word for "lamb", arnion, appears 29 times in Revelation. In 13:11 it is used of the appearance of the beast that rose out of the earth and tried to pass himself off as the Lamb of God, but in every other case it is used of the resurrected and victorious Christ.

These various sevens are a device employed by John to depict the completeness and perfection of Jesus Christ. By the use of other symbols, he has taught us that Christ, who is of the tribe of Judah and of the line of David, is both omnipotent and omniscient (that is all-powerful and all-knowing), just like God himself, and that he was victorious through his atoning and sacrificial death. In this passage we have a wonderful combination of ultimate power and ultimate self-sacrifice. It is no wonder that John saw the whole creation prostrated in deepest reverence before God and his Christ, and singing out loud a new song about the worthiness of the one who was slaughtered and who by his blood has ransomed us for God. The Lamb rightly shares the throne of God and receives equal praise with him. He will now break the seals and open the book of destiny, and we shall then be able to understand the history of our Christian era, to interpret what is happening in our own day, and to discern what must soon take place.

John Stott summed up the remarkable way in which Christ, the Lamb of God, illumines history, past, present and future, as follows:

(a) The Lamb speaks of victory. A lamb was a sacrificial offering, but Christ's sacrifice made possible his victory. In the New Testament the cross is represented not as a defeat but as a victory, not as a tragedy but as a triumph. On the cross, Christ dethroned and disarmed the rulers and authorities of evil. He made a public example of them, triumphing over them (Col 2:15). What seemed a completely abject and humiliating defeat was in fact the decisive victory of good over evil. The Lamb of God is *Christus Victor*, and if we are in Christ and participate in his sufferings, we shall undoubtedly share his glory and even his throne (3:21).

(b) The Lamb speaks of redemption. The frequent use of the title "the Lamb" is a reminder of the Jewish Passover. Just as the Passover lamb was sacrificed, its blood sprinkled and the people of Israel spared, so Christ our Passover has been sacrificed for us (v 9, 1 Cor 5:7-8) in order that we might be redeemed *from* sin and *for* God. History has a double plotline: there is world history (which deals with the rise and fall of empires), and there is salvation history (the story of God's acts of redemption). The key that explains the former is found in the study of the latter. What God is doing against the background of world history is to call out a people for himself and then present them as his own royal people and as his holy priests (1 Pet 2:9). What has made this possible is Christ's death on the cross.

(c) The Lamb speaks of suffering. The sufferings of Christ were unique in their redemptive power, but they were also a prototype of the sufferings of God's New Testament people (which includes us). Just as Christ suffered, so we are called to suffer (Rom 8:17). Just as he went to the cross for us, so we are to deny ourselves, take up our cross and follow him (Mk 8:34). Some of us may be called to make the ultimate sacrifice and be martyrs for his sake (2:10, 13; 6:9-11). There are too many churches today that make it their top priority to avoid causing offence. The message of the gospel will always be offensive (1 Cor 1:18-25). If we live godly lives and bear faithful witness to Christ, we shall be persecuted (2 Tim 3:12). In the New Testament, affliction is viewed as the normal experience of a Christian. For example, the apostles strengthened the souls of their converts and encouraged them to continue in the faith, saying, "It is through many persecutions that we must enter the kingdom of God" (Acts 14:22). Indeed, affliction and persecution were a sign that God was making those who endured them worthy of his kingdom, for which they were suffering (2 Thess 1:4-5). Affliction and persecution were helping them to cultivate endurance and steadfast character. They could even be a source of joy, because they stimulated Christian hope and the awareness that God was pouring his love into their hearts through the Holy Spirit (Rom 5:3-5).

(d) The Lamb speaks of weakness. There is power in weakness. God favours the weak and the needy. He chooses them in order to shame the strong. He picks out what is low and despised in the world, things that are not, in order

to reduce to nothing things that are (1 Cor 1:26-31). We are not to boast in our wisdom, nor in our might, nor in our wealth, but only in our understanding and knowledge of God (Jer 9:23-24). Simply to know God and his Son Jesus Christ is eternal life (Jn 17:3). The more closely we follow Christ, the more we shall learn the truth that the Apostle Paul expressed memorably in the words, "Therefore I am content with weaknesses, insults, hardships, persecutions, and calamities for the sake of Christ; for whenever I am weak, then I am strong" (2 Cor 12:10).

XV

6:1-8 The four Horsemen of the Apocalypse

John now sees the Lamb opening the seals that have kept hidden the secrets of the book of destiny. The picture that they reveal is grim but unsurprising. Those who know world history and study the news will recognise the themes brought to light by the four horsemen. Conquest achieved at all costs, war waged by or on obsessive megalomaniacs, rampant inflation, and ruinous famine or pestilence. But there is something new that follows, and that is the place of the church. As Leon Morris pointed out, the martyrs are singled out in verses 9-11, there is a fearful reminder of the Day of Judgement in verses 12-17, and then chapter 7 is given over to the great multitude of the redeemed. "John sees God as in control of the whole process, and he is concerned for his people. So, though apocalyptic judgements be loosed against all mankind, God's people need never be dismayed. They will be preserved no matter what the tribulation. That is the precious new revelation". The purpose of the first four seals is to demonstrate the self-defeating character of sin. Leon Morris goes on, "When the spirit of self-aggrandisement and conquest is abroad, all God need do is let events take their course, and sinners will inevitably be punished". Conquest is followed by war, and war gives way to inflation, famine and pestilence. The people of God are called to trust in him to deliver them from evil whenever tribulation becomes the common lot of all.

1. Once again *John saw*. He saw *the Lamb open one of the seven seals*, and reveal the contents of one of the scrolls. We learn that the saving work of the Lamb of God includes an element of judgement (Jn 12:31).

Leon Morris wrote, "Christ's death was not only salvation *from* sin, but also condemnation *of sin*". *John then heard one of the four living creatures call out, as with a voice of thunder, "Come!"* A voice of thunder aptly describes a heavenly voice (Jn 12:28-29). The command to come was addressed to the first horseman, who promptly appeared.

2. As the seven scrolls were opened, John saw their content in a series of visions. Here *he looked, and behold!* The word *behold* is conveyed by a lone exclamation mark in the New Revised Standard Version, here and in 4:1; 6:5, 8; 14:1, 14 and 19:11 (in 7:9 even the exclamation mark is omitted). John wished to convey that what he saw was startling. *There was a white horse, and its rider had a bow.* In the book of Revelation the colour white is often associated with victory. There is some similarity here with Christ the rider of the white horse in 19:11-16, but this horseman is not Christ. *He was awarded a victor's crown*, and was obsessed with *conquering, for his intention in coming out was to conquer*. The bow he carried was a symbol of war in the Old Testament (e.g. Isa 41:2). Sometimes God broke bows and thereby destroyed military power (Ps 46:9, Ezek 39:3, Hos 1:5). The first rider was a warlike conqueror on his way. Any nation that followed such a man would inevitably unleash bloodshed, famine and destruction. Henry Swete wrote in his commentary, "The lust of conquest which makes great empires was the first and most momentous of the precursors of the final revelation".

3. *When the Lamb opened a second seal* and thus revealed the contents of another scroll, *John heard the second of the four living creatures call out, "Come!"* The second horseman heard his summons and promptly appeared.

4. *Out came another horse*, this time *bright red* in colour, symbolising bloodshed, and *its rider was given* a destructive power. The sovereignty of God is seen when he uses the events of human history to judge human history, and thereby works out his purposes. The power God gave this rider was the *permission to take peace from the earth*. The rider *was given a great sword*, and *people then slaughtered each other*. Just as the first rider was a victorious megalomaniac bent on conquest, so the second was an inveterate fighter intent on war. William Barclay observed that between 67 and 37 BC 100,000 men died in rebellions

in Palestine, while the revolt in Britain in AD 61 associated with Queen Boudicca saw the deaths of 150,000. Historical events such as these form a sombre background to the second horseman's work of bloodshed through war, civil strife or persecution (Mt 10:34). This second woe appears to repeat the warlike character of the first. This may be because John is copying Christ, since the repetition of war occurs in each report of our Lord's discourse of the last times (Mt 24:6-7, Mk 13:7-8, Lk 21:9-10).

5. *The Lamb opened the third seal* and made it possible to read another scroll, and *John heard the third of the four living creatures call out, "Come!"* Just as before, a third horseman appears. John is startled, for *it was a black horse*. It symbolised famine (Lam 4:8), for *the rider carried a pair of balances in his hand*. The scales would be used to weigh grain, and the quantity needed for a loaf might command as much as a day's wages in times of famine (Lev 26:26, Ezek 4:9-10, 16).

6. John then *heard what seemed to be a voice*. It came *from the midst of the four living creatures* so it must have been the voice of God from the throne (4:6b). The words that came were *"A quart of wheat for a day's pay, and three quarts of barley for a day's pay"*. This was a famine price, but not yet a starvation price. It was unfair on the poor, for although bread shot up in price, *the rich person's olive oil and wine were unaffected*. Leon Morris observed that "The necessities of life for the poor will be in short supply, while the luxuries of the rich will not cease. All this adds up to a famine which is not yet a disaster. It is in the nature of a warning. Things are difficult, but the end is not yet".

7. *The Lamb opened the fourth seal* and made it possible to read the fourth scroll, and *John heard the fourth of the living creatures call out, "Come!"* This is the cue for the fourth of the horsemen to make his appearance.

8. Once again John is startled, for *he looked and there was a pale green horse*. The Greek word *chloros*, from which we get *chlorine*, denotes a yellowish green colour, possibly describing the bare skin of a mangy horse. The colours of the four horses, white, red, black and pale green, are reminiscent of the colours of the four horses in Zechariah's vision (Zech 6:1-3), although there they were drawing chariots sent by God to patrol the earth, while here their function is more sinister, and they are ridden by horsemen. The first three riders held a bow, a sword and

a pair of scales, but *the fourth is identified by his name, which is Death. Hades followed with him* (1:18). In medieval illuminated apocalypses *Hades* follows behind the rider called *Death*, and Hades is depicted as the mouth of hell, in which the wicked perish in the lake of fire.

Death and Hades *are given authority over a quarter of the inhabitants of the earth.* God disposes his power as he wills, and they are given destructive power *to kill with sword, famine and pestilence, and by the wild animals of the earth.* These four agents of Death are the same as those sent by God in Ezekiel's vision of the judgement with which God visited his people in 586 BC (Ezek 14:21). Henry Swete sums up this passage by saying that "The first group of seal-openings, now completed, describes the condition of the empire as it revealed itself to the mind of the Seer. He saw a vast world-wide power, outwardly victorious and eager for fresh conquests, yet full of the elements of unrest, danger, and misery; war, scarcity, pestilence, mortality in all its forms, abroad or ready to show themselves. This series of pictures repeats itself in history, and the militarism and lust of conquest, which it represents both in their attractive and repellent aspects, are among the forces set loose by the hand of Christ to prepare the way for his coming and the final publication of the secrets of the sealed book".

Meditation: Who is the first Horseman?

Three interpretations have been proposed for the rider on the white horse (6:1-2). One is that he is Jesus Christ himself. Another is that he represents the progress of the gospel throughout the Christian era. The third is that he represents warlike conquerors and megalomaniacs who are intent on conquest. These interpretations go back a long way and have a well-established pedigree. Which one is correct?

John Stott is one of those who believed that the first rider is Jesus Christ. He wrote, "The first horse was white; and its rider held a bow, was given a crown, and 'rode out as a conqueror bent on conquest'. Because he belongs to the series of apocalyptic horsemen, many commentators conclude that he too symbolises disaster, in his case military conquest. But throughout Revelation white stands for righteousness; crowns and conquest belong to Christ; and in 19:11-16 the rider on a white horse is named 'Faithful and True', 'the Word of God' and even 'King of kings and Lord of lords'. So we are assured that, before the other horsemen spread the horrors of war, famine and death, Christ rides first at the head of the cavalcade, resolved to win the nations by the gospel. And he succeeds! For in chapter 7 we see a countless multitude standing before God's throne, drawn from all the nations, the fruit of his international mission".

George Eldon Ladd went to great lengths as he sought to establish the case that the rider represented the progress of the gospel. He wrote, "The rider is not Christ himself but symbolises the proclamation of Christ in all the world". He also made much of the prophecy of Jesus that "The good news must first be proclaimed to all nations" (Mk 13:10, see also Mt 24:14), and he suggested that "The course of the age is not to be one of unrelieved evil when God's people are surrendered helplessly and passively into the hands of hostile powers".

F.F. Bruce, on the other hand, opted for the more commonly held belief among recent scholars, and wrote, "One long-established interpretation understands this of the victorious progress of the gospel, the rider on the white horse being Christ, as in 19:11. But the analogy of the other horsemen, and the fact that this horseman is equipped with a bow (like the mounted archers of the Parthian army), suggests rather invasion from beyond the eastern frontier of the Roman Empire".

George Beasley-Murray summed up two of these views and then opted for the more common interpretation: "Many interpreters regard the conquering horseman as Christ and compare him to the returning Lord in the vision of 19:11-16. It must be admitted, however, that the only thing in common with the two pictures is the *white horse*, which is a symbol of victory. Others hold that the ride represents the triumph of the gospel, and cite Mark 13:10. This suggestion is more plausible, but in view of the similarity of the four riders it seems more natural to interpret all of them as portraying divine judgements".

Leon Morris summed up all the arguments succinctly. He believed that "Christ would surely not appear merely as one of the Four horsemen of the Apocalypse". He added, "Some see in the [first] horseman a symbol of the victorious progress of the gospel. But there is nothing to indicate this. The four horsemen must surely be taken together, as they all indicate destruction, horror, terror. This one surely stands for war, triumphant war of conquest".

In a footnote, Phil Moore agrees with Leon Morris: "Some people assume from 19:11-16 that the rider of the white horse must be Jesus, but it is a mistake to see him playing such a minor role. He has the leading role in this scene, as the Lamb breaking the seals". In their commentaries, Robert Mounce and Tom Wright also interpret the first horseman as personifying the lust for military conquest.

But there is another reason for believing that the first horseman is symbolic of warlike conquerors and megalomaniacs who are intent on conquest. As he wrote the Book of Revelation, John made use of a recurring device in order to point out that certain enemies of the gospel will come disguised as Christian leaders. John was following in the footsteps of Christ himself, who in the Sermon on the Mount warned his followers to be wary of false teachers who appear in sheep's clothing, but inwardly prove to be ravenous wolves (Mt 7:15). We may be deceived by them initially, for they do resemble the real thing, but we shall ultimately see through their disguise, for we will "know them by their fruits" (Mt 7:16-20). This is a lesson that John will try and teach us several times.

(a) Here he says that the first horseman rides a white horse, as Christ will do later.

(b) He will tell us that the beast from the earth has two horns, like a lamb (13:11).

(c) He will likewise describe Satan and the beast from the sea as displaying seven heads, for they will feel free to misappropriate the divine number (12:3, 13:1).

(d) He will demonstrate that the beast from the earth is an evil and false prophet because he falls short of the perfection of God, for his number is 666 (13:18).

(e) He will depict the whore of Babylon drinking from a golden chalice, full of the wine of her abominations and impurities (17:3-6).

XVI

6:9-11 The Longing for just Retribution

John is watching, his attention rapt as the Lamb opens one by one the seals that keep the contents of the scrolls of destiny hidden from view. The picture that they reveal is grim but unsurprising. The first four seals have announced woe upon the earth. When the Lamb opens the fifth seal, we must consider the difficult matters of vindication and retribution. This is our study today. The sixth seal that follows is the terrifying prelude to the Day of Judgement. The final seal stands alone, and will be kept back until 8:1. It will usher in the next major heptad, when the seven trumpets will follow the seven churches and the seven seals. This pattern of four, two and one is going to recur with the trumpets and, later on, with the bowls.

9. *The Lamb proceeds to open the fifth seal.* In another vision, *John sees the souls of the martyrs under the altar.* The altar is part of the heavenly temple, and is also mentioned in 8:3, 5; 9:13; 11:1; 14:18 and 16:7,

a total of seven times (which is another heptad). The Lamb has already offered himself as the sacrifice that puts away our sin, so this must be the altar of incense, which symbolises worship and the offering of prayer. The fact that the souls of the martyrs are under it indicates that they have offered up their lives to God as part of their worship. They have been put to the sword, but this has only hastened their entrance into glory. John says that *they had been slaughtered for the word of God and for the testimony they had given.* What had led to their deaths was their faithfulness to the message of scripture and their public witness to Jesus Christ as Lord. Leon Morris rightly observed that "throughout history there has been a persistent hostility towards deeply committed Christians on the part of those wielding power", and those who wield power include senior church leaders who are unfaithful to biblical truth and take much of the glory that is due to Christ for themselves. They are deceitful and false teachers, wolves in sheep's clothing, and they await a terrible judgement.

10. *The martyrs cry out to God with a loud voice.* They address him as *"Sovereign Lord, holy and true"*. The word translated "Sovereign" is *Despotes*, used of God in Luke 2:29, Acts 4:24 and 2 Tim 2:21, and of Christ in 2 Pet 2:1 and Jude 4. It is the word for a master of slaves and it emphasizes God's absolute power. He is not like a human despot, however, for he is also *holy and true* (3:7). He is worthy of our trust, even in times of bewilderment and perplexity. The martyrs are indeed bewildered and perplexed. If God is holy and true, how can he, in his complete goodness allow unholy and untrue people to mete out unjust treatment on the saints? Surely, they insist, *God should judge and avenge their blood on the inhabitants of the earth.* Notice that it is the martyrs who are crying out for justice to be done. George Eldon Ladd understood this verse as meaning that "It is the blood of the martyrs crying for vindication, and not the martyrs themselves crying for personal vengeance". This may sound tidy, but it is plainly not what the verse is saying. There is a deep longing for justice in every human heart, and the martyrs have every reason to request it from God, who is not only holy and true, but also perfectly just. But *how long will it be before it comes?* A time must come for the righting of all wrongs and the redressing of all righteous grievances. That time is not yet. Nevertheless God promises that come

it will, and we shall begin to see the answer to the martyrs' prayer very shortly, and then more clearly in 19:2.

11. *The martyrs were each given a white robe.* These white robes have been seen as a reference to their justification by God, and they are *given* because people do not justify themselves, but are instead justified by God. Alternatively, the robes may be white because this colour represents victory (6:2, 19:11), and although it might look as if the martyrs had been defeated, in fact God has awarded them the triumph. *They were told to rest a little longer*, and this opportunity to rest further from their labours in the bliss of blessedness (14:13) would have been welcome. The end of the age would not come *until the number would be complete, both of their fellow servants and of their brothers and sisters, who were soon to be killed as they themselves had been killed.* As Leon Morris wrote, "God has determined who are to be martyrs, and he waits until his plan for them is accomplished. The problem of God's failure to punish sin here and now was one which exercised the first Christians. They found part of the answer in the cross. The cross does not mean the abolition of judgement. It means that [people] will be judged by their attitude to the sacrificial love of God shown on Calvary. But the cross shows that God has no truck with evil. Finally it will be totally overthrown. God waits until the number of the martyrs is complete. But then the destruction of evil is certain. It is not a question of 'Whether?' but of 'When?'"

Meditation: It is God himself who will dispense fair Justice

The phrase "the inhabitants of the earth" occurs nine times in Revelation (3:10; 6:10; 8:13; 11:10; 13:8, 12, 14; 17:2, 8). It always seems to refer to those who are not true followers of God, but are instead their opponents and persecutors. In verse 10 of our passage it occurs in a cry for divine retribution on such people: *"How long will it be before you judge and avenge our blood on the inhabitants of the earth?"* There is a similar prayer for divine justice in Luke 18:7-8, which is attributed by Christ to God's people in this life, and which he promises will be answered speedily: *"And will not God grant justice to his chosen ones who cry to him day and night? Will he delay long in helping them? I tell you, he will quickly grant justice to them"*. In both of these passages there is no question of a Christian seeking personal vengeance. It is quite clear that in the Bible, both Old

Testament and New, vengeance belongs to God alone. In the Jewish law we read that *"You shall not take vengeance or bear a grudge against any of your people, but you shall love your neighbour as yourself: I am the Lord"* (Lev 19:18). God also says that *"Vengeance is mine, and recompense"* (Deut 32:35).

Moreover, God declares in no uncertain terms that he will execute retribution: *"A jealous and avenging God is the Lord, the Lord is avenging and wrathful; the Lord takes vengeance on his adversaries and rages against his enemies. The Lord is slow to anger but great in power, and the Lord will by no means clear the guilty. Who can stand before his indignation? Who can endure the heat of his anger? His wrath is poured out like fire, and by him the rocks are broken in pieces. The Lord is good, a stronghold in a day of trouble; he protects those who take refuge in him"* (Nah 1:2-3, 6-7). This very robust teaching about God was summed up by the Apostle Paul in the words, *"Beloved, never avenge yourselves, but leave room for the wrath of God; for it is written, 'Vengeance is mine, I will repay, says the Lord'"* (Rom 12:19). Retribution is not only a divine prerogative, but also a duty that a holy and just God must and will perform.

Some Christians indignantly protest that the prayer of the martyrs in our passage falls short of Christ's teaching in the Sermon on the Mount, *"Love your enemies and pray for those who persecute you, so that you may be children of your Father in heaven; for he makes his sun rise on the evil and on the good, and sends rain on the righteous and on the unrighteous"* (Mt 5:44-45). They also point to the prayers of forgiveness spoken by Stephen and by Jesus Christ as they were being put to death: *"Lord, do not hold this sin against them"* (Acts 7:60) and *"Father, forgive them, for they do not know what they are doing"* (Lk 23:34). But the fact remains that God is not only loving: he is both holy and loving. He is light and he is love (1 Jn 1:5, 4:8). He loves all of us with a holy love. He therefore wants the very best for us, and has gone to great pains to make it possible for us to be saved from our pride and our deceit, sending his Son Jesus Christ to die for our sins on the cross. But if we spurn his holy love, disdain the sacrifice of his Son, and reject his gracious provision for us, he must respect our choice. He has given each one of us free will and he will never abuse our freedom to choose or to reject him. So the same Christ who loved us and gave himself for us may have to destroy us in the winepress of his wrath (Isa 63:1-6, Rev 19:11-16). Leon Morris wrote, "The cry [of the martyrs in v 10] is intelligible only on the basis that the supreme power in the world is God's power, and that he exercises it in a moral way".

The persecution of God's people is still going on, and in its subtlety it is stronger than ever. Wolves dress up in sheep's clothing and water down the truths about God. Then they sideline the sheep, and so open up paths whereby they are able to attain positions of power in the church. From these lofty positions they accuse the sheep and sideline them even further. Many of God's people feel rejected and cry out in anguish, "Sovereign Lord, holy and true, how long?" One day all these persecutions will have run their course. Only then, when the full measure of the martyrs is completed, the prayers of the saints, both dead and alive, will be heard, and an angel will cast fire from the altar onto the earth in judgement (8:3-5).

Tom Wright put it like this: "What has to happen, it seems, is for evil to do its worst, to reach its height, and so to be at last ripe for the judgement that wise and faithful people know, in advance, it deserves". God will not judge evil until it is fully and thoroughly deserving of judgement. "The evil represented by the four horsemen must reach its height with the martyrdom of yet more believers. That martyrdom will itself be part of the means of God's judgement. As we shall see, this is how the Lamb's victory is worked out in practice".

XVII

6:12-17   The terrible Discovery that it is now too late

As John keeps looking, the Lamb opens the sixth seal. This is it. This is a vision of the end of the world. This is what it will be like for those who have disdained Jesus Christ and opposed his holy remnant. What will strike us most vividly will be the fact that of all people, the lost are the ones most to be pitied. The prospect of their utter terror at having to face the one on the throne and the Lamb is written by John with restraint and sobriety. Apocalyptic imagery signals the end of the age, and there can be no salvation for those who persistently refused to repent and never turned to God in faith. They will face the holy and irresistible wrath of God.

12. After the Lamb *opened the sixth seal*, some cosmic disturbances are depicted: *There came a great earthquake* (already a sign of the end in Ezek 38:18-20); *the sun became black as sackcloth, and the full moon became like blood.* This is apocalyptic language similar to Joel 2:30-31. It announces the imminent arrival of "the great and terrible day of the Lord" which the prophets often spoke about. The New Testament refers to it as *the day of our Lord Jesus Christ* (1 Cor 1:8), *the day of the Lord Jesus* (2 Cor 1:14), *the day of Christ* (Phil 1:10), or *the day of the Lord* (2 Thess 2:2). It is also called *the day of wrath* (Rom 2:5) or *the day of redemption* (Eph 4:30). The *locus classicus* for a depiction of the Day of the Lord in vivid apocalyptic imagery is Isaiah 2:8-22, which we shall be studying shortly.

13. The prelude to the great day continues. *The stars of the sky fell to the earth as the fig tree drops its winter fruit when shaken by a gale.* Unseasonal winter figs are no match for a strong wind, and will drop off in a gale. The regularity of stars and other heavenly bodies was something that ancient people could trust as being utterly dependable. So Jewish people were taught to imagine the end of the world as being accompanied, or even ushered in, by certain cosmic irregularities. It is, of course, unfeasible for stars to fall to earth, and the graphic wording of verse 14 makes it impossible to restrict such a star-fall to a shower of meteorites.

John is saying that when the terrible day is about to dawn, its arrival will be heralded by the collapse of well-established authority, symbolised by catastrophic events in the heavens. In his discourse about the last things, Christ used similar apocalyptic language (Mt 24:29-31, Mk 13:24-27, Lk 21:25-28). Martin Kiddle aptly pointed out that this vision of complete ruin in the sixth seal was "a restatement of beliefs already held on supreme authority. What the faithful Witness at one time had said on earth, he now repeats from heaven".

14. The universe is now imagined as being *rolled up like a scroll* and taken away, as in Isaiah's vision of God's judgement on the nations (Isa 34:4). As John looked, *the sky vanished like a scroll rolling itself up, and every mountain and island was removed from its place.* The movement of the mountains may have been inspired by Jeremiah's vision of the day of the Lord's fierce anger (Jer 4:23-26): "I looked on the mountains, and lo, they were quaking, and all the hills moved to and fro". For those who disdain Christ and his followers, the day will arrive when every dependable reference point will be removed. There will be very frightening social and political upheavals. The lost will find themselves alone – together with God and Christ. Nothing else will count. It will be utterly terrifying.

15. Fear will fall on the inhabitants of the earth, as well it might. John subdivides all people into seven classes – another heptad. First come *the kings of the earth*, then *the magnates and the generals and the rich and the powerful*. The less well-off are there also, for *everyone, even the slaves and the freed*, are included. The focus is on those who are great and powerful, for John is at pains to make it clear that even the greatest will not be spared in the Judgement. Everyone who is guilty before God will seek to *hide in the caves and among the rocks of the mountains*. This is Old Testament imagery, coming no less than three times in Isaiah chapter 2 (verses 10, 19, 21), as we shall shortly see.

16. John hears the guilty *calling to the mountains and the rocks*. The reality they must face is so terrible that anything else, however horrible, is preferable. They beg the mountains and the rocks to *fall upon them* (Hos 10:8, and see also Christ's words in Lk 23:28-30) *and hide them from the face of the one seated on the throne and from the wrath of the Lamb*. As Henry Swete wrote, "What sinners dread most is not death, but the revealed presence of God". What terrifies these proud people is the gaze of their Creator and the anger of their Saviour. To look on the face of the one on the throne, perfectly holy and perfectly loving, is unbearable for those who have ignored and spurned his advances. It was so in the beginning (Gen 3:8-10), and it will be so at the end.

But even more frightening is the wrath of the Lamb. This phrase, *the wrath of the Lamb*, comes only once in the Bible, in this verse. Thomas Torrance wrote forthrightly in his commentary, "Who ever heard of a lamb being angry? What a terrible thought – the gentlest of all God's creatures angry! It is the wrath of love, the wrath of sacrificial love which, having done the absolute utmost for us and our salvation, tells us as nothing else could the certainty with which evil awaits its doom at the hand of God". The book of Revelation has much to say about wrath. There are two Greek words used for it: *orge* (used in 6:16-17, 11:18, 14:10, 16:19 and 19:15), and *thumos* (occurring ten times). As Leon Morris wrote, "John is in no doubt but that the divine wrath is a grim reality. People must reckon with it in the end".

17. The guilty finally articulate the awful reality that has appeared before them so suddenly, inescapably and terrifyingly: *The great day of their wrath has come, and who is able to stand?* John can only describe the last day as the great day of the wrath of God and of the Lamb. As F.F. Bruce helpfully observed, "This wrath is the retribution which must operate in a moral universe such as God's. It is the response of his holiness to persistent and impenitent wickedness. It is indeed his *strange work* (Isa 28:21) to which he girds himself slowly and reluctantly (Isa 63:1-6), in contrast to his proper and congenial work of mercy; but where his mercy is decisively repudiated, people are left to the consequences of their freely chosen course. If here the wrath of God is also 'the wrath of the Lamb', it is because that wrath is not detached from the cross; indeed, it is best understood in the light of the cross".

This great day of divine wrath will be the day of reckoning for all evildoers. Nobody will be able to stand before God (Joel 2:11, Zeph 1:18). This message of doom for the guilty is also a message of reassurance for those who belong to God, who have been reckoned to be righteous by their faith in the Lamb. John is telling us that God is completely in control. He will work out his purposes and on the last day, when the present world order and the vast universe pass away, evil will be seen to be defeated and every wrong will be put right.

Meditation: The great Day of their Wrath has come

One of the highlights of the book of Isaiah is the vision of the great day of the Lord in 2:8-22. In a poem of extraordinary power the prophet depicts the fate that awaits the proud and arrogant. He begins by painting in the background: "Their land is filled with idols; they bow down to the work of their hands" (Isa 2:8). The consequence is that God must intervene to humble human pride, and we listen to some voices in heaven suggesting that there are certain things that God cannot forgive (Isa 2:9). And so the day will come when people will seek to hide behind rocks, and in caves or holes, in a vain attempt to run away from the wrath of God and from his incinerating, white-hot glory.

Two ominous refrains appear in the poem. The first is "Enter . . . and hide . . . from the terror of the Lord and from the glory of his majesty" (Isa 2:10, 19, 21). God in person will rise and terrify the earth. This will be the final consequence of proudly delighting in the superficial glory of celebrities, of relying on our own achievements, and of bowing down to idols. The second ominous refrain is that "Haughty eyes shall be brought low (Isa 2:11, 17, and see Prov 6:16-19, 21:4), and the pride of everyone shall be humbled". On the great and final day, only one person will capture everyone's attention. Only one being will have the spotlights of glory shining on him. The radiance of all the universe will light up his majesty. He alone "will be exalted on that day" (Isa 2:11, 17; Rev 4:11, 5:13).

This being is God, but what is his name? Isaiah often calls him Yahweh, which was the familiar name by which he revealed himself in a personal way to his people. They knew him as Yahweh; he was their God (Ex 6:7, Jer 32:38). In our day, God makes himself known to us by the familiar name of Jesus Christ. He is the same God, even though he is a person distinct from Yahweh. This is because there are three different persons within the plural Godhead, which consists of God the Father who was known as Yahweh, God the Son whom we know as Jesus Christ or the Lamb of God, and God the Holy Spirit.

In Isaiah's vision Yahweh, who commands all the armies of heaven, "has a day" which he has appointed as the final day of reckoning, and he alone knows when it will be (Mk 13:32). Today's church disdains its privilege of feeding the people of God with nutritious spiritual food, because its message lacks the vital eternal dimension. Very seldom nowadays is the solemn truth of the final day mentioned from the pulpit. Christian people would rather not think about the final reckoning, when perfect justice will be seen to be done. This day is defined as being "against" various groups of people and their proud attitudes. God will be seen to oppose all who are proud and lofty, all who are lifted up and high. To be high and mighty could well be regarded as an advantage now, but it will be a terrible liability on the last day. Why? Because God hates human pride. He will not bless those who are proud, but instead he will actively oppose them (2 Sam 22:28, 1 Pet 5:5).

He will pronounce against those who stand out among their peers and receive glory from them – celebrities who are epic heroes, like the prover-bial cedars of Lebanon, lofty and lifted up, and like the lesser-known oaks of Bashan, long-lived and mightily dominant – giants among people, who are like high mountains or lofty hills, marked out by an apparently impregnable solidity, seemingly quite impervious to attack – but this invincibility of theirs will be blown away by a single exhalation from the God of armies, and they will fall – Alexander the Great, Napoleon, Hitler, and their successors today. God will also bring down those who are like a high tower or a fortified wall: now they may look down on other people from a great height, treating them as insignificant ants, but this is not pleasing to the God and Father of the One who went around doing acts of kindness on behalf of the needy and marginalised.

Even the insignia of escapist security, the mighty ships of transport, war or hedonistic living, will be brought low by being sunk. Those who are both arrogant and affluent (Lk 12:13-21) will be judged for storing up treasures for themselves. On the great day of the Lord all the material things will be stripped away and we shall see the one who creates and upholds all things. Then the attention will not be on the bright lights, nor on the superficial glamour of this world's celebrities, nor even on the great achievements of mankind. The haughtiness of people will be humbled, and their pride will be brought low; and God alone will be exalted on that day (Isa 2:12-17).

Not only human pride will bite the dust. So will man-made religion. Idols are often man-made things which have become objects of worship. Idols can also be fallen humans who have attained celebrity status and are being worshipped. All idols will utterly pass away (Isa 2:18). Only God is worthy of our worship, for all glory rightly belongs to him and to him alone, and so it is he who will be exalted and adored on that day (Rev 4:8-11; 5:8-10, 11-14).

Three times Isaiah mentions those who will hide away in caves and under rocks (Isa 2:10, 19, 21). The Bible teaches that fallen man is incapable of enduring the sight of God in his perfection and holiness. God had said to Moses, "You cannot see my face; for no one shall see me and live" (Ex 33:20). He then put Moses in a cleft in the rock to enable him to survive (Ex 33:21-23); this is the first clear parallel with Revelation 6:15-17. Isaiah's vision of the great day of Yahweh is built around a recurring scene of madness and panic. People are trying to escape the divine presence by entering caves in the rocks or holes in the ground. They are utterly unable to think in their terror. They want to hide "from the terror of the Lord and from the glory of his majesty", for God has risen in order to terrify the earth. Who are these pitiable people? They are the proud of this world. There is no terror like that of proud people who know that they are about to be brought low. They realise that they will lose all their power, position and privilege. They will be humbled. It would have been better if they had humbled themselves.

The proud will throw away the idolatrous images they have made. They will throw all their idols of silver and gold to the moles of the ground and the bats of the caves (Isa 2:20). They had made them in order to worship them, and on the day of the Lord these idols will be tangible evidence of rebellion against God. They ignored and disobeyed him. They acted as if he did not exist. They had an innate desire to worship something, but they did not wish to worship

God – so they worshipped their idols, perhaps they worshipped themselves. None of them gave themselves to the only one who was the rightful object of their adoration.

What is the lesson that Isaiah wanted his readers to learn from this awesome vision of God in his majesty? Could it be that only God may occupy the supreme place in our thoughts? When it comes to resting the full weight of our trust on someone, we are to turn away from mortals, who have only breath in their nostrils, for of what account are they? (Isa 2:22). Other people's hold on life is as slender as ours, and if it is eternal life that we are after, only God's Son Jesus Christ can be depended upon for the truth. He alone gives us eternal life, and he does so as a free gift – even though it cost him his very life blood (Jn 10:28, 3:16).

We should not miss the fact that on the great and final day the terror will stem not only from the wrath of God but also from the wrath of the Lamb, mentioned in Revelation 6:16 and by implication in verse 17. What a terrible concept is this wrath of the Lamb! It sounds like a contradiction in terms. What picture does the Lamb of God bring to your mind? He is the one who gently and meekly allowed others to lead him to the cross, where he took away the sin of the world. But is he also covered in wool, ever-soft towards us, and one whom we may occasionally stoop down to cuddle? That is the impression given of him today in most English churches. We are led to believe that he is utterly inoffensive. By implication we are taught that not only would he never be as ill-mannered as to say anything that might offend us, but also that he is so considerate that he would never take offence at anything that we might think, say or do – and therefore all is peace between us.

But what if this soft and cuddly Jesus Christ is just the modern creation of false teachers in the church? What if the Lamb who died in weakness did so because he was truly the strongest of the strong? What if the one who emptied himself for our sakes has been given the name that is above every other name? What if the Lamb of God who was slain for our sins is in fact the fierce and indomitable Lion of the tribe of Judah (5:5)? Let's realise something before it is too late: the Lamb of God is *not safe*. Let's realise this before he sets off on his mission to vindicate and avenge the martyrs. Let's realise this before the great and terrible day arrives when he will destroy the proud in God's wine press (Isa 63:1-6, Rev 19:11-16).

"Pride goes before destruction, and a haughty spirit before a fall" (Prov 16:18). "Humble yourselves therefore under the mighty hand of God, so that he may exalt you in due time" (1 Pet 5:6). "All who exalt themselves will be humbled, but all who humble themselves will be exalted" (Lk 18:14).

XVIII

7:1-8 The Sealing of the Servants of God

Six of the seven seals have been opened, but now there is an interlude before the seventh one is opened in 8:1. In the meantime God's special care for the security of his servants is demonstrated by the fact that he seals them. In this section we shall consider who exactly are the sealed, and what their sealing consists of. Then John will share with us another amazing vision (in 7:9-17) of the multitude from every nation who stand before the throne and before the Lamb.

1. *After this*, the opening of the first six seals, *John saw four angels standing at the four corners of the earth.* This does not mean that the earth has four corners, nor that first century cosmology included a belief in a rectangular world, but that these four angels between them had a view of everything that took place on planet earth. They were similar to the horses that God had sent forth to "patrol the earth" (Zech 1:7-11), or the seven lamps or eyes of the Lord, which "range through the whole earth" (Zech 4:2, 10b), or the four chariots that were told to "Go, patrol the earth" (Zech 6:1-7). Likewise, these four angels were scrutinising everything that was happening everywhere on the earth. In particular, they were *holding back the four winds of the earth so that no wind could blow on earth or sea or against any tree.*

   The four winds are metaphorical and could refer back to the four horsemen of the Apocalypse (6:1-8). John is concerned about the harm that God's people may suffer at the hands of war-mongering conquerors, and from the pestilence, inflation and famine that usually result from their initiatives. Just as strong winds can damage trees by uprooting them or destroying their main branches, so God's people are vulnerable to the winds of judgement that are bound to follow after the major apocalyptic tribulations. When they blow against us, as they most certainly will, what will our fate be? Has God done anything in order to protect us?

2. *John also saw another angel ascending from the rising of the sun.* Here the east may represent the source of God's blessing. The magi came from the east with the good news of Christ's birth (Mt 2:1-2), and John may be thinking of them. This angel who came up from the east *had the seal of the living God.* In antiquity seals were a mark of ownership. Here the divine seal would mark the people who were sealed with it as belonging to God, and thanks to it they would be preserved from destructive judgements that would affect others (see Ezek 9:1-11; note also the prototype in Ex 12:23). In the book of Revelation God's people bear this mark on their foreheads and are protected by it; it is called "the name" of the Lamb and of God (9:4, 14:1, 22:4).

Those who are impenitent evildoers are also marked, but in their case it is a different mark. It will bring them some benefits in this life, but it will not spare them from the wrath of God, either in this life or on the great and terrible day of judgement (13:16-18, 14:9-11, 16:2, 19:20, 20:4). *The angel with the seal called with a loud voice to the four angels.* We learn that the latter *had been given power to damage earth and sea,* and that the angel with the seal had the duty of informing them of God's plan for the protection of his own people.

3. The angel with the seal said, *"Do not damage the earth or the sea or the trees, until we have marked the servants of our God with a seal on their foreheads".* The Greek word for "servant" is *doulos,* normally used for "slaves", and here it means those who are utterly devoted to God. All of his servants are marked with the seal. This brings about a great restraint on the forces of destruction. In his book "The Apocalypse Today", Thomas Torrance argued that this is "the great master-thought that informs this book [of Revelation]. Every moment on the earth is made to serve the redeeming purpose of God for mankind. The four winds from the four corners of the earth cannot blow and vent their rage as they like, but only as they are made to serve the church of Jesus Christ".

4. *John heard the number of those who were sealed.* "Sealed" is in the perfect tense and this means that they are sealed forever: God does not change his mind about who his servants are. The number was 144,000. Some, like the Jehovah's Witnesses, have taken this number literally and made it a core belief. This will be invidious if their group is bigger than

144,000 (the Jehovah's Witnesses claim over eight million members worldwide). But 144,000 is obviously symbolic. It is twelve times twelve multiplied by the cube of ten. Twelve is the number of God's people twice over – the twelve tribes of Jacob in the Old Testament, and the twelve apostles of the New. Ten is the number of completeness, so that the Ten Commandments represent the entirety of God's law. The Holy of Holies was a perfect cube (I Ki 6:19-20). Therefore 144,000 stands for the totality of God's people in their sanctified state.

In 14:3 they are defined as those "who have been redeemed from the earth". In verses 5-8 they are assembled like soldiers in battle formation, threatened and constantly under enemy attack, for they are the church militant here on earth. *They are sealed out of every tribe of the people of Israel.* In the New Testament the church is often spoken of as the twelve tribes of Israel (Mt 19:28, Lk 22:30, Jas 1:1). Similarly, any Christian is a true *Jew* (Rom 2:29), and the collective of all Christians, which we call the church, is the true *Israel of God* (Gal 6:16), the true *circumcision* (Phil 3:3), as well as being *a chosen race, a holy nation,* and *God's own people* (1 Pet 2:9).

5. The tribes are now listed in an unusual order. This is hardly surprising, since there are 18 different orders among the 20 or so in the Old Testament, and none of them agrees with the order in Revelation. It begins *Judah, Reuben, Gad.* Judah comes first because Christ was a member of that tribe (Heb 7:14). In this scheme each tribe is said to contain exactly *12,000* people, and this is numerically tidy. Everyone who belongs to the Israel of God is *sealed* with the divine seal.

6. The order continues *Asher, Naphtali, Manasseh.* It is strange to find Manasseh listed separately, since the tribe of Joseph is listed in verse 8, and it included both Ephraim and Manasseh. Instead we would have expected Dan to feature in the list, but it is omitted. Some of the earliest commentators believed that Dan was not included because it was thought, following an exposition by Irenaeus of the Septuagint version of Jeremiah 8:16, that the Antichrist was to come from that tribe. F.F. Bruce declared that "This roll-call of the tribes is schematic; we are not dealing with a census tribe by tribe as in Numbers 1:20-47 or 26:5-51, and need not be over-concerned about the inclusion of Manasseh or the exclusion of Dan".

7. The order continues with *Simeon, Levi, Issachar*. After each tribe, comes the repeated number that symbolises their totality: *12,000* people.

8. The order ends with *Zebulun, Joseph and Benjamin*. Each of the tribes included *12,000* people, and they were all *sealed*, as we are told at the beginning and end, in the cases of Judah and Benjamin. But what exactly did this sealing consist of?

Meditation: The distinctive Mark of the true Christian

The background to this sealing of God's servants is in Ezekiel 9:1-11, where God gave his prophet a vision of Jerusalem in 592 BC, six years before its destruction by the Babylonian army in 586 BC. The divine judgement would certainly come, and God summoned six angelic executioners to carry it out. Before doing so, God instructed one of them, who was clothed in linen and had a writing case, to place a mark (it might have been a Hebrew *tau* that looked like a cross) on the forehead of anyone who was deeply troubled by the sins of Jerusalem. This mark would be a sign that would protect those who had it from the judgement that would soon be meted out on the city. Those without the mark would not be spared, but would be dealt with pitilessly. The mark was like the seal in Revelation 7, whose purpose was to ensure protection for true believers from the terrible judgement of God.

All true Christians belong to the church, which is the Israel of God. We are the servants of God, usually under attack and battle-weary, but nevertheless safe. We enjoy divine protection as those who have been sealed with "the seal of the living God". What is this seal? Like every seal, it has a threefold function. It is a *stamp of ownership*, a *mark of genuineness* and a *guarantee of security*. What more does the New Testament teach about this seal? Interestingly, God first set his seal on Christ (Jn 6:27). Christ himself was the prototype of those who have the seal of God upon them. The sealing of Christians is further described as an "anointing" whereby "God establishes us in Christ, by putting his seal on us and giving us his Spirit in our hearts as a first instalment" (2 Cor 1:21-22). Something similar may be found in the Epistle to the Ephesians, where the Apostle Paul explained that "in [Christ] you also, when you had heard the word of truth, the gospel of your salvation, and had believed in him, were marked with the seal of the promised Holy Spirit; this is the pledge of our inheritance toward redemption as God's own people, to the praise of his glory" (Eph 1:13-14, and see also Eph 4:30).

So the way God seals us is with his Holy Spirit, who comes and dwells within our bodies (1 Cor 6:19-20). In his book on Revelation, Richard Bewes wrote that "God's presence, by the Holy Spirit, is what marks out the true disciple from the merely nominal Christian. How can you tell if you are sealed? There are a number of telltale signs. Are you someone who has a trust in Jesus Christ, and a love for him? Do you find yourself more and more wanting to meet with others who are in his church? Does the truth of God exert an increasing, magnetic pull on you? Do you find yourself in distress when you fall into the old wrong habits? Is it *difficult*, living as a Christian and fighting against evil? If the answer is 'Yes', it is a good sign! You are in the church militant".

Preaching on Ephesians 1:13-14, John Stott said that "All who have heard the gospel and believed in Christ have been sealed with the promised Spirit, who is the guarantee of our inheritance. This indicates that the sealing took place when we believed. It is something that has happened. It is something that God has given us. A seal is a mark of ownership. Whether it be the affixing some personal seal to a legal document, or the stamping of your name on some tool or instrument, or the branding of sheep or cattle with a hot iron, the purpose of sealing is to mark something as belonging to us. And God's seal, with which he brands us as belonging forever to him, is the Holy Spirit himself. The Holy Spirit is the identity tag of the Christian. If the Holy Spirit dwells within you, you are a Christian. If he does not, you are not a Christian. For when we believed in Christ, God sealed us with the seal of the Holy Spirit himself, who dwells within us. This seal is an indelible seal: it cannot and will not be erased. We have been sealed 'for the day of redemption' (Eph 4:30). Until the final day, when our bodies will have been redeemed, God has branded us with his seal, the Holy Spirit, and will never take him away from us. This divine seal is God's guarantee that we shall enter into our heavenly inheritance one day. What a reassuring blessing this is! There is so much uncertainty and insecurity in the world. The very survival of human civilisation is in jeopardy. There are many men and women whose hearts are failing them for fear, and there is deep insecurity. But if we have trusted in Christ, God has sealed us for eternity with the Holy Spirit".

There is one further text about the significance of this seal. In 2 Timothy 2:19, the seal or inscription of God is "The Lord knows those who are his" and "Let everyone who calls on the name of the Lord turn away from wickedness". Here are two further aspects of what it means to be the true servants of God.

Phil Moore suggested that there were three lessons that we might learn from the first eight verses of Revelation 7, and they will bring comfort and reassurance to us during the very troubled years in which we live.

(a) However bad the trials and tribulations may be that come our way, God has clearly placed his seal on those whom he has redeemed, and once we are sealed, we are and shall continue to be under his protection.

(b) All who are God's servants are sealed, and God will keep and protect every single one of us from evil. The number 144,000 is not a precise total, but instead it symbolises the completeness of God's true church. Neither death, nor Satan, nor any other evil power, nor any man or woman who follows evil in any form, will be able to separate us from the love of God in Christ Jesus our Lord.

(c) The number of those saved will be large. We are about to encounter them once more, not as the church militant in earthly peril marching in well-ordered ranks as to war (7:1-8), but as a great multitude that no one can count, worshipping God and giving to him all the blessing and glory and wisdom and thanksgiving and honour and power and might that are rightly his (7:9-17).

XIX

7:9-17 The great Multitude that no one can count

The interlude continues prior to the opening of the seventh seal. The redeemed have to face opposition and persecution for the sake of Christ and the gospel, but they are sealed and therefore they are safe. Now in this new vision we find them in the bliss of heaven, after the end of this present age. They are gathered together before the throne and the Lamb. Their tribulation is past. Eternal glory lies before them, and full of amazement they declare their gratitude and heartfelt worship.

9. John wishes to express the vivid nature of his new vision and says, *After this I looked, and there was a great multitude that no one could count.* There were very many redeemed people there, more than John expected, and so vast was the crowd that it would have been impracticable to count all of them. They came *from every nation, from all tribes and peoples and languages.* These four categories of God's people appear five times in Revelation (5:9, 7:9, 11:9, 13:7, 14:6), and always in a different order. Their universality inspired the amazing enterprise of the church.

The costly worldwide mission, which seemed humanly speaking unrealistic but was commissioned by Christ himself (Mt 28:19-20), had as its aim to win for him a universal crowd of holy people.

The vast multitude was *standing before the throne and before the Lamb.* Once again Christ is mentioned in the same breath and is accorded the same status as God the Father. The crowd were all *robed in white,* made perfect with the righteousness that Christ has freely gifted to them. They held *palm branches in their hands,* an emblem of victory. It was won by Christ, through his saving work on the cross, and it is he who provided them with the white robe of righteousness (Isa 61:10). When we are faced by men and women who attain their own ends by means of their own manipulative tactics, it is good to remember that our final victory will be the result of a quiet trust in God. This lesson comes often in the Old Testament (e.g. in Ps 37:3, 5; Isa 30:15).

10. The great multitude *is crying out in a loud voice.* They have something that they wish to celebrate publicly. It is welling out of their innermost beings and it is worth our while to listen to it. *They say, "Salvation belongs to our God who is seated on the throne, and to the Lamb!"* They ascribe their salvation to both God and the Lamb. Not to one or to the other, but to *both.* God is on the throne, so he is sovereign. Therefore Leon Morris concludes that "Salvation then comes from the sovereign act of God in Christ".

11. The angels, who did not sin and so did not need to be redeemed, join with the redeemed in their song. *All of the angels stood around the throne and around the elders and the four living creatures.* As they listen to the cries of the redeemed, the mere thought of God's grace and kindness towards beings who had disobeyed him causes the angels to *fall on their faces before the throne, and worship God.*

12. The angels begin by singing *"Amen!"* Full of joy at God's saving act, they then proceed to ascribe seven qualities to God, each of which is preceded by the definite article in the Greek: *"The blessing and the glory and the wisdom and the thanksgiving and the honour and the power and the might be to our God forever and ever! Amen".* This heptad of qualities that belong to God is almost the same as the heptad that is ascribed to Christ in 5:12, except that *thanksgiving* replaces *wealth,* and the order of the seven is quite different. The angels end with the words "forever

and ever", which lifts up their statement to the realm of eternal verities, and then close their contribution with a second "Amen!"

13. At this stage an animated discussion takes place when *one of the elders addressed John. He asked him, "Who are these, robed in white, and where have they come from?"* He asked John because he thought it was important that John should know what characterised the redeemed, and what their background was.

14. John threw the ball back into the elder's court, saying, *"Sir, you are the one that knows"*. No doubt someone from heaven would express the truth that follows more clearly. *The elder* proceeded to do so, and *said, "These are they that have come out of the great ordeal"*. The Greek word used for "ordeal" is more often translated as "tribulation". *The great ordeal* may refer to a time of acute suffering just prior to the end of the age, but it must also refer to the sufferings that are to befall all Christians, for everyone in this vast multitude *came out of it*. F.F. Bruce wrote, "The tribulation of our present passage is the persecution of the followers of Christ which broke out in such intense malignity in John's day and continues until the ultimate triumph of Christ".

   In other words, it is the normal Christian life, together with the afflictions that are certain to accompany it. We shall look more closely at this idea in our meditation. The elder continued, *"These"* who are robed in white *"have washed their robes and made them white in the blood of the Lamb"*. This statement is paradoxical but very memorable. Our robes symbolise our inner nature, what we are really like. How can we become clean and pure? The answer is – by washing ourselves, once and for all, in the blood that was shed by the Lamb of God. And this of course means, by appropriating for ourselves all the benefits of Christ's death for our sins on the cross. This declaration proclaims the complete efficacy of Christ's atoning death.

15. Therefore, *for this reason*, the multitude can *stand before the throne of God, and worship him day and night within his temple*. Heaven will not consist of lots of clouds bearing harp players. It will be a new earth, which is in continuity with the present earth, but wonderfully renewed (Isa 65:17-25; Rev 21:1-2, 10-27). A problem arises from the mention of a heavenly temple in this verse, because later John will state that he saw no temple in the heavenly Jerusalem. But he will also add that

the temple *is* the Lord God the Almighty, and the Lamb (21:22). Leon Morris wrote that "Probably the whole of heaven is being regarded as a sanctuary in which all God's people are priests (1:6, 5:10) and enjoy the immediate presence of God".

Furthermore, *the one who is on the throne will shelter them.* The word translated "shelter" is *skenosei*, which is closely related to *skene* ("tabernacle") and *shekinah*. The immediate presence of God in his glory will surround God's people in the new earth (21:3). He himself will be our tabernacle. He will shelter us because we shall be dwelling *in him*. This is a truly wonderful prospect for the people of God. Robert Mounce said, "Without doubt it is one of the most exalted portrayals of the heavenly state to be found anywhere in scripture. The lyric prose of verses 15-17 is charged with a spiritual excitement that has caused the faithful of all ages to yearn for that final redemption".

16. The bliss of the redeemed is put across in terms of a series of negatives, mostly taken from Isaiah 49:10. *They will hunger no more, and thirst no more; the sun will not strike them, nor any scorching heat.* Every desire of ours will be satisfied, but the promise goes beyond mere physical privation. As Robert Mounce wrote, "It points to that ultimate satisfaction of the soul's deepest longing for spiritual wholeness. 'Blessed are those who hunger and thirst for righteousness', said Jesus, 'for they will be filled' (Mt 5:6). And again, 'Whoever comes to me will never be hungry, and whoever believes in me will never be thirsty' (Jn 6:35; see also Jn 4:14, 7:37)". Furthermore, in the age to come the sun will no longer scorch us. There will be neither global warming, nor skin cancer. We shall experience some torments in this life, but there will be none in the life to come. Why is this?

17. It is because *the Lamb at the centre of the throne will be our shepherd, and he will guide us to springs of the water of life.* All of the blessings of the next life, the positive ones because of what will be there and the negative ones because of what will not be there, will be ours thanks to the Lamb. There will be a reversal of roles, for the Lamb will be our shepherd, and he will lead us to springs of living water (Ps 23:2, Jn 4:10). The redeemed people of God will always thirst for him, but in the life to come this thirst will continually be satisfied. Finally, *God will wipe away every tear from our eyes.* With his gentle fingers, he will remove

every hurtful memory and so fulfil one of the promises that was first made in Isaiah 25:7-8, and which is repeated in 21:4.

Meditation: Out of the great Ordeal, with Robes washed and clean

On a first reading, the people of God in the second half of chapter 7 appear to be different from the group mentioned in the first half. The first group is numbered, but the second is too big to count. The first seems to consist of the tribes of Israel, but the second involves all the Gentile nations. In fact, both are pictures of all the redeemed people of God, but viewed from different perspectives. In verses 1-8 we see them as the true Israel of God, vulnerable to the winds of history, but we learn that they will be eternally safe because they have been sealed as God's own treasured possession. In verses 9-17 we see them as a multitude worshipping God in heaven, forever freed from the afflictions that befall God's people in this life. We learn from the first picture that if we belong to God, then we are numbered and protected. What do we learn from the second?

The people of God, who include Old Testament saints as well as true Christians, will stand before God's throne, clothed in righteousness and holding the symbols of victory. They will sing loud songs of worship, ascribing salvation to God and to the Lamb. The next life will be one long continuous celebration of joy. Earthly choirs and orchestras are only rehearsing for the future gala concert. This makes us wonder how we may be sure that we will be numbered among God's people. One of the elders helpfully asked John the two questions that often come to our minds, "Who are these, robed in white, and where have they come from?" John replied, "Sir, you are the one that knows", and the elder then proceeded to supply model answers to his own questions in verse 14.

1. *These are they who have come out of the great ordeal* (or tribulation). This cannot be a reference to a specific historical time of great persecution, since this is a condition applying to *all* the redeemed who stand before God's throne. They are said to have come out of the great ordeal. In Greek, the word used is *thlipsis*, which may be translated as "tribulation", "pressure", "oppression", "affliction", "ordeal" or "persecution". "The great ordeal" must be a description of the normal Christian life. All true believers, when they reach heaven, will be described as having come out of the great tribulation. This is consistent with the teaching in the rest of the New Testament. Here are four of the many examples of this:

(a) At the end of his discourse in the upper room, Jesus said to his disciples, "In the world you face persecution (*thlipsis*). But take courage; I have conquered the world!" (Jn 16:33). Any follower of Jesus Christ will necessarily face *thlipsis*.

(b) When Paul and Barnabas were returning from their first missionary journey, they visited the churches that they had established in the Galatian cities. There they strengthened the disciples, saying, "It is through many persecutions (*thlipsis*) that we must enter the kingdom of God" (Acts 14:22). Without enduring it, they would not be able to "come out of the great *thlipsis*".

(c) In his letter to the church in Rome, Paul encouraged all the Christians, asking them, "Who will separate us from the love of Christ? Will hardship, or distress, or persecution (*thlipsis*), or famine, or nakedness, or peril, or sword?" Then he quoted from Psalm 44:22, "For your sake we are being killed all day long; we are accounted as sheep to be slaughtered". Paul thought that *thlipsis* was the norm for all Christians, and he believed that this was prophesied in the Old Testament.

(d) At the start of the book of Revelation John introduced himself to his readers as their brother, who shared with them in Jesus "the persecution (*thlipsis*) and the kingdom and the patient endurance" (1:9). John knew what he was talking about.

It is clear from these examples that suffering is an integral part of the Christian life. Far from sparing us from tribulations and persecutions which are expressions of the fierce hatred of Satan for God's people, God allows them for our good, so that we may grow in faith and humility. As Dietrich Bonhoeffer wrote in his book *The Cost of Discipleship*, "Suffering is the badge of true discipleship. The disciple is not above his Master. It is therefore not at all surprising that Christians should be called to suffer. In fact it is a joy and a token of his grace". Paul made a similar point when he wrote to the Romans: "We boast in our sufferings, knowing that suffering produces endurance, and endurance produces character, and character produces hope, and hope does not disappoint us, because God's love has been poured into our hearts by the Holy Spirit that has been given to us" (Rom 5:3-5; see also Mt 5:10-12, Jas 1:2-4 and especially Rom 8:16-17).

Preaching forthrightly on Revelation 7, John Stott said, "It is through suffering that we enter into glory. All Christian people, if they are uncompromisingly loyal to Jesus Christ, will know what it is to suffer for their loyalty. We shall probably not be martyred, but we may be ridiculed, we may be made to feel like fools for Christ's sake, and we may be spoken against or boycotted or slandered in some way. For example, if we take our stand, without compromise, on the uniqueness of Jesus Christ as the only Saviour of sinners, we are bound to be opposed by any who affirm pluralism, and so support the independent validity of every religion. The uniqueness of Jesus Christ is today one of the most unpopular truths of the Christian gospel. Because it is true, we cannot abandon it, and its unpopularity is neither here nor there. Again, if we take our stand, without compromise, on the truth that salvation is a free gift, that not only are we unable to earn it but we are also unable to contribute to it by anything that we are or do, we shall find that this undermines people's self-righteousness and their self-esteem, and they hate us. Or again, if we take our stand, without compromise, on purity and self-control in an age of increasing sexual promiscuity, we shall again suffer for it, we are bound to arouse opposition, even within the church". So this is the first condition for standing before God's throne. We shall "come out of the great ordeal" because we are willing to take our stand for Christ and, if necessary, to suffer for him.

2. *They have washed their robes and made them white in the blood of the Lamb.* Dirty robes disqualify us from standing before the throne, and banish us from the presence of the divine majesty. We cannot stand before God in the tattered rags of our own morality. We have to wash our robes so that they become white. Only then will we be fit to enter the presence of God and to stand before him. Of course, to launder our robes in the blood of the Lamb is not to be taken literally. Washing clothes in red blood does not make them shining white. But the interpretation of this image is easy. The Lamb is Jesus, indeed it is Jesus who died as the Lamb of God in order to take away the sin of the world (Jn 1:29). Like the Passover lamb, he died in our place to enable God to pass over our sins (Ex 12:1-13). The blood of the Lamb represents the permanent power and effectiveness of the atoning death of Jesus Christ. To wash our robes in the blood of the Lamb means to come to the crucified Saviour, to beg him to have mercy on us and to make us clean and fit for his presence. There is no other way whereby we can get right with God and be saved (Acts 4:12). In God's sight, even our righteous deeds are like a filthy cloth (Isa 64:6). Like the high priest Joshua, we need to have our filthy clothes taken off us, for they represent our guilt before God, and then replaced by clean festal garments and clean headgear (Zech 3:1-5).

So those who are robed in white and stand before God's throne are those who have washed their robes in the blood of the Lamb, and who have made their stand for Christ and come out of the great ordeal. Therefore, "for this reason, they are before the throne of God" (v 15). Had they not fulfilled these two conditions, they would not be standing there in God's presence, worshipping him, forever happy and grateful in the bliss and perfection of heaven.

XX

8:1-5 The Lamb finally opens the seventh Seal

Finally we come to the moment when the Lamb opens the seventh seal. There is an uneasy silence which seems to be a sign that something momentous is about to happen. Indeed, it leads to fire from the heavenly altar being thrown upon the earth, and to a further series of seven visions, this time of divine judgement, which are announced by angels with trumpets. It is remarkable that the prelude for this is the prayers of God's people. The latter are often considered to be insignificant by worldly men and women, and their prayers can only be the object of godless derision. Nevertheless these prayers move the hand that moves the universe, and open the way for the holiness of God to express itself in righteous judgement.

1. After a long interval *the Lamb opens the seventh seal.* The result is that *there was silence in heaven for about half an hour.* This was an awe-inspiring moment, the silence before the storm, but what caused it? The answer is that the prayers of the saints were about to be offered to God (v 3-4). The saints may seem to be of little earthly use to other people, but in God's sight they matter. The moment has arrived for their prayers for vindication to rise before God (6:9-11). The praises of the angels (7:11-12) give way to silence so that the prayers of the saints may be heard. Silence reigns in heaven as a result of the sense of awe at God's fiery holiness (Hab 2:20). He is about to launch severe judgements on worldly people, and heaven is hushed for about half an hour. Christ taught that God is to be feared, for he can destroy both soul and body in hell (Mt 10:28, and see also Lk 12:5). The right response to this solemn truth is a time of silent meditation (Isa 41:1).

2. *John* then *saw the seven angels who stand before God.* Who are these seven angels? They must be important and senior heavenly beings, for they stand before God and are about to be entrusted with the execution of divine judgements upon the wicked. In Luke 1:19 Gabriel identifies

himself as one of these, and in one of the apocryphal books seven angels are mentioned who also present the prayers of the saints and go in before the glory of the Holy One (Tobit 12:15). In another apocryphal book their names are given: Gabriel, Michael, Raphael, Uriel, Raguel, Saraqael and Remiel (1 Enoch 20:2-8). In the book of Revelation we find seven references to a group of seven angels (a heptad of heptads), but after this chapter they refer to the angels with the seven bowls, whose outpouring would lead to the seven last plagues. The later angels with the bowls may or may not be the same as those mentioned here.

Seven trumpets are given to them. F.F. Bruce wrote that the day of the Lord will be heralded by eschatological trumpet blasts (e.g. Isa 27:13, Joel 2:1, and see also Mt 24:31, 1 Cor 15:52, 1 Thess 4:16). When the final trumpet is to be sounded, it will not be a surprise if the Church of England, ever watchful for correctness, sets up a committee to examine its tonal characteristics.

3. Before the angels blow the trumpets, the prayers of the saints are offered. John watches as *another angel with a golden censer came and stood at the altar. He was given a great quantity of incense to offer with the prayers of all the saints on the golden altar that is before the throne.* A better translation would be "incense which *consists of* the prayers of the saints" (5:8). The heavenly altar is golden and is situated before the throne. These two facts are an indication of the importance of our prayers. Moreover, they must be heard by God before his judgements are released on the earth.

4. When incense is burnt, smoke visibly rises, and John says that *the smoke of the incense, with the prayers of the saints, rose before God from the hand of the angel.* Again, this would be better translated as "the smoke of the incense that *consists of* the prayers of the saints". The fact that our prayers go up from the hand of the angel implies that earth and heaven join together when we pray. As Leon Morris wrote, "Prayer is not the lonely venture it so often seems to be. There is heavenly assistance and our prayers do reach God. It may be significant that there is mention of an altar in connection with this, for it signifies that there is something sacrificial in true prayer".

5. As John keeps watching, *the angel took the censer* (which had just been used to offer the prayers of the saints in v 3) *and filled it with fire from the*

altar and threw it on the earth. The same censer that he used for purposes of intercession he now uses for purposes of judgement. As a direct consequence, *there were peals of thunder, rumblings, flashes of lightning, and an earthquake.* The fire is taken from the same altar on which the prayers of the saints have been offered. Leon Morris believed that "This surely means that the prayers of God's people play a necessary part in ushering in the judgements of God". George Eldon Ladd agreed: "This verse dramatically pictures the fact that it is in answer to the prayers of the saints that God's judgements will fall upon the earth". Thomas Torrance put it forthrightly: "What are the real master-powers behind the world, and what are the deeper secrets of our destiny? Here is the astonishing answer: the prayer of the saints and the fire of God. This means that more potent, more powerful than all the dark and mighty powers let loose in the world, more powerful than anything else, is the power of prayer set ablaze by the fire of God and cast upon the earth".

Some Christians pray daily that God's name may be held to be holy, that his kingdom may come, and that his good and perfect will may be done on earth as it is in heaven. Such prayers are answered in ways that we cannot imagine.

Meditation: The perfumed Prayers that please God

Phil Moore has written that in ancient times perfumes were known as "incense". They were invented in Egypt, and were made by mixing gum resin, frankincense and myrrh, together with a few other spices that gave them their individual scent. The mixture was burned as a sweet fragrance in Pharaoh's palace and also in the temples. The word "incense" comes from the Latin word *incendere*, which means *to set on fire*, and the word "perfume" likewise comes from the Latin words *per fume*, which mean *through the smoke*. Incense has a long history of being used in worship, and in the Law of Moses there are precise directions for when and how to use it, as well as a special recipe for making it (Ex 30:1-10, 34-38).

As early as the time of King David, incense smoke was a picture of our prayers rising to God (Ps 141:2), and in Revelation 5:8 the heavenly incense is said to be the prayers of God's people. At first sight Revelation 8:3-4 appears to distinguish the incense from the prayers, but as F.F. Bruce pointed out, the dative case used in the Greek may be a dative of definition, so that "incense *with* the prayers of the saints" is equivalent to "incense *consisting of* the prayers of the saints". This makes 8:3-4 harmonise with 5:8, and underlines the point that God is delighted when we pray. So much so, that his choice of a picture for the prayer of his people is the fragrance of the fine perfume of rising incense smoke. Because our prayers please him, we should be like the prophet Samuel and say, "Far be it from me that I should sin against the Lord by ceasing to pray for you" (1 Sam 12:23).

God's people in Old Testament days had to prepare their incense using the right ingredients, and offer it to God in the approved manner. On one occasion two of the priests burnt incense using their own unholy fire, and paid for this with their lives (Lev 10:1-2). Similarly, it is important that *we pray as Christ taught us.* We are to pray to our Father who is in heaven, full of confidence because we are his children – chosen, loved and adopted. We should not think of prayer as a work of the flesh, as if we were trying to get something from a reluctant God. God is much more willing to give than we are to pray. Prayer is a gift of God's grace and not a human activity that depends on our own efforts and exertions.

The humble prayers of God's people, offered up with humility and fervour to our heavenly Father, are powerful and effective (Jas 5:16-17). The opening of the seventh seal teaches us that our prayers are vital to further God's purposes. The fire from the heavenly altar that was poured out upon the earth had far-reaching consequences. It led to "peals of thunder, rumblings, flashes of lightning, and an earthquake" (v 5). This was all in direct response to the prayers of the righteous.

We have already seen this pattern. The souls of the martyrs prayed to God, their blood crying out for divine retribution (6:9-10). They were told to rest for a while longer (6:11). But the time would arrive when terrible cataclysms would strike the earth, and those who had considered themselves to be rich and powerful would be unable to escape the gaze of the Holy God and of the Lamb, and their efforts to scuttle away and hide in caves or under rocks would be in vain (6:12-17). The *dies irae*, the day of God's wrath, would surely arrive. As F.F. Bruce wrote, "The cry 'How long?' of 6:10 is answered at last". Furthermore, the message of the seven trumpets and the seven bowls is that divine judgement is not reserved for the final day, but it begins here and now, as a result of our prayers.

George Eldon Ladd has written that "The wrath of God is not merely judicial; it also embodies a merciful purpose. It is designed to drive people to their knees by harsh experiences while the time for decision remains, before it is too late.

This is hinted at in several passages" (9:20; 16:9, 11). "If it were possible to drive people to repentance, the plagues of the trumpets and bowls would do so".

The prayers of God's people clearly play an important part in the outworking of God's purposes. When we work, we work. When we pray, God works.

XXI

8:6-13 The first four Trumpets

God has heard the prayers of his saints, and now he will proceed to execute some of his temporal judgements. The seven trumpets, like the seven bowls that come later, cover similar ground to the seven seals, and indeed to the warnings in the letters to the seven churches. Leon Morris put it like this: "For John the End is the significant thing. He does not take in the whole in any one vision or any one series of visions. He deals with different aspects, sometimes covering the same ground from different points of view, and sometimes taking in different features of the landscape. Thus we may legitimately expect some matters to recur in the visions, but always new details will make their appearance". John Stott wrote, "It is important to remember, as the drama develops, that the breaking of the seven seals and the blowing of the seven trumpets are not consecutive, but symbolise the same period, between the two comings of Christ, although seen from different perspectives". He added that the distinctive perspective of the trumpets is to act as explicit divine warnings, "for their overriding purpose is to jolt the unbelieving world out of its complacency and self-centeredness, to summon it to repentance, and to warn the impenitent of the righteous judgement of God". He then wrote that "We can understand the seals, the trumpets and the bowls as relating to the same period, between Christ's comings, but from a different point of view. The seals describe what Christ *allows* in his world (since events happen only as he breaks the seals). The bowls (still to come) describe how Christ *judges* his world. But the trumpets (which come between the seals and the bowls) describe how Christ *warns* the world and summons people to repentance". The first four of the seven trumpets are concerned with natural disasters which are reminiscent of some of the plagues just prior to the Exodus (v 7-12), the next two with demonic assaults on the human race (9:1-21), and the seventh will follow after a heavenly interlude (11:15-19). We saw an identical 4-2-1 pattern in the seven seals.

6. This follows from verse 2, where the trumpets were given to the seven angels. *Now the seven angels who had the seven trumpets made ready to blow them.* They raised their instruments and were all set, heightening the sense of expectation.

7. *The first angel blew his trumpet,* and there was a fierce outburst of lightning, as in a violent thunderstorm, although here it was more like a giant fireball. The result was widespread bloodshed, and many died. *There came hail and fire, mixed with blood, and they were hurled to the earth.* The consequence was devastation: *a third of the earth was burned up, and a third of the trees were burned up, and all green grass was burned up.* Although the whole earth was not destroyed, a significant part of it was, and the alarm that was caused would certainly act as a warning to many to repent. As Leon Morris wrote, "God sends his plagues on evil people. This is true throughout the ages and it will be so until the End".

8. *The second angel blew his trumpet.* This time *something like a great mountain, burning with fire, was thrown into the sea.* This could refer to a large asteroid that catches fire as it plummets through the atmosphere and then lands on the sea. It could also describe a large volcano on an island, which suffers a violent eruption, causing most of it to break off and fall into the sea. In either case the result would be a giant and catastrophic tsunami. John proceeds to describe the devastation.

9. *A third of the sea became blood, a third of the living creatures in the sea died, and a third of the ships were destroyed.* In a significant part of the sea people and sea creatures died. A large proportion of the waters may have been polluted with sulphur and other toxic minerals, and the sea temperature may have risen. In any case, this would constitute another major manifestation of divine judgement.

10. *The third angel blew his trumpet.* This time it is not the salty waters of the sea that are affected, but the fresh waters on the land. *A great star fell from heaven, blazing like a torch, and it fell on a third of the rivers and on the springs of water.* What is going on here? This great star falling down to earth is evocative of the great fallen angel, Satan, who was cast out of heaven (Isa 14:12, Lk 10:18). But a star from heaven, blazing

like a torch, could also be a series of nuclear missiles. We might think this a trifle far-fetched, but John is about to say something that has provoked people in our own day to think furiously about our world.

11. *The name of the star is Wormwood.* Wormwood is a very bitter substance that is disagreeable to ingest, but it has medicinal uses and is not poisonous. And yet *a third of the waters became wormwood, and many died from the water, because it was made bitter.* John may be using the word "wormwood" to refer to any bitter substance which is poisonous (Jer 9:15, 23:15). There may also be an unconscious prophetic element here (2 Pet 1:20-21), since the Ukranian word for *Wormwood* is *Chernobyl.* In April 1986 a major nuclear accident occurred in the number 4 reactor of the Chernobyl Nuclear Power Plant, near the city of Pripyat in north Ukraine. Much of Europe was affected, and humans, animals and plants suffered. The ecological damage caused was immense, and Chernobyl itself continues to be a radioactive site to our own day (this is being written in 2023).

12. *The fourth angel blew his trumpet.* This time it is the heavenly luminaries that are affected, and a dark gloom descends on the earth. *A third of the sun was struck, and a third of the moon, and a third of the stars, so that a third of their light was darkened; a third of the day was kept from shining, and likewise the night.* There is a pollution of the skies that is beginning to affect countries with dirty industries, whose tall chimneys keep on expelling dense smoke. Eventually twilight prevails, and residents have to wear masks so as not to breathe in the dirty air. These first four trumpets all portend disasters that will not affect the whole earth but only *one third* of it. These judgements are not final like those that are to be poured out from the bowls (15:1). The trumpet blasts are just severe preliminary warnings.

13. *John is looking* at the desolation, and *he hears an eagle crying out with a loud voice as it flew in mid-heaven.* Eagles or vultures, being sinister birds of prey, are often a sign of disaster (Mt 24:28). This eagle was flying in the heights of mid-heaven, from where it proclaimed, *"Woe, woe, woe to the inhabitants of the earth, at the blasts of the other trumpets that the other angels are about to blow!"* The phrase "the inhabitants of the earth" occurs often in Revelation (3:10; 6:10; 8:13; 11:10; 13:8, 12, 14; 17:2, 8), and refers to those who oppose and persecute God's people. The ravages of nature, visited by God on evil people, are bad enough, but worse is to follow. We shall see that the greatest afflictions are to arise from man's inhumanity to man. This does not mean that they may not be classed among God's temporal judgements, for God has always used the evil actions of those in power to bring his own purposes to fulfilment. The brutality of Nebuchadnezzar's army resulted in the destruction of Jerusalem and the exile to Babylon of the surviving Jews, and God used it to purify and reform his rebellious people. But it was a very bitter pill to swallow, and this bitterness was the theme of the book of Habakkuk.

Meditation: The Plagues of Egypt are repeated

It is interesting to notice the echoes of some of the ten plagues of Egypt in these verses. F.F. Bruce wrote, "The hail and fire, mixed with blood, which follows the first trumpet, may be compared with the seventh plague of Egypt (Ex 9:22-26); the admixture of blood is probably a purely apocalyptic portent (Joel 2:30). The great mountain, burning with fire, which was thrown into the sea when the second trumpet sounded, so that a third of the sea became blood, recalls the first plague of Egypt (Ex 7:17-23), but the undrinkable character of the fresh water (Ex 7:24) is paralleled in the effect of the great star called Wormwood, which fell on a third of the rivers and springs of fresh water after the third trumpet-blast. The darkness which follows the fourth trumpet is reminiscent of the ninth Egyptian plague (Ex 10:21-23); it is not caused, however, by a mere passing sandstorm like Egypt's *darkness to be felt*, but by a disturbance of the heavenly luminaries (Lk 21:25-28). These four plagues destroy one third respectively of earth, sea, fresh water and natural light". The catastrophes of 3,400 years ago are being repeated today.

The plagues arising from these first four trumpets are ecological disasters of a type that is very much in the news in our 21st century. We may be tempted to see them as simply man-made, and therefore unnecessary if we educate one another to treat our world with more care. But our passage teaches us that these disasters are also God's temporal judgements which he brings to us because of our wicked selfishness. God works through the damage caused to nature by selfish people.

F.F. Bruce was way ahead of his time when he wisely pointed out in 1969 that "These four judgements remind us that the sin of man can and does adversely affect the rest of creation in a way that reacts disastrously upon his own life. John would have agreed with all that Paul says about the creation's bondage to decay and frustration (Rom 8:20-23), and he later expresses the same hope as Paul's for that 'revealing of the sons of God' which will liberate creation from this bondage, when he envisages the manifestation of a new Jerusalem, the glorified community of the people of God, accompanied by the appearance of 'a new heaven and a new earth' (Rev 21:1-27). But before that, judgement must work itself out to the bitter end". So we must do good, but the Bible implies that life will get worse before it gets better. In the end, by God's grace, it will be altogether perfect.

XXII

9:1-12 The fifth Trumpet and first Woe

As in the case of the last three seals, we now move away from physical afflictions that are the consequence of wars or disturbances of the natural world, and enter instead into the realm of the spiritual. But while the opening of the last three seals concerned the realities of heaven, the blowing of the last three trumpets will result in terrors emerging from the bottomless pit, demonic attacks affecting multitudes of people, and the just outpouring of God's wrath on those who are bent on evil.

1. *The fifth angel blew his trumpet*, and John witnessed a supernatural vision. To begin with, *he saw a star that had fallen from heaven to earth*, and this star (it was an angelic being) *was given the key to the shaft of the bottomless pit*. Who was this star or angel? Most commentators believe that the words "fallen from heaven to earth" imply that he was a fallen angel, possibly even Satan himself (Mt 25:41, Lk 10:18, Rev 12:9). But some suggest that he was a good angel, and perhaps even Jesus Christ. If a good angel, he may be the same as the angel who will later come down from heaven with the key to the bottomless pit (20:1). Leon Morris wrote, "With the experts so divided it is unwise to be dogmatic". Whoever he was, he had been given a key.

   With this key, he was able to open *the shaft of the bottomless pit*. The pit is a broad place whose top is like a narrow well that was usually kept locked. It is an exceedingly unpleasant place, and the demons in the Gadarene pigs were very keen not to be sent there (Lk 8:31). It is a place that is inhabited by harmful spirits but is firmly under God's control. It is a prison for fallen angels (2 Pet 2:4) and also for Satan himself (20:1-3). It is mentioned seven times in Revelation (another hidden heptad, 9:1, 2, 11; 11:7; 17:8; 20:1, 3).

2. The star-angel *opened the shaft of the bottomless pit.* It would have been better if he had opened the mythical Pandora's Box, for this bottomless pit is real, and *from the shaft rose smoke like the smoke of a great furnace.* This is reminiscent of the destruction of Sodom and Gomorrah (Gen 19:28), and it brought darkness and gloom. *The sun and the air were darkened with the smoke from the shaft.* The sunlight was extinguished (as in Ex 10:15, Joel 2:2), and the gloom spread in *the air,* which is where evil spirits were thought to dwell (16:17, Eph 2:2).

3. *Then from the smoke came locusts on the earth.* Much has been written about the precise nature of these locusts, and we shall investigate it in the meditation that follows. Perhaps they are referred to as locusts because locusts constituted the eighth plague in Egypt just before the Exodus. *They were given authority like that of scorpions of the earth.* They had no authority of their own; it was *given* to them by God, just as the key was *given* to the star-angel. What is the authority of scorpions? Quite simply, to administer exceedingly painful stings with their tails.

4. The locusts were then given a divine command. *They were told not to damage the grass of the earth, or any green growth or any tree.* They cannot have been real locusts, since the natural diet of locusts was forbidden to them. Instead, the target for their sharp teeth – or maybe for the sting in their tails – was to be *those people who do not have the seal of God on their foreheads.* Hence the sealing in 7:3-8, so that those who belong to God would be safe from these demonic attacks.

5. *They were allowed to torture them for five months, but not to kill them.* Their purpose was to inflict pain rather than to kill. The period of five months may refer to the lifespan of a locust (spring and summer). But as Leon Morris pointed out, the number five occurs frequently in the Bible as a small, indeterminate number, and he suggested that here it might imply a limited but undefined period of time. Moreover *their torture was like the torture of a scorpion when it stings someone.* The words "torture" and "scorpion" both point towards extreme pain.

6. People will be in very great agony, but they will be unable to kill them-selves. *In those days people will seek death but will not find it.* Their pain will be so sharp that *they will long to die, but death will flee from them.* Bodily death would give them an escape from physical agony, but not from the torment of an accusing conscience. We may learn that in the long run, it pays to be godly. Those who know and love God will be sustained by him in their afflictions, until they "come out of the great ordeal" (7:14). But those who do not know and love God will find that living becomes more and more painful in this life, and if they do not repent they will duly be cast into the lake of fire, which is the second death (20:11-15).

7. John proceeds to describe these locusts. He paints an impressionist picture, and every attempt to make the details fit with natural crea-tures will lead to impossible hybrids. *In appearance the locusts were like horses equipped for battle.* Locusts have heads that resemble those of horses, and their compact ranks look a bit like lines of cavalry (Joel 2:4). *On their heads were what looked like crowns of gold.* They possessed a regal authority that made them appear majestic. *Their faces were like human faces.* When angels appear to people, they look human, and it may be the same with fallen angels. These locusts are described as if they were supernatural beings. There is something disturbing and uncanny about them.

8. *Their hair was like women's hair*, presumably long and wavy, and this might give them a certain alluring charm. *Their teeth were like lions' teeth* (Joel 1:6), which made them ferocious and fearfully destructive, to be avoided at all costs.

9. *They had scales like iron breastplates*, which gave them total protection. Like crocodiles, they constituted formidable opponents, who could not be pierced by ordinary arrows or spears. Furthermore, *the noise of their wings was like the noise of many chariots with horses rushing into battle*, like a vast army (Joel 2:5). Their approach was audible, like that of an army with chariots and cavalry troops.

10. As the scene before his eyes becomes increasingly vivid, John switches to the present tense: *They have tails like scorpions, with stingers, and in their tails is their power to harm people for five months.* Their sting is in their tail. Five months was the length of time during which they could

torture people (v 5). It is a limited period, but the acute pain inflicted would make it seem like an age.

11. Unlike natural locusts (Prov 30:27), these demonic beings *have a king over them*. This is none other than *the angel of the bottomless pit*, possibly (according to F.F. Bruce) a reference to the angel-star as in verses 1 and 2. Whoever this king is, he is an evil angel who commands the demonic hordes. We are told his name in two languages. *In Hebrew he is called Abaddon*, the transliteration of a Hebrew word meaning "destruction" (see Job 28:22, 31:12; Ps 88:11; Prov 15:11, 27:20). And *in Greek he is called Apollyon*, which means "destroyer". These names make it clear that the objectives pursued by the angel of the bottomless pit and his cloud of locusts are not positive at all. They are hell-bent on destruction.

12. The eagle had announced that the fifth, sixth and seventh trumpets would bring woe to the inhabitants of the earth (8:13). We have seen the outcome when the fifth angel blew his trumpet. *The first woe has passed*. But the troubles of most men and women are far from over. *There are still two woes to come*.

Meditation: The Locusts from the Pit of Hell

Leon Morris wrote that "The symbolism of the locusts is horrible and strange. It is not surprising that it has been interpreted in a variety of ways. It is unwise to be dogmatic, but the most probable understanding of it refers it to the preaching of the gospel. When people fail to respond to God's gracious invitation and set themselves in opposition to his purposes, then they become the prey of horrifying demonic forces. They suffer the consequences of their choice. Not that they are defeating God: his sovereignty is clear to John. God is not mocked. Even in the demonic horrors he works out his purposes. But people must abide the results of their choice". God has so arranged the universe that actions have consequences.

In his book *The Apocalypse Today*, Thomas Torrance interpreted the passage in a similar way. He identified the key with the preaching of the word of God, for nothing "opens the bottomless pit of human nature" like the gospel. "Preach the gospel and keep on preaching it, and either people are ashamed and converted or the bottomless pit is opened. Surely that is what has happened in Europe, as well as in [other parts of the world]. The cross of Jesus Christ has provoked such a reaction against it, that all the latent evil in people has been pushed to the surface in unbelievable wickedness and bloodshed. The very bottomless pit has been opened in our midst, so that heaven and earth have been darkened with its fumes and the whole character of the world has been poisoned". There are indeed latent evils festering away in the depths of our human nature, but when people hear the gospel, their deep sinfulness is revealed to them. Much of the time it lies hidden, but sometimes, when it is disturbed, it rises to the surface and makes itself known in numerous horrible ways. This was clearly taught by Jesus Christ (Mk 7:20-23). Tom Wright believes that this inner depravity "is the black hole inside us all". John Stott wrote forthrightly that the gospel "convicts us painfully of sin, for there is no pain more painful than that of a tormented conscience. It leads some people to repentance and faith, but others to harden their hearts and so perish".

But John is surely conveying more in this vision. There exist other evil forces apart from those that are latent in our innermost beings. There are demonic forces which come to the fore when people reject the gospel and turn away from God. Commenting on the locusts, James Love wrote that "Such a picture etches forever on the soul one of the most terrible truths of life. It is this: whenever people go beyond their own humanity in committing their crimes, whenever they become so debased that they let themselves be possessed by a force of evil greater than human nature itself could conjure up, then human sin becomes inhuman, people behave like the offspring of beasts, and judgement lashes the soul with its most unspeakable terrors".

Ultimately the demonic forces represented by the locusts result in the terrifying excesses of what Robert Burns called "man's inhumanity to man". By this he was referring to the cruel behaviour that people sometimes show to each other. In the worst of cases, it will set off a chain reaction of cruelty leading to revenge, which in its turn will spark off greater cruelty, and so the vicious circle continues. This is hell on earth. No wonder Jean-Paul Sartre wrote in his play *No Exit* that "Hell is other people". Hellish behaviour is conceived deep inside the human heart, it is fostered by human disobedience to the message of the gospel, and it is then made worse by terrible locusts from the pit of hell. The result is tribulation for everyone. God promised to lead his own people out of the great ordeal and he will certainly keep his word. But what of those who ignore the gospel and disdain the grace of God? The message of the fifth trumpet is that it will be far worse for them. They will have no relief from the sharp stings of scorpion tails.

XXIII

9:13-21 The sixth Trumpet and second Woe

The first woe brings extreme pain, but only for a limited period. As a result of it, some who are affected may come to terms with themselves and with God, and repent (Lk 15:17-19). But for those who remain impenitent, a more severe woe is on the way. Whereas the blowing of the fifth trumpet brings forth locusts that torture, the blowing of the sixth trumpet will unleash four deadly angels and their great army of troops who are mounted upon strange but very fierce horses, which will then proceed to exterminate a sizeable proportion of humanity.

13. *The sixth angel blew his trumpet*, and before the fresh vision was revealed to him, *John heard a voice from the four horns of the golden altar before God.* We have already met the heavenly altar in 6:9 and 8:3-5. At its four corners are four horns, like the horns of a bull. They symbolise strength (Ex 30:1-3). This altar is said to be before God. It is the altar under which the martyrs are crying out for retribution (6:9-11), and on which the prayers of all the saints are offered to God (8:3-5). The prayers of the righteous are powerful and effective (Jas 5:16), and it is in answer to them that God's permission is given for the temporal judgements that are to follow. It is a sobering thought that God's vindicating interventions are made possible because of the power and effectiveness of our own prayers, for it is prayer that moves the hand that moves the universe. The voice from the altar may be God's own, for it is a voice of command that is instantly obeyed.

14. The voice addressed *the sixth angel who had the trumpet, saying, "Release the four angels who are bound at the great river Euphrates".* We do not know who these four angels are. They are not the four angels at the four corners of the earth (7:1). They are together, at the Euphrates. The fact that they are *bound* there suggests that they are fallen angels who have been restrained and tied up so that they do not cause harm. It is ominous news that they are now being released. The Euphrates is described as *the great river* (16:12). It was part of the ideal limit of the Promised Land (Gen 15:18, Deut 1:7, Josh 1:4), so these four angels were just outside Israel. In the first century this would have suggested an invasion by the Parthian army, whose mounted archers were held in dread by other nations (6:2).

15. *The four captive angels were duly released*, presumably by the angel with the sixth trumpet. We are informed that *they had been held ready for the hour, the day, the month, and the year*. In the Old Testament the day, month and year were sometimes specified (e.g. Num 1:1, Hag 2:10), but only here in the whole Bible is the *hour* spoken of as well. John writes about the outworking of God's purpose. God is planning to execute judgement on godless people, and specifically *to kill a third of humankind*. Here "humankind" means those who are hostile to God (as in 6:10; 8:13; 9:4, 20-21), and "a third" means a very large number, but not a majority. The divine judgement is strict and very severe, but it is not yet final.

16. It now emerges that the four angels are in charge of a vast and mighty mounted army. *The number of the troops of cavalry was two hundred million*. This is an enormous number, far exceeding those of the largest armies mentioned in the Old Testament. It is not just twice ten thousand (Ps 68:17), but twice ten thousand *squared*. Unlike the numbers in 5:11, here it may be an exact figure rather than poetic hyperbole, for John says that *he heard their number*.

17. John now proceeds to describe the details of *his vision*, a great deal of which was bizarre. It is difficult for us to decide what we may learn from its symbolism. He writes, *This is how I saw the horses*. First he describes the appearance of those who rode them: *the riders wore breastplates the colour of fire and of sapphire and of sulphur*, so the cavalry uniforms were reddish, greyish blue and yellow. As for *the horses, their heads were like lions' heads, and fire and smoke and sulphur came out of their mouths*. They were as ferocious as lions, and like the mythical Leviathan (Job 41:1, 19-20), their mouths belched forth flames together with dark, toxic fumes, which would also have been red, greyish blue and yellow.

18. These horses would be the harbingers of *three plagues*, which would lead to very many casualties: *a third of humankind was killed, by the fire and smoke and sulphur coming out of their mouths*. At this stage it becomes clear that the horses are not natural creatures but demonic visitations. But worse news is to come:

19. These terrifying horses are able to kill people at either end. *For the power of the horses is in their mouths and in their tails*. Fire, smoke and sulphur emerge out of their mouths, and *their tails are like serpents*, *having heads; and with them they inflict harm.* Just as with the locusts in the previous vision, their tails had stingers like those of scorpions (v 10). This vision is like the last, but more severe. It is not just about enduring sharp pain for a limited period, but also about seeing the peril and subsequently being mortally hurt by it. F.F. Bruce wrote, "However symbolically they may be portrayed, there is no doubting the reality of these demonic forces which thrive on people's unbelief and are bent on their ruin; but those who are allied to their Conqueror are immune against their malignity".

20. Not everyone will be killed by this lethal cavalry led by the four angels who had been bound at the Euphrates, only a sizeable fraction, less than half. Would the rest of them learn from what had happened, repent, and put their faith in God who created them and in his Son Jesus Christ who redeemed them? Very sadly, it seems that the answer is "no". *The rest of humankind, who were not killed by these plagues, did not repent of the works of their hands or give up worshipping demons and idols of gold and silver and bronze and stone and wood, which cannot see or hear or walk.* Idolaters find it almost impossible to turn away from their idols to the living and true God, though there are exceptions (1 Thess 1:9). The trouble is that those who worship idols often find themselves worshipping demons as well. It is so stupid to worship man-made idols, for they are blind, deaf and incapable of moving by themselves (Ps 115:4-8, 135:15-18; Isa 40:18-20, 44:9-20; Dan 5:23). But it is equally stupid to idolise people like sports stars, politicians, musicians, and other celebrities. Nor is it any good to worship money. Phil Moore points out that "As soon as money becomes our goal, our security, or the driving factor in our decision-making, it has become the false god Mammon to us, and we have fallen for the oldest trick in the demons' book. We may not look as if we are worshipping 'idols of gold and silver and bronze and stone and wood, which cannot see or hear or walk', but demons are just as happy to receive worship as idols of bricks and mortar, steel and rubber, and the numbers on a bank statement". As we shall see, even good angels are not worthy of our worship; only God and his Son Jesus Christ (19:9-10, 22:8-9, and see also 5:13-14).

21. John now turns from false gods to the sins of the ungodly, and he singles out four. *They did not repent of their murders or their sorceries or*

their fornication or their thefts. Ungodliness issues in all kinds of sinful behaviour (Rom 1:18-32, 2 Tim 3:1-5). In the Sermon on the Mount, Christ taught that *murder* includes the thought as well as the deed (Mt 5:21-22). *Sorcery* or witchcraft, spiritual abuse, or any other form of manipulating people, is a sin that blinds sinners and leads to their downfall (21:8, Gal 5:19-21). *Fornication* or any other form of sex outside marriage is likewise condemned (1 Cor 6:9-10; for Christ's definition of marriage see Mk 10:6-9). *Theft* includes taking what belongs to another and making it your own (2 Sam 12:1-4), but also borrowing without returning what was borrowed.

Meditation: The Seriousness of Sin

John Stott summed up the blowing of the sixth trumpet and what it brought forth as follows: "Once again this is not a description of literal events, but nor is it to be explained away as meaningless. The sixth trumpet seems to symbolise violent death, whether by war or terrorism, and has a special relevance to us who have lived through much of the 20th century, perhaps the most violent of all centuries. One would also have hoped that the horrors of war would bring unbelievers to repentance. But John records in his vision that those who survived death did not repent either of their idolatry (the worst breach of the first table of the law) or of their other sins (mostly those in breach of the second table)".

It needs to be pointed out that there is a purpose of love behind the judgements. In this vision there is some emphasis on people's failure to repent. This is tragic, because the judgements that God is sending upon the wicked are an opportunity, maybe the last, for them to realise the seriousness of their sins, to turn away from them, come to God and be saved. But if they remain impenitent, they are not to think that they have triumphed over God. He remains sovereign and in supreme control. People may resist his will, but this will only be to their own hurt.

George Eldon Ladd suggested that "Throughout the course of the ages, people have been able to pursue a path of sin and to defy God with apparent impunity and safety. As the end approaches and the time of judgement draws near, God pours out on them a taste of his judgement and wrath; but this is not because he takes pleasure in wrath but in order to warn them that the way of sin and defiance of God can lead only to disaster".

Tom Wright pertinently observed that "If [God] allows people space to repent, to come to their senses, to worship him as the source of life rather than demons and idols which are the source of death (v 20, 21), then that patient mercy always risks the possibility that people will use the breathing space to make matters worse". While discussing God's salvific purpose behind major catastrophes, F.F Bruce wrote that "Plague and similar disasters, which bring out the best qualities in some people, also bring out the worst in many others. Samuel Pepys speaks of the Plague of London in 1665 as 'making us more cruel to one another than if we were dogs'; Thucydides made a similar observation in the Plague of Athens over 2,000 years earlier. God has pledged his ready pardon whenever a glimmer of repentance is shown, but what if people persist in impenitence?"

What exactly are these horses that breathe out flames and noxious fumes, and have mortal stings in their tails? To John's first century readers they might have recalled the Parthian cavalrymen, who would twist their horses' tails so that they looked like stings, and whose skill at archery was legendary. By turning around on the saddle, they could fire their arrows either forwards or backwards. These facts may have helped to form John's imagery, but he was not describing Parthian horsemen. In his vision, what he saw was demonic forces.

Tom Wright put it like this: "If the locusts and the fiery riders are symbols, then what are they symbols of? What does John suppose will be the reality, on earth, which corresponds to these lurid visions? Here we must be cautious. There is a whole spectrum of speculation at this point, ranging from those who see these passages as prophecies of actual warfare in the Middle East (if the locusts can be seen as helicopters, the horses of verses 17-19 could be seen as armoured vehicles or tanks) right through to those who stress that the true reality to which these images point is entirely 'spiritual', with the torture and threat being carried out in the hearts, minds, imaginations and consciences of rebellious and sinful humans".

Do these weird horses symbolise war? Perhaps their origin at the Euphrates is a reminder of Assyria and Babylon, those ancient nations that were symbols of furious aggression and conquest. If so, then Christians may see war as being part of God's purpose. Indeed, war sometimes reminds unbelievers of their insecurity apart from Christ. It has often been said that many people come to Christ in times of war, and C.S. Lewis wisely observed, "How hard it is to turn our thoughts to God when everything is going well with us". However, the passage also teaches us that true repentance is a rare phenomenon. Richard Bewes put it succinctly: "The 'God get me out of this trench and I'll believe in you' type of prayer can be forgotten very quickly once the threats are lifted".

The present writer believes that since the book of Revelation was written for all of God's people throughout the Christian era, the horses and the locusts are bound to mean different things to different believers at different times. For some they will represent war, but for others they will represent other disasters. They may even represent different things to the same people at different times.

For example, in Europe most people were led to think about the sixth trumpet during the years 1347-1351, when the Black Death resulted in over a third of the population dying. In the twentieth century, where one world war followed another with increasingly destructive weapons, from rifles to atomic bombs, people said that the sixth trumpet was war. In more recent times, the Coronavirus pandemic resulted in anxiety and a widespread fear of death in most countries, even though the proportion of those who actually died was much smaller than one third. This pandemic was followed, in quick succession, by the war unleashed by Russia on Ukraine, which plunged a significant fraction of the population of the world into even greater poverty and suffering than they had experienced previously.

The locusts of the fifth trumpet and the lethal horses of the sixth may therefore represent all those great disasters that are allowed by God, and which inflict harm on large numbers of people. Even in Christ's day, when he was asked about two local disasters that had taken place in Jerusalem, he suggested that God's purpose in allowing them was that of prompting unbelievers to exercise penitence and faith: "Unless you repent, you will all perish just as they did" (Lk 13:1-5). Repentance and faith in God were often the twin spearheads of his message.

One further point should be made. Great disasters are part of life, and we must come to terms with them. As Leon Morris put it, "John was not writing to or for the pagan world. He was writing for the Christian church. Believers must live in this world, not in an imaginary world of their own choosing. John is making plain to a little group of persecuted believers that they must not expect to live in a world that understands them and welcomes their witness. No matter how severe the judgements of God upon it, the world will continue with its idolatries and its manifold sins. Believers must not delude themselves. This world that John depicts, with sinful people resisting God to the limit no matter how much they hurt themselves in the process, is the world we must live in. There is no other".

XXIV

10:1-11 The open Book that was for eating

As was the case with the seven seals, there is an interlude between the sixth and seventh trumpets. This will keep us in suspense. What could possibly come next, after the locusts and the cavalry of death? But there may be more to it than this. Leon Morris believed that this was not simply a literary device: "It is part of life. People cannot predict how God's judgements will operate. They take unexpected courses. There are delays which give opportunity for repentance". The interlude concerns an open scroll or book. John was told to eat it, after which he was asked to "prophesy again about many peoples and nations and languages and kings". Here, then, is a message to the church, which has duties to attend to and afflictions to endure. In particular, it is called to proclaim the good news to all nations. As it does so, its members will be hated by many people because of Christ's name. But those who endure to the end will be saved (Mk 13:9-13).

1. *Another angel* enters the stage, and as in other cases (5:2, 18:21) he is described as being *mighty. John saw him coming down from heaven* (18:1, 20:1)*, wrapped in a cloud* (clouds signify the holiness of heaven, e.g. Ezek 1:4-5)*, with a rainbow over his head* (possibly part of the rainbow in 4:3, in which case this angel had duties around the throne, i.e. very close to God himself). *His face was like the sun* (this happens to those who are very close to God, e.g. 1:16 and Ex 34:29-35), and *his legs were like pillars of fire.* A pillar of fire was a symbol of God's presence with his people (Ex 13:21-22). In spite of his divine attributes, commentators on the whole agree (John Stott being a notable exception) that this angel is not Christ, for in Revelation Christ is never called an angel. Moreover, he is not worshipped. If he had been, he might have pointed the worshipper to God (19:9-10, 22:8-9).

2. This angel *held a small scroll open in his hand.* Leon Morris noticed that "The perfect participle rendered *open* carries the suggestion of permanence. The book is not concealed and is not likely to be". The angel *set his right foot on the sea and his left foot on the land*, proving that he was mighty indeed, for he could stand over both, had mastery over both, and had a universal message that was for both.

3. The angel *gave a great shout, like a lion roaring.* One of the previous angels had a loud voice (5:2), but this one shouted, and it was a mighty roar, fit for the king of the jungle. Such was its volume that *when he shouted, the seven thunders sounded.* Commentators struggle to identify who or what the seven thunders are. One suggestion is that they follow up a theme from Psalm 29, which describes a great thunderstorm. On seven occasions the psalm uses "the voice of the Lord" to refer to frightening peals of thunder, and if this is the reference here, then the seven thunders might be an alternative to "the seven spirits" as a designation of the Holy Spirit. At any rate, the thunders spoke out a definite message.

   F.F. Bruce thought that the seven thunders might be another heptad of divine visitations, rather like the seals, trumpets and bowls, but the revelation which they conveyed (unlike the one in the little scroll), was unsuitable for some people to hear in this life. Therefore John is told to seal up their utterance instead of writing it down. By contrast, in 22:10 he will be instructed to make the book of Revelation public.

4. *When the seven thunders had sounded, John was about to write* what they had said. He clearly felt that this was important. George Eldon Ladd wrote, "The only hint we have as to the message of the seven thunders is to be found in the fact that in all other passages in Revelation where thunder occurs, it forms a premonition of coming judgements of divine wrath (8:5, 11:19, 16:18). *But he heard a voice from heaven saying, "Seal up what the seven thunders have said, and do not write it down".* John did not have to destroy what he had written. He was just to roll up the scroll and seal it so that its writing should remain concealed.

   Certain truths are written and open to view so that anyone may read them (v 2), but other truths must be kept sealed and hidden (or else not written down at all) to prevent anyone from reading them (Dan 12:4, 2 Cor 12:2-4). As Leon Morris said, "Not all the counsel of God is open to everyone. Our knowledge that the thunders are sealed serves as a warning against the kind of date-fixing which has characterised some schemes of prophecy based on this book. On John's own showing we do not have all the information. God has kept some things back from us, so let us beware of proceeding as if all has been revealed".

5. *The angel whom John saw standing on the sea and the land* now proceeds to proclaim on oath the imminent fulfilment of God's eternal purposes.

He raised his right hand to heaven. In antiquity this was the usual gesture you would adopt when you swore an oath (Deut 32:40, Dan 12:7).

6 It is clear from the prolonged description of God that this was a particularly solemn oath, for *the angel swore by him who lives forever and ever, who created heaven and what is in it, the earth and what is in it, and the sea and what is in it.* The angel is about to speak in God's name, and to highlight the importance of what he is about to say, he describes the eternity of God and his sovereign work as Creator. Leon Morris observes that God does not need to react in surprise at the machinations of evil people and evil spirits, for "He is supreme over time and over creation. He fulfils what he plans". Martin Kiddle wrote, "The last days, no less than the first, are in his hands".

The angel begins with an assurance that time is running out: "*There will be no more delay*". God has delayed the *dénouement* in order to give people opportunities to repent, but he will not delay much longer. He will remove his restraints and the Antichrist will be revealed (2 Thess 2:3-12). God's apparent slowness in the past was due to his patience with the impenitent. Not wanting any to perish, but all to come to repentance (2 Pet 3:9), he provided them with further opportunities to repent. But now their time is running out.

7. Quite soon *the days* will arrive *when the seventh angel is to blow his trumpet*, and this will herald the moment *when the mystery of God will be fulfilled*. Here a mystery is something that we cannot work out for ourselves, so God has to reveal it to us. Left to ourselves, we would never have discovered the wonder of God's amazing rescue plan (1 Cor 2:1, 4:1; Eph 1:9, Col 2:2), *which he has announced to his servants the prophets* (Amos 3:7, Rom 16:25-26). Who are these prophets? Leon Morris wrote, "It is possible that we should understand *prophets* here to mean the New Testament prophets as well as those of the old dispensation. God has had one purpose through the ages and it reaches its climax at this point. From the very beginning God has planned to bring his people to salvation, and thus his whole purpose is coming to its culmination. It involves the judgement of evil, but also the deliverance and vindication of the people of God. John's readers are to reflect that the mighty world forces they saw, far from being triumphant, are about to be overthrown decisively. A purpose that God has planned before the world and has matured throughout all ages will not lightly be jettisoned. The mystery of God will indeed be fulfilled".

8. *Then the voice that he had heard from heaven (v 4) spoke again to John.* After the mighty angel's oath, what follows has to be important: *"Go, take the scroll that is open in the hand of the angel who is standing on the sea and on the land".* Once again the angel's mastery over both land and sea is underlined, as is the fact that the book he was holding was open. The revelation was not hidden.

9. John obeyed the divine command. *He went to the angel and asked him to give him the little scroll.* The angel did so and said to John, *"Take it, and eat; it will be bitter to your stomach, but sweet as honey in your mouth".* The verb translated *eat* means "devour it" or "take its contents into your innermost being". Two of the great Old Testament prophets, Jeremiah and Ezekiel, had vivid experiences of this. Jeremiah tells us that he found God's words and ate them. They became a joy to him and the delight of his heart (Jer 15:16). Ezekiel was commanded to eat a scroll of God's word and he did so. In his mouth it tasted as sweet as honey (Ezek 3:1-3). As it was then, so it is today. God's word is always sweet-tasting for any believer (Ps 19:9-10, 119:103). But because it includes firm denunciations and woes on evildoers (Ezek 2:10), it is also bitter. The little scroll contains the message that John must proclaim.

Leon Morris put it well: "The true preacher of God's word will faithfully proclaim the denunciations of the wicked it contains. But he does not do this with fierce glee. The more his heart is filled with the love of God, the more certain it is that the telling forth of 'woes' will be a bitter experience". The wickedness of people grieved God in his heart (Gen 6:6), and the true preacher of God's word must enter into this suffering to some degree.

10. *John took the little scroll from the hand of the angel and ate it.* Twice John was urged to *take* the scroll, and he did so. The revelation from God needs to be appropriated personally by every individual believer. John took its contents into his heart of hearts. He found that *it was sweet as honey in his mouth, but when he had eaten it, his stomach was made bitter.*

11. Then *they* – the mighty angel and the voice from heaven – *said to John,* *"You must prophesy again about many peoples and nations and languages and kings".* Revelation is not for a special group of people such as

the church, or a particular country, or those who speak Greek, or the middle class. It is for all people. This has been wonderfully fulfilled over the centuries. Even kings and world rulers must encounter the word of God spoken and written by his servants (Jer 1:9-10).

Meditation: The secret Things and the revealed Things

There was an important message between the openings of the sixth and seventh seals. It concerned God's people. Although they are presently in danger, they are completely secure because they have God's seal upon them (7:1-8). One day they will come out of the great ordeal, their redemption will be complete and they will then worship God before the throne (7:9-17). There is also an important message between the blowing of the sixth and seventh trumpets. Its importance could not have been made clearer – it was heralded by the mightiest and most radiant of all the angels, and he did so after taking a solemn oath in the name of the one true God who is both eternal and the Creator of all that exists.

The first part of his very important message is in our present passage (10:1-11). It concerns divine truth. Some of it is hidden from us, because God knows that it would not be helpful for us to read it (v 4). But much of it is open (v 2, 8) and it is revealed to us so that we may read it and profit from it. As we study it in depth, it will prove to be both sweet and bitter – sweet, because it is a word from God; and bitter, because it contains messages about the judgement of unbelievers and the great ordeal that the believing church must pass through. The Bible is not an easy read. It never guarantees that believers will always be delivered from being martyred. But for those who are called to die for their Christian faith, it promises that out of martyrdom they will emerge to a glorious resurrection. The great angel begins his message by declaring that the final act in the drama of salvation is now imminent (v 6b). When the seventh angel blows his trumpet, the eternal purpose of God will be fulfilled, and there will be no further delays. This is indeed sweet news, for it means that the days of struggle will come to an end. But the final act will involve disagreeable conflicts with evil, and this is a bitter pill to swallow.

Moses had already taught the people of Israel that "The secret things belong to the Lord our God, but the revealed things belong to us and to our children forever, to observe all the things of this law" (Deut 29:29). God has withheld some truths from us (for example, the dates of our death and the return of Christ), because it would not be good for us to know them. These hidden truths are "the secret things that belong to the Lord our God". But the "revealed things" are all made available to us in the Bible, for it is an open book, like the little scroll in the hand of the mighty angel. These "revealed things" belong to us and to those to whom we pass them on. Nobody can take them away from us. They are ours forever.

Moses also declared that "One does not live by bread alone, but by every word that comes from the mouth of the Lord" (Deut 8:3). This was quoted by Christ as he battled with the devil during his temptations in the wilderness. The Bible is the word of God, and is often compared to food (Ps 119:103, 1 Cor 3:1-2, 1 Pet 2:2). All that we need to know in order to be saved and to live in a way that is pleasing to God is to be found in it, and much else besides. It is good to heed the angel's words to John and "Take it and eat" (v 9), and to do this regularly, as one regularly eats food. This is a very important lesson, and the angel put it across memorably by adding the rider that the word of God will prove to be both bitter and sweet.

It is interesting to compare the commission given to John with the one given to Ezekiel, which we have already referred to (see the commentary on v 10 above). When Ezekiel had obediently eaten his scroll, he was told to "Go to the house of Israel and speak my very words to them" (Ezek 3:4), but when John ate his own scroll, he was told, "You must prophesy again about many peoples and nations and languages and kings" (v 11). There is a difference between the tasks given to Ezekiel and John. Ezekiel was sent to God's people, and not to "many peoples of obscure speech and difficult language" (Ezek 3:5-6). John's message, on the other hand, was for "many peoples and nations and languages and kings".

It would seem that John had the more difficult call. He was to continue the task of worldwide mission entrusted by Christ to his followers (Mt 28:18-20). Which is easier, to preach to God's own people, or to those who have never heard about him? Usually it is the former. It was John who was told about the bitter side of God's word, because it was he who would preach it to many peoples and nations. But when the church lives in denial of the Bible, as has sometimes been the case during its history, and is certainly the case with some churches in certain countries today, then it can be even harder to preach God's word to members of the church. We are assured that Ezekiel, for example, had the harder task. God's word to him was, "Surely, if I sent you to [peoples of obscure speech and difficult language], they would listen to you. But the house of Israel will not listen to you, for they are not willing to listen to me; because all the house of Israel have a hard forehead and a stubborn heart". God encouraged Ezekiel and prepared him for his difficult task, advising him that he should go to his own people and say to them, "Thus says the Lord God", whether they heard or refused to hear (Ezek 3:6b-11).

Phil Moore has some helpful comments on the bittersweet quality of God's word. As for its sweetness, "Sometimes we let the amazing transforming power of God's word become so familiar that we forget it is 'sweeter than honey, and drippings of the honeycomb' (Ps 19:10). The gospel proclaims that Jesus is King of kings and that he has conquered sin, death, Satan and sickness. It promises us new relationship with God, new purpose in God and new partnership with God, both now and beyond the grave. We must never lose our wide-eyed wonder at the good news of Jesus Christ. The gospel is deliciously sweet". As for its bitterness, "Sometimes we forget that too. The message that Jesus is King of kings means life for those who accept it, but it also means *death* to them. The gospel is a bold command to fall into line with the reality that [Christ] is Lord of the universe, and to surrender freely to him before he comes back to enforce his rule. It is not simply the offer of a better life, but a call to die to our old life". Christ insists that if we want to be his followers, we should deny ourselves, take up our cross, and follow him. If we insist on retaining our old way of life, we shall lose it; but if we lose it for his sake and the gospel's, we shall save it (Mk 8:34-35).

If we miss out the sweetness of the gospel, our message to unbelievers will lose its zestful appeal. If we miss out its bitterness, we may please people but will not have the lasting disciples that God is looking for. The gospel is sweet *and* bitter.

XXV

11:1-4 Measuring the Temple in the Light of the two Witnesses

We have just learnt three lessons from the Bible. First, it is an open book, so that all believers may avail themselves of the helpful truths it contains. Secondly, any delays will speedily come to an end, because the fulfilment of God's purposes is imminent. Thirdly, we are to pass on the bittersweet message of the gospel to the world without shirking either its sweetness or its bitterness. Before the seventh angel blows his trumpet, there are two more visionary episodes. In the first, John is told to go and measure the temple. In the second, we are introduced to the two witnesses, whose history will be presented to us.

1. *John is given a measuring rod like a staff*, presumably by God, who then tells him to *come and measure the temple of God, and the altar and those who worship there*. So far John has been a spectator of visions, but now he is to take an active part. It is clear from verse 2 that the temple in question is not the heavenly one. It represents the church here on earth, which in the New Testament is described as God's temple (1 Cor 3:16, 2 Cor 6:16, Eph 2:21). John is to *measure* it or assess it. He is to use a measuring rod like a staff, which symbolises God's yardstick for evaluating churches. Christ himself used it as he composed his letters to the seven churches in chapters 2 and 3. The divine standard has to involve the *altar* (which speaks of sacrifice, Rom 12:1), and *those who worship* (which in turn speaks of consecration, 7:9-10). The believers who are measured and approved are the same ones as those who are sealed and under God's care. They will be protected during the great ordeal (7:2-3). They may be called to give their lives for Christ, but they will never perish (Jn 10:27-29). Christian martyrs have eternal life.

2. *John is not to measure the court outside the temple*, however. *He is to leave it out*. It may represent the nominal church, which *is given over to the nations*, who *will trample over the holy city for forty-two months*. There is to be a persecution of the holy city (which means the people of God), and among the persecutors will be those in the court outside the temple. These are nominal Christians, wolves in sheep's clothing, who form part of the visible church, but oppose the true church. The period of *forty-two months* (here and in 13:5) is equal to three and a half years (12:14). If we take one month to equal thirty days, this is 1,260 days (v 3 and 12:6). This is the traditional duration of the great ordeal (Dan 12:7, and see also Dan 9:27 where one week equals seven days equals seven years, divided equally between the time before Christ and the Christian era). We shall meet this symbolic period of three and a half years a number of times in Revelation. On one occasion it is expressed as three and a half *days* (instead of years, in v 9, 11), but it always refers

to the period between Christ's first coming in weakness and his final return in glory, which we refer to as the Christian era.

3. Suddenly two major characters are introduced by the voice of God: *I will grant my two witnesses authority to prophesy for 1,260 days, wearing sackcloth*. Who are the two witnesses? Medieval commentators interpreted them as being Moses (v 6b, see Ex 7:14-18, Ex 8:1-2) and Elijah (v 5-6a, see 2 Ki 1:9-12, 1 Ki 17:1). Nowadays there is widespread agreement that they are symbolic of the witnessing and suffering church. They are given authority to prophesy (that is, to preach the gospel) for 1,260 days (that is, throughout the whole Christian era). They wear sackcloth, which indicates mourning. Because they are prophesying doom, their attitude is sombre and penitent. The church is only powerful when its message includes the coming judgement of God. If Christian believers preach the love of God without mentioning the holiness of God, they may well live comfortably, but they will lack power to stir the world either to salvation or to opposition.

4. The witnesses are described as *the two olive trees and the two lampstands that stand before the Lord of the earth*. The two olive trees refer back to Zechariah's vision and symbolise the presence of the Holy Spirit with God's two chosen and anointed ones, the High Priest Joshua (Zech 3:1) and the governor Zerubbabel (Zech 4:6-7). God had spoken, saying, "Not by might, nor by power, but by my Spirit" (Zech 4:3-6). In Zechariah's vision the olive trees represent two servants, set apart for God, who "stand by the Lord of the whole earth" (Zech 4:14). John's words are very similar. Zechariah also mentions a lampstand (just one, Zech 4:2), but John specifies two, a plural number just as in 1:12, 20, where he saw the seven lampstands that represented seven churches. Leon Morris wrote, "The witnesses are collective rather than individual, and stand for the church. But as there are seven lampstands in 1:12 and only two here, it is only *part* of the church that is meant". Since only two of the seven churches receive no blame, perhaps John is thinking primarily of the witnessing church, exemplified by Smyrna (2:8-11) and Philadelphia (3:7-13). Also, both the word used for 'witnesses' (*martures*), and the death of the two witnesses in verse 7, point to those members of the church who are wholeheartedly faithful, even unto death. The verse ends with a reference to *the Lord of the earth*. John will

not let us forget that Christ is the Lord, to whom all authority has been given in heaven and on earth (Mt 28:18).

Meditation: How to assess the Church rightly

(a) What does the temple symbolise? In this difficult passage Tom Wright agreed with most other commentators, and wrote that "John's 'measuring of the temple' has nothing to do with the Jerusalem Temple, or with the heavenly temple or throne room of chapters 4 and 5. By the time John was writing – indeed, this was true from very early on in the Christian movement – the followers of Jesus had come to see themselves as the true temple, as the place where God now lived by his powerful Spirit". So the temple here symbolises the Christian church.

(b) What does the measuring of the Temple symbolise? The present author does not agree with the prevailing view, which is that it is symbolic of the guarding and protecting of the temple, i.e. the church. Such a view is based on a thoughtful reading of Old Testament passages such as Zech 2:1-5 or Ezekiel chapters 40-43, where the idea of protection is present but not prominent. To measure something involves examining it and assessing it. At the beginning of 11:1-4 John is given a measuring rod or yardstick with which to measure the church. This is a reference to Christ's standard. We have noted Christ's assessment of his church in chapters 2 and 3. As he scrutinises and compares the seven local churches, he knows their works. In some cases he commends them, and in others he has something critical to say against them. He has been "measuring the temple".

In our present passage we are given further hints concerning Christ's standard. John is to measure the altar, which is the place of *sacrifice*. Christ gave himself for the church; is the church giving itself for him? It is as if he were saying to all the members, "All this I did for you. What are you doing for me?" John is also to measure those who worship. Worship is the activity and the way of life of those who are *consecrated* to Christ. Those who worship in the church are to be holy, just as God is holy (1 Pet 1:15-16). Also, it is significant that the two witnesses are introduced at this point in the book. Is the church *bearing unflinching witness* to Christ as its Saviour and Lord? Are its members willing to lose their lives for his sake and for the sake of the gospel? If we are ashamed of him and of his words in this adulterous and sinful generation, then Christ will be ashamed of us when he returns in the glory of his Father with the holy angels (Mk 8:35, 38).

The church repeatedly manages to get itself into a terrible mess, and in our own day, in affluent countries, it appears to have done so once more. It urgently needs true witnesses to testify to the radiant holiness of God and of his Son Jesus Christ. Many churches are playing with fire nowadays, and unless they repent and return to the works they did at first, their lampstand will be removed (2:5).

(c) What do the two witnesses symbolise? Tom Wright helpfully thinks that they "are a symbol for the whole church in its prophetic witness, its faithful death, and its vindication by God. The church is to prophesy, 'wearing sackcloth' as a sign of mourning for the wickedness of the world and the evil that it will bring on to itself". What is said about the witnesses echoes the experiences of Moses (v 6b) and Elijah (v 5-6a), who represent the law and the prophets. Both the law and the prophets bear witness to Christ (Lk 24:27, 44), so here we have another pair of witnesses. The reason why there are *two* witnesses in our passage is because in the Old Testament a minimum of two witnesses was needed to validate testimony in a court of law (e.g. Deut 19:15, and see also Jn 8:17). It was for this reason that Christ sent his 70 followers to testify about him *in pairs* (Lk 10:1-3).

(d) What do the 42 months and 1,260 days symbolise? We have seen that seven is the number of perfection and completeness. As a result, a period of seven years symbolises the complete duration of humankind in this age. This period is divided into two parts, before Christ and after Christ, each of three and a half years or "a time, times and half a time" (12:14), which equals 42 months (11:2, 13:5) or 1,260 days (11:3, 12:6). In Revelation this refers to the Christian era, throughout which the church will witness, be persecuted and be protected. The intense mockery and gloating goes on constantly, though in any particular case it is termed three and a half *days* (11:9, 11). John's intention is that his readers should realise that their ordeal will be of measurable duration, and that they will be delivered from it.

XXVI

11:5-14 The History of the two Witnesses

The two witnesses have made their appearance. They symbolise the suffering and witnessing people of God, and as we study their history, we shall learn about the unremitting opposition faced by God's people throughout the ages, and especially during the Christian age. The witnesses bear unflinching testimony to Christ, but they are battling the antichrist. It may seem as if they are overwhelmed by him, but the reality is that God will vindicate them and reward them with final victory.

It is important to interpret all of the details in this passage symbolically. If we do so, we shall find that it puts across the same truths that are found throughout the Bible. Therefore the book of Revelation is not a weird one-off book that seeks to put across a message of its own. Its teaching is consistent with the teaching that we find throughout the rest of scripture, but it is presented in a way that is helpful and appropriate for Christian believers who are undergoing persecution.

5. In verse 3 we learnt that the two witnesses had been given authority to prophesy for 1,260 days, wearing sackcloth. They symbolise the witnessing and suffering church throughout the Christian era. Their message is bitter as well as sweet, because God is holy as well as loving. Here we are informed of their great power. *If anyone wants to harm them, fire pours out of their mouth and consumes their foes: anyone who wants to harm them must be killed in this manner.* The message they put across concerns a holy God, and it has a fiery aspect to it (Jer 5:14). It is to be hoped that in some cases the good news of Christ will transform their foes so that they become their friends. In this sense they will destroy their foes. But any who hear the good news and refuse to repent should take note. Just as Elijah was vindicated by God, who is holy and answers by fire, so a second death must await the impenitent in the lake of fire (1 Ki 18:24, 38; 2 Ki 1:9-12; Rev 21:8).

6. The two witnesses have a privileged position. *They have authority to shut the sky, so that no rain may fall during the days of their prophesying* (like Elijah, in 1 Ki 17:1 and Jas 5:17). Moreover, *they have authority over the waters to turn them into blood, and to strike the earth with every kind of plague, as often as they desire* (like Moses, in Ex 7:20 and Ex 8, 9, 10, 12:29-32). Leon Morris writes that "There are other references to the power given to the servants of God, a power limited only by lack of faith" (e.g. Mk 11:23, Jn 15:7). Here John may also have in mind that "the church's faithful performance of its duty is itself one of the ways in which the judgements of God are set in motion against an evil world" (see 8:5). Our resources for the prophetic work of telling the

good news of Christ are not the same as those given to Moses and Elijah, but they are equally powerful.

7. *When they have finished their testimony*, however, *the beast* or antichrist *that comes up from the bottomless pit will make war on them and conquer them and kill them.* When the witnesses have accomplished the task that God has set them, the beast, who is introduced here but will feature prominently in later chapters, will oppose them and seemingly overthrow them. This beast is said to come up from the bottomless pit (9:1), and this suggests that his nature is altogether evil. Having suffered as a result of the powerful testimony of the witnesses, the beast will make war on them in nasty and vindictive ways. Eventually he will kill them, and he wants their death to be as humiliating and as painful as possible.

8. In antiquity, the most terrible death was one in which the bodies of those who died were left unburied, so that their enemies would gloat. It would be like this for the two witnesses. *Their dead bodies will lie in the street of the great city that is prophetically called Sodom and Egypt, where also their Lord was crucified.* The great city cannot be Sodom and Egypt (which is not a city) and Jerusalem at the same time. Sodom was proverbial for wickedness (Isa 1:9-10), Egypt is where God's people were oppressed (Ex 1:8-14), and Jerusalem rejected and crucified Christ (Mt 23:37-39). The judgement of God struck all three of them: Sodom was destroyed (Gen 19:24-28), Egypt was utterly ruined by the ten plagues (Ex 10:7), and Jerusalem was besieged and razed to the ground amid unparalleled suffering (Mt 24:21). The *great city* appears again in 16:19, 17:18, and 18:10, 16, 18, 19, 21. Leon Morris interpreted it as "the earthly city in opposition to the heavenly city of chapters 21, 22. It is people in organised community and in opposition to God". It is a symbol for godless, worldly people who will face God's judgement.

9. In this case *for three and a half days* means a limited period in each individual case, but the cases will recur throughout the whole Christian era. *Members of the peoples and tribes and languages and nations* means representatives of the whole world: clearly John is not thinking of only one earthly city. These worldly people *will gaze at the dead bodies* of the two, *and refuse to allow them to be placed in a tomb.* All are entitled to a proper burial, so by this refusal the worldly not only revel in their triumph but also heap shame on the deceased (Ps 79:3).

10. *The inhabitants of the earth* is a phrase that recurs nine times in Revelation (3:10; 6:10; 8:13; this verse; 13:8, 12, 14; 17:2, 8). It seems to refer to those who are not true followers of God, but instead oppose and persecute those who are. In this case they *gloat over the corpses of the witnesses and celebrate and exchange presents.* The defeat of the witnesses brings great rejoicing to their enemies, and one wonders what could justify such rejoicing in evil (1 Cor 13:6). The reason is *because these two prophets had been a torment to the inhabitants of the earth.* Their prophesying had unmasked the hollow lives of the godless. As F.F. Bruce observed, the witness of the godly is a condemnation to the ungodly (1 Ki 18:17). Leon Morris observed that "The faithful preaching of the gospel is never soothing to the impenitent, so that the removal of an outstanding preacher is commonly a matter of rejoicing for those whose consciences he or she has troubled".

    Thomas Torrance was prompted to ask some searching questions: "Why does the church of Jesus Christ today sit so easy to her surroundings? Why do Christian people live such comfortable and such undisturbed lives in this evil and disturbed world? Surely it is because we are not true to the word of God".

11. *After the three and a half days,* a limited period of time, *the breath of life from God entered them.* Although still in the future when he wrote it, in John's mind the renewal and revival in God's church was so certain that he spoke of it as if it had already happened (Ezek 37:10). *The witnesses stood on their feet.* After lying dead and being despised and disparaged for a period of time, the representatives of the true church were now very much alive again, *and those who saw them were terrified.* They suddenly realised that they had been wrong and the witnesses had been right all along, and that now the God about whom the witnesses had testified would exercise judgement on his enemies and vindicate his friends (1 Sam 2:30).

12. *Then they* (meaning the witnesses) *heard a loud voice from heaven saying to them, "Come up here!"* Christ was vindicated by his resurrection and ascension (Rom 1:4, Acts 1:9-11), and it will be the same for his servants. *And they went up to heaven in a cloud while their enemies watched them.* Robert Mounce wryly observed that "Since murder is the last resort of people, what can be done about those who rise from the dead?"

If the inhabitants of the earth were terrified at the resurrection of the witnesses, what would they feel as they watched them being lifted up to heaven in a cloud? But something even more ominous and frightening was about to happen to the world in which they lived.

13. *At that moment there was a great earthquake.* When *terra firma* starts to move to and fro, it is no longer safe to stand on anything. A great panic would seize all the people. *A tenth of the city fell, and seven thousand people were killed in the earthquake.* A tenth is a sizeable proportion, and because it was God's will, *seven* thousand (a complete number of thousands) denotes the totality of the casualties. *The rest* of the people *were terrified and gave glory to the God of heaven.* We are not told that their hearts were hardened (as in 9:21), but nor are we told that they repented. Leon Morris wrote, "These happenings were so striking and so clearly from God that even sinful people could not forbear from ascribing glory to him". Martin Kiddle believed that "the great mass of mankind will have committed the unpardonable crime of deifying evil, and they must give glory to God when they are compelled by overriding terror to recognise that the true Lord is Christ and not antichrist". The terror of the last day is also depicted powerfully in 6:12-17.

14. In 8:13 the eagle announced that the fifth, sixth and seventh trumpets would bring woe to the inhabitants of the earth. After the blowing of the fifth trumpet we were told in 9:12 that the first woe had passed and two were yet to come. Then came the blowing of the sixth trumpet with its catastrophic consequences, after which there was a brief interlude with the measuring of the temple and the history of the two witnesses. Now *the second woe has passed. The third woe is coming very soon.* Indeed, the seventh angel is about to blow his trumpet.

Meditation: The History of the witnessing Church

In this section of the book of Revelation we have a vivid account of two enigmatic witnesses, who remind us of two powerful figures from the Old Testament, Moses and Elijah, who represent the law and the prophets, which point forward to Christ. Here they symbolise the true church, which loses its life for the sake of Christ and his word. The witnesses are given a powerful prophetic ministry which is to last for 1,260 days, symbolising the whole Christian era that spans the period between the two comings of Christ. The true church is likewise given a ministry to witness in Christ's name to all the nations, and it is provided with a remarkable power. The weapons of its spiritual warfare are not merely human, but they have divine power to destroy strongholds. They destroy arguments and every proud obstacle raised up against the knowledge of God, and they take every thought captive to obey Christ (2 Cor 10:4-5).

The message of the true church is the good news of Christ, known as *the gospel*. Christians are not ashamed of the gospel, for it is the power of God for salvation to everyone who has faith, whether they are religious or have no creed. In the gospel God's way of making people righteous in his sight is revealed. It is attested by the law and the prophets, and is attained by people as soon as they put their faith in Jesus Christ (Rom 1:16-17, 3:21-22). The power of the gospel is immense. There is no other message in the world whereby men and women may get right with God. The heralds of the gospel are not only given the most powerful message of all, but are also regarded by Christ as members of his family. The way in which other people respond to the witnesses is identical to how they would respond to him, and Christ will judge them by their response (Mt 25:40, 45).

Throughout the period of their prophetic ministry the two witnesses will be persecuted and protected simultaneously. But once their testimony is finished, the beast that comes up from the bottomless pit will be allowed to attack, defeat and kill them. This beast or antichrist may be a single exceptionally evil individual at the end of time, but he could also symbolise the succession of persecutors of the church over the centuries. The bodies of the witnesses will lie, not in state but in disrespectful ignominy, on the street of the worldly city which is known by three symbolic names: Sodom (immoral and not helpful of the needy – Jude 7, Ezek 16:49), Egypt (oppressive and impenitent – Ex 2:23-25, 8:15) and Jerusalem (unbending and the city that crucified Christ – Lk 13:34-35, Mt 27:35-37). They all symbolise communities of people in organised opposition to God.

For a certain period of time the representatives of all unbelieving peoples will not only refuse the witnesses burial, but also gloat over their defeat and celebrate their murder. This is because the faithful testimony of the true church caused them great torment in their minds and consciences. But after this limited interval, the martyred and silenced church will be brought back to life by God. Its witness will become powerful once again, causing terror to the observant world, and finally it will be exalted to heaven, to the consternation of its embittered enemies. As Leon Morris put it, "History has often seen the church oppressed to the very verge of extinction, but it has always seen it rise again from that proximity to death. Each such resurrection strikes consternation into the hearts of her oppressors". Henry Swete wrote that, "[The final vindication] has been partly anticipated in the sight of the world by the tribute paid to the victims of a persecution, sometimes within a few years after their dishonour and death. Paganism saw the people it had hated and killed caught up to heaven before its eyes".

At this stage a devastating disaster will take place, causing widespread damage and numerous casualties. A few people will realise that God is behind all this, and they will give glory to him. Hopefully they will do so by repenting and coming to him in fear, sorrow and faith, but otherwise they will have to suffer the fate of all the impenitent. On the day of judgement those who do not repent will hear those sad and terrible words of Christ, "I never knew you; go away from me, you evildoers" (Mt 7:23). After that, according to the book of Revelation, they will be thrown into the lake of fire, which is the second death (20:14-15). According to the Old Testament psalmists, they are doomed to destruction forever (Ps 92:7), and the very memory of them will perish (Ps 9:6).

XXVII

11:15-19 The seventh Trumpet and the third Woe

When the seventh seal was broken, we expected severe judgements to unfold, but instead there was half an hour of silence and then the prayers of the saints were offered to God as incense, and they rose to him. Now at last the seventh trumpet is blown, and again there is a hiatus. But on this occasion, instead of silence, there are loud voices in heaven; and instead of the prayers of the saints, there are two choruses of heavenly praise. Also, just as the seventh seal served to introduce the seven trumpets, so the seventh trumpet will lead on to a series of seven significant signs. They are unnumbered, but they form a heptad – how could it be otherwise?

15. *Then*, after an interval for reflection on the assessment of the church and on its history throughout all the Christian era, *the seventh angel blew his trumpet.* Would there be another silence in heaven for prayers to ascend to God, as after the opening of the seventh seal? No, *there were loud voices in heaven.* The theme was worship, and the worshippers were many celestial angels. *They said, "The kingdom of the world has become the kingdom of our Lord and of his Messiah"*. The secular power, represented by the beast, would no longer domineer the saints. The worldly spirit, so opposed to Christ and his witnesses, would no longer rule. God and his Messiah will reign. Christ in person will be King of kings and Lord of lords (19:16). F.F. Bruce wrote, "The sovereignty of God has never ceased, but now it is universally manifested and acknowledged; at last the time has come for the full realisation of the divine purpose that at the name of Jesus, 'every knee should bend and every tongue confess that Jesus Christ is Lord' (Phil 2:10-11)".

The angels use the past tense – *it has become* – because the change of sovereign rule is absolutely certain, as sure as if it had already occurred. Moreover, this is not to be a temporary phenomenon. *"He will reign forever and ever"*. This eternal message was wonderfully put to music by Georg Friedrich Handel in his inspired oratorio "Messiah". A marvellous new age is about to begin, and that is a fact.

16. We first met *the twenty-four elders who sit on their thrones before God* in 4:4 and they reappeared in 5:8 and 7:11. Again they take centre stage. They know all about adoration, and at the mention of the establishment of God's eternal reign they *fell on their faces and worshipped God*. The worship of God is the highest activity that we humans may engage in, and the angelic elders do so repeatedly.

17. The elders *sang* in unison, *"We give you thanks, Lord God Almighty, who are and who were"*. They worship God for his power and for his eternity (1:8). It is no longer necessary to add the future clause *and who is to come*, since this is the moment of consummation, and God has come. The elders continue, *"You have taken your great power and begun to reign"*. The tense of the two Greek verbs indicates that God has taken power permanently. Through the death of Christ evil had already been dealt a mortal blow, but now God has taken over the reins of power. He has overthrown the evil one and begun his benign rule.

18. The elders continue their victory anthem. *"The nations raged, but your wrath has come, and the time for judging the dead"*. The nations have indeed conspired and set themselves against God and his Anointed One (Ps 2:1-2), but the great day of God's wrath has finally come (6:17). Leon Morris wrote, "The punishment fits the crime. God's wrath is not

irrational, but the fitting reaction to the conduct of the nations". It is true that the judgement cannot take place until the time is ripe for it, but the dead *must* be judged. The elders worship God because the right time has arrived for the judgement. The final day is to be a day of judgement, but it will also be a day of vindication. The elders sing that it is a time *"for rewarding God's servants, the prophets and saints and all who fear your name, both small and great"*. Obedience and perseverance will be honoured. The people of God will be recognised for their acts of service (Mk 10:45), their encouraging words (1 Cor 14:3), the holiness of their lives (1 Pet 1:15-16), and their attitude to God, whom they fear with all reverence (Ps 128, Phil 2:12-13).

Whether they worked in a low-key way or in the limelight makes no difference, for God will reward his people *both small and great*. Our importance or unimportance has nothing to do with whether we opt for good or evil, and are duly rewarded or punished. It is intriguing that people "both small and great" will be among the saved and also among the lost. There are four references to "both small and great" in Revelation. Two of them refer to the saved (11:18 and 19:5), and two to the lost (13:16 and 20:12). So, even though the world may think otherwise, what really matters is not whether you are important or unimportant, but whether you are one of the saved or one of the lost. For the terrible truth remains that God must also *destroy those who destroy the earth*. He takes note of what people do to the world or to the church (1 Cor 3:17), and his punishments will fit the crimes of the impenitent.

19. *Then God's temple in heaven was opened.* It was important that John (and via his eyes, we too) should see something that was inside it. *The ark of his covenant was seen within his temple.* Leon Morris informs us that "In the Old Testament this was the very symbol of God's presence. Jeremiah hoped for a time when the people would know God so intimately that they would not miss the ark" (Jer 3:15-18). The ark was almost certainly destroyed or lost when Jerusalem fell to the Babylonians in 586 BC. Here the sight of the heavenly archetype of the ark in the heavenly temple symbolises a wonderful truth. It is that the way into God's holy presence is now open for all those who have been made holy (Heb 10:19-22). Previously the curtain of the temple had hidden the ark from view (Heb 9:8), but the death of Christ on the cross had changed everything (Mt 27:51). The ark of God's covenant is not missed by Christians, because the new covenant has made its presence unnecessary. But when history finally reaches its climax, the symbol of God's steadfast love and covenant faithfulness will be publicly disclosed. It will mark the prelude to the Day of Judgement. So important is this moment that heaven proceeds to burst into life with an ominous and phenomenal *son et lumière* display, in which we who attend may hear and see *flashes of lightning, rumblings, peals of thunder, an earthquake, and heavy hail.*

Meditation: It's all over bar the Shouting

It was made clear that the blowing of the seventh trumpet would be followed by the third woe (8:13, 9:12, 11:14) and, sure enough, we find this woe, in summary form, in verse 18: "The nations raged, but your wrath has come, and the time for judging the dead . . . and for destroying those who destroy the earth". The details of the final judgement are, however, reserved until later on. John has brought us to the very eve of it, just as he did in 6:12-17 and in 8:3-5. Before we are shown its sad course, a few details of human history remain to be fleshed out.

In one sense the passage we have been studying is a summary of what has been written so far and an introduction to what is to come in the second half of the book. The declaration of God's reign by the loud voices in heaven, and the anthem of praise by the worshipping elders, serve as a summary of chapters 1-11, as well as an introduction to chapters 12-22. The special use of the past tense makes the final victory of good over evil absolutely certain: God *has taken* his great power and *begun to reign*. We might well say, "It's all over bar the shouting", and indeed loud voices of victory are already sounding in heaven. The Lord God Almighty *is* and *was*, for he is eternal, but there is no longer any question that *he is to come*, for so certain is his coming that it is spoken about as if it had already taken place.

The storyline of the Bible concerns the great transfer of the dominion and rule of this world from its present raging overlords to God and his Christ, who are to reign forever and ever. There is to be a great eschatological event whereby this transfer, already made absolutely sure by Christ's victory over evil on the cross, will be finally and universally consummated. This is a recurring theme in the Old Testament. It is foreshadowed in the law (e.g. Gen 12:2-3, Deut 28:1-2), predicted in the prophets (e.g. Isa 60:1-3, 61:4-6, 62:2-4; Zech 14:6-9) and celebrated in the wisdom writings (e.g. Ps 96, 97, 98 and 99). Christ came to destroy the works of the devil (1 Jn 3:8) and to overcome the worldly opposition to God and his people (Jn 16:33). Because he resisted the devil's temptation to worship him and thereby gain all the kingdoms of the world, he receives kingship and rule over all nations as a consequence of his obedience to God's will. The result is that the darkness of sin is passing away (1 Jn 2:8), as is the world and the desire for it (1 Jn 2:17).

All is now ready for the imminent consummation, which will bring about an absolute and inevitable division of humankind. Indeed, the final day will feature what can only be described as the ultimate polarising event.

Verse 18 speaks of the great separation of all people into two classes on the Day of Judgment. On one side are the destroyers of the earth. For them it will be a day of wrath when God destroys them. On the other side are the faithful. For them it will be a day of blessing when God rewards them. These divine rewards are all of *grace* (Lk 18:13-14, Eph 2:8-9), but they vary according to what each person has *done* (Lk 19:16-19, 1 Cor 3:8). John has given us a wonderful definition of the faithful. They are "God's servants, the prophets and saints and all who fear his name, both small and great". We who are followers of Christ are to serve God by speaking prophetic words of edification, encouragement and consolation to other people, and by leading holy lives. And all of us, both small and great, are to fear God's name. John will repeat most of this in 19:5, when he will report a heavenly voice as saying, "Praise our God, all you his servants, and *all who fear him, small and great*". Interestingly, part of this definition comes in one of the psalms where, in the midst of various blessings, the psalmist says, "He will bless *those who fear the Lord, both small and great*" (Ps 115:13). The fear of the Lord is a quality that is highly commended throughout the Old Testament (Ps 111:10), and Christ himself also enjoined his followers to fear God (Mt 10:28, Lk 12:5).

The climax of the temporal judgements will be elaborated in the pouring out of the seven bowls (15:5-16:21), and in the fall of the great whore and of the great city (chapters 17 and 18). After that will come the judgement of the beast and the false prophet (19:17-21), and Satan will also be captured and doomed (20:7-10). Last of all there will be the Day of Judgement, in which the criterion of the final assessment will be the works that people have done and their attitude to Christ (20:11-15, Mt 25:31-46). This great Day will also be the time when the faithful will receive their ultimate reward and vindication (chapters 21 and 22).

We have reached the halfway point in our studies in the book of Revelation. Of its 22 chapters, we have examined the first 11. The blowing of the seventh trumpet makes us feel, not for the first time, that the end of history has arrived. Again we are on the brink of the final judgement, and again John will break off and take us through the great story of human history. We shall read further revelations about the church and the world that opposes it, and once more we shall do so at an even deeper and more challenging level than before.

XXVIII

The seven significant Signs

After the breaking of the seventh seal, there was the briefest of intervals – half an hour of silence, during which the prayers of the saints rose before God – and then the blowing of the seven trumpets followed immediately. We might have thought that it would be similar after the blowing of the seventh trumpet. There was again a brief interval in which loud heavenly voices proclaimed that the kingdom of the world has been transferred to God and his Christ, and the elders worshipped God and sang. So, do we now move straight on to the pouring of the seven bowls?

The answer is no. Instead there is to be a lengthy interval for us to reflect further about the church, and in it John will share with us seven visions concerning the troubles and tribulations of God's people. Following Leon Morris, we may think of these visions as seven significant signs. They are not numbered, but they are clearly seven in number, and John could well have intended that we should take them as another of his major heptads. The seven significant signs are:

(a) The woman clothed with the sun (12:1-6). From among God's people there would be born a male child, Jesus Christ, who will rule all the nations. Satan tried his utmost to devour him, but utterly failed in his attempts. So he concentrated on making life difficult for all true Christians. This means that they must suffer a wilderness experience throughout the Christian era, but God would find ways to provide spiritual nourishment for them and to build them up in their faith.

(b) Satan is thrown out of heaven (12:7-12). At some stage in the cosmic battle between good and evil, Satan was thrown down. He is the

mastermind behind the forces of evil, and is called the deceiver and the accuser of the brothers. But the latter will be able to overcome him, and a loud voice from heaven instructs them concerning the threefold means by which they are able to do this.

(c) The war between Satan and the people of God (12:13-17). Satan is fully aware that he has been defeated, and this has provoked him to wage a furious and hateful war against God's people. But when the latter are struggling against the flood-tide of evil spewed out by Satan, God steps in. He gives his people wings like eagles in order that they may flee from Satan. This may lead them to further isolation from the rest of the world, but it is precisely when they flee obediently to the wilderness that they will be wonderfully nourished with the bread of life.

(d) The beast from the sea (13:1-10). We have met the beast before in 11:7, but now John expounds upon the history and present power of this quintessentially anti-Christian being. It gradually becomes clear that the beast is plural and that it presents itself as a God-substitute. Again we read with some alarm that the beast is allowed "to make war on the saints and to conquer them".

(e) The beast from the earth (13:11-18). This second beast is the henchman of the first, and to a greater extent than the first it represents the false and apostate church. The second beast deceives anyone who is inclined to oppose God, and gives them reasons for worshipping the first beast instead of God. Just as all true believers are sealed with God's Holy Spirit, so all followers of the beast are sealed with the mark of the beast, which is the intriguing but revealing number 666.

(f) The Lamb on Mount Zion (14:1-5). Whereas the beast stood on sand (13:1), the Lamb stands on the rocky ground of Mount Zion. There he is worshipped by the true believers who were sealed with the name of God and of the Lamb. Every person who was sealed is now victoriously singing a new heavenly song; not one has been lost. This is a vision of life after the great consummation, and we shall be able to recognise four distinguishing marks of the worshippers.

(g) The harvest of the earth (14:6-20). Three angels now fly past in mid-heaven and proclaim judgement. This acts as a call for the saints to endure until the great harvest of the earth takes place. When the time is right and the harvest is ripe, the angels will come and reap the harvest.

The wicked will be the grapes of wrath. At the vintage they are collected together and thrown into the great wine press of the wrath of God. When they are trodden, a huge volume of blood flows from the press. But blessed are those who have died in the Lord: their deeds follow them.

These seven vivid visions are all highly significant signs that God is completely in control of events here on earth. He allows evil to spread and do its destructive work. At times it may seem to us as if wickedness is winning the day. We should not be hoodwinked by the deceivers whom we bump into, nor by those wolves in sheep's clothing who have wormed their way into the church. God is able to bring good out of evil. He is using the forces of antichrist to purify and refine his people. He is working out his purposes even while Satan is doing his worst and his forces are blaspheming Christ by taking his holy and loving name in vain.

Meditation: The Conflict with Wolves in Disguise

When we interpret any part of the Bible, be it merely a verse or two, or a chapter containing several verses, or a whole book, it is important not to wrench any text out of its context. Nor should we attempt to adjust the rest of the context, let alone the rest of the Bible, so that it fits our interpretation of an isolated text. We should seek to interpret every text in the light of its immediate context and of the whole Bible. It is a good principle to interpret the parts in the light of the entirety, the confusing in the light of what is plain, and the obscure in the light of what is clear. Before we study in detail the seven significant signs in chapters 12-14, we must consider certain features of the book of Revelation, and also certain difficult truths that are put across throughout the whole Bible.

(a) *The book of Revelation is a book of conflict.* By means of a series of visions it depicts the continuing conflict that is going on throughout the period between the first and second comings of Christ. This conflict is between good and evil, between God and Satan, between the Lamb and the devil, between the city of God and the great city of Babylon and, alas, sometimes between the true church and the wolves in sheep's clothing who have wormed their way into it. The whole book of Revelation tells of this conflict, and we shall necessarily be engaged in it if we are faithful followers of Jesus Christ.

(b) *The book of Revelation is a book of victory.* The outcome of the conflict is not an open question. John has no doubt about it. We are assured that the Lamb wins and the devil loses. Jesus Christ has overcome evil through his death on the cross, and God has publicly vindicated him by raising him from the dead on the third day. The devil fights on ruthlessly with great fury because he knows that his time is short. He is a defeated foe. We who know and love God and his Son have a part to play in the final mopping-up operations of this age-long conflict between good and evil, but the final result is certain. If we are with Christ, we are on the winning side. Our part is to give a faithful witness about Christ before an evil and adulterous generation. We shall conquer the devil by the blood of the Lamb and by the word of our testimony. We shall not cling to life even in the face of death.

(c) The book of Revelation is a book of celebration. It celebrates the victory of Christ over the devil. The commentators have observed that the whole book is a *sursum corda*, a call for God's people to lift up their hearts to God and to celebrate with joy and gladness all the mighty works of God in Jesus Christ. Time and again the story of the ongoing struggle between the true church and the forces of evil is interrupted for a heavenly interlude. We hear either a heavenly voice, or the four living creatures, or the twenty-four elders, or the whole host of heaven, as they sing in worship, praising God for the great triumph he has secured through Christ on behalf of his people. As we do so, we learn how to sing and how to worship.

(d) The book of Revelation is represented as a spiral staircase. It rises inside a tall circular tower with windows. As we climb up step by step, we have ever more panoramic views of the landscape. Through the windows we see the same views each time we do a complete circle, but as we come round again we see each view from a greater height. John is not shy about discussing the same topics again and again – the mission of Christ, the mission of the church, the spiritual battle, how we may defeat the devil, the setbacks we experience along the way, the certainty of victory, and how we can celebrate it as we go along. These themes recur in the major heptads – the churches, the seals, the trumpets, the significant signs and the bowls. The heptads do not form a chronological sequence. They are like a piece of music called a *perpetuum mobile*, in which the same tune is repeated several times, but in this case with increasing intensity, as in Ravel's *Bolero*. The tune is the story of the true people of God throughout the Christian era.

(e) The whole Bible teaches that God's people will have difficult times. It was difficult for them in the Old Testament. People of faith like Abraham and Ruth, leaders like Joseph and Moses, true prophets like Elijah, Isaiah and Jeremiah, the psalmists and the common people, all led extremely difficult lives.

Christ himself was persecuted and attempts were made on his life. He was (and still is) despised and rejected by men. He was a man of sorrows and acquainted with grief (Isa 53:3, King James Version). Right at the end he was falsely accused, unjustly sentenced, painfully scourged and cruelly crucified.

He promised his followers that a similar treatment would be certain to come their way: "If the world hates you, be aware that it hated me before it hated you. If they persecuted me, they will persecute you; if they kept my word, they will keep yours also. But they will do all these things to you on account of my name, because they do not know him who sent me" (Jn 15:18, 20b-21). All true believers in Christ must suffer on account of him (Mt 5:11-12). Christ calls each one of us to deny ourselves, take up our cross, and follow him. We are to identify ourselves fully with him, just as he identified himself fully with us. We are to lose our lives for *his sake*, and not be ashamed of *him* or of *his words* (Mk 8:34-35, 38).

(f) Both the Old Testament and the New warn us that some of the most insidious and deadly opposition will come from within the body of God's people. The Old Testament prophets faced some of their most concerted opposition from ordained Jewish priests (e.g. Isa 28:7-13, 29:13-14; Jer 20:1-6; Amos 7:10-17) and schools of false prophets (e.g. 1 Ki 22:1-40; Jer 5:30-31, 6:13-15, 23:9-40). This ungodly opposition in godly garb was so pernicious that it led to a corrective strand of Old Testament teaching, which affirmed that what really matters is to know and obey God. This comes first, ahead of the good habit of engaging in public worship with sacrifices (1 Sam 15:22, Ps 50:7-15, Isa 1:11-17, Hosea 6:4-6, Micah 6:6-8).

When Christ began his three years of ministry here on earth, some of the *state* authorities felt threatened by him. At first they wanted to capture him in order to control him, but later they intended to kill him (Lk 9:7-9, 13:31-33). But the bulk of the opposition he experienced came from the *religious* authorities – the priests, the scribes, the Pharisees and the Sadducees. They hounded him at every turn, sometimes asking him for a sign to prove his credentials (Mt 16:1-4). Even when he did perform miracles, they criticised him for working them on the day of rest (Mt 12:9-14), or accused him of working them with the power of the devil rather than the power of God (Mt 9:32-34, 12:22-32). On several occasions Christ saw fit to warn his disciples to beware of false teachers inside the church, whom he referred to as wolves in sheep's clothing (Mt 7:15-20, 10:16-22).

In its early days the church was often under attack from false teachers. Most of the New Testament epistles were written to warn Christians about errors that had crept (or could creep) into the church as a result of this false teaching (e.g. 2 Cor 11:12-15, Jude 4-19). To correct and prevent errors, all the writers of the epistles continually and consistently urged their readers to be loyal to the early, inspired and inscripturated apostolic teaching (e.g. 1 Cor 15:1-2, Gal 1:8-9, Phil 4:9, Col 2:6-7, 2 Thess 2:15, 1 Tim 6:20, 2 Tim 3:14-17, Titus 1:9, Heb 13:7-9, 1 Pet 1:23-25, 2 Pet 1:12-15, Jude 3 and 1 Jn 2:7, 2:24-26, 3:11, 4:6).

In the book of Revelation John presents the same message. False teachers will spread false teachings in the church. John has his own way of putting this across. In Revelation he tells us his visions, and clothes the truth in symbolic dress. He has already warned us about the different perils that beset the church in chapters 2-3, and in one of his visions he exemplifies how we may assess the condition of the church in our age, just as he did in his (11:1-2). He will now proceed to teach us about the serious attacks on the church, and how Christians are to meet them, by means of the seven significant signs in chapters 12-14.

XXIX

12:1-6 The Woman and the Dragon

As far as we know, John's imagery was not derived from pagan sources. His great source-book was the Old Testament. It was the Genesis account of the dreams of Joseph that inspired the imagery of the woman clothed with the sun, who in turn stands in contrast to the great whore of 17:1-6. Leon Morris believed that "John was an artist in words with a divinely-given message. We must not degrade him to the level of a copyist of ill-digested pagan myths. Moreover it is plain from his whole book that he abominated paganism. It is thus most unlikely that he would borrow significantly from that source, or that pagan religion will give us the key to his ideas. We must let his own usage be our guide".

1. *A great portent appeared in heaven.* The word for *portent* means a *sign* and it was used of Christ's miracles in John's Gospel. Here it means a significant person or personification, namely *a woman clothed with the sun, with the moon under her feet, and on her head a crown of twelve stars.* Who exactly is this woman, or whom does she represent? Many Roman Catholics understandably regard her as being the Virgin Mary who gave birth to the Christ child (v 2, 4-5). But Mary

was not persecuted as this woman was (v 13-16), and this woman had numerous other children (v 17). Indeed, our passage suggests that the woman is not an individual at all, but a corporate figure representing the true people of God, both in the Old Testament (v 1-2) and in the New (v 17). The *sun, moon* and *twelve stars* are reminiscent of Joseph's dream in Genesis 37:9-11, where Joseph saw his father, mother and eleven brothers bowing down before him. In John's vision the number of stars is twelve, because Joseph himself would join Jacob, Rachel and his eleven brothers, and together as a body of patriarchs they would all bow down before the male child who would be born out of the people of God (Rom 9:5).

2. *The woman* here represents the saints of the Old Testament. She *was pregnant and was crying out in birth pangs, in the agony of giving birth.* Israel was sometimes symbolised by a woman in labour (Isa 26:17-18, 66:7-8; Micah 4:10, 5:3). Her longing was to give birth to the Messiah, but her efforts would only be fulfilled when the fullness of time had come (Gal 4:4). Before that, she suffered one labour pain after another, and her agonising contractions included bondage in Egypt, wilderness wanderings, attacks on the nation, and the crushing blow of exile. The birth of the Messiah would climax a lengthy period of expectant hope, but it would itself bring forth agonising cries of pain (Mt 2:16-18). John describes the Christ event using the vivid language of childbearing. As regards the identity of the woman, Leon Morris put it clearly: "For the early Christians there was an important continuity between the Old Israel and the church, the true Israel. Here the woman is undoubtedly Israel who gives birth to the Messiah. But in the later part of the chapter she is the church who is persecuted for her faith".

3. *Then another portent appeared in heaven: a great red dragon.* The dragon is undoubtedly Satan, and this will be made explicit later in the passage (v 9). His colour is red, just as the beast on whom the whore will sit is scarlet (17:3). Red symbolises the murderous personalities of Satan and his henchmen (Jn 8:44). The dragon has *seven heads and ten horns, and seven diadems* or crowns *on his heads.* Seven is God's number and the number of perfection, so the *seven heads* are the dragon's attempt to become like God and like Christ. They also point to his great vitality.

Like the hydra, it is not easy to kill him. If you succeed in cutting off one of the dragon's heads, he has six others with which he can inflict huge damage. Likewise, the dragon's opposition to the church is persistent. When you snuff him out here, he rears another of his ugly heads there.

A horn is a symbol of strength, so the dragon's *ten horns* represent great power. He seems unstoppable. Indeed, if you try to stop him by the use of brute force or deceit, you are in fact using his own weapons against him, so the result will inevitably be another victory for him, and defeat for the powers of good. This unholy monster will only be overcome with the weapons of righteousness, by those who live holy lives (2 Cor 10:3-5). His *seven diadems* are in fact royal crowns, for he exercises a certain sovereignty over the nations. Indeed, we are told that the whole world lies under the power of the evil one (1 Jn 5:19). At first sight, it appears impossible to defeat such great evil. But there is good news. The dragon has been defeated by Christ (v 9-10), and Christ's followers may play a vital part in the mopping up operations (v 11).

4. *The dragon's tail swept down a third of the stars of heaven and threw them to the earth.* Whatever the source of this imagery may have been (and Dan 8:10 is one possibility), here the reference is to the angels who were involved in Satan's fall, whose existence is attested in 2 Pet 2:4 and Jude 6, and one of whom may be the star-angel mentioned in 9:1. Leon Morris suggested that this sweeping down of a third of the stars with his tail was only a warming-up exercise, little more than an initial flexing of the dragon's muscles. He was really after a vulnerable infant. *Then the dragon stood before the woman who was about to bear a child, so that he might devour her child as soon as it had been born.* We know that Jesus Christ was the object of destructive and satanic hostility while he was an infant (Mt 2:13-15), and this continued until he died on the cross. The bitter opposition he faced throughout his life had been prophesied in the Old Testament (Isa 53:3). While he lived on earth, the forces of evil continually sought to devour him.

5. *The woman gave birth to a son, a male child.* The adjective is unnecessary, but there may be some emphasis here on the fact that the Messiah was a man and not a woman. This child was destined for world dominion, for we read that *he is to rule all the nations with a rod of iron* (19:15, see also Ps 2:9). The verb which is translated *to rule* means "to shepherd",

and the *rod of iron* speaks not of tyranny (as in normal English usage) but of firmness. *But her child was snatched away and taken to God and to his throne.* John does not enter into details. In fact here he omits all the events of Christ's life between his birth and his ascension. The one point he seeks to make through this vision is that God protects the incarnate Son from destruction. Throughout chapter 12 John is focussing on the church rather than on Christ. Leon Morris wrote, "The incarnation gives encouragement to believers. Satan tried hard to destroy Christ. But he did not succeed. Christ came right through to the ascension. Let believers take heart. God always effects his purpose". But Christ is not alone in receiving divine protection.

6. *The woman fled into the wilderness.* She too was protected from the dragon, although in quite a different way. She now represents the New Testament people of God, and *God has prepared a place for her.* This is the place of protection. In it the woman would be safe. There *the woman would be nourished for 1,260 days.* We should notice that the place is *in the wilderness.* Every true believer in Christ has his or her own little hermitage to which he or she may retreat periodically, in order to receive spiritual nourishment. In the Old Testament this is foreshadowed by the *physical* nourishment received, first by the Israelites and then by Elijah, in the wilderness (Ex 16, 1 Ki 17:4). Later, some prophets had personal wilderness experiences where they were *spiritually* nourished (e.g. Ps 27:4-5, Isa 8:13-18, Jer 1:4-19). The interval of time mentioned here is 1,260 days, which represents the whole Christian era. In this form it echoes the period during which the two witnesses prophesied (11:3). There is a link between the two. God both nourishes and protects his true church during the time of her witness.

Meditation: Welcome to the nourishing Wilderness

(a) A brilliant idea. The image of the wilderness is a masterstroke on John's part. With it he vividly captures the sensation of loneliness and difficulty that all God's people experience from time to time, sometimes for prolonged periods. The life of faith has a communal side to it, involving membership of a supportive church. But another part of it is individual, concerning our one-to-one dealings with God and his Son Jesus Christ, dealings made real in our experience by the Holy Spirit who dwells in the heart of each individual Christian.

(b) A symbol of encouragement. The woman represents every true follower of Christ. The symbolism is wonderful. Just as God wraps himself in light as with a garment (Ps 104:2), so the woman is clothed with the sun. The world may well despise God's holy people and hold them in very low esteem, but God perceives the woman as a radiant bride in the wilderness (Jer 2:2). Also the moon under her feet suggests dominion, and the crown of twelve stars royalty. When we receive Christ we become sons and daughters of the King. We are now royal princes and princesses (Jn 1:12-13). If we conquer, we shall be given a place with him on his throne (Rev 3:21); if we endure, we shall also reign with him (2 Tim 2:12a).

(c) A challenging task. We are called to be unashamed of Christ before an evil and adulterous generation (Mk 8:38, 2 Tim 2:12b). Christ has identified fully with us. He himself bore our sins in his own innocent body on the tree, and was made a curse for us (Deut 21:23, Gal 3:13, 1 Pet 2:24), so we in our turn are called to identify fully with him. We may do this by being, like him, men and women from outside. He calls us to come out of the world (2 Cor 6:17), but at the same time we are to remain in it (Jn 17:15). We are to be *in the world* but not *of the world.* The purpose of the vision of the woman is partly to inspire us, like her, to adopt a new quality of life. It is also to reassure us, if we are being sidelined or cast out, that God has prepared for us a place of spiritual refuge in the wilderness. There he will nourish us and strengthen us, so that we will be able to resist the dragon's attempts to devour us. We shall not be "among those who shrink back and so are lost, but among those who have faith and so are saved" (Heb 10:39).

(d) A magnificent example. Out in the wilderness we shall find time to consider him who endured such hostility against himself from sinners. In this way we shall not grow weary or lose heart (Heb 12:3). This is part of what it means for God to nourish us. He has given us, in his Son, a noble and uplifting example to follow. Like Christ, we have been called to endure when we do right and suffer for it. We will then be imitating Christ, and this will lead to God's approval (1 Pet 2:20b). We have been called to this, because Christ also suffered for us, leaving us an example, so that we should follow in his steps (1 Pet 2:21).

Unjust suffering is a necessary part of our calling as Christians. This is taught throughout the New Testament. Christ taught it plainly, for example in the eighth beatitude. There he said that those who were *persecuted for righteousness' sake* were blessed, for the kingdom of heaven was theirs (Mt 5:10). In his discourse during the last supper, he said to his disciples, "If they persecuted me, *they will persecute you"* (Jn 15:20). The apostles reflected this faithfully in their letters. Paul wrote that God has graciously given to every Christian two privileges. First, of believing in Christ, and secondly of *suffering for him* (Phil 1:29). It is only *if we suffer with him* that we shall also be glorified with him (Rom 8:17). For all who want to live a godly life in Christ Jesus *will be persecuted* (2 Tim 3:12). Peter likewise taught that *Christians must suffer;* in every chapter of his first epistle he wrote this plainly (1 Pet 1:6-7, 2:19-21, 3:13-17, 4:12-16, 5:8-10). And in the last book of the Bible, which we are studying, the great multitude before the throne of God consists of those who have *come out of the great ordeal.* Suffering is the badge of true discipleship, as the modern martyr Dietrich Bonhoeffer said.

We shall now take a look at Christ's magnificent example of unjust suffering. He was personally blameless, for "he committed no sin, and no deceit was found in his mouth" (1 Pet 2:22). He did no wrong to anyone, either in deed or in word. Even Pilate who judged him declared that he was innocent, saying not once but three times, "I find no case against him" (Jn 18:38, 19:4, 6). Although Christ was abused verbally and suffered physically, he did not return the abuse nor did he threaten his tormentors (1 Pet 2:23a). Instead, and this is an inspiration for us who follow him, "he entrusted himself to the one who judges justly" (1 Pet 2:23b). He committed himself and his righteous cause to God, who is the righteous judge. The reason why Christ refused to defend his rights was not because he did not care about justice, but because he recognised that it was not his prerogative but God's to avenge injustice. He commended his cause to God, leaving room for the divine wrath (Rom 12:19). And then he waited, he trusted, he suffered, and he died. It was in the time of his greatest weakness that his divine glory was revealed to the greatest degree (Jn 12:27-28, 17:1, and especially 1:14).

(e) The location of the wilderness. It is wherever we meet with God and with his Son Jesus Christ. The Holy Spirit facilitates these meetings and welcomes us to them. They may happen in a church building, in a private room in our house, in a crowded commuter train, or in a favourite secluded spot in the countryside. They will feature the means of grace. The two most important ones are Bible reading and prayer, but there may also be hymns or psalms sung, sacraments enacted, and the word of God explained and expounded. The wilderness is separate from the world. Sometimes we may find ourselves there on our own, but if so, we shall not be alone – God will be with us. After a period of resisting the devil, we shall need to recharge our batteries. We shall long to submit ourselves once again to God. We shall draw near to him, and he promises to draw near to us (Jas 4:7-8).

So where have we got to in the book of Revelation? Tom Wright put it like this: "The stage is set. The woman will be with us, in one way or another, right through to the end of the book, though there will be another woman, a horrible caricature of this one, who will occupy plenty of attention along the way. The dragon, too, will be with us much of the way, and part of the whole point of chapters 12-20 is to enable the churches to whom John is writing to understand how the dragon operates and how, therefore, his power must be overthrown. The church needs to know that its present struggles and sufferings are not a sign that God has gone to sleep on the job. They are the sign that a great, cosmic drama is being staged, in which they are being given a vital though terrible role to play". The role of the true Christian is indeed vital, and at times it will be very difficult. But "terrible"? Presumably it is the role of the false teachers in the church that is terrible.

How right was Richard Bewes when he wrote, "The way is never easy for God's people. The woman is under pressure now, out in the wilderness. Have you felt this at times? The solitude of your Christian position; the pressure, the adversity? *It is very biblical to feel this.* For how long? 1,260 days, a period when we are fed and maintained in the wilderness. At times it seems as if the light is about to be extinguished. Persecution, false teaching and godless materialism are taking their toll in every century. But somehow it seems that the frail church, with all its human failings, is destined to survive its wilderness ordeal and overcome".

XXX

12:7-12 The Overthrow and Conquest of the Dragon

John turns to the wider struggle between good and evil. He wants us to know that our role, crucial though it is, is part of a cosmic conflict in which good angels are also involved in the struggle against the dragon and his allies. There are mighty angelic forces on God's side, just as there are rulers and authorities and cosmic powers on the side of evil (Eph 6:12). Likewise, we who love and follow Christ may join together with him in his cause, just as the extremely misguided enemies of God join together with the dragon and his allies.

7. *War broke out in heaven.* This did not make the headlines on planet earth, but it is important news, and God's people need to be aware of it. On one side were *Michael and his angels*. Michael is an archangel (Jude 9), whose divine calling may involve being militant and warlike (Dan 10:13, 21; 12:1). He and his angels were out against *the dragon and his angels*, and *fought against* them. *The dragon* was intent on causing maximum harm to God's cause, so *he and his angels fought back*. The word angel means "messenger". Some are good and some are fallen.

8. The outcome of the war was that *the dragon and his angels were defeated*. The consequences of this defeat were devastating. *There was no longer any place for them in heaven*. For a while, after their rebellion, it seems that they were still able to attend the meetings of God's council (1 Ki 22:19-23; Job 1:6-12, 2:1-7). But after a while this had to stop, for there was no longer any place for them.

9. *The great dragon was thrown down*, expelled from heaven. At this stage we are given a fivefold description of him. He is *the great dragon*, which speaks of his ferocious longing to devour Christ and to cause harm to Christ's people. He is *that ancient serpent*, the devious tempter who fooled Eve into disobeying God and so brought about the fall (Gen 3:1-7). He is called *the Devil*, which is a legal term meaning "slanderer". He is clearly at work when God's people are arraigned for fearing God, or for loving his word and taking it at face value. He is a devious liar who seeks to persuade people that white is black and black is white (Jn 8:44). He is also called *Satan*, which means "adversary". This later became synonymous with "accuser" or "denouncer" (Job 1:9-11, Zech 3:1). William Barclay linked this with the *delator*, the paid informer of Roman days whose job it was to accuse people before the authorities. Such a hateful practice would vividly bring to life the portrait of Satan as "the accuser". Finally, he is said to be *the deceiver of the whole world*. Can we be sure that he exists? Yes, because there is no doubt that there is a being who is continually pulling the wool over people's eyes, deceiving them into thinking that good is bad and bad is good, and trying in every way to prevent anyone from coming to Christ. That being is the evil one, and he is ever awake and vigilant so as to favour evil and oppose good. It is he who *was thrown down to the earth, and his angels were thrown down with him*.

10. *John then heard a loud voice in heaven*. The plural pronouns that follow may mean that the speakers are angels. They exclaim triumphantly,

"Now have come the salvation and the power and the kingdom of our God and the authority of his Messiah". It is an impressive list of blessings, and they have come and are coming to us here on earth. *The salvation* – from the penalty of past sin, from the power of present sin, and from the presence of sin in the future. *The power* – of God, for salvation, through the message of the gospel (Rom 1:16), because Christ is in us, and the one who is in us is greater than the one who is in the world (1 Jn 4:4). *The kingdom* – meaning the rule of God, which comes to us in ever greater measure in answer to prayer (Mt 6:10). *The authority of God's Messiah* – over all things in heaven and earth, an authority given to Christ by God after his victory on the cross (Mt 28:18). There is therefore now no condemnation for those in Christ (Rom 8:1), and no one may bring any charge against God's elect (Rom 8:33).

For the accuser of our brothers has been thrown down, who accuses them day and night before our God. The implacable hostility of Satan, accusing many confused believers day and night before God, is a fact of life. However, it cannot harm their standing before God, for God has thrown Satan down through the victory of Jesus Christ on the cross. But if the power of Satan's accusations against Christians has been broken, other aspects of his destructiveness remain. His ability to intimidate all people as a fierce dragon, to tempt them as a cunning serpent (2 Cor 11:3), and particularly to deceive them, are still evident. He tries to lead astray the followers of Christ. He succeeded with Judas (Jn 13:2), and got close with Peter (Lk 22:31). He continues to be an implacable opponent for the time being, but he has been thrown down (Lk 10:18).

11. The amazing truth that John now spells out is that Christian believers, sinners though they surely are, also have their part to play in this titanic struggle, in which Christ has emerged as the victor over evil and death, and in which Michael and the heavenly host also played their part. Moreover, the part to be played by God's people is vital for them. They have been given a threefold empowerment to share the victory of Christ, and this will enable them to say that *they have conquered Satan.* As Christ's followers they will conquer the enemy, first and foremost, *by the blood of the Lamb.* There is power and efficacy in the atoning death of Christ on the cross. Believers need to stand on victory ground, resting their faith on the completed work of Christ.

They will conquer the enemy, in the second place, *by the word of their testimony*. Christians not only share their Saviour's victory but also spread the news of it throughout the world by their testimony to his saving power in their lives. This often includes a mention of how he bore their sins in his body on the cross.

And they will conquer the enemy, thirdly, thanks to their courageous stand for Christ. Bold and unashamed, *they do not cling to life even in the face of death*. John has martyrs in mind. In the hour of trial, God is able to give amazing courage to those who are called to die for their faith in Christ (2:10, 13). But this requirement to be willing to pour out one's life for Christ is not restricted to the martyrs. Leon Morris put it clearly: "The same quality of devotion is required from all the followers of the Lamb" (Lk 14:26, Jn 12:25).

12. These wonderful truths, of the victory of Christ over the accuser in verse 10, and of the means by which Christians may overcome Satan in verse 11, provoke a great chorus of rejoicing in heaven, where all the angels are invited to sing the words *"Rejoice then, you heavens and those who dwell in them!"* But although the final absolute victory of the saints is completely assured, and their *citizenship* is in heaven, the time has not yet arrived for them to bask in the *joy* of heaven. There is a paradox here. *"Rejoice you heavens – but woe to the earth and the sea, for the devil has come down to you with great wrath, because he knows that his time is short"*. There is great joy in heaven, but a woe is pronounced to the earth, because the devil has come down here, full of fury because he knows that his time is short. As Leon Morris put it, "The troubles of the persecuted righteous arise not because Satan is too strong, but because he is beaten. He is doing all the harm he can while he can. But he will not be able to do so for much longer".

Meditation: The Blood, the spoken Word and the Death to Self

The second of the seven significant signs is all about the war between good and evil. Part of the war took place in heaven. It is difficult to try and assign a date to this heavenly warfare. John Stott wrote that "This second vision does not depict events subsequent to those of the first, but is superimposed on it as its heavenly counterpart". Some commentators believe that it may refer to a primordial battle describing the fall of Lucifer. Others see in it a conflict towards the end of time that explains why fierce persecution must befall God's people. But the clearest clue about the date of this war comes in verse 11. It is also the first of the three secrets of victory in our own spiritual warfare given in this verse.

(a) They conquered him by the blood of the Lamb. In the history of redemption, the victory over Satan and his fallen angels was won by Christ when he shed his blood on the cross. F.F. Bruce put it like this: "Jesus' ministry involved [Satan's] overthrow, for his kingdom could not stand against the inbreaking kingdom of God, and he received his *coup de grâce* through the cross, the crown of Jesus' ministry" (Col 2:15). So the final victory over evil is thanks first and foremost to Christ's finished work on the cross. But even after a war has been won, there are mopping-up operations to be undertaken. Angels had their part to play in heaven. God's people have a part to play here on earth.

(b) They conquered him by the word of their testimony. Christ's blood shed on the cross is the prime cause behind the victory of the saints, but the spoken word of their testimony will confirm its efficacy in their lives. Not only will this be a help and encouragement to them, but as they pass on to unbelievers the good news that Christ bore our sins on the cross, it may be that Christ's victory will also free those who hear it from the sin of unbelief. When people respond to Christ and put their trust in him, the guilt of their sins is immediately taken away forever. The grip of their sins will also begin to be broken in their lives as they set out on the wonderful adventure of knowing Christ as their Companion, Saviour and Lord.

(c) They conquered him by being willing not to cling to life even in the face of death. The third factor that will result in our overcoming the evil one is basically a profound commitment to Christ. The good news is a powerful message in itself (Rom 1:16), but it becomes invincible if the messengers are so given over to their Lord that they are willing to die for his sake and for the sake of his victorious cause. A deep commitment such as this will bring upon believers all the vindictive and malicious fury of the dragon. He will proceed to attack God's people with misunderstanding, contempt, hatred and persecution. He may cause them to be put to death, although this would be counter-productive. As Tertullian wrote in AD 197, "the blood of the martyrs is the seed of the church". F.F. Bruce wrote that "The dragon's downfall means an intensification of his malignant activity on earth, during the brief interval before he is put out of harm's way" (20:10).

The intention of this passage is to reassure Christians who meet satanic evil that Satan really is a defeated foe, in spite of the many suggestions to the contrary. He knows that his power is broken and his doom is certain, and this explains his final convulsive efforts to crush the church and destroy the saints.

Phil Moore has introduced many people to the following tract, which he quotes in his commentary. Its provenance is unexpected and its authorship is uncertain. It sums up the right attitude for any Christian to adopt if he or she means business, and it could be entitled "Who am I?"

The die has been cast. The decision has been made. I have stepped over the line. I will not look back, let up, slow down, back away or be still. My past is redeemed, my present makes sense, and my future is secure. I no longer need pre-eminence, prosperity, position, promotions, plaudits, or popularity. I don't have to be right, or first, or top, or recognised, or praised, or regarded, or rewarded. My face is set, my gait is fast, my goal is heaven, my road is narrow, my way is rough, my companions are few, my Guide is reliable, my mission is clear. I will not be bought, compromised, detoured, lured away, turned back, deluded or delayed. I will not flinch in the face of sacrifice, hesitate in the presence of adversity, negotiate at the table of the enemy, pander at the pool of popularity, or meander in the maze of mediocrity. I will not give up, shut up, let up or slow up until I have stayed up, stored up, prayed up, paid up and spoken up for the cause of the One who shed his blood for me. Who am I? I am a disciple of Jesus Christ.

XXXI

12:13-18 The spiritual Warfare intensifies

The hostility of the dragon towards God's people intensifies. Christ won the war against him after seeming to lose it. On the cross Christ suffered for our sins once for all, the righteous for the unrighteous, in order to bring us to God (1 Pet 3:18). There he died, and for a brief moment it seemed as if Satan had won the war. But death could not hold Christ (Acts 2:24), because he had always trusted God, and on the cross he had entrusted himself to the one who judges justly. On the third day God raised him from the dead (1 Cor 15:3-4), thereby vindicating him and adjudging him the victor over death and Satan.

13. The final outcome is certain. The dragon has been beaten. He has lost the war that broke out in heaven in connection with his ambition to devour the woman's male child. *So when the dragon saw that he had been thrown down to the earth, he pursued the woman who had given birth to the male child.* The dragon's only desire now is to bring as much misery as possible to God's people in what remains of his evil existence. As we read in our previous study, he has come down to the earth in great wrath, because he knows that his time is short. He can no longer be the heavenly accuser of the brothers, so he will concentrate all his efforts on being their deceiver and tempter here on earth, and the persecutor of God's people.

14. *The woman,* who previously represented the people of God in Old Testament times, now symbolises those of the New. *She is given the two wings of the great eagle so that she could fly from the serpent into the wilderness.* Leon Morris wrote that having two wings of a great eagle meant that she could flee easily and swiftly. She needed to, for the serpent was in hot pursuit of her, with alluring and insidious temptations. She had to fly from the great city (11:8, 18:4-8) into the wilderness.

Leon Morris observes that this was prefigured in the Exodus, when the people of Israel fled out of slavery into the wilderness (Ex 12:29-14:31). Here verse 14 tells us about God's people who live *in* the world, in "the great city", but they do not belong *to* the world. They dwell physically in a worldly environment, but their true home and their sure refuge is far away in the wilderness, in which they will enjoy the privacy they need in order to meet with God. It is interesting that in the wilderness of the Exodus, God spoke to his people and said, "you have seen ... how I bore you on eagles' wings and brought you to myself. Now, therefore, if you obey my voice and keep my covenant, you shall be ... for me a priestly kingdom and a holy nation" (Ex 19:4-6, and see also Isa 40:31).

Out in the wilderness, the woman would be in *her place, where she is nourished.* God would provide for her, but we are not told whether it would be through other like-minded believers or directly through his word. This would be the case *for a time, and times, and half a time.* This means one year + two years + half a year = three and a half years, or 42 months, or 1,260 days, which represents all of the Christian era. God has always provided a refuge for his people to retreat to. Even in Old Testament days there was a deep longing among the godly for a wilderness retreat such as this (Ps 55:6-8, Jer 9:1-2).

15. At this stage *the serpent* thought up a novel way of killing the church. From his mouth he *poured water like a river after the woman, to sweep her away with the flood.* This may be an echo of the Old Testament idea that there are times when God's people have to struggle against flood waters of evil that threaten to overwhelm them and sweep them away (Ps 18:4, 16-19; 69:1-2, 15). In our own day a flood of worldliness is seeking to drown the church, and the comfortable but unacceptable response to it is to say, "I like to go with the flow". This cannot be an option for a live Christian. It is the dead trout that float downstream. The ones that are alive will always swim against the current (Rom 12:2).

16. There are occasions when help comes from unexpected sources. John tells us that *the earth came to the help of the woman; it opened its mouth and swallowed the river that the dragon had poured from his mouth.* There are times when the earth opens its mouth and swallows up God's enemies, be it on water (Ex 15:12, which looks back to Ex 15:4-5) or on dry land (Num 16:23-35). Such occasions are very rare nowadays. This may help our nervous systems, though their present paucity could lead us to irreverence. But there may be other less obvious ways in which the earth comes to the rescue of the suffering church. Creation is itself on the side of God and his people: it was made by God and, like ourselves, bears the stamp of his nature. It may be that on a few occasions the moral order established on earth will intervene and help the Christian church, although it has to be said that there are also times when the main enemy of the true church is the false one. Ultimately God himself will help God's people, and he will do so in many ways.

17. *The dragon, angry with the woman* because he could not drown her with the torrents of water that came out of his mouth, *went off to make war on the rest of her children.* This is the fulfilment of a very early prophecy (Gen 3:15). Satan is at war with all of God's people, in the Old Testament and the New, and with "the rest of her children", who represent ordinary Christians, among whom hopefully may be numbered you the reader and I the writer of this commentary.

Satan has tried to destroy the church, but he has not succeeded in doing so. The church will never be destroyed because the principle of faith on which it is built makes it secure from the gates of hell (Mt 16:17-19). So it will continue, doubtless with many imperfections in most of its local gatherings, but Satan will never, ever destroy it. Frustrated and in great fury he now goes off to attack the individuals that belong to it. John sums them up as follows.

In the first place, *they keep the commandments of God*. This is very basic, but extremely important (14:12). If God's people disobey his commands, they will get nowhere. Usually, as time goes by, they will eventually do an about turn and return contritely to him. But when God's people obey his commands there will be steady and encouraging progress. The kingdom of God will come, both in their own lives and in the lives of those around them.

The second thing John says about each individual man or woman of God in the church is that they *hold the testimony of Jesus*. This is the very activity for which John was in exile (1:9). All his fellow Christians, together with the angels, likewise hold this testimony, which is the spirit of prophecy (19:10). We have seen how the two witnesses bore prophetic testimony. They were given great authority for their ministry, but they were conquered and killed by the beast (11:3, 7). The true church is always the suffering church. It is bound to suffer for being true to Christ. Its truth is evidenced by its two distinguishing marks, which are first, a thoroughgoing obedience to God's commandments (1 Jn 2:3-6) and secondly, an unashamed loyalty to Christ's testimony (Mk 8:38. Rom 1:16).

18. After his attacks on Christ's followers, *the dragon took his stand on the sand of the seashore*. In a vain attempt to fulfil his antichristian purposes, the dragon stood on a sandy beach in order to call forth from the deep the beast who would be his primary instrument in the persecution of true Christians. This beast will feature prominently in chapter 13. Before that, we should not fail to notice that unlike the Lamb, who is standing on the rocky ground of Mount Zion (14:1), the dragon is seen to be standing on shifting sand. He will do what is evil for a while longer, but he cannot offer any true stability or sure foundation to those whom he seeks to deceive. Everything about him is unreliable. It is just a tissue of lies.

Meditation: The Woman and her Children

This section may appear repetitive, going over the ground that has already been covered in verses 1-12. There are two new points being made, however, and they are important. The first is that the ongoing survival of the true church is assured, but the personal safety of individual Christians is not. Each one finds himself or herself involved in a bitter war against the dragon, which may result in a costly martyrdom. But until their witness is over, they have a place to which they may retreat and where they will be nourished. The second is that two things mark them out from other people: they obey God and they testify about Christ. Notice also:

(a) *The woman, her male child, and the rest of her children*. In this chapter, the woman initially represents the Old Testament people of God. From them was born a male child who was the long-awaited Christ (v 1-2, 5). The dragon wished to devour the child, but this proved to be impossible (v 4-5). Later in the chapter she represents the church, which is the New Testament people of God. They were persecuted by the dragon (v 13), but were given help to flee from him to a safe place where they would be nourished and strengthened (v 14). The dragon tried to sweep away the church by a flood of afflictions (v 15), but God provided a means of escape from an unexpected source (v 16). He thereby ensured that the church would never be destroyed. So the dragon, full of anger, tried to cause harm to the rest of the woman's children, meaning those individuals that make up the church and bear witness (v 17). We have already read about them in 11:3-13. God gives them authority to prophesy, but when they have finished their testimony the forces of evil will get the upper hand and conquer them and kill them. This means that a number of faithful Christians will be sidelined and not allowed to witness any more. It means that some good churches will be taken over by self-seeking enemies of Christ and the gospel. It may even mean that certain churches will be destroyed completely and become synagogues of Satan. But as for the worldwide church, it will never, ever be destroyed.

(b) *The dragon's intense anger and hatred*. The dragon is not to be pitied. He is to be hated. For he is hate personified. To begin with, he hated God's people and accused them in order to discredit them (Job 1:6-12, 2:1-6). Then for a while he concentrated his hatred on Christ, the male child to whom the woman had given birth. He tried to devour him while he was human and vulnerable (12:4), and it was then that his hatred was at its cruel and destructive height. He thought he had succeeded in killing Christ, but in fact Christ was then more alive than ever, and it was the dragon who had been dealt a death blow, being banished from heaven and thrown down to the earth (12:7-9). The dragon knew that he was now dying and that his days were few. He had come down to earth with great wrath, because his time was short (12:12). In his fury he caused trouble upon trouble to come to the woman, seeking to persecute her, but God then provided a wilderness retreat in which she would be safe (12:13-14). The dragon tried to drown her with trials, but God then provided help from an unexpected quarter. God made sure that the woman, who is the worldwide church, would never, ever be killed or wiped away (12:15-16). The dragon was then angry with the woman, and went off to make war on the rest of her children, the individual members of the church (12:17). But God would protect them and give them power during their witness.

We learn from this that at each stage of his destructive career, Satan has been driven by hatred. He hates God's church and the individual people in it, just as he hated Christ. Indeed, he hates God's people precisely because he hated Christ. As Henry Mounce observed, "It is important to note that the antagonism directed against the church has its origin in the hatred of Satan for Christ. Jesus taught his disciples that they would receive the same hostile treatment from the world that he had received". This is true. Christ said, *"If the world hates you, be aware that it hated me before it hated you. If you belonged to the world, the world would love you as its own. Because you do not belong to the world, but I have chosen you out of the world – therefore the world hates you. Remember the word that I said to you, 'Servants are not greater than their master'. If they persecuted me, they will persecute you; if they kept my word, they will keep yours also. But they will do all these things to you on account of my name, because they do not know him who sent me. Whoever hates me hates my Father also"* (Jn 15:18-21, 23).

(c) The obedience of God's people. God's people have always found a profound sense of contentment and joy as they "keep the commandments of God" (12:17). In the Old Testament there are many examples of this. "Moses did everything just as the Lord had commanded him" (Ex 40:16). In one of the psalms there is a prophecy of the Messiah, who would say, "I delight to do your will, O my God; your law is within my heart" (Ps 40:8). In Psalm 119 the psalmist expresses his wish to obey God's commandments in most of the 176 verses of this beautifully composed ode to the word of God. Likewise in the New Testament there are great blessings promised for those who keep God's commandments. On the night that he was betrayed, Christ said to his disciples, "They who have my commandments and keep them are those who love me; and those who love me will be loved by my Father, and I will love them and reveal myself to them" (Jn 14:21).

(d) The testimony of Jesus. This could conceivably mean the testimony borne *by* Jesus, which is found primarily in the four gospels, but also in Revelation. There are some Bibles that are printed with the words spoken by Christ in red, and in the last book of the Bible the passages in red are 1:11, 17-20; all of chs 2 and 3; 4:1; 16:15; 22:7, 12-13, 16. But most scholars believe that in 12:17 "the testimony of Jesus" does not mean the testimony borne *by* Jesus, but the testimony borne by his followers *about* Jesus. They are said to *hold* it, for they carry it around with them, because it is in their hearts. They do not need to prepare beforehand what they are going to say. They know the word of God, and Christ himself will give them words and a wisdom that none of their opponents will be able to withstand or contradict (Lk 21:15). At the heart of their testimony are the great truths that Christ bore their sins on the cross; that he was raised from the dead on the third day; that they now know him and he knows them; that they speak to him in prayer and he speaks to them through his word, the Bible; and that they cannot keep from speaking about what they have heard and read about Christ. For doing this they will be hated and persecuted, but they know that if they remain unashamed and persevere to the end, they will be saved (Lk 21:16-19).

XXXII

13:1-10 The Worldly Beast from the Sea

In chapter 13 the book of Revelation explores the depths of the evil that we come across here on earth. This does not make for easy reading. As we study it, we will feel distressed and uncomfortable, but ultimately what we learn will be liberating. As Jesus said in the middle of the most disturbing chapter of John's Gospel, "If you continue in my word, you are truly my disciples; and you will know the truth, and the truth will make you free" (Jn 8:31-32). Throughout the New Testament it is made clear that in the interval between the two comings of Christ there will be some very nasty outbreaks of the power of evil. Sometimes they will be associated with individuals, who are designated by names such as "antichrist"

(1 Jn 2:18) or "the lawless one" (2 Thess 2:3). Here, in verses 1-10, John speaks of "a beast", and proceeds to tell us in picturesque detail just how evil it is.

1. The dragon took his stand on a sandy beach in order to call forth evil from the deep waters. *John saw a beast rising out of the sea.* In ancient times people would associate evil with the depths of the sea. Dreadful monsters dwelt there, so woe to the people of the earth if one of them emerged and began to play a part in their affairs. This beast *had ten horns and seven heads.* We have seen this before. The dragon had the same features (12:3). But whereas the dragon had seven diadems, one on each head, *the beast had ten diadems, one for each horn.* The dragon liked to see his heads crowned, for he was big-headed and wished to be on a par with God. But the beast would be given power by the dragon (v 2), so it is on the *horns* that it bore its crowns as visible insignia of its mighty dominion. *The beast had blasphemous names inscribed on its heads.* When it spoke it would blaspheme the name of God and of those who dwelt in heaven (v 5-6). With the blasphemies already written on him, it would be natural for him to do this.

2. *The beast that John saw was like a leopard, its feet were like a bear's, and its mouth was like a lion's mouth.* John is making use of several features of the beasts mentioned in Daniel 7:1-8, so that his composite beast is both horribly fierce and frighteningly grotesque. The leopard may represent cruelty and cunning, the bear intimidation and strength, and the lion ferocity and mercilessness. The beast has no power of its own, for *the dragon gave it his power and his throne and great authority.* As a result, the beast possessed brutal might, imperial prerogatives and ample freedom to destroy. It was very dangerous.

3. And now John saw something strange and alarming. *One of its heads seemed to have received a death-blow, but its mortal wound had been healed.* This death-blow was delivered by a sword (v 14). We do not know who delivered it or why. The important thing as far as John is concerned is that it was a mortal wound, and yet the beast was healed. This recovery had a disturbing effect. *In amazement the whole earth worshipped the beast.* What exactly is the significance of the head that was wounded? Some commentators refer to the *Nero redivivus* myth, which was the belief that Nero would return from the dead after he committed suicide on June 9, AD 68. He would appear at the head of the Parthian

army, and continue his evil reign. This myth was widely accepted until almost the end of the second century, and many charlatans pretended to be Nero returning to life. But there is also a timeless interpretation of this fatally wounded head that was healed, which we shall consider in the meditation. At present we should notice that people as a whole followed the beast. But that is not all that they did.

4. *They worshipped the dragon, for he had given his authority to the beast.* The world saw that it would be pointless to resist the beast since it had such strength and authority, so they worshipped the source of its power, namely the dragon. But *they also worshipped the beast, saying, "Who is like the beast, and who can fight against it?"* These words are a parody of the ones used in the Old Testament as a form of worship of God himself (Ex 15:11, Ps 35:10). And since we have just read that Michael helped to defeat the dragon (12:7-8), this may be a worldly and defiant attempt to pour scorn on the name "Michael", which means "Who is like God?" For the principal objective of the beast is to capture the imaginations and loyalties of people and to divert them from worshipping God.

5. *The beast was given a mouth uttering haughty and blasphemous words.* It may be that the beast should be thought of as an evil spirit that takes hold of certain people. The origin of its pride and its blasphemies is the dragon. Pride is a sin that God hates and will punish very severely (Isa 2:11-17), and blasphemies are insults against God that vilify his holy nature. We are told that the beast *was allowed to exercise authority for forty-two months.* It has leave to infect people with its pride and blasphemous speech during the time permitted by God, which is the Christian era. Its power is limited by God, and it is encouraging to know this.

6. *It opened its mouth to utter blasphemies against God.* It is evil to blaspheme, and such speech will distress those who love and serve God. Certain blasphemies will not be forgiven (Mk 3:28-30). Here the beast was *blaspheming God's name and his dwelling, that is, those who dwell in heaven.* Here "his dwelling" means "those in whom God dwells", so that the blasphemies are directed against God's person and nature – what he is like – and against the people whose bodies are the temple of the Holy Spirit (1 Cor 6:19-20). One way of blaspheming God is to stress that he is loving (1 Jn 4:8) without ever mentioning the complementary

truth that he is holy (1 Jn 1:5). One way of blaspheming God's people is to accuse them of being unloving when they try to obey Christ's commands (Jn 14:21).

7. *Also it* (the beast) *was allowed to make war on the saints and to conquer them.* This is an echo of Daniel 7:21-22, which then limits the extent of this war "until the Ancient One came". It is also a repetition of 11:7, "the beast that comes up from the bottomless pit will make war on [the two witnesses] and conquer them and kill them". The result of the unholy war is that the beast *was given authority over every tribe and people and language and nation.* There is a worldly power that is diabolical. It manifests itself everywhere on earth (1 Jn 2:15-17, 5:19).

8. The terrible truth is that there is no *via media.* Every person is either one of the few who walk on the narrow and hard way that leads to life, or one of the many who walk on the wide and easy way that leads to destruction (Mt 7:13-14). John has his own way of putting this across. *All the inhabitants of the earth* (meaning all who do not know and love God and Christ) *will worship the beast, everyone whose name has not been written from the foundation of the world in the book of life of the Lamb that was slaughtered.* The worship of the beast means putting it first, above God and neighbour. "The beast" could assume all manner of worldly forms – a politician, a film or pop star, a career, a sport, a hobby, any person or pastime that occupies the supreme place in life, the place that should be reserved for God and for his Son Jesus Christ.

Thomas Torrance wrote, "Again and again there emerge bestial forces out of the filmy depths of the nations that fascinate and mesmerise humanity until all the world wanders after and worships the beast, except those whose names are written in the Lamb's book of life". Many people willingly devote themselves to the beast, and set themselves in opposition to God. But as Leon Morris observed, "The significant thing is that their names are not written in the book of life. John wants his little handful of persecuted Christians to see that the thing that matters is the sovereignty of God, not the power of evil. Those whose names are written in the book of life will not be forgotten. Their place is secure". This is a most fortifying message.

The idea of a divine register goes as far back as the time when Moses met God on Mount Sinai (Ex 32:32-33, and it also appears in Ps 69:28,

87:6; Dan 12:1; and Mal 3:16. In the New Testament it is mentioned in Lk 10:20, Phil 4:3, and five other times in Revelation – 3:5, 17:8, 20:12, 20:15 and 21:27). It is a book containing the names of all those who belong to God. It is important not only that our names are *written in the Lamb's book of life*, but also that this has been the case *from the foundation of the world*. Christ is able to save us because he is the Lamb of God that takes away the sin of the world, and his salvation is part of God's eternal purpose for his people (Eph 1:4).

9. In the light of all this, John writes, not for the first time, *Let anyone who has an ear listen*. This same admonition ends each of the seven letters in chapters 2 and 3. From whom did John learn this familiar phrase? (Mt 11:15, 13:9, etc).

10. John follows this up with two couplets. The first teaches an acceptance of the realities of life: *If you are to be taken captive, into captivity you go*. If providence dictates exile and slavery for God's people, then it is for a divine purpose and it will happen (Jer 15:2). The second couplet teaches that the end does not justify the means: *If you kill with the sword, with the sword you must be killed*. Had John heard Christ say these words on the night of his arrest? (Mt 26:52). Leon Morris wrote, "If the Christian takes the sword he will not establish the faith, for the truth of Christ cannot be defended by violence. He will simply perish by the sword. But when persecuted he can know that the final word is not with his persecutors". In times of persecution this is a message of great comfort. As John himself wrote, *Here is a call for the endurance and faith of the saints*. Because the beast seems to have unlimited power to destroy the saints, they must all the more put their trust in God. God is God. He is holy and he rules. His kingdom is over all.

Meditation: Pure Evil

(a) Satan and his agents. Two extremely wicked allies of the dragon now appear on the scene. The first is called the beast from the sea (13:1-10). The second has two names, the beast from the earth and the false prophet (13:11-18). Just as God makes himself real to us in three persons, the Father, the Son and the Holy Spirit, evil likewise manifests itself to us in the guise of the dragon, the beast, and the false prophet. These three spirit beings are a diabolical parody of the Trinity. At the time when John wrote the Revelation, the two beasts represented

the city and empire of Rome. The first beast stood for Rome as a persecuting power, and the second stood for Rome as a religious system of idolatry. In later times, they have kept on acting as symbols, but their significance has changed so that it is no longer primarily linked to the Roman Empire, which is now a thing of the past.

In our own day the first beast represents worldliness as it captivates, enslaves and domineers people, gradually compelling them to bend to its power. The false prophet represents all forms of idolatrous worship, including the false church in its many guises. Between them these two inspire the antichrists of the world, and their spirit is possessing people everywhere, seeking to drive a dangerous wedge between them and Christ (1 Jn 2:18, 4:3).

(b) The beast from the sea. In this chapter there is little about the dragon. He may be in the background, but he is doing his work through men and women who are driven by the spirit of the beast from the sea. What John is writing about is evil deeds done by people, but in the back of his mind he is thinking of a superhuman spirit who has been spawned by the dragon. William Hendriksen wrote that the beast is symbolic of "worldly government directed against the church", and its seven heads may symbolise different manifestations of the secular attacks on the church down the ages. One might mention Egypt, Assyria and Babylon in ancient times, and Hitler, Stalin, Mao Zedong and Pol Pot in more recent ones. Henry Mounce wrote that "The beast has always been, and will be in a final intensified manifestation, the deification of secular authority".

(c) The seven heads. The beast and the dragon resemble each other. Both have seven heads, which is very striking in this book, for there are numerous heptads in Revelation. Seven is the number of perfection and completeness. We might even say it is God's number, for many of the heptads are connected with the Lamb (see 5:6 and the meditation for section XIV on p. ???). How can it be, then, that Satan and his principal assistant blasphemously appear with seven heads, just like the Lamb? Surely it is because they want to be regarded as worthy replacements for God. The beast is also known as the antichrist, and the Greek preposition *anti* can mean "instead of" as well as "against". The beast represents itself as a God-substitute, and John tells us that it longs that people might worship either it or the dragon (v 4). This is why it blasphemes the name and the people of God (6).

(d) The ten horns. There is another way in which the beast is very much like the dragon. Both have ten horns, and a horn is a symbol of power. Whereas the

dragon has seven crowns, the beast has ten. The dragon has crowns on each of his heads, but the beast has them on each of its horns. The dragon retains the trappings of royal and divine majesty by virtue of his crowned heads (19:12), but he has given his tenfold power to the beast, who displays it with its ten crowned horns. These horns represent ten kings or world leaders, to whom the beast will in due course delegate its power for waging war on the Lamb and on God's people (17:12-14).

(e) The blasphemous names on the beast's heads. The beast would claim divine prerogatives (Dan 7:25, Mt 24:15, 2 Thess 2:4) and expect to be worshipped by people (v 4). Self-deification by the emperor was common in the Roman Empire, the most explicit claims being made by Domitian who reigned during AD 81-96. He demanded that others address him as *"Dominus et Deus"*, Lord and God. But self-deification is not confined to Rome and its emperors. In every age there are cruel and despotic leaders who have imposed totalitarian regimes, and persecuted anyone who did not bow the knee or prostrate themselves in their presence.

(f) The apparent mortal wound. The beast seemed to have been dealt a death blow (v 3), but it came right back from apparent death in a parody of Christ, who suffered real death but was raised from the dead after being crucified (5:6). Leon Morris wrote that those who equate the beast with the Roman Empire understand John as saying that *the head* died and was restored. In fact it was *the beast* that suffered a deadly wound, located in one of its heads, and was healed. There is no suggestion that the head was restored. We may conclude that there exists an evil which comes ultimately from the dragon, and is found both in individual human hearts and in communities. Apparently it cannot be slain and eradicated. When wounded, it will rise again, and it will keep on doing so to the end of time, to the great astonishment of all. One thinks of the problems that western governments face today. They realise that a certain action is evil, so they take steps to stamp it out. The same action then reappears in a slightly different guise, and life becomes far worse than it was previously (Mt 12:43-45). Examples of this are theft, fraud, bullying, physical and spiritual abuse – and almost any other crime.

(g) How we should react to the beast. If we have ears to hear, let us hear! God's permission to the beast is to make war on God's people and to conquer them. If we are numbered among the saints, that will include us (v 7). If we are part of the witnessing church, we will be part of the suffering church (11:3-7).

If we are part of the true church, we will be part of the church militant (12:10-11). In the war against evil, we shall experience numerous hurtful setbacks, and the glorious day may arrive when we shall be counted worthy to make the ultimate sacrifice for Christ and for the truth (Heb 12:3-4).

If this means poverty or captivity or martyrdom, we may be assured that God is in control. He has allowed the beast to afflict us in this way. God has his purposes, and he will reward his servants when they suffer unjustly for Christ's sake. Of course we should never respond to harshness and injustice with violence. Instead we are to put our trust in God who judges justly. As William Barclay commented, "It is an intolerable paradox to defend the gospel of the love of God by using the violence of man".

XXXIII

13:11-18 The Ecclesiastical Beast from the Earth

If the first half of chapter 13 made us feel uncomfortable, our discomfiture will be even greater as we study the second half. Here we have evil every bit as nasty as anything we have encountered so far, with an added component that is almost too horrible to contemplate. In agreement with his Saviour's teaching, with the history of the early church in the book of Acts, and with the turbulent background of the New Testament epistles, John now describes a vision of the unthinkable beast from the earth, also known as the false prophet. With its appearance, writes F.F. Bruce, "The unholy trinity of dragon, beast and false prophet is completed. As the true Christ received his authority from the Father (Mt 11:27, 28:18; Jn 13:3), so antichrist receives authority from the dragon (v 4); as the Holy Spirit glorifies the true Christ (Jn 16:14), so the false prophet glorifies antichrist (v 12)". John uses symbols and numbers to express what has been implicit since chapters 2 and 3, but which he has found difficult to put into words.

11. John continues his account. The beast from the sea was not alone. *Then I saw another beast that rose out of the earth.* This puts us at ease. We are familiar with the earth; it is the sea that makes us anxious. *It had two horns like a lamb*, so it is not as fearsome as the first beast with its ten horns. It is said to be "like a lamb", so we naturally associate it with *the Lamb.* Could it perhaps be allied to the Lamb? Is the second beast perhaps a way of representing the true church? No, because John goes on to say that *it spoke like a dragon*, and the fact that it is "like a lamb" therefore implies that this beast from the earth is a diabolically motivated imitator of true religion. Later it will be called "the false prophet" (16:13, 19:20, 20:10). It will speak and preach like a prophet, but its teaching and its prophecies will be false. It may look like a plausible version of the truth, but it will prove to be false.

12. *It exercises all the authority of the first beast on its behalf.* The dragon gave its power to the first beast, who in turn delegated it to the second beast. So this second beast speaks with great authority, with the result that *it makes the earth and its inhabitants worship the first beast, whose mortal wound had been healed.* The two beasts are not rivals but close allies. Leon Morris wrote that the second beast appears to have a priestly function, allied in some way to the current worldly regime. At the time John wrote, his readers would have seen the Roman imperial power as an illustration of the first beast, and the Roman imperial priesthood and cult in the second. In our time, we might see a corrupt national government as the first beast and its apostate national church as the second. But the corrupt national government had a mortal wound which had been healed. Perhaps it suffered from a terrible scandal, but then recovered – in an apparently miraculous way.

13. *The second beast performed great signs.* In the first century pagan priests used to perform counterfeit miracles in order to impress those who were gullible. The Greek word used for *signs* is *semeia*, and it is used in Revelation for some of the visions seen by John (12:1, 3; 15:1), and also for the miracles performed by evil beings (here and in v 14, 16:14, 19:20). Interestingly, this is the same word that is used in John's Gospel for the miracles of Jesus (Jn 2:11, etc.), and Leon Morris believed that this is a further case of evil powers engaging in a parody of the good. False miracles are part of Satan's plan of deception (Mk 13:22, 2 Thess 2:9).

The second beast *even made fire come down from heaven to earth in the sight of all.* The purpose behind such a spectacular celestial fireworks display was only to take hold of people's imaginations by arousing their admiration. This was not the reason for Christ's miracles (Mt 16:1-4, Lk 23:8-9). False priests and prophets may perform great signs but they will not bear good lasting fruit (Mt 7:15-20). They may claim to be filled with the Holy Spirit, when in fact they are inspired by the ecclesiastical beast from the earth. If so, they will be guilty of blaspheming the Holy Spirit (Mt 12:31-32), and in the final day Christ will declare to them, "I never knew you; go away from me, you evildoers" (Mt 7:21-23).

14. *By the signs that it is allowed to perform on behalf of the first beast, it deceives the inhabitants of the earth.* Its signs are a performance, and their purpose is solely to deceive. The phrase *the inhabitants of the earth* always seems to refer to those who are not true followers of God, but are instead their opponents or persecutors. We should note that this second beast can only deceive unbelievers. Leon Morris draws the important lesson that those who love God and Christ with all their being will never be taken in by the empty miracles of the deceiver. It is when they begin to drift away from God that they may predispose themselves to believe the lies of this second beast, and worship the first one. Indeed, the second beast *will tell them to make an image for the first beast that had been wounded by the sword and yet lived.* Once more we are told that the first beast is characterised by its amazing recovery from a deadly wound (v 3, 12, and here).

15. Now follows another spurious miracle by the second beast. *It was allowed to give breath to the image of the first beast so that the image could even speak and cause those who did not worship it to be killed.* In antiquity there were numerous stories about idols that spoke. Martin Kiddle reflected that the breath of life was something that belonged exclusively to God the Creator, so "when the priests of antichrist have thus animated their idol, they have acted a blasphemy exceeding that of all previous idolaters; this is the magician's most impious usurpation of God's power". Here it is a case of people being compelled, possibly in the name of God, to worship a false God. To do this is not just to take God's name in vain; it is to blaspheme the name, and God will not hold guiltless those who do this.

16. The beast from the earth also *causes all, both small and great, both rich and poor, both free and slave, to be marked on the right hand or the forehead.* Every kind of person had to go through this, regardless of achievement, riches or status. No one was exempt. They had to bear the mark of the beast conspicuously, on the right hand or forehead.

Richard Bewes has pointed out that "It is when people's actions (the right hand) and thinking (the forehead) are controlled by a philosophy alien to Christ, that you could say that the beast has stamped itself upon their lives". Very simply, they are branded like sheep with their owner's mark.

William Barclay has suggested various interpretations of this marking. From the branding of slaves, it could be that they were slaves of the beast. From soldiers branding themselves with the name of their favourite general, it could be that they were devoted followers of the beast. From the use of seals in contracts, it could be that they were bound to accept the law and the authority of the beast. From the mark stamped on coins, it could be that they were the property of the beast. From the certificate that a person had sacrificed to Caesar, it could be a mark certifying that they worshipped Caesar and denied Christ. It is possible that many or all of these different ideas were in John's mind as he used the word *mark*.

17. Why did the beast cause everyone to be branded in this way? *So that no one could buy or sell who did not have the mark.* This total prohibition would make it impossible for those who were not marked to get even the basic necessities of life, like food and clothing. Their existence would become an obscure battle for survival. What exactly does the mark consist of? It is *the name of the beast or the number of its name.* We should bear in mind that someone's *name* is their basic nature. For example, God's name is *holy and loving* because he is like this.

18. John urges us to think. *This calls for wisdom: let anyone with understanding calculate the number of the beast, for it is the number of a person. Its number is 666.* It is likely that what John wrote was χξϛ, for the Greeks did not use either Arabic or Roman numerals. The first nine letters of the alphabet represented the units, the next nine the tens, and the rest (plus a few other signs because there are less than 27 Greek letters) the hundreds. Chi (χ) is 600, Xi (ξ) is 60, and Sigma (Σ or ϛ) is 6, and so χξϛ is 666. But what is meant by calculating it? John gives us some hints. We are to use *wisdom* and *understanding*. Because we are to *calculate* it, some basic arithmetic may be needed. It is *the number of a person*, which may mean "of any person" – so we should ask what it is that all people have in common? It is *the number of the beast*, never mind

which of the two. What is the solution? How do we arrive at 666? The method should be clear and simple.

Meditation: 666 and all that

One way of approaching the conundrum of what 666 means is to seek for a name whose letters add up to 666. This kind of reckoning of numerical values of words and names was a pastime of well-off Greeks and Romans, and also of the Jews, who called it "gematria". Most people favour the solution "Nero Caesar", but this does not quite work. As Leon Morris pointed out, in order to get it to work, it is necessary to use the Greek form of the Latin name, transliterate it into Hebrew characters, and use a variant spelling that omits the letter y from qysr. Any Maths teacher will tell you that this is a fudge. By resorting to similar fudges, you may prove to your own satisfaction that 666 means three different Roman Emperors, several popes or Martin Luther. In modern times, 666 has been shown to be Adolf Hitler, Joseph Stalin or Saddam Hussein. If you find the right alphabet and juggle around a bit, you can end up with lots of other names. If there is someone whom you dislike intensely, try to show that his or her name gives 666, and see if you succeed. You may use the three rules for yielding the number 666 propounded by George Salmon in his *Introduction to the New Testament*: "First, if the proper name by itself will not yield it, add a title; secondly, if the sum cannot be found in Greek, try Hebrew, or even Latin; thirdly, do not be too particular about the spelling". In our day there is no reason why you may not use either the English alphabet or a slightly different one from another language. You may even decide to apportion numbers to each letter of the alphabet according to a new rule, which you may choose so as to fulfil your objectives. Have fun! Here is an example, just to tickle your fancy. We will work in English, where we feel at home, and use the system A = 100, B = 101, C = 102, and so on. Then the letters of the name *Hitler* add up to 107 + 108 + 119 + 111 + 104 + 117 = 666.

A few commentators have suggested an altogether different approach, which is consistent with all the hints that John gives us in verse 18, as well as harmonising perfectly with the numerical symbolism in the book of Revelation. This approach regards the number not as "six hundred and sixty-six" but as "six, six, six". Here follows a presentation of it which is hopefully clear enough to understand.

(a) In Revelation, 7 is the number of perfection or completeness. In several ways it is God's number. It is the number of the churches he patrols, of the seals in his book, of the trumpets blown by his angels, of the significant signs for his people, and of the bowls of his wrath. It is also the number of the Lamb, who has seven horns and seven eyes, and who alone is worthy to break the seven scrolls. In the book of Revelation he is called "Christ" seven times, "Lord" seven times, "Jesus" fourteen times, and "the Lamb" twenty-eight times. Seven is also the number of the Holy Spirit, who is called "the seven spirits". There is something good and divine about the number seven. Moreover, God is one being but he is also three persons − Father, Son and Holy Spirit. He could therefore be assigned the number 777, meaning not seven hundred and seventy-seven but seven, seven, seven.

(b) It comes as a shock, therefore, to see that both the dragon and the first beast have seven heads, aping the Lamb, and to read that the second beast has two horns like a lamb. They are an evil parody of one who is absolutely good. The second beast is also called the false prophet. It appears in a priestly guise, and it performs signs in order to deceive the inhabitants of the earth. Here we have three spirit beings, all of whom wish to take the place of God in the lives of ordinary people.

(c) They use every means in order to rise to the heights of God, for they want to usurp his place, and their objective is that people may worship them as if they were God. But they fall short of the glory of God. They cannot reach the heights of seven, seven, seven. So the essential nature or name of the evil one is summed up by its number, which is six, six, six. Thomas Torrance put it in his own words, "This evil trinity 666 apes the Holy Trinity 777, but always falls short and fails".

(d) Leon Morris suggested that the number does not refer to a specific individual, but to a persistent falling short. This is likely to be correct if we take "the number of a person" to mean "the number of any person". John is then teaching the very unpalatable truth that those who are not God's people persist in evil. They bear the mark of the beast in a prominent way, and show it off in all they do. Human civilisation without Christ is necessarily under the dominion of the evil one.

(e) The implications of 666 may be worse. Any reader who finds it difficult to come to terms with reality should not read this paragraph. We have seen that the second beast has priestly connotations. At various times in the past 2,000 years it has taken over the leadership of a church in its guise as the false prophet. As he drew to the climax of his Sermon on the Mount, Jesus Christ warned us that this would happen. Wolves love to dress up in sheep's clothing (Mt 7:15-20). In the early church problems often arose from the pernicious influence of false teachers. Most of the New Testament epistles are written against this background. Of the seven churches in Revelation, four were seriously affected in this way.

How do false teachers get rid of the true Christians? It is always the same. God's people are told that they may not continue to influence the church because they do not have the correct credentials, meaning the mark of the beast. Instead, God's people have a seal, for they have been sealed with the Holy Spirit. In the church, those with the mark of the beast will carefully tweak the internal politics of how the church is run, and proceed with the boycott and social ostracism of those who have the seal of the Holy Spirit. The false Christians will take over the important functions of the church from the true ones. The latter will be confused. In their innocence many will feel uncomfortable, thinking that they may have gone wrong in some way. In fact their discomfort has arisen because they are no longer being nourished with God's word. Moreover, they are being sidelined. Nevertheless they remain faithful, hoping for a return to better times, but things will only get worse. Having given an inch or two to the beast's agents, they will then be asked to give a mile. They will not realise until it is too late that they now have to operate as the agents of the resistance in a totalitarian regime.

It has often happened in the history of the church that the greatest problems it has faced have been occasioned by false teaching within the church itself. There have been a few times when the greatest enemy and persecutor of the church has been the church leadership. God's people in the 21st century English church are finding themselves caught up in the middle of such a time. God is faithful, and he will provide the way of escape according to his promises. He will look after his own people in a special place in the wilderness, and there he will nourish them.

XXXIV

14:1-5 The Lamb is praised on Mount Zion

In the book of Revelation, as in life, there are some wonderfully happy interludes in which we glimpse the glory and the joy of heaven. This is one of the loveliest. Its positioning in the book is significant. We have just been given a vision of the unrelenting spiritual battle in chapter 12, and of the horrifying reality of evil in chapter 13. With relief we now turn from the beasts to the Lamb; from the great ordeal on earth to security on the heavenly Mount Zion; from the imperfection of 666 to the completeness of 144,000; and from those who have on their foreheads not the mark and number of the beast but the name of God and the Lamb.

1. The scene is presented vividly. The Greek requires the translators to use either the word *behold* or an exclamation mark: *Then I looked, and there was the Lamb, standing on Mount Zion!* In the Bible, Mount Zion sometimes represents the idea of divine deliverance (e.g. Ps 48, Isa 33:2-6, Joel 2:32) and this may also be the case here. This is a glimpse of the final triumph of Christ, the Lamb of God. It is noteworthy that whereas the dragon took his stand on the shifting sand by the sea, the Lamb stands on the stable and solid rock of Mount Zion. The Lamb possesses rocklike dependability, but the dragon is a deceiver and the father of lies.

   John saw that *with the Lamb were one hundred and forty-four thousand who had his name and his Father's name written on their foreheads.* We have already been introduced to the 144,000 in 7:4. There we saw that they stand for the totality of God's people in their sanctified state. They are, in fact, a "great multitude that no one could count" (7:9). They will shortly be defined in verse 3 as those "who have been redeemed from the earth", and John will proceed to describe four of their distinguishing marks in verses 4-5. But here in verse 1 there is a note of fulfilment: as Martin Kiddle put it, "A hundred and forty-four thousand were sealed, a hundred and forty-four thousand were saved". Leon Morris observed that "They were on earth, confronted by enemies. Now they are in heaven and not one of them has been lost". God is faithful and looks after his own. Also the names of God and of Christ written on their *foreheads* explain the nature of the seal on their *foreheads* in 7:3. God's people have, imprinted in their minds, details of God's essential being. Their great delight is to think about him and learn new truths about him. They love to hear the Bible being faithfully expounded.

2. Not infrequently in Revelation John hears an unidentified heavenly voice. *And I heard a voice from heaven.* He proceeds to describe the voice

in three ways. *It was like the sound of many waters*, resembling the voice of Christ (1:15), and also the voice of God according to the Prophet Ezekiel (Ezek 43:2). It was also *like the sound of loud thunder*. Anyone who has been outdoors in a thunderstorm and has experienced a clap of thunder close by will know that it is exceptionally loud (6:1). John also describes *the voice* he heard *as like the sound of harpists playing on their harps*. Leon Morris writes that it was melodious and attractive, and that it was probably the voice of the 144,000. The alternative is that it is angels who are singing. Since it is a song of redemption (v 3) it is likelier that the singers are the redeemed, who are giving full voice to their great joy.

3. We might well ask what kind of song they were singing. *They sing a new song before the throne and before the four living creatures and before the elders.* The Greek word for *new* means entirely fresh and unprecedented. The Lamb's work in achieving and then consummating our salvation creates a completely new state of affairs. It calls for a completely new type of worship song. It is a song about redemption, sung before God, with some senior angels present. They have never fallen and do not need to be redeemed, but they may listen and wonder and adore. *No one could learn that song except the one hundred and forty-four thousand who have been redeemed from the earth.* It is only fallen humans who have sinned and then been redeemed who can sing the songs of redemption. Leon Morris points out that they have been redeemed *from the earth*, from the futile worldly ways they inherited from their ancestors. The cost of redemption was the precious blood of Christ, the Lamb without defect or blemish (1 Pet 1:18-19).

4. But who are these redeemed people? What are their characteristics? How can you tell if someone is redeemed? John proceeds to give us four tell-tale signs that define them. The first is that they are *these who have not defiled themselves with women, for they are virgins*. This is a curious expression. After a first reading it is difficult to apply the first clause to a godly woman, nor does the second clause fit appropriately with most men. Moreover the Bible never suggests that proper sexual relations are defiling. Instead, it teaches that marriage is a commendable estate, and sexual relations are a necessary part of it (1 Cor 7:2-5). Nor does the Bible encourage perpetual virginity. Sex is the Creator's

wonderful gift to us. It is likely, therefore, that John is here using virginity not in its literal sense but as a symbol for the avoidance of idolatry. This is a common usage, both in the Old Testament (2 Ki 19:21; Jer 3:6, 18:13; Lam 2:13; Ezek 16:1-63; Hosea 2:5; Amos 5:2) and in the New (e.g. 2 Cor 11:2; Eph 5:31-32). John himself backs up this interpretation by his repeated use of the Greek word *porneia* (meaning fornication or any illicit sexual activity). He uses it as he describes the idolatrous worship of the beast (14:8; 17:2, 4; 18:3, 9; 19:2). Therefore the 144,000 are undefiled and virgins in the sense that they refused to participate in *porneia* or the worship of the beast. They kept themselves pure by dedicating themselves to God instead of devoting themselves to the world, the flesh and the devil.

The second sign of redeemed people is that *these follow the Lamb wherever he goes*. It is not they who decide the occasions or the place where their service will lead them. It is the Lamb who leads. Their part is to follow him (Mk 1:17-18).

The third sign is that *they have been redeemed from humankind as first fruits for God and the Lamb*. They have been *redeemed* at the high price of the blood of the Lamb (5:9). Because they have been purchased *from humankind*, they no longer belong to this world (Jn 15:19). They have been bought *as first fruits*, so they are holy to God (Ex 23:19, Neh 10:35, Jer 2:3). In the New Testament the idea of first fruits is used to refer to God's people (2 Thess 2:13, Jas 1:18). The true church is God's. The calling of God's people is to consecrate themselves to him. Once again John mentions *the Lamb* together with *God*. What belongs to one belongs to the other. There is an indissoluble link between them (Mt 11:27).

5. The fourth sign that a person is one of the redeemed is that *in their mouth no lie was found*. This also distinguished the godly of the Old Testament (Zeph 3:13), and is part of the testimony borne to Christ in the Bible (Isa 53:9, 1 Pet 2:22). The world has never been marked out by people with a strict regard for the truth. The modern church in wealthy countries is in desperate need of truthful people, for the false prophet is busily speaking its haughty and blasphemous words through the mouths of false church leaders. By contrast, those who have been redeemed by God *are to be blameless*. The Greek word *amomoi* means

without blemish or fault, and is used of sacrificial animals or victims (1 Pet 1:19). Leon Morris wrote that "there may be a hint here that Christian service is sacrificial".

Meditation: How to tell the difference

In this section we are presented with a number of contrasts between the few who are on the hard road that leads to life, and the many who are on the easy road that leads to destruction (Mt 7:13-14). It is good to keep our eyes and ears open when we interact with people. If we remember these contrasts while we do so, we shall spot some clues as to which road they are on. This is particularly important with regard to churchgoers. There is no need to assess those who are outside the pale of the church, but we may observe church members and leaders (11:1-2), so as to see how our church fits into the general scheme of churches (chapters 2 and 3).

(a) What is written on their foreheads? Is it the name of God and of Christ (v 1), or is it the name and number of the beast? (13:16-17). In either case, it is written on the forehead, so it affects all their thinking, whether for good or for evil. We may learn that *the redeemed love to think about their Redeemer.*

(b) Do they have a new song to sing? Is it a hymn about God's great redemption, secured by Christ when he suffered for our sins once for all (v 3, 1 Pet 3:18), or is it a sugary mood-enhancing song about "Peace, peace" when there is no peace? (Jer 6:13-15). How much better it is to sing the praises of God and to delight in the gift of his Son (Jn 3:16), than to be restless and face the prospect of torment (v 9-11). We may learn that *the redeemed rejoice in their Redeemer* (Ps 37:4).

(c) To whom do they belong? Is it to God, who purchased them at the great cost of the life-blood of his Son (this is what it means to be redeemed, v 3), or to the second beast who manipulates them as he wills, controlling even what they buy and sell? (13:16-17). Do they have the seal of the Holy Spirit (7:1-8) or do they have the mark of the beast? (13:16). We may learn that *the redeemed are not their own; they have been bought with a price by their Redeemer* (1 Cor 6:19-20).

(d) What is their worship like? Is it pure and uncontaminated by idolatry (v 4), or is it defiled by being idolatrously directed to the first beast at the instigation of the second? (13:8, 12). Archbishop William Temple provided a fine definition of true worship in his *Readings in St John's Gospel*: "Worship is the submission

of all our nature to God. It is the quickening of conscience by his holiness; the nourishment of mind with his truth; the purifying of the imagination by his beauty; the opening of the heart to his love; the surrender of the will to his purpose. And all this is gathered up in adoration, the most selfless emotion of which our nature is capable and therefore the chief remedy for that self-centredness which is our original sin and therefore the source of all actual sin". God's people must be spiritually chaste. Their ultimate devotion is for God alone. We may learn that *the redeemed are faithful to their Redeemer* (Mk 8:38).

(e) Whom do they follow? Is it Christ or is it the world, the flesh and the devil? (v 4, Eph 2:1-3). The gospel message at its simplest is a call to follow Christ. At the start it is a matter of turning one's life around to walk in the same direction as Christ. Later it is a matter of following him wherever he goes. Sometimes he does not explain everything we want to know, but says, "What is that to you? Follow me" (Jn 21:22). Nothing else should come before our following (Mt 8:22). We may learn that *the redeemed are disciples of their Redeemer* (Mt 11:29, Jn 13:13).

(f) Are they losing their lives for Christ? Are they first fruits offered willingly as a living sacrifice to God (v 4, Rom 12:1), or are they holding back on account of peer pressure for fear of losing themselves? We may learn that *the redeemed give their lives as a sacrificial offering to their Redeemer* (Mk 8:35).

(g) What is their speech like? Is it always transparently truthful (v 5), or is it a tissue of deceitful half-truths? (22:15, Rom 1:25). Are they genuine or just acting a part? Do they ring true or lack conviction? Christ spoke the truth with majestic authority (Mt 7:28-29). Nobody else has spoken like him (Jn 7:45-46). We may learn that *the redeemed speak the truth with integrity, like their Redeemer.*

Richard Bewes wrote, "The message is a sobering one. You can take any group of people and – invisibly – there will be a line drawn down the middle. Some are going to go God's way. Others will go their own way, and in so doing will identify themselves with the opposition; in short with the beast. The contrast is strong".

XXXV

14:6-20 The Implications of the coming Judgement

In this, the last of the seven significant signs, we are once again given a vision of the final judgement of God, as in 6:12-17, 8:1-5 and 11:15-19. This sign contains two heptads: there are seven visions or calls that relate to the coming judgement (in verses 6-7, 8, 9-11, 12, 13, 14-16 and 17-20), and there are seven different angels who either proclaim judgement or play a part in bringing it about (in verses 6, 8, 9, 14 & 16, 15, 17 & 19, and 18). The final vision is horrifying. John sees an enormous wine press, but what is being crushed is not grapes but wicked people, and instead of wine, it is a flood of blood that is poured out on the earth.

6. To begin with, *John saw another angel flying in mid-heaven*, different from all the other angels he had seen, and like the eagle which pronounced the three woes (8:13), he flew in the middle of the sky. *He had an eternal gospel to proclaim to those who live on the earth*. The word *gospel* means "good news", and the good news is that there is a way of escaping from the divine judgement (Jn 5:24). *Those who live on the earth* are in desperate need of this good news. It is *eternal*, so it has permanent effects. It is to be preached everywhere, *to every nation and tribe and language and people* (see 5:9, 7:9, 10:11, 11:9, 13:7, 17:15). This is one of John's favourite phrases, describing the extent of the Christian mission. With minor variations, it comes seven times in the book of Revelation – another heptad.

7. *The angel spoke in a loud voice*, so that he would be heard throughout the earth. He called on people *to fear God and to give him glory*. Christ told his disciples to fear God (Lk 12:4-5), and those who have never responded to the gospel have far more reason to fear God than those who know him. They are not only to fear him but also to give glory to him. One day they will have to do this anyway, on bended knee, but it will be of no benefit to them unless they obey voluntarily before then (11:13, Phil 2:9-11). Two reasons why everyone should fear and glorify God are *because the hour of his judgement has come*, and *because he created heaven and earth, the sea and the springs of water*, and is therefore *worthy of worship*. The true God is awe-inspiring, for he is the great Creator and he will be our Judge.

8. *Another angel, a second one, followed* the first. His announcement is, *"Fallen, fallen is Babylon the great!"* This is the first of six mentions of this city, and each time it is called *great*. Babylon symbolises the communities of proud and worldly people who live in indifference and opposition to God (Gen 11:1-9). Babylon's fall had been predicted from of old (e.g. Jer 51:7-9), and the reason given for it is her corrupting influence. *She has made all nations drink of the wine of the wrath of her fornication.* The worldly spirit represented by Babylon infects all peoples with idolatrous impurity, and this worldliness in turn brings on them the wrath of God (Jer 25:15). Many people raise their cups and drink the wine of Babylon's fornication only to discover that they are drinking the wine of God's wrath.

9. *Another angel, a third, followed them.* He too *cried in a loud voice*. He too had a message about God's judgement, and it was about *those who worship the beast and its image, and receive a mark on their foreheads or on their hands* (13:16).

10. Such people *will also drink the wine of God's wrath, poured unmixed into the cup of his anger*. The Greek words *thumos* and *orge* are used here for the anger and wrath of God. The first implies a passionate outburst and adds an appropriate tone to John's vivid vision, while the second denotes anger that is prompted by a settled opposition to evil. John is saying that God's anger will be *unmixed* with any favourable dispositions. It will be totally unmitigated. As a result, those who worship the beast *will be tormented with fire and sulphur in the presence of the holy angels and in the presence of the Lamb* (Isa 34:8-10). Their fate is terrible.

Leon Morris writes, "This is to be taken symbolically but seriously. The modern vogue of dispensing with hell has no counterpart in Revelation. John is quite sure that the consequences of sin will follow sinners into the life to come. Here on earth they may rejoice over their misdeeds. There they will suffer for them". Also, just as some of the suffering of God's people in this life is public, so the suffering of the impenitent will be public in the life to come. It will be viewed with sadness by the holy angels and even by the Lamb (Lk 12:9). As Julian Love put it in his Layman's Bible Commentary, "The deepest sting that an embittered conscience is dealt is that it must suffer while utter purity looks on".

11. How long will this torment last? *The smoke of their torment goes up forever and ever.* It is not the *torment* that goes *on* forever, but the *smoke* of it that goes *up* forever. In the Bible, rising smoke means accomplished destruction. After the destruction, only smoke remains, a reminder of God's complete and just triumph over evil. It is a reference to the destruction of Sodom and Gomorrah, after which dense smoke rose from the land for centuries. It is in this life that *there is no rest day or night for those who worship the beast and its image, and for anyone who receives the mark of his name.* Worshipping the beast may make you wealthy and it may bring you power and influence, but it will not give you peace and you will not sleep well. There is no rest day or night for these unhappy people. Only Jesus Christ can give anyone true rest (Mt 11:28-30).

12. John wants all of God's people to realise that these visions of the judgement are given for a purpose. *Here is a call for the endurance of the saints.* To see the fate of the wicked will help them endure to the end, and so be saved (Mk 13:13). It is vitally important to be numbered among *those who keep the commandments of God and hold fast to the faith of Jesus.* John is focusing on obedience and trust. The saints are to trust and obey, for there's no other way to be happy in Jesus.

13. Once again *John hears a voice from heaven.* It says, "*Write this: Blessed are the dead who from now on die in the Lord*". John is told to write this in his book. It is the second of seven blessings in Revelation (the others are in 1:3, 16:15, 19:9, 20:6, 22:7 and 22:14). Leon Morris wrote that "God's people may be grossly maltreated even up to and including the death penalty. But they, and not their tormentors, remain blessed". Because this beatitude has been written, *from now on* they may be encouraged by it. God the Holy Spirit now steps in with one of his rare interventions in this book. "*Yes*", says the Spirit, "*they will rest from their labours, for their deeds follow them*". The word *labour* here means "work to the point of painful weariness". It is not that work has ceased in heaven, but rather that pain no longer exists. It is worth noting that their deeds follow them to heaven: this gives dignity to all the work done by God's people.

14. Three angels have announced the judgement (v 6-11). Two comments about it have been made (v 12-13). *Then John looked, and there was a white cloud, and seated on the white cloud was one like the Son of Man, with* *a golden crown on his head, and a sharp sickle in his hand!* The crowned figure was seated on a *white* cloud. This colour is associated with God in the book of Revelation, but the figure is not necessarily Christ. We are told that he is someone *like* the Son of Man, so he may be a mighty angel. John found it difficult to distinguish between certain angels and Christ (19:9-10, 22:8-9). It is unlikely that Christ would have received commands from another angel (v 15). Moreover, he himself had taught that it would be the angels who would collect the harvest (Mt 13:39, 41).

15. *Another angel,* the fifth of seven in this chapter, *came out of the temple.* He had been in the presence of God and was told that the moment had arrived, so *he called with a loud voice to the one who sat on the cloud, "Use your sickle and reap, for the hour to reap has come, because the harvest of the earth is fully ripe".* In antiquity the sickle was the instrument used for reaping the grain harvest.

16. *The one who sat on the cloud* obeyed the command. He *swung his sickle over the earth, and the earth was reaped.* This probably refers to the harvest of souls, after which the weeds would be separated from the wheat (Mt 13:30, 38, 40-43). The weeds would be burned, but the wheat would be taken to God's barn.

17. John has not spelt out the fate of the weeds, because he wants to use another image to describe it. He therefore moves on, from the harvest of the wheat to the vintage of the grapes. *Then another angel came out of the temple in heaven, and he too had a sharp sickle.* We are about to be told the fate of the wicked.

18. *Then another angel,* the seventh in this series, *came out from the altar.* The altar is where the prayers of the saints are offered, and the consequent judgement then begins (8:3-5). Leon Morris wrote that the judgement is God's final answer to the prayers and sufferings of his saints. This seventh angel *has authority over fire,* the fire that will consume the wicked (20:15). *He called with a loud voice to him who had the sharp sickle, "Use your sharp sickle and gather the clusters of the vine of the earth, for its grapes are ripe".* A sickle was not used in viticulture, but John uses its grim overtones to alert us to the coming retribution (Joel 3:13).

19. The punishment of the wicked is now vividly depicted by John, who uses the prophetic image of God's wine press (Isa 63:1-6). *So the angel* swung his sickle over the earth and gathered the vintage of the earth, and he threw it into the great wine press of the wrath of God. The impenitent will be like grapes being pressed.

20. And the wine press was trodden outside the city. At this stage John does not tell us who did the treading, though he will later (19:15-16). Nor does he tell us the name of the city, but it may well be the New Jerusalem, which has a repository for the corpses of the wicked just outside it (Isa 66:24). And blood flowed from the wine press, as high as a horse's bridle, for a distance of about two hundred miles. In Greek the distance is written down as 1,600 stadia. This number is four squared multiplied by ten squared. Four is the number of the earth (7:1), which is the dwelling of the wicked (3:10, etc.), and ten is a number of completeness. Leon Morris writes that "Blood stretching for 1,600 stadia thus stands for the complete judgement of the whole earth and the destruction of all the wicked".

Meditation: Seven Visions about the Judgement

(a) How we should live in the light of the coming judgement (v 6-7). The hour of God's judgement has come. The Greek word for *judgement* means separating or sifting the true from the false. If we are true, this will show in our lives as we fear God and give him glory. There is great blessing in this life for those who fear God (Ps 128), and there is something deep within us which longs that all the glory may be given to the one to whom it is due (Ps 115:1). Because he created heaven, earth and the waters, people are to worship God as the great Creator (Acts 14:15).

(b) Worldly idolatry, with all its impurity, is fallen (v 8). It is symbolised by the worldly and adulterous city of Babylon. Its fate is deserved, decided and definite. So certain is it that the prophetic past tense is used: "Fallen, fallen is Babylon the great!" Her greatest sin was to infect all nations with her worldly allure: the desire of the flesh, the covetousness of the eyes, and the pride in riches. The world and its desire are passing away, but those who obey God live forever (1 Jn 2:16-17).

(c) The punishment of the wicked will be severe and terminal (v 9-11). Evil may at times seem to have the upper hand, but its triumph will be short-lived. It is a struggle for John to put across a most fearful and final reality which words cannot describe. Those who disdain Christ and instead give themselves devotedly to

the beast will drink the wine of God's righteous anger poured out in its full strength, not moderated or lessened in any way by his grace or mercy. They will suffer the punishment of painful and permanent destruction in the presence not only of the holy angels, but also of Christ himself, the Lamb of God. He died to take away their sins, but they contemptuously rejected his loving favour.

(d) **Those who persevere to the end will be saved** (v 12). The trials and sufferings inflicted on God's people by Satan, the beast and the false prophet are a difficult test which could discourage them. The judgement is certain to come to evildoers, and ultimate vindication is also certain for the godly. They are both scheduled to happen at the end, at a time which God has appointed. Although sometimes their final fulfilment may seem unlikely, its certainty may be apprehended by faith. This is the hope of godly people, and it is a sure anchor for their souls (Heb 6:19).

(e) **God's people die well** (v 13). They may die as martyrs. They may labour under adverse circumstances and see little fruit. They may give their lives to Christ and the gospel, but be sidelined by false teachers, who detest them because they speak the truth. They may be part of that rare miracle, a good church (2:8-11, 3:7-13), and if so, they will feel the full weight of opposition from the loveless and worldly establishment. It may seem that they have been conquered by the beast and yet, in spite of the outward appearances, God's blessing rests on them. Whatever their circumstances may be, as they die they will know where they are heading. There will be no more tiresome battles with the many-headed beast for them. In the life to come their good deeds will follow them; each and every one will be rewarded.

(f) **The harvest of the earth** (v 14-16). History is not ruled by a meaningless fate that leads nowhere. God is controlling it, and under his hand it is moving towards a climax. By the time this arrives, all people will have made their decision: either to lose their life for Christ and for the sake of the gospel, or to devote it to the worship of the beast. It is then that an angel will announce that "the hour to reap has come, because the harvest of the earth is fully ripe". If we who are followers of Christ firmly resolve to live for his glory, this will accelerate the end.

(g) **The gathering of the vintage** (v 17-20). This is not a preview of the final judgement. That will come later (20:11-15). Here we have Christ's return in glory to wind up this present age and to "tread the wine press of the fury of the wrath of God the Almighty" (19:15). Interestingly, Christ will do this work of treading the grapes of wrath on his own and unaided (Isa 63:3). This terrible and inevitable retribution, perfectly just and fully deserved, will take place "outside the city", perhaps because Christ's own blood was shed "outside the city" (Jn 19:20, Heb 13:12-13). It is the eschatological punishment of all those people who have been wicked, spurned Christ's blood and remained impenitent. It will fully and finally destroy every vestige of evil and hostility to the reign of God.

XXXVI
Further Thoughts about the seven significant Signs

In chapters 12-14 we have been studying seven significant signs: the woman and the dragon, the overthrow and conquest of the dragon, the fearsome and intense spiritual warfare, the worldly beast from the sea, the ecclesiastical beast from the earth, the Lamb on Mount Zion, and seven brief visions of the coming judgement. John has presented us with some vivid and memorable images. In this section we shall recapitulate some of them, and consider their bearing upon the state of the church in certain well-off countries in the 21st century.

(a) An image of hatred: the dragon's attempt to devour the child (12:3-5). The dragon hates the people of God, but this is only a side effect of his real hatred, which is directed towards Christ and, ultimately, towards God. The bitterness of his hatred is such that he tried hard to devour the new-born Christ child, but failed. He then tried to destroy Christ during the years of his ministry, and the time came when he thought he had succeeded. It proved to be the time of his own defeat.

(b) An image of defeat: the great dragon is thrown down (12:7-10). After Christ had triumphed over him on the cross, there was no longer a place for the dragon in heaven, so he and his fellow fallen angels were cast down. Christ had earlier looked ahead to this event when he said, "I watched Satan fall from heaven like a flash of lightning!" (Lk 10:18). It was while he hung helplessly on the cross that Christ disarmed the fallen angelic rulers and authorities. It was while the Lamb was being slaughtered that he made a public example of Satan and his henchmen, triumphing over them in his time of greatest weakness (Col 2:15).

(c) An image of encouragement: God's people conquer the dragon (12:11). It is amazing that God gives sinners like ourselves a role to play in the

conquest of evil. Our sanctification is incomplete, and yet we are enabled, thanks to the blood of the Lamb which means the completed work of Christ on the cross, to overcome the devil who slanders Christians. We are also enabled to pray and speak out so that the devil will relinquish his hold on the lives of unbelievers. We do this by the word of our testimony concerning Christ. We are called to devote our lives to the supreme adventure of serving him and passing on the good news about him.

(d) An image of growth under highly unfavourable conditions: the place of nourishment in the wilderness (12:6, 14). We shall grow as strong and as tall as an oak tree provided that, like an oak tree, our roots are spread as deep and wide as our branches are high and leafy. The secret of the oak lies in its roots, and its roots are invisible. The place of nourishment should be our church, but if Christ and the cross are not clearly preached there, we may have to find our nourishment in a less obvious way. Nothing can stop us from meeting Christ on our own or with a like-minded friend. God's principal way of speaking to us is through his word. As we read it, he feeds us, and then we respond in prayer.

(e) An image of wounded pride: the devil has come to the earth with great wrath (12:17). He lost his greatest battle, and also the war, just when he thought he had won. His fury is such that in the present he can only think of stealing, killing and destroying. He vents his anger on Christ's people, many of whom will be called to suffer as Christ himself did. The devil's main henchman is the beast, who has been given permission to conquer and even kill those whose testimony is finished. If you or I are given the privilege of suffering because we have done what is right, we shall most certainly receive God's approval.

(f) An image of arrogant, unrestrained verbal abuse: the blasphemies uttered by the beast (13:5-6). You can tell when church leaders are motivated by the spirit of the beast when they blaspheme God's name by denying either his holiness or his love, or when they blaspheme the saints, in whose hearts God is pleased to dwell. They accuse the godly of being unloving because they do not tolerate what God has called evil. False teachers can end up by referring to good as evil, and to evil as good. This is perilously similar to the unforgivable sin (Mk 3:22-30).

(g) An image of falsehood: the priestly role of the false prophet (13:12-15). It performs miraculous signs, even causing fire to come down from

heaven to earth in the sight of all. It uses these signs to deceive people into making an image of the beast. It then animates the image of the beast so that it speaks out compelling everyone to worship it. Anyone who refuses to worship the image of the beast is liable to be killed. Likewise, when the false prophet begins to infiltrate a church, the saints in that church will inevitably begin to feel uncomfortable and uneasy. If they do not conform, they will be deeply hurt by being marginalised, and then they will see their church gradually slip into error and spiritual adultery.

(h) An image of complete inability to please God: the mark and number of the name of the beast (13:16-18). The false prophet causes the godless inhabitants of the earth to be marked with the number of the beast, 666, so that in every way they fall short of the glory of God, symbolised by 777. The false prophet also has power to prevent any who refuse to be marked on their foreheads in this way from giving and receiving good things. They will be forced to flee into the wilderness of suffering, where they will find a place in which God will nourish them.

(i) An image of fire and brimstone: the terrible judgement of those who worship the beast (14:9-11). Fire and sulphur used to be translated "fire and brimstone", and they present such a vivid picture of the judgement that they are out of fashion nowadays. They are associated with the Victorian years, but in fact they should be linked to all the historic revivals of true religion that have taken place in the British Isles. Preachers are now strongly advised never to mention the judgement and – surprise, surprise – we have no more British revivals. We need to remember that no one has ever preached the terrors of hell as starkly as Jesus Christ during his three years of ministry. Therefore preachers who in their sermons avoid any mention of hell and judgement dishonour Christ, who said that heaven and earth would pass away, but his words would never pass away (Mk 13:31). It is a fact that in the Sermon on the Mount alone, he spoke about hell and judgement no less than eight times (Mt 5:20, 22, 29, 30; 7:13, 19, 21-23, 27). Furthermore, the large majority of his parables were parables of sifting and of judgement.

(j) An image of light shining in darkness: how God's people stand out. They are completely different from "those who live upon the earth" and do not belong to God. They keep the commandments of God and hold the testimony of Jesus (12:17). From the foundation of the world their names

have been written in the book of life of the Lamb that was slaughtered (13:8). They have faith in God, and so they endure (13:10). They have the Lamb's name and his Father's name written on their foreheads, and this reflects the way they think (14:1). They steer clear of idolatry and thereby remain chaste for their marriage with the Lamb, following him wherever he goes. They are redeemed from mankind as first fruits dedicated to God and the Lamb (14:4). They are completely straightforward in their speech, and therefore they are blameless before God (14:5). They endure, because they keep God's commandments and hold fast to the faith of Jesus (14:12). Whatever the outward appearance of their death, they are greatly blessed because they die in the Lord. After death they will no longer suffer hurts inflicted on them by the ungodly, and all their good deeds will follow them (14:13).

Meditation: How vulpine Speech is made to sound sheepish

It is not easy for God's people to come to terms with the truth that "when they have finished their testimony, the beast that comes up from the bottomless pit will make war on them and conquer them and kill them" (11:7). It seems strange that the beast is "allowed to make war on the saints and to conquer them" (13:7). It is a fact of experience that, once they are strong in faith and in the scriptures, many of God's saints are taken out of the field of play and forced to be spectators of the spiritual conflict. They are no longer given the opportunity to bring God's word to others. At best, they become unacknowledged prayer warriors.

Their sidelining is part of a remarkable take-over process which is well under way today in first-world countries like the United Kingdom. False teachers have wormed their way into many churches. They stress the love of God at the expense of his holiness, and do so to such an extent that a tolerance of false-hood permeates the atmosphere of many churches. It then becomes possible and even natural for the false teachers to marginalise those who are faithful to Christ and his word, accusing them of intolerance and lack of love towards those who hold different views. The godly are made to feel uncomfortable and unwanted. There are now no meaningful roles for them to play in their church. Everything is different from what it was in the good old days – the preaching and even the catchphrases.

The preaching is notable for being completely different from what it was fifty years earlier. This is because the preachers shrink from declaring to their hearers the whole purpose of God, and are very selective when it comes to preaching from Bible passages. Among the absolute no-nos are the truths of God's radiant holiness, the universality of human sin, the inevitability of judgement, the gift of our salvation through Christ's death on the cross, Christ's great commission that we should go and make disciples of all nations, God's requirement that we should be holy just as he is holy, and the future return of Christ in glory.

It is quite a stupendous miracle when anyone converts to Christ today. Sin is being reduced to a sense of ennui and of estrangement from other people, with no mention of the way it brings forth the wrath of God. The righteousness that can be ours thanks to the cross is being reduced to an inner healing such as that which is on offer from psychotherapists. All the humiliation and pain that Christ endured in his passion and crucifixion are reduced to a pointless and empty expression of divine love. The coming judgement is not mentioned and when pressed, today's clergy reply that although judgement is necessary, and God must punish certain people like Hitler, it is vital nowadays to be tolerant of other people's views and not to be unloving. But how can the Holy Spirit convict the world of sin when the seriousness of human sin is always minimised in sermons? How can he convict the world of the possibility of righteousness if the revealed righteousness of God is never preached? How can he convict the world of judgement if people remain unaware of its inevitable approach? In many of today's churches the good news of Christ is not preached. Furthermore, there can be no good news if the bad news is not understood first. If neither the bad news about people nor the good news about Christ is being preached, what are we being given in sermons today?

(i) Today's message is not good news for unbelievers, but false news that God's people need to change their beliefs in order to fit into today's world. The church rightly seeks to help people with their economic and social problems, but it argues that all in the church should demonstrate Christian love by always empathising with the fringe, even if those in the fringe live unholy lives and have no intention of turning away from their sin or of facing the cost of following Christ.

(ii) The message preached today is not the truth about how hard it is to swim against the current of this world, but the half-truth that there has been a coming together by Christians of different backgrounds resulting in unity and purpose. But the unity that Christ enjoined among his disciples (Jn 17:21) was to be based on truth (Jn 17:8, 17), holiness (Jn 17:15-17, 19) and mission (Jn 17:18,

21, 23). It was never Christ's will that unity should include compromise with the worldly spirit of the beast and the deceitfulness of the false prophet. Unity with the devil's henchmen and their followers is not Christian unity. There can be no reality or lasting encouragement in a message of "Peace, peace!" when there is no peace.

(iii) The message preached today is not about our obedience which proves that we love Christ (Jn 14:15, 21), but about the feel-good factor we may enjoy if we have a tolerant disposition. We are advised against reading the Bible in case this makes us judgemental. Instead of encouraging each other to follow the truth, which may be seen as negative, we are urged to be happy and to go with the flow.

(iv) The message preached today about those who are persistently disobedient to God is not that they are under his wrath and will be judged, but that God will find a way to forgive everyone. This is the heresy called universalism. The Bible consistently teaches otherwise. Those who believe in Christ have eternal life, but those who disobey Christ will not see life, for the wrath of God remains on them (Jn 3:36). They will drink the wine of God's wrath poured unmixed into his cup.

XXXVII

15:1-8 The Angels with the seven last Plagues

John has already confronted us with God's judgements, both temporal and final. On several occasions he has made it plain that God not only intervenes in human history, but that he will one day bring this age to an end. His judgements cannot be resisted. John now uses the imagery of seven angels pouring out the contents of seven golden bowls in order to present God's temporal judgements to us once again, but this time he stresses their finality. These are the *last* plagues, for with them the wrath of God will reach its end (v 1). They may, however, occur at any time during the period between Christ's first and second comings. As William Hendriksen put it, "Whenever in history the wicked fail to repent in answer to the initial and partial manifestation of God's anger in judgements, the *final* effusion of wrath follows". Before proceeding to describe these last plagues, John stresses God's majestic sovereignty over the whole process of history.

1. John the seer again sees. He writes, *I saw another portent in heaven, great and amazing.* This sign stands out among all the signs that he saw, and John will soon reuse the adjectives he employs to describe it as he turns to consider the deeds of God (v 3). But first he tells us about the nature of this portent. It concerns *seven angels with the seven plagues.* John has already used the word *plague* in 9:18, 20 and 11:6, but these seven plagues have a certain finality about them, because *they are the last, for with them the wrath of God is ended,* for it has reached its target.

2. John *saw what appeared to be a sea of glass mixed with fire.* He has seen this sea of glass before, in front of the throne of God (4:6), but this time it was *mixed with fire,* for it was going to reveal the wrath and judgement of God. This may be another reminder of the Exodus, a kind of heavenly Red Sea which the godly have crossed, but which will now proceed to drown their persecutors. John sees the godly, and describes them as *those who had conquered the beast and its image and the number of its name.* Their struggle against the beast consisted of refusing to pay homage to its image, and rising above the persistent falling short that is the consequence of being marked with the number of its name. The evil forces were unable to defeat the godly, who now *stand beside the sea of glass with harps of God in their hands.* In heaven the musical instruments are even more sonorous and distinctive than on earth, for they are made by God (1 Thess 4:16).

3. John listens to the godly playing their harps; they *sing the song of Moses, the servant of God, and the song of the Lamb.* There are two songs of Moses, whose lyrics are found in Exodus 15:1-18 and Deuteronomy 32:1-43. The former was a victory song after the drowning of the Egyptian army during the Exodus; the latter was a judgement song. Both may have helped to inspire the heavenly song we find here (Deut 32:4 is echoed by the song's beginning in verse 3b, and Ex 15:11 by its continuation in verse 4a). The heavenly song is described as being *of Moses and of the Lamb,* in order to indicate the harmony between the different parts of God's revelation. Moses and Christ are in complete agreement (Mt 5:17-19), just as the law was our disciplinarian until Christ came, so that we might be justified by faith (Gal 3:24). Moses is the servant of God just as Christ was prophetically called the servant of the Lord (Isa 52:13-53:12). The great deliverance that God provided

under Moses is the pattern or type of the greater deliverance that God provided through his Lamb. The song sung by the godly celebrates both. It begins with the words, *"Great and amazing are your deeds, Lord God the Almighty! Just and true are your ways, King of the nations!"* Here John is probably drawing on the Psalms, where God's deeds are described as great and amazing (e.g. Ps 111:2, 139:14), and his ways as just and true (Ps 145:17, 18:30). The inhabitants of the earth may marvel at the beast and its wonders, but they are little more than trifling distractions. It is the deeds and ways of God the King that are truly marvellous, for he is the *Almighty Lord God*, whose power is incomparable, and also the *King of the nations*, whose rule is characterised by perfect justice and truth. At a time of tribulation John loves to dwell on God's universal sovereignty (Jer 10:6-7, 10).

4. In view of God's incomparable greatness John marvels at the possibility that anyone might fail to give him the reverence that is his due: *"Lord, who will not fear and glorify your name?"* The song ends with three causal clauses addressed to God, which explain why he is to be feared and glorified. The first is, *"For you alone are holy"* (1 Sam 2:2). Here John uses a Greek word that means "perfectly pure". The second is, *"All nations will come and worship before you"* (Ps 86:9, Mal 1:11), underlining the universality of God's rule. And the third is, *"For your judgements have been revealed"*. Here the judgements of God are his judicial sentences regarding the nations. They either pronounce mercy towards those who fear him and repent, or else condemnation towards those who persist in pride and impenitence. These judgements *have been revealed* (Ps 98:2), but many people – even in the church – disdain and ignore them, with disastrous consequences.

5. After hearing the heavenly song of the godly, John proceeds to describe a scene of imposing solemnity. Seven bowls filled with the wrath of God are about to be distributed to seven angels. *John looked, and the temple of the tent of witness in heaven was opened.* The tent of witness was where Moses and Aaron ministered during the Exodus. In it dwelt the very presence of God. Its heavenly counterpart is the divine throne room, from where God will now reveal his judgements to all.

6. As soon as it had been opened, *out of the temple came the seven angels with the seven plagues.* Leon Morris observed that "These plagues thus

come with the fullest divine sanction, for they are brought by angels who have come from the very presence of God". John tells us in some detail how these seven angels were clothed: they were *robed in pure white linen, with golden sashes across their chests.* The pure white linen is indicative of the spotless purity of those who will pour out the divine wrath upon the world, and the golden sashes suggest that theirs is a priestly function. What is about to happen is in no way tainted by the passions of fallen and sinful human anger. Instead it arises out of a pure longing for justice.

7. The distribution of the bowls takes place. *Then one of the four living creatures gave the seven angels seven golden bowls full of the wrath of God, who lives forever and ever.* The everlasting God inhabits eternity (Isa 57:15) and is attended by four living creatures, who were introduced to us back in chapter 4, and appear seven times in the book of Revelation, another heptad (4:6-8, 5:6, 6:1, 7:11, 14:3, 15:7 and 19:4). They resemble a lion, an ox, a man and an eagle, but we do not know which one is in action here. At any rate, this living creature gave a bowl to each of the seven angels. The same word was used in 5:8 for the bowls filled with incense that represented the prayers of the saints. These prayers acted like a fuse that ignited the judgements of God, and now these bowls are filled with the wrath of God. F.F. Bruce noticed the contrast between bowls filled with the prayers of the saints and bowls filled with the wrath of God, "and yet the outpouring of wrath on the earth-dwellers is the response to those prayers" (6:10, 8:3-5). Leon Morris likewise wrote that "the prayers of God's people which seem so insignificant are important. They may initiate great divine judgements. They have a part to play in bringing about the final state of affairs".

8. At this point *the temple was filled with smoke from the glory of God and from his power.* In the Bible the glory of God is sometimes manifested in dense smoke (Ex 40:34-35, 1 Ki 8:10-11, Isa 6:4). The glory of God is also closely associated with his power, and this is especially appropriate in the book of Revelation, which speaks of his great might. *No one could enter the temple until the seven plagues of the seven angels were ended.* The holy presence of God is too dazzling even for the godly. If he was to mark iniquity on the last day, then who could possibly stand? But there is forgiveness with God, so that he may be feared (Ps 130:3).

Meditation: Where, O Death, is your Victory?

Leon Morris observed that "nothing evil can triumph over God's people". In the early church the day of martyrdom of the godly was called the day of their victory, while in medieval martyrologies it was called the day of their birth. For those who die in Christ, the day of death is the day of victorious rebirth. As William Barclay observed, "the real victory is not to live in safety, to evade trouble, cautiously and prudently to preserve life; the real victory is to face the worst that evil can do, and if need be to be faithful unto death". This little-known and greatly misunderstood chapter has some very important lessons to teach us.

(a) *These seven plagues are the last: with them the wrath of God is ended* (v 1). As John Stott thoughtfully pointed out, "The previous judgements (the seals and the trumpets) were partial; those of the bowls are final. It could be expressed thus: the eye of faith sees in the breaking of the seals the permissive will of God, in the blowing of the trumpets the reformative purpose of God, and in the pouring out of the bowls the retributive justice of God". Richard Bewes added, "We read now of the seven bowls with their portrayal of God's final judgement. No, we are not contemplating the last, universal and ultimate judgement here. What we are being warned of is the approach of judgements in history which are final in their nature, with no redress. These are the 'last' plagues because 'with them the wrath of God is ended'. They take the form of events that bring people's lives to an end. At that point there can be no further appeal and no intercession. This may be why no one may enter the temple to pray, until the judgements are complete".

(b) *What makes a wonderful song of worship* (v 3-4). Christ taught that the time would come when true worshippers would worship in spirit and truth, for God is seeking for worshippers such as these (Jn 4:23). George Eldon Ladd believed that "This song is one of the most moving expressions of faith in the entire biblical literature". The song of Moses was a song of praise to God because he delivered the Israelites from their Egyptian slave masters. The song of the Lamb is a song of praise to God for delivering true Christians from the hatred and hostility of the beast. The victors sing the song of Moses, the servant of God, *and* the song of the Lamb. This is a song of triumph which the saints of both the Old and the New Testaments know how to sing, because both rejoiced in the mighty deliverances of the same God. The victors sing with amazement of the utter inappropriateness of failing to fear and glorify God's name. Why, the very idea is ridiculous! For God alone is holy, he will be worshipped by people from all nations, and the news of his temporal and final judgements has been clearly revealed in the Bible.

(c) God's judgement is absolutely pure and holy (v 5-7). The pouring out of the seven last plagues is entrusted to seven angels who are robed in pure bright linen, with priestly golden sashes across their chests. One of the four guardians of the throne of God distributes the seven golden bowls full of the wrath of God, who lives forever and ever. All this means that God's judgement is *right*. Amazingly, some churchgoers in well-to-do countries feel free to disagree with God and the heavenly host. Phil Moore has perceptively written that "Although people who live in safety, luxury and peace complain that God should not send people to hell, those who live in war-torn or poverty-stricken lands generally do not. They tend to look heavenwards with eyes that have stared human wickedness in the face, and to cry out, *'Where is the God of justice?'* Many of the psalms were written in the face of injustice, and the writers plead with God passionately, forcefully and repeatedly that he might settle the score. I hope that you have not experienced such wickedness in your own life, but if you have, it is quite normal to cry out for God's retribution. All of the Christian martyrs did so, when the fifth seal was opened: 'Sovereign Lord, holy and true, how long will it be before you judge and avenge our blood on the inhabitants of the earth?' (6:10). Christ gives us good news that his vengeance is indeed coming".

(d) There is a time when intercessory prayer is no longer appropriate (v 2a, 8). The sea of glass is now mixed with fire. The smoke that fills the heavenly temple indicates the presence of God in all his glory and power. The time has come for him to carry out his judgement actively upon wickedness. Until the seven plagues are finished, no one may enter the temple. The time for the last plagues has come. No one can now stop God's hand. The time for intercession is past. It is interesting to note that in the book of the prophet Jeremiah there are three occasions when God instructed his servant not to pray for Judah (Jer 7:16; 11:14; 14:11). Things had deteriorated so much that the judgement of God was inevitable: nothing could prevent it. May God have mercy on us if similar circumstances now apply to our own country, and if the divine judgement it deserves has begun. God knows that many people even in the church have made up their minds to reject him. In his unapproachable majesty and power he has declared that this must end. Christ no longer knocks at the door. He is now acting in sovereign judgement.

XXXVIII

16:1-9 The first four Bowls of God's Wrath are poured out

One by one, the seven angels now proceed to pour out their bowls on the earth, and so the seven last plagues are released. The first four have some similarities with the judgements that followed the blowing of the trumpets, but they also have features of their own. The fourth plague has an unprecedented aspect which gives it a contemporary feel. Henry Swete pointed out that "while the first four trumpet judgements affect only a third of the earth, the sea, the fresh water supply and the lights of heaven, no limitation appears in the account of the seven plagues about to be described. They are not tentative chastisements, but punitive and final".

1. After the distribution of the bowls full of the wrath of God, *John heard a loud voice from the temple speaking to the seven angels*. The announcement that the seven last plagues were to be released was audible to anyone with ears to hear. It came from the temple, for it originated with God. Indeed, the speaker must have been God himself, since no one else could enter the temple until the seven plagues were ended (15:8). The voice said, *"Go and pour out on the earth the seven bowls of the wrath of God"*. There is a striking Old Testament parallel: "A voice from the temple! The voice of the Lord, dealing retribution to his enemies!" (Isa 66:6). Here the bowls were *phiales*, broad and flat like a soup plate. The wrath of God is his settled and unchanging anger caused by his unrelenting opposition to evil.

2. *So the first angel went and poured his bowl on the earth*. The angel obeyed God and carried out his command. There was a dramatic result. *A foul and painful sore came on those who had the mark of the beast and who worshipped its image*. These loathsome and malignant ulcers are reminiscent of the plague of boils in Egypt prior to the Exodus (Ex 9:8-12). Once again they do not affect the people of God, but only those men and women who, under the domineering influence of the beast, have given themselves over to opposing God and his people.

3. *The second angel poured his bowl into the sea*. Once again the result was clear and dramatic: *it became like the blood of a corpse* (Ex 7:14-21). Salty sea water became gloopy and livid. It felt unpleasant. It was toxic, *and every living thing in the sea died*. At the blowing of the second trumpet,

one third of the sea became blood, and one third of the living creatures in it died (8:9). But now *every* living thing in all the sea died, for these last plagues result in widespread death.

4. *The third angel poured his bowl into the rivers and the springs of water. And, like the sea, they also became blood.* At the blowing of the third trumpet, a third of the fresh waters became bitter wormwood (8:10-11). But at the pouring out of the third bowl, they all became blood. Fresh drinking water was now unavailable. On turning the tap, a viscous reddish liquid came out which was disgusting. With no water to drink, the future was bleak for the inhabitants of the earth (Ps 78:44).

5. *John then heard the angel of the waters speak.* The Jews believed that angels were responsible for specific areas of the creation. We have read about the angels of the winds (7:1) and the angel of fire (14:18), but in no other first century text is there a reference to the angel of the waters. He said, *"You are just, O Holy One, who are and were, for you have judged these things".* He describes God as being *just*, as befits the only being who is perfectly holy and who inhabits eternity. But what is the divine justice like? The angel addresses himself to this question.

6. God's justice is fair, since the punishment fits the crime: *"because they shed the blood of saints and prophets, you have given them blood to drink. It is what they deserve!"* Since they saw nothing wrong in shedding other people's blood, it is fitting that they should now have to drink blood. Leon Morris believed that this could mean that those who had shed innocent blood would later be caught up in fighting one another and shedding each other's blood, for the forces of evil do not present a united front: there are hatreds, divisions and strifes among them (17:16). Bloodshed leads to blood drinking, and bloodshed deserves this. There is often a grim and obvious aptness in the ill effects of an ill cause.

7. At this stage *the altar of God responds* (9:13). As we have seen, there is a link between the altar and the prayers of the saints (8:3), which are like the spark that ignites the judgements of God (8:5). And the altar agrees with what the angel of the waters had said: *"Yes, O Lord God, the Almighty, your judgements are true and just!"* The altar places its own emphasis on God's great *might*, and describes his judgements as being

true and *just*, the same adjectives used of God's ways by those who have conquered the beast (15:3).

8. *The fourth angel poured out his bowl on the sun*. Because of this *the sun was allowed to scorch people with fire*. This permission is a timely reminder that God controls the whole process of judgement, including the effects of the sun. In the early stages of judgement, some of the sunlight is darkened (8:12), but when the last plagues are poured out, the sun becomes an unrelenting fiery scourge.

9. *The inhabitants of the earth were scorched by the fierce heat*. We have yet to experience the extremes of global warming and climate change, but all the early signs are that they will be deadly and ruinous. Will people respond rightly to God as a result of the sun's scorching? Some of the inhabitants of the earth may learn to control carbon dioxide emissions, and some may adjust to a diet that contains less red meat and more fruit, salad and vegetables. These are good responses if they are accompanied by a change of heart towards God. What is the attitude of most people to him? We read that *they curse the name of God, who has authority over these plagues*. They curse the one who is forever blessed. They view white as black and refer to good as evil. Can such hard and embittered people change? No. *They do not repent or give him glory* (9:20-21).

Meditation: Not tentative Chastisements but final Punishments

Commentators have noticed both the similarities and the differences between the chastening judgements of the first four trumpets, and the respective last plagues of the first four bowls. All God-fearing Bible scholars put over the same thoughts, but express them in their own words, offering slightly different insights.

F.F. Bruce commented that "There is a remarkable parallelism between most of the seven trumpet-judgements of chapters 8-11 and the last plagues of chapter 16. In the first four of each series the earth, sea, fresh water and sun are respectively affected; but the judgements here are more severe than the 'trumpet' counterparts; where the former judgements affected one third of the area in question, these affect the whole". He also describes the resemblances between the last plagues and the plagues of Egypt, and observes, "Unpalatable as the work of judgement may be, it is inseparable from a moral universe. 'Is God unjust to inflict wrath on us?' asks Paul. 'By no means!' is his reply. 'For how then could God judge the world?' (Rom 3:5-6). Symbolical as the details of these plagues are, they denote terrible realities. More terrible than the plagues themselves, however, is the way in which those on whom they fall are only hardened in their impenitence".

As he wrote about the first four plagues John Stott also noted that "Talk about earth, sea, fresh water and sun has a modern sound in our era of environmental sensitivity. We are concerned about the earth's biodiversity, the plankton of the oceans, the availability of clean water and the preservation of the ozone layer to protect us from radiation and its harmful effects. This priority given to life on planet Earth is also a necessary preparation for the coming renewal of all things. As Bishop Paul Barnett has written, 'the destruction of the old heavens and earth is now being completed, clearing the way for the new creation of God'".

Richard Bewes astutely observed that we read here of incurable diseases (v 2), sea disasters (v 3), calamities in inland rivers (v 4-7), and drought and scorching (v 8-9). Are all the people who are struck by disease or natural disaster under the judgement of God? Or, for that matter, all those in countries plagued by drought? The answer must be No. Of course we all die one day. It is possible that in certain countries drought is the actual means by which some people's lives come to an end. In other countries it might be an environmental disease or a deadly virus. So what might for *some* be the catastrophe that brings the judgement of God to them, will for *others* prove to be the gateway that leads to eternal life with Christ beyond the grave. It is interesting that it is said of those who come out of the great ordeal that "they will thirst no more, and the sun will not strike them, nor any scorching heat" (7:13-16). We should therefore be thankful that it is God who is the judge, and not a fallen and flawed human being.

Tom Wright wrote that the point at issue in the first four plagues is fairly simple: "God will allow natural elements themselves (earth, sea, rivers and sun) to pass judgement on the human beings who have so grievously abused their position as God's image-bearers within creation. They are supposed to be looking after God's world, and caring for one another as fellow humans. But God will call the natural elements to turn on them and judge them for their wickedness". Those who selfishly disobey God's mandate to be fruitful and multiply, to fill the earth and subdue it, and to exercise a benevolent dominion over every living creature, will find that the earth and its creatures will hit back at them in irresistible fashion, which is exactly what they deserve.

We are now deep into judgement territory in the book of Revelation. We began with a terrifying glimpse of how people who rejected Christ will react on the great day when they finally realise that they have missed out on life, and must look into the face of the one whom they have disdained (6:12 17). Then we heard and saw the thunder and lightning, and felt the rumblings and the earthquake as the great day was dawning (8:5). The seven trumpets announced temporal judgements or tentative chastisements of a reformative nature (8:6-9:21), culminating in another display of thunder and lightning, of rumblings and an earthquake, and with some heavy hail added on for good measure (11:15-19). Before the seventh trumpet we saw the witnessing church come back to life. This striking portent was followed by another earthquake, after which some terrified people gave glory to the God of heaven (11:11-13). The last of the seven significant signs was itself a sevenfold vision of the coming judgement, with the grim news that the followers of the beast will drink the undiluted wine of God's wrath and then be tormented with fire and sulphur in the presence of the Lamb, after which the smoke of their torment will rise as a perpetual reminder that the rejection of God's grace and mercy will only lead to destruction (14:9-11). At the end of the age the wicked will be like grapes of wrath. They will be gathered and trodden down in the great wine press of the wrath of God (14:17-20). These have all been glimpses of the end, given to us as a warning so that we may respond to God's tentative chastisements, in order that we may escape from his final punishments.

We are now studying the pouring out of the seven last plagues. They are final. They are deadly signals of what will happen at the end. After these plagues we shall view the final judgement of that evil triumvirate, the world, the flesh and the devil (17:1-19:10, 19:17-20:10). In the middle of all this, Christ, who is the judge and the warlike rider with four names, will return in glory and consummate his victory (19:11-16). Last of all will be the great final judgement of all people before the great white throne (20:11-15). All of these judgements *must happen* because we live in a universe in which actions have consequences, and in which persisting in impenitence and in rejecting God's appointed way of righteousness is alto-gether unforgivable. But then, at the last, will come the fulfilment of all the hopes of God's people. It is not just a matter of evil being punished and destroyed. In the final winding up of all things, good will be rewarded and God's people will be vindicated (chapters 21 and 22). We must not miss out on this. It will be sheer bliss. There is some bad news here, because the reality is that things are bound to get worse before they get better. But there is also a lot of wonderfully good news, because when things get better they will be forever perfect. The victorious Lamb will be there with us, and we shall see him face to face.

XXXIX

16:10-21 The final three Bowls of God's Wrath are poured out

These last plagues are universal and deadly. They point us to God's over-throw of all that is evil. But that is not all. As Leon Morris wrote, "There is another point. Though there is stress on the severity of these plagues, we should not ignore the implied call for repentance. John keeps on pointing out that people reacted in the wrong way, refusing to repent of their evil". Instead, they cursed God (verses 9, 11, 21). All true followers of Christ will wish to participate in the universal appeal for every person to repent (Mk 1:14-15, Acts 17:30-31, 2 Pet 3:9). We shall all share in God's grief when the large majority respond badly to this appeal.

10. *The fifth angel poured his bowl on the throne of the beast.* He attacked the citadel of evil (2:13). The results were unexpected. *The kingdom of the beast was plunged into darkness* (9:2). In Exodus 10:21-23 a similar plague is described as "a darkness that could be felt". In this darkness *the people gnawed their tongues in agony.* We are not told what caused the pain, but it could have been ulcers from the first plague (v 2) or scorching heat from the fourth (v 9). In any case, they were in the dark and they were in great pain. The fifth trumpet plague was similar, with smoke from the bottomless pit darkening the sun and the air, and with those frightening locusts that tortured people with scorpion-like stings.

11. As previously when the fourth bowl was poured out, people reacted wrongly. *They cursed the God of heaven because of their pains and sores.* The inhabitants of the earth blasphemed the glorious God of heaven. Leon Morris wrote that they "could not recognise the majesty of heaven when they saw it". They were taken over by their pains and ulcers. As a result, *they did not repent of their deeds.* Not even agonising pain could awaken them to the reality of their situation.

12. John goes into greater detail as he describes what happened when *the sixth angel poured his bowl on the great River Euphrates.* The sixth

trumpet was also linked to this River, with its order to release the four avenging angels who were to kill one third of all people (9:13-15). In this case, the result of the pouring of the bowl was that *the river waters were dried up to prepare the way for the kings from the east.*

Just as at the Exodus the waters of both the Red Sea and the River Jordan were parted for the Israelites to cross (Ex 14:21-22, Josh 3:14-17), and just as King Cyrus diverted the waters of the Euphrates so as to enable his Persian army to enter Babylon and overthrow it, so in some way that is not explained, the great river would dry up to allow "the kings from the east" to cross it. John does not elaborate further on this, but he may have had the Parthians in mind. In his day people dreaded an invasion by them. They were seen as destructive agents on the far side of the Euphrates, on the north-east frontier of the Roman Empire. But something far worse was troubling John, namely the perversion of the minds of those in authority by destructive demonic powers, and he turns to consider this.

13. *John saw three foul spirits like frogs coming from the mouths of the dragon, the beast and the false prophet.* The false prophet is the same as the beast from the earth (13:11, and compare 19:20 with 13:14). The unclean spirits that emerge from the evil triumvirate are *like frogs*. This may be a reminder of the plague of frogs prior to the Exodus (Ex 8:3), but it is also saying that the words people find most evil and fearful are nothing more than the meaningless croaks of slimy and ugly creatures of the night, which in the end will achieve nothing that is lasting. The three spirits are lying spirits, like the one that enticed King Ahab into suicidal battle (1 Ki 22:19-23). But this time they are mesmerising most of the world.

14. They are lying spirits with power to deceive because *they are demonic spirits, performing signs.* They can work extraordinary and meaningful miracles that will lead people astray. We may learn from this that the dragon, the beast and the false prophet are engaged in a worldwide confidence trick (Mt 24:24). *They go abroad to the kings of the whole world, to assemble them for battle on the great day of God the Almighty.* They influence rulers and great thinkers, including worldly church leaders and theologians. Through them they hope to reach everyone on Earth, and gather them together for the final spiritual battle.

They think it will be their great day, but they are mistaken. It will prove to be the great day of God the Almighty (Isa 2:10-12, 17; 2 Pet 3:11-12). Leon Morris wrote, "This is the most resounding description of the last day. *Great* distinguishes it from lesser days. It is the day of *God*, not of man or of the antichrist. *Almighty* reminds us that even in the face of the might of all the world, God's power is supreme".

15. The narrative of the bowls is interrupted by an important interjection from Jesus Christ himself: *"See, I am coming like a thief!"* He had said similar words to the church at Sardis: "If you do not wake up, I will come like a thief, and you will not know at what hour I will come to you" (3:3). During his earthly ministry he had said, "If the owner of the house had known in what part of the night the thief was coming, he would have stayed awake and would not have let his house be broken into. Therefore you also must be ready, for the Son of Man is coming at an unexpected hour" (Mt 24:43-44). The point is that Christ will return in great power and glory to wind up this present age, "but about that day and hour no one knows, neither the angels of heaven, nor the Son, but only the Father" (Mt 24:36). The return of Christ will be unheralded and totally unexpected (1 Thess 5:2). It is because of this that Christ now adds, *"Blessed is the one who stays awake and is clothed, not going about naked and exposed to shame"*. He exhorts us to remain watchful for his return (Mk 13:32-37, Lk 21:34-36), but also to stay *clothed*. If we are justified, we have been clothed with garments of righteousness (Isa 61:10), so at the critical moment we should not be unprepared, or we may be found naked and exposed to shame like those who are stout of heart and ungodly (Amos 2:16).

16. Returning to the demonic spirits of the dragon, the beast and the false prophet, *they will assemble the kings* and their people for battle *at the place that in Hebrew is called Harmagedon.* John says that it is a Hebrew word, which could mean the mountain of Megiddo, but there is no such mountain. In Old Testament times some battles were fought at or near the plain of Megiddo (Judg 5:19, 2 Ki 23:29, 2 Chron 35:22). Harmagedon appears only here in the Bible. More familiarly known to us today as Armageddon, it seems certain that John means us to take it symbolically and not literally. It represents the decisive battle in the spiritual war between good and evil. There are dark times

when the forces of evil will seem to have an overwhelming numerical advantage, but however hopeless the prospects for God's people may appear, we are to continue trusting in God. It is by faith that we shall obtain Christ's victory. We shall not conquer Satan by our great exertions, but by the blood of the Lamb and by the word of our testimony (12:11). Then, with our own eyes, we shall see the overthrow of evil.

17. We now reach the climax. John tells us that *the seventh angel poured his bowl into the air.* The air is the dwelling place of evil spirits (9:2-3, Eph 2:2), who are being attacked in their own element. Significantly, *a loud voice came out of the temple, from the throne, saying, "It is done!"* The voice was probably that of God himself (15:8, 16:1), or of Christ. It spoke one word in the Greek, *gegonen,* which means "Done!" (21:6). In its context (chapters 15-20 of Revelation) this must be a reference to God's judgement. It has finally been administered once for all. Its previous manifestations (the seals and the trumpets) were partial, but now God's judgement has appeared in its final form, the bowls filled with the last plagues, which have been poured out to punish evil. God is declaring that this time he has answered the innumerable prayers for justice that have been offered at his altar (6:9-10, 8:3-4). He is now able to reply to his people, "You have been patiently asking me to do something. Here you are, *it is done!*"

18. Immediately the repercussions were evident. *There came flashes of lightning, rumblings, peals of thunder, and a violent earthquake.* Some natural phenomena, particularly earthquakes, are symbols of divine judgement (6:12; 8:5; 11:13, 19), but this particular earthquake was extraordinary. *It was such as had not occurred since people were upon the earth, so violent was it.* This was a solemn moment.

19. *The great city was split into three parts.* This "great city" represents worldly people in organised community and in opposition to God (11:8). It symbolises the pride of human civilisation and achievement, and the folly of those who put their trust in people rather than in God. This "great city" is now dealt a shattering blow. It splits up into three parts, which stand for its complete break-up. And with its disintegration, *the cities of the nations also fell.* The consequences were global. *God remembered great Babylon* (the symbolic name for the great city), *and gave her the wine-cup of the fury of his wrath.* Leon Morris' comment was

apt: "This speaks of utter destruction. It does not say that all people will be killed. They are yet to face Almighty God for judgement. But this bowl means the fragmentation of earthly life. John leaves us in no doubt that Babylon is to receive the most wholehearted opposition conceivable from an all-powerful and all-holy God". It will be the end of all happiness that depends on the material things of this world.

20. The reverberations continue. *Every island fled away, and no mountains were to be found.* We have already seen these two physical cataclysms as harbingers of the final judgement (6:14). Islands are peaceful havens in the ocean of trouble, but they have all fled away – none are left. Mountains are there to be climbed and at their summits new visions are granted – but no mountains remain after the huge earthquake, only endless dreary and dry plains, nothing to please the eye.

21. There is a further detail of the devastation. *Huge hailstones, each weighing about a hundred pounds, dropped from heaven on people.* Have you ever putted the shot? Imagine such shots falling from heaven. These metal spheres weigh 16 pounds. The hailstones John mentions are six times as heavy. Would they suffice to humble proud, ungodly people? Sadly, no. *They cursed God for the plague of the hail, so fearful was that plague.* For the third time in chapter 16 we read that people blasphemed God (v 9, 11 and here). It was, indeed, a fearful judgement, whose purpose was to bring forth repentance. But some people's hearts are harder than granite, and nothing on earth or even in heaven will soften them.

Meditation: Dark Forces gather together and are destroyed

What lessons may we learn from the fifth, sixth and seventh plagues?

(a) Fact: When the fifth angel pours out his bowl on the throne of the beast, the kingdom of the beast is plunged into darkness (v 10-11). This makes life utterly unbearable for the beast's followers. Things are already very bad, with their foul and painful sores, a lack of good food from the sea, no pure water to drink, and scorching burns inflicted on them by the sun. But now they are totally in the dark and unable to take any steps in any direction. They will lose the ability to see and react, and they have no guidance as to what to do. Who are they? They are the godless world and the false church, who now sit "in darkness and in gloom, prisoners in misery and in irons, for they [have] rebelled against the words of God, and spurned the counsel of the Most High" (Ps 107:10-11).

Lesson: We are to keep our eyes on the triune God, who is light and from whom comes light. God the Father revealed himself as the one who is our light and our salvation, so that if we fear him we need fear no one else (Ps 27:1). God the Son is the true light that enlightens everyone (Jn 1:9). The light shines in the darkness, and the darkness could not overcome it, although it tried to do so (12:4, Jn 1:5). Christ said that he was the light of the world (Jn 8:12; 9:5; 12:35, 46). God the Holy Spirit loves to shine his spotlight on Christ, glorifying him by revealing him to us (Jn 16:14). The Holy Spirit does this by means of the Bible. In the past he inspired all the scriptures (2 Tim 3:16-17), which testify to Christ. And now he illumines them so that we see Christ in them (Jn 5:39-40).

(b) Fact: Many people are being gathered together to oppose God (v 12-16). The great river has dried up, and so there is a scarcity of the spiritual refreshment from the living water that Christ offers (Jn 4:10, 13-14). People are afflicted by a sense of dryness and thirst (Lk 16:24), and this drives them to look for human solutions, which in turn opens the way for them to be deceived by manipulative propaganda from the dragon, the beast and the false prophet. And so they gather together for the great spiritual battle in the place that in Hebrew is called Armageddon, or Har-Magedon, which means Mount Megiddo. But Megiddo is not a mountain at all – merely an elevated town that looks over a great flat plain, on which great battles have been fought since time immemorial. The implication is that Armageddon is not a literal place but a symbolic one. Phil Moore suggested that we could think of Armageddon as "the battlefield where God judges". He also wrote that there have been several Armageddons throughout AD history leading up to one great Armageddon at the end of history, just as there have been several antichrists in history leading up to one great antichrist at the end (1 Jn 2:18). Armageddon is symbolic of those dark periods when Satan and his two beastly henchmen stir up the people of the earth to oppose and blaspheme Christ and his holy people.

Lesson: Christ himself warns us to stay awake and never to take off our clothes of righteousness (v 15). We know for sure that he will return in power and great glory, but we know nothing about the day when this will happen. Therefore, we must stay awake and be watchful so as not to be caught unprepared. In the words of Martin Luther, "we should live every day as if Christ died yesterday, rose from the grave today and is coming back tomorrow". Soldiers in the midst of the battle cannot afford to take some days off. Christ's interjection is very appropriate. The church is under severe attack. The big battle is approaching. The camp of the saints and the beloved city will be surrounded (20:7-9). We should trust in Christ unceasingly. We are promised that he will win a mighty victory.

(c) Fact: A terrible earthquake will destroy the world, and those who are proud and worldly will have to drink the wine-cup of the fury of God's wrath (v 17-21). Huge hailstones will fall on them, but instead of repenting and turning to Christ they will curse God. This is not a welcome message in any age. People love to think that there are three possible outcomes. They agree that there is a holy remnant consisting of people who know and love Christ, and whose longing is to trust and obey him. They concede that there are a few extremely evil people who deserve the ultimate punishment. But they believe that the majority of people, including themselves, will be accepted with all their sins by a merciful God on the last day. This is not what the Bible teaches. When it comes to salvation, there is no middle way. It is all or nothing. A few have entered by the narrow gate and are on the hard road that leads to life, but many have unknowingly passed through the wide gate and are on the easy road that leads to destruction (Mt 7:13-14). This is the climax of the Sermon on the Mount. Christ did not mention a third way.

Lesson: Because the coming judgement of God will be just and retributive, we are to fear God and flee from the coming wrath. Christ taught his followers not to *fear people*, who can only kill the body, but instead to *"fear him* who, after he has killed, has authority to cast into hell" (Lk 12:4-5). John the Baptist saw many religious leaders coming for baptism. He was troubled by their casual attitude to God's judgement, and said to them, "You brood of vipers! Who warned you to flee from the wrath to come?" (Mt 3:7). Paul wrote to one of his churches, who took seriously the warnings of coming judgement, and he commended them for turning to God from idols, to serve the living and true God, and to wait for his Son from heaven, whom he raised from the dead – Jesus, who rescues us from the wrath that is coming (1 Thess 1:10).

XL

17:1-8 The Whore of Babylon

A new character steps onto the stage of the book of Revelation. She is the whore of Babylon. If Babylon stands for ungodly worldliness, the whore symbolises the sinful lack of faith that characterises godless or worldly behaviour. She possesses great earthly splendour, but she is very evil and implacably opposed to the people of God. She may be compared to Jezebel in 2:20-23, but is at the very opposite pole to the woman of chapter 12 and the bride in chapters 21-22.

1. *Then one of the seven angels who had the seven bowls* (never mind which one) *came and spoke to me.* This description is repeated in 21:9. Here it concerns the judgement of the whore; there the reward for the Lamb's bride. As Leon Morris put it, "Out of God's final judgements there emerges a single purpose which includes both the destruction of evil and the appearance of the New Jerusalem". The angel said, *"Come, I will show you the judgement of the great whore who is seated on many waters".* Her judgement will duly be told in chapter 18, but first a few preliminary matters need to be discussed. This wicked woman was full of earthly glory (v 4), but by nature she was a spiritual prostitute. Deeply hostile to God, her chief objective was to seduce people from their proper allegiance to him. In the Old Testament the metaphor of sexual laxity is often used of God's people. Because they were God's bride, every unfaithfulness on their part was tantamount to adultery (Jer 3:9, Ezek 16:32). And when it was habitual, it was equivalent to prostitution (Isa 1:21, Jer 2:20, Ezek 16:15-16, Hosea 2:5).

   Here the whore is described as sitting *on many waters*, which represent peoples or nations of the world (v 15). In the Old Testament Babylon was addressed as "you who live by mighty waters" (Jer 51:13), partly because the Euphrates flowed through the city and it was the centre of a network of canals, and partly because Babylon had become a world empire that exercised dominion over many subject nations. In John's time Babylon had been replaced by Rome (v 9): the beast was the Roman Empire and the false prophet was the imperial cult.

2. *The kings of the earth* had business and cultural dealings with Babylon, but as far as John was concerned, *they had committed fornication with the whore.* Leon Morris wrote that "Their commerce with Rome involved them in the same basic attitude to the things of God as she had". Likewise *the inhabitants of the earth had become drunk with the wine of her fornication.* They were happy to be lulled into a drunken stupor, and they liked to boast that they had been seduced by her.

3. John had heard about the whore from the angel, but then he saw her. *The angel carried him away in the spirit into a wilderness, and he saw a woman sitting on a scarlet beast.* John was "in the spirit" (1:10) and therefore open to visions from God. He was taken into a wilderness, so as to be detached from the attitudes and worldview of the great city (12:6, 14). Previously he had seen her sitting on many waters, but now she was sitting on a scarlet beast, the one that rose out of the sea (13:1). She domineered many nations *and* she was an evil force supported by the beast. The beast was scarlet, a similar colour to that of the red dragon. It was the colour of splendour, but also the colour of sin (Isa 1:18). *The beast was full of blasphemous names.* Blasphemy characterised it (13:1, 5-6), and it blasphemed in fullest measure. As in 12:3, *it had seven heads and ten horns.*

4. The whore was royally *clothed in purple and scarlet*, which are colours of great splendour and magnificence. In particular, purple had imperial connotations. The purple dye was extracted at great cost from the shell-fish called *murex*. The whore was not only lavishly dressed, but also luxuriously *adorned with gold and jewels and pearls, holding in her hand a golden cup* (Jer 51:7). Might this be full of some refreshing drink, like cold water or chilled fruit juice? No, because we are told that it was *full of abominations and the impurities of her fornication.* Leon Morris wrote, "The attractive cup is revealed as no more than an enticement to people to join the glittering harlot in her evil ways. It is her means of seducing them from God. The picture is vivid, combining regal state with utter moral and religious corruption".

5. *On her forehead was written a name.* It is common in Revelation for people to have a name inscribed on their foreheads. God's servants were sealed in this way (7:3, 9:4), as were the servants of the Lamb (14:1, 22:4). But the same was true of the followers of the beast (13:16, 14:9 and 20:4). So here the harlot displays her name or nature on her forehead, for everyone to see. *It is a mystery: "Babylon the great, mother of whores and of earth's abominations".* She is herself a harlot, and she spawns other harlots and also every kind of evil abomination. William Barclay commented, "John's picture of Rome is not in the least exaggerated; it is actually restrained in comparison with some of the pictures which the Romans themselves drew of their own civilisation". It has been

rightly said that Roman civilisation, as a corrupting influence, rode on the back of Roman military power.

6. *John saw that the whore was drunk with the blood of the saints and the blood of the witnesses to Jesus.* It must have taken a considerable number of martyrdoms to make her drunk. She must have rejoiced in shedding the blood of many saints, just as a drunkard rejoices in his vintage wines. She must have drunk the blood of many witnesses. They had indeed borne costly witness, and had given their lives for the faith. She was not ignorant of the deeper issues. She knew what she had done, and was guilty before God. John writes of his sense of wonder. *When he saw her, he was greatly amazed.* He had been invited to look at the judgement of the whore (v 1). Instead he saw her marvellously arrayed, and perhaps was glimpsing the allurement of the worldly city for the first time.

7. All was about to be explained by the angel of the bowls, who *said to him, "Why are you so amazed? I will tell you the mystery of the woman, and of the beast with seven heads and ten horns that carries her"*.

8. He began by explaining the mystery of the beast. *"The beast that you saw was, and is not, and is about to ascend from the bottomless pit and go to destruction"*. Who was it who was and is not? First of all, in John's time – who was it that was about to ascend from the bottomless pit and go to destruction? *Nero Redivivus*. Leon Morris put it like this: "Nero lived out his evil life. He died. And in Domitian there appeared one who might be called a second Nero, Nero all over again. That the beast *was* means that he had put in an appearance on the earth. That he *is not* signifies that he is no longer in evidence. But this does not mean that the last has been heard of him". No, indeed – *He is about to ascend from the bottomless pit and go to final destruction*. But the second Nero would fail, and the Lamb would win. Secondly, at various stages during the Christian era, the beast is that satanic power that, having received a death-stroke in one of his heads and yet survived (13:3, 12, 14), returns and attacks the people of God with renewed fury (12:12).

Of course, not everyone understands this. It remains an insoluble conundrum to *the inhabitants of the earth, whose names have not been written in the book of life from the foundation of the world*. Robert Mounce wrote, "John is not teaching a form of determinism (according to 3:5

names may be blotted out of the book of life), but emphasizing the great distinction that exists between the followers of the Lamb and those who give their allegiance to the beast". The ungodly cannot discern God's eternal purpose, and *they will be amazed when they see the beast, because it was and is not and is to come.* The beast is utterly evil. It personifies the spirit of worldliness, and is able to amaze and fascinate people with a worldly disposition. We may well ask how people can be so stupid as to follow the beast. Here is the answer. They have been amazed, charmed and captivated.

There is more to come in the unravelling of the mysteries of evil with regard to the beast and the whore of Babylon. But this must wait until our next section.

Meditation: The golden Cup filled with Abominations and Impurity

(i) The fascination of evil. There is something strangely captivating about evil. It allures and entices. It is like a large serpent closing in on its motionless victim, which seems to be hypnotised. In fact there is no evidence to support the claim that snakes charm their prey, though small animals and birds do seem to suffer from a form of physical paralysis when a large snake like a cobra approaches them. In ancient times and in the Middle Ages it was thought that the serpent had charmed them. But now scientists believe that, if they are confronted by snakes, the victims are "frozen with fear". They are so terrified that they do not know what to do, and so they wait for the snake to consume them – but they have not been charmed by it. Something similar happens when we are tempted. Temptation cannot charm or hypnotise us, but if we are not abiding in Christ it can paralyse our weakened spiritual defences. The whore of Babylon may appear to us in three guises: the world, the flesh and the devil. Each of these can be very captivating.

(a) The world. Most people are on the easy road that leads to destruction. It seems natural to follow the course of this world. We do not like to be oddballs who stick out like a sore thumb. It is easier to go with the flow than to resist peer pressure. The desire of the eyes can be dauntingly strong. We see a beautiful and desirable object glittering in a shop window, and we know that we shall not be happy until we can say "It is mine". Boasting about what we have or what we do is also a major snare. We boast about our wisdom, our might and our wealth, when in fact we should not boast about any of them (Jer 9:23-24). We love to

meet important people and be noticed by them. We long more than anything else to be part of the fashionable crowd. We crave to be accepted by other people.

(b) The flesh. We all have appetites, which are given to us by God and are good. But we may abuse our appetites. When this happens we cease to be in control of them and they begin to take control of us. A gift of God, when abused, turns into a domineering monster. Hunger becomes gluttony, thirst becomes alcoholism, sex becomes lust, mental stimulation becomes drug addiction, physical exercise becomes hyperactivity, and rest becomes sloth.

(c) The devil. Was it he who committed the original sin of pride? (Isa 14:12-15). Certainly pride is the besetting sin of most people. The Lord hates pride. "He has a day against all that is proud and lofty, against all that is lifted up and high. The haughtiness of people shall be humbled and the pride of everyone shall be brought low; and the Lord alone will be exalted on that day" (Isa 2:12-17).

(ii) The disgusting contents of the whore's cup. She holds in her hand a golden goblet. Does it contain sparkling wine? No, in fact it is full of abominations and the impurities of her fornication. But the appearance of the goblet is fascinating, and we feel we shall be deeply satisfied with its contents. And so we drink and, ugh! It is disgusting, even worse than slimy excrement mixed with vomit.

The pleasures of the world are fleeting, and then comes the darkness of guilt and the awareness of separation from God. The glittering object in a shop window is not cheap, and yet we spend our hard-earned money on things that do not profit.

The desires of the flesh promise fulfilment and joy, and indeed they do provide a temporary thrill in the very short term. But it is all deceit. Twisted appetites are insatiable hounds that tear away at our soul. In the end there is little if any pleasure and, as with a sugar-coated pill, there is an awful after-taste.

The devil promises power, influence and adulation. He offers us pre-eminence, if only we first bow down and worship him. He wants us to be proud of our own achievements. But the reality is that our pride will make us ugly. Our life will be unsatisfying when our self is at the centre and we are trapped in the dark little dungeon of our own ego. If our concern is the growth of our kingdom, our lives will slowly wilt; but if we pray "Your kingdom come", then we shall be fulfilled.

(iii) Victory over temptation. Christ was tempted just as we are (Lk 4:1-13). How did he emerge victorious? What were the secrets of his success?

(a) He loved God. He loved his Father with all his heart, soul, mind and strength (Mk 12:28-30). He always did what was pleasing to him (Ps 40:7-8, Jn 8:29).

(b) He submitted to scripture. He fed on it as on food (Deut 8:3, Ezek 3:1-7). As far as he was concerned, what scripture said, God said.

(c) He immediately refused the devil's offers. There was no discussion or truce; only a firm rebuke, an instant refusal and a summary dismissal (Mt 4:10).

(d) He built up his resistance to evil over time. He kept on resisting the devil, and each time he did this, it became more natural to do so (Jas 4:7-8).

XLI

17:9-18 The Beast carries and destroys the Whore

The angel who has been speaking to John (v 1, 7) now urges both him and us to use our minds and to be wise. He provides us with some further clues about the significance, not only in John's time but also in ours, of the beast and the whore who rides on it. After this the angel springs a major surprise on us, informing us that the beast is going to hate the whore, and it will proceed to use its power in a ruthless and public way, first to disgrace her and then to destroy her.

9. The angel who has been speaking to John urges those who are wise to use their minds and think: *This calls for a mind that has wisdom.* The matters that he is expounding are not obvious truths which are immediately apparent to everyone, but the wise can work them out. *The seven heads* of the beast *are seven mountains on which the woman is seated.* It is now clear that the whore is being identified with Rome, whose seven hills were often referred to in ancient literature. This was the significance of the whore in John's time, but she has a similar significance for subsequent readers, including those in the 21st century.

Leon Morris wrote, "As we have seen, the great city is every city and no city. It is civilised people, organised apart from God. It has its embodiment in every age". In a similar vein, William Hendriksen observed that "Babylon, then, is the centre of seduction at any moment of history, particularly during this entire present dispensation. The harlot, Babylon, always opposes the bride, new Jerusalem". In the first century, Rome was a striking realisation of what Babylon means in the book of Revelation. In Rome, as nowhere else, Christians saw a worldly city bent on its blasphemous way, opposing the people of God and the way of God with all its power. *Also, they are seven kings.* The heads of the beast symbolise both hills and rulers.

10. Of these seven kings, *five have fallen, one is living and the other has not yet come; and when he comes, he must remain only a little while.* If the kings stand for emperors, the five who had died are probably Augustus, Tiberius, Caligula, Claudius and Nero. The sixth is Vespasian (though this leaves out Galba, Otho and Vitellius who only ruled for a few months), and John may have written the Revelation during Vespasian's rule (AD 69-79), although it is usually dated to Domitian's rule 10-15 years later. The seventh who had not yet come would then be Titus, who would only rule for two years. A quite different interpretation is that the seven kings represent seven empires. The five that had fallen would then be the Old Babylonian, the Assyrian, the New Babylonian, the Medo-Persian and the Greco-Macedonian. The one in John's time was the Roman, and the seventh and future one would be all the anti-Christian governments after the fall of Rome. Leon Morris suggested that "Either interpretation is possible. Both remind us of the continuing power of the beast".

11. *As for the beast that was and is not* (see v 8 and 13:3), the angel declares that *it is an eighth but it belongs to the seven.* If we continue with the most common interpretation involving Roman emperors, the eighth one is Domitian, who was likened to Nero by both pagan and Christian writers. Leon Morris suggests that "Domitian was Nero all over again. A difficulty in the way of this interpretation is how to apply 'was and is not' to Domitian. The answer may be that in one sense he was, and in another he was not Nero". If the eighth is Domitian, who was held by some to be *Nero Redivivus*, he could have been thought of as one of the seven, Nero, who had returned to haunt his old enemies. Then, while being the eighth, he would also have belonged to the seven. But the angel does not say enough for us to arrive at a firm identification. His interest is not in the career of the eighth king, nor in his power, but in his overthrow: *it goes to destruction.*

12. The angel now explains the meaning of the beast's ten horns. *And the ten horns that you saw are ten kings who have not yet received a kingdom, but they are to receive authority as kings for one hour, together with the beast.* Because they had not yet received a kingdom, they were future,

after John wrote, so some of them may be alive in our own day in the 21st century. In verse 16 they will go on to destroy the whore. Their number *ten* may be exact, or simply a symbol of completeness. They will be *powerful* kings, for a horn was a symbol of power. They will receive authority as kings for *one hour*. Leon Morris wrote that "Their reigns would be short as God counts time. To people they may appear great, but to God they reign for only one unimportant hour. They are associated with the beast. Their day will be as brief as his". They will reappear in 19:19-21.

13. We should not consider these ten latter-day kings apart from the beast. *These are united in yielding their power and authority to the beast.* They do not think independently. They are united for they are willing collaborators with the beast.

14. The angel prophesies that *they will make war on the Lamb, and the Lamb will conquer them, for he is Lord of lords and King of kings.* John will spell out some further details of this eschatological victory in 19:11-21. Against such a righteous warrior as the Lamb, the servile underlings of the beast have no chance at all. This is a comforting message for the persecuted followers of the Lamb, who are described as *those with him, who are called and chosen and faithful.* There are times when Christ's people think they are fighting against seemingly insuperable odds. They may then reflect that *they are with him.* They have been *called* and *chosen*, so they are to get on with the task the Lamb has given them. Because he is guarding them as the apple of his eye (Ps 17:8, Zech 2:8), they will be *faithful.* Their success depends on their divine election and on their resulting loyalty.

15. *The angel briefly explains* the meaning of *the waters that John saw, on which the whore is seated.* They represent many *peoples and multitudes and nations and languages.* The harlot has a great empire. In verse 7 the angel promised to explain the mystery of the harlot and of the beast. So far he has spoken mainly about the beast. What about the harlot? The angel has a big surprise up his sleeve.

16. Evil is a terrible mystery; we cannot fully understand it. But part of its very nature is that there is a deep disunity among the forces of evil. The angel makes use of some picturesque language and expresses this fact memorably: *And the ten horns that you saw, they and the beast will*

hate the whore; they will make her desolate and naked; they will devour her flesh and burn her up with fire. As Leon Morris put it, "It is easy to think of the forces of evil as one united phalanx. But there is no cohesion in evil. Wicked men are not just one happy band of brothers. Being wicked, they give way to jealousy and hatred. At the climax their mutual hatreds will result in mutual destruction. There will be hatred between *the ten horns* and *the whore*, a hatred which will issue in deeds. They will make her desolate and naked, which means that they will strip her of every resource (cf. the punishment of the harlot Oholibah, Ezek 23:25-30). They will *devour her flesh*, i.e. they will prey upon her and consume her. And they will *burn her with fire.* She will be completely destroyed".

17. The reason why evil will be a kingdom divided against itself (Mt 12:25-26) is quite simply because it is God's wish that evil will defeat itself in this way. *For God has put it into their hearts to carry out his purpose by agreeing to give their kingdom to the beast, until the words of God will be fulfilled.* The ten horns or latter kings *agree.* They will not bicker or break up their coalition, for then the whore might escape. She is destined for destruction because God has willed it, and God will give them a semblance of unity until they have fulfilled his *words.* It might be argued that the beast will be guilty of treachery against the woman who sat on it (v 3). But this is in accordance with God's purposes. The beast may overthrow its own supporters, but even this base action will fulfil God's purposes. This verse denies the possibility of any dualism. As Henry Mounce put it, "In the final analysis the powers of evil serve the purposes of God".

18. So who was *this harlot that John saw?* Her identity is now revealed. *She is the great city,* and *she rules over the kings of the earth.* She represented Rome in John's time, but during the Christian era she stands for the essence of worldliness, i.e. for godless people living in organised community against God and his people.

Meditation: A Message for our own Time

It is tempting to use Chapter 17 to support a preterist interpretation of Revelation. This is a way of looking at the book by regarding it primarily as referring to the past – to the rise of the Christian movement, to the opposition it encountered from Rome, and to the eventual defeat of the Roman Empire. There can be no doubt that John was thinking of Rome as he wrote this chapter. F.F. Bruce was forthright about this: "Even if the imperial police missed the reference to Rome elsewhere in this vision, the proverbial seven hills, the *septimontium*, could not be mistaken. Rome was first a conurbation of seven hill-settlements on the left bank of the Tiber, the principal settlement being that on the Palatine hill".

This cannot be the whole story, however. Richard Bewes advised us to study this chapter with humility. "Let's not get too clever. It is possible to plunge into the extravagant imagery of this chapter, to come up with an impressive display of nimble and even convincing explanations, and to think that you have then solved the mystery of the woman astride the scarlet beast, together with the seven heads, seven hills, seven kings, Babylon and the rest. It isn't that I disagree with the findings of the Bible commentators. I can nod sagely when told that the seven kings represent the seven anti-Christian empires of Ancient Babylonia, Assyria, New Babylonia, Medo-Persia, Greco-Macedonia, Rome, and finally all the other such empires rolled into one. I nod again when I learn from a different source that they represent seven Caesars – Augustus, Tiberius, Caligula, Claudius, Nero, Vespasian and Titus. But then I wonder what this would all mean to a Bible reader in the Amazon basin, or to a new believer whose historical knowledge is restricted to that of the Ming dynasties of China? Is it essential for them to bone up on the history of Europe in order to make sense of Revelation 17? Or will a working knowledge of the Bible alone prove sufficient guidance?"

What we have here are visions, not brain-teasers. The woman in this chapter is presented to us firstly as the great whore with whom the kings of the earth have committed fornication (v 1-2). She stands for worldly power in all its seductive and sensual fascination. Then we find written on her forehead her name, Babylon the great (v 5). She is the proud city, who from the first rebelled against God and pandered to the vanities of cruel and manipulative despots like Nebuchadnezzar. Then John refers to her as the city she personified in his own day, a city built on seven mountains which must be Rome (v 9). As F.F Bruce wrote, "John reminds us, with reference to the empire that he knew best, that imperial dominion does not endure, and that any power that sets itself against the Lord and his anointed (Ps 2:2) signs its own death-warrant". But John then jumps fast forward to the future, which includes our time. The ten horns of the beast symbolise ten rulers who will exercise authority for a short time, together with the beast. They will be profoundly anti-Christian, and will make war on the Lamb (v 14). There will be an extraordinary and unexpected twist in that the harlot will suffer at the hands of the beast and its minions.

So what may we learn from this for our own witness to Christ in our own day?

(a) We must resist the allurements of the harlot. She is glittering and her worldly pride has an almost irresistible appeal. She occasionally dresses in Christian garb (Mt 7:15-20). She offers us the world as our oyster. She tells us that we are the pearl in the middle. She has an obsession with power, which she promises to share with us. But all her approaches are false, appealing to our sinful cravings, the lust of our eyes and the boasting of what we have and do. She just wants to seduce us from what is holy and pure. Her golden cup might seem to be full of popularity, position, pleasure and sensual passion, but it contains not one drop of the living water that Christ gives in his rich abundance to those who are spiritually thirsty. Therefore we will do well if we say a brief and very clear "No" to her.

(b) We shall see the terrible fate of the harlot. Hanns Lilje has pointed out that "the turning of the beast upon the woman who sits on it speaks of a terrible and mysterious law of political history, according to which every revolutionary power contains within itself the seed of self-destruction". Anyone who manipulates and destroys other people will in turn be manipulated and destroyed. Babylon will be judged, and now we must turn to consider her judgement in terrible detail.

XLII

18:1-8 God's righteous Judgement is visited on Babylon

Time is up for Babylon. John writes vividly and unforgettably of the judgement that has finally arrived for the great city. Terrible is her fall, and terrible its effect on those who put their trust in her and devote their lives to furthering her cause. The language is reminiscent of that of the Old Testament prophets in describing the falls of Babylon (Isaiah chapters 13, 14, 21; Jeremiah chapters 50, 51) and of Tyre (Ezekiel chapters 26, 27, 28). Leon Morris observed that "John has caught the spirit of the prophetic doom songs". Martin Kiddle wrote aptly, "We cannot grasp anything like the full power of John's words unless we are familiar with the passages to which he alludes. The song in Revelation is a resounding echo of the passionate faith and stormy exulting in the doom-songs of the great prophets. Chapter 18 is at once 'a new song' in that it has passed through the fire of the prophet's imagination, and also a summary of all prophetic oracles on the doom of unrighteous peoples". It is clear that John is not thinking of the fall of just one city, be it Tyre or Babylon or Rome, but of the collapse of civilisation. The final judgement will entail the overthrow of everything that opposes itself to God.

1. After the visions of chapter 17, *John saw another angel coming down from heaven.* This angel was outstanding on account of *his great authority.* In the book of Revelation authority is often said to be given to various forces of evil, but here, to the relief of all students of the book, it is given to a good angel who was so endowed with divine glory that *the earth was made bright with his splendour.* He had just departed from God's presence and so he lit up the dark earth with a blaze of light. God dwells in unapproachable light (1 Tim 6:16) and covers himself with light as with a garment (Ps 104:2), and because of this those who emerge from his presence retain a lingering radiance in their features (Ex 34:29-35).

2. *He called out with a mighty voice,* announcing the fall of the great city. *"Fallen, fallen is Babylon the great!"* (Isa 21:9). We know that this fall will be brought about by evil forces (17:16-18), but the angel does not repeat this. He is interested in the result. The city's doom is still future, but so certain is it that the angel speaks about it as if it had already happened: *"It has become a dwelling place of demons, a haunt of every foul spirit, a haunt of every foul bird, a haunt of every foul and hateful beast".* People no longer live there, only demons. It is the cage or prison of every unclean spirit. The foul birds of the desert haunt it, as do detestable beasts that steer clear of human beings (Isa 13:21-22, 34:11-17).

3. Why must Babylon suffer this utter desolation? Because of the outrageous sins she committed by corrupting others, *for all the nations have drunk of the wine of the wrath of her fornication* (14:8). In Revelation, *fornication* is the worship of the beast instead of the Lamb. Babylon's corrupting influence was incalculable. The worldly spirit represented by Babylon has infected all peoples with idolatrous impurity, and this worldliness inevitably brings down on them the wrath of God

(Jer 25:15). Leon Morris wrote, "Not content with sinning herself, she brought others to share in her sin", and this is why *the kings of the earth have committed fornication with her, and the merchants of the earth have grown rich from the power of her luxury.* When the kings of the earth wallowed in impurity, the people they ruled over had little choice but to imitate their royal role models. And the merchants of the earth made themselves filthy rich through her wanton power.

4. The people of God were persecuted and harassed. They must have tried to come to terms with the great city. It was difficult being surrounded by selfishness and worldly values. Unacceptable and detestable attitudes and actions were constantly encroaching on their feeble attempts to live a holy life that was fully pleasing to God. Moreover, Babylon was forever offering riches and comfort. Maybe there was room for a little compromise here and there? Leon Morris observes that "It is important to see the issues for what they really are, and have nothing to do with unclean things. So [the people of God] are called to come out of her". *John heard another voice from heaven, saying, "Come out of her, my people, so that you do not take part in her sins, and so that you do not share in her plagues".* This voice may have been that of another angel, or possibly (in the light of v 5) that of Christ himself. Similar calls were made to God's people in the Old Testament (Gen 12:1, 19:12-14; Num 16:23-35; Isa 48:20, 52:11-12; Jer 50:8, 51:6, 45; Zech 2:6-8).

   Such calls were not limited only to God's people before Christ (2 Cor 6:14-18, Eph 5:11, 1 Tim 5:22), for compromise with worldliness is always fatal. God's people are called to be *in the world*, but not *of the world* (Jn 17:15-18). They must play their full role in the community while keeping themselves separate from corrupt worldly values. This verse is in some ways the key to the whole of chapter 18. John is not delighting in the city's downfall. He is appealing to his Christian readers to see the reality of their situation and to act accordingly. For them as for all people in all ages, to share in the world's wickedness is to reap its recompense.

5. The reality concerning the worldly city is that *"her sins are heaped as high as heaven".* Jeremiah had prophesied that "her judgement has reached up to heaven and has been lifted up even to the skies" (Jer 51:9). The heavenly voice pictures her sins as heaped up in a pile,

and the top of the pile is sky high. The description continues, *"and God has remembered her iniquities"*. There is a terrible contrast between this and the central promise of the New Covenant, "I will forgive their iniquities, and remember their sin no more" (Jer 31:34). But this is not for those who refuse to repent. Leon Morris comments that "From the standpoint of the persecuted church it might seem that evil men were getting away with their sins. From the standpoint of heaven it is plain that God is not mocked. He remembers".

6. The voice now calls for just retribution for the worldly city. *"Render to her as she herself has rendered"*. If Christ is the speaker, he has turned from addressing his people to instructing the ministers of judgement. He commands them to do to the city what she has done to others (Jer 50:29). Indeed, she is to be punished in fullest measure: *"repay her double for her deeds; mix a double draught for her in the cup she mixed"*. It is not a question of revenge but of just requital. Leon Morris has observed that "There is tremendous depth of feeling against the guilty city. There is also the recognition that the simple 'an eye for an eye and a tooth for a tooth' is not sufficient. In view of Babylon's full culture and enlightenment, a more severe punishment is required. She has mixed a cup for others, so the voice calls, 'mix her a drink of double strength'".

7. The voice continues to call for a fitting and deserved retributive punishment. The city arrogated for itself the glory that belongs to God and lived in luxury at the expense of the poor. This must be taken into consideration: *"As she glorified herself and lived luxuriously, so give her a like measure of torment and grief"*. She had a deep-seated but misguided awareness of herself as a royal figure who was untouched by suffering and who was to be feared as if she was God : *"In her heart she said, 'I rule as a queen; I am no widow, and I will never see grief'"* She was expecting her pleasant state to continue (Isa 47:7-8). She suffered from the delusion of those in every age who are materially prosperous.

8. This is the reason for her sudden punishment: *"Therefore her plagues will come in a single day – pestilence and mourning and famine – and she will be burned with fire"*. There will be no warning and no delay. Four disasters will hit her in one day (Isa 47:9): a deadly virus or plague, terrible sorrow and suffering, wasting famine, and destruction by fire.

This will most certainly happen, because *"mighty is the Lord God who judges her"*. It will not be an arbitrary display of power, for God will be behind it. It will not be a gentle rap on the knuckles, for it will be exactly what she deserved. This is divine and merited *judgement*.

Meditation: What the Future holds and what we should do now

The prophecy we are studying is about the future, although the fall of the worldly city is written prophetically in the past tense, as if it had already happened. We may find certain truths about verses 1-8 instructive:

(a) *Past prophecies fulfilled.* (i) The fall of Babylon was prophesied early on by Isaiah and then later by Jeremiah. The autocratic ruler they mention was probably Nebuchadnezzar, for it was he who would conquer and destroy Jerusalem in 586 BC. The Bible gives us a mixed review of him. Jeremiah was a contemporary of his and he suggests that Yahweh longed for him to repent and for Babylon to be reformed. Some attempts may have been made to bring this about (Jer 51:8-9). In the book of Daniel (chapters 2, 3 and 4) a vivid picture is painted of the pride and despotism of King Nebuchadnezzar. Nevertheless, we read there that God was at work in his heart. This led the King of Babylon to suffer a fit of insanity which lasted seven years, after which he recovered his mind, praised God and declared him to be the Most High, saying "I, Nebuchadnezzar, praise and extol and honour the King of Heaven, for all his works are truth, and his ways are justice; and he is able to bring low those who walk in pride" (Dan 4:37). Did Nebuchadnezzar repent? Some theologians no longer consider the first half of the book of Daniel to be a historical account. His insanity is not mentioned in contemporary writings, although we are told that in his final years he began to behave irrationally, paying no attention to his sons or daughters, and becoming very suspicious of them. It is tempting to speculate that Nebuchadnezzar may have been humbled in some way that prompted the narrative of Daniel. This would explain the merciful end of the city of Babylon in spite of the terrible prophecies of its doom. It was captured by Cyrus in one night, and there was no major blood-bath as a result. But then God does promise that he will meet a humble and repentant sinner more than halfway (Jer 18:7-8, Ezek 18:21-23, 2 Chron 33:10-13).

(ii) By the first century Babylon had been deserted and nobody lived there. John had identified Babylon of old with Rome the prostitute and persecutor, and he went on to describe her overthrow. It would not take place in its finality for some 320 years, until in AD 410 Alaric the Goth would sack the city. Yet throughout chapter 18 John used the prophetic past tense, expressing the certainty of God's judgement as if it had already taken place: "Fallen! Fallen is Babylon the great!" He said this in spite of the prevailing view that Rome was "the eternal city" and that the empire was invulnerable. Moreover Rome was then the only superpower, her frontiers were safe, and her subject-peoples were compliant. Pirates were banished from the sea and bandits from the country-side. There were elegant cities along the Italian coasts and also in many inland regions. But John predicted the fall of Rome with certainty, partly because he believed in the judgement of God upon evil, and partly because he knew that the Old Testament prophecies of the fall of Babylon had all been fulfilled (e.g. Isa 13:19).

(b) The terrible prophecy about the future. Isaiah prophesied, "Fallen, fallen is Babylon" (Isa 21:9). Some 150 years later, the Persians and Medes captured the city, but they did not immediately destroy it. It gradually lost its glory and in due course it was abandoned, to become the haunt of sinister animals and birds. John repeated the words of Isaiah, "Fallen, fallen is Babylon the great!" (v 2). He was referring in the first instance to Rome and indeed, some 320 years later Rome did fall. But John's prophecy was ultimately not about Babylon or Rome. It was about any civilisation or worldly system of values that is resolutely hostile to God. John looked ahead to the day which God had appointed against all who are proud and lofty. On that day the haughty eyes of people will be brought low, and the pride of everyone will be humbled. Most important of all, the Lord alone will be exalted on that day (Isa 2:11-12). It is interesting that the divine judgement that must fall upon the worldly city is something that she has brought upon herself, and that her judgement is not arbitrary but fully deserved and just. The retribution will not be brought about through the agency of God's people, for as Tom Wright pointed out, "vengeance is too dangerous a weapon to be handled by the followers of the Lamb" (Deut 32:35, Rom 12:19). It is the beast itself that will act as God's agent in the destruction of the whore (17:16-18), but the judgement will all be God's own work. He will cause wickedness to destroy itself, and will allow arrogance to reach a giddy height from which it will inevi-tably crash helplessly to earth.

(c) The call to come out of the world. Phil Moore wrote, "The spirit of Babylon's full-frontal attack is to embed herself so deeply within a culture that Christians will think her way, even after conversion. She is in the slave business, and she is

determined to recapture those whom Christ has freed from her clutches. She will whisper promises of sex, wealth and pampered luxury – whatever it takes to catch their eyes and ensnare their hearts. If necessary, she will put on religious clothes, driven on by her unquenchable thirst to replace living faith with dead religion. She will turn Christian ministry into a springboard for power, fame and self-fulfilment, and will even trick the most passionate builders of the New Jerusalem into laying bricks for Babylon. Her dirty fingerprints stain 2,000 years of Church history, and her feet still trample the Church just as Jesus predicted in 11:2. No wonder Christ cries out at this point fervently from heaven, 'Come out of her, my people!' Christians need to resist her full-frontal attack, because if they share in her sins, they will also share in her judgement".

The task that God has given to his people is exceptionally difficult. They are to be fully in the world, just as God became fully human in Christ and partic-ipated in its activities. And yet they are to be different from worldly people, just as Jesus Christ was different. The great difficulty is, how do you join in with people in all sorts of everyday activities related to study, work, recreation and culture, and yet remain distinct from them? The wrong approach is to withdraw completely from activities that have some marks of Babylon in them, but could still be redeemed. The nation's schools, industries, professions, music, media and politics are all in desperate need of Christians to join in fully with them, acting as salt that prevents corruption and as light that brings hope and vision. We long to bring the goodness of Christ to these areas of life, but can we be part of them and yet be different? The answer is yes, and we do this by living lives that are guiltless and totally free from guile.

This is what is entailed by the call to come out of the world, for the instruction in verse 4 is "Come out of her, my people, *so that you do not take part in her sins*" – because if you do then you will also share in her plagues. Christ put it clearly in his prayer for his disciples on the evening that he was betrayed: *"I have given them your word, and the world has hated them because they do not belong to the world, just as I do not belong to the world. I am not asking you to take them out of the world, but I ask you to protect them from the evil one. They do not belong to the world, just as I do not belong to the world. As you sent me into the world, so I have sent them into the world"* (Jn 17:14-16, 18). Phil Moore went on to say, "God calls his people to withdraw from the *contamination* of Babylon so that they will not share in both her sins and her judgement, but he then calls them to a strategy of *infiltration*, not of *isolation*.

He calls us to take our place within our towns, cities and communities, and to build Jerusalem instead of Babylon at the heart of our nations".

This world's culture may be thought of as being at the junction of two rivers. One is the muddy river of Babylon, which is full of Babylon's effluent and which pollutes all who bathe in it. The other is the river of the water of life which flows out of the hearts of all who know and love Christ and who come to him and drink (Jn 7:37-39). We are called to stay in the clean and clear water, and to help those around us to wash and to keep clean. It is a marvellous challenge!

XLIII

18:9-19 Rich People lament the Fall of Babylon

We have read of the inevitable fall of the great city, and of the call to God's people to come out of her so that they will not take part in her sins and need not share in her plagues. We have pondered the perfect justice of the severe judgement that God will visit on her. Her fall will be accompanied by four plagues – pestilence, mourning, famine and burning with fire. But what of the mighty, the wealthy and the prosperous who work for her because of what they can get out of her? Her fall will also have a catastrophic effect on them. They will lament, grieve and cry in distress. Then they too will fall, and their fall will be tragic and irreparable.

9. The fall of the great city would bring untold distress to *the kings of the earth, who committed fornication and lived in luxury with her.* These kings are not the ten mentioned in 17:12-17 but other kings, closely associated with her in the sins that brought about her fate, especially her idolatry and her complacency. Like her, they were proud, they overate, and they prospered in ease, but they did not help the poor and needy. They were haughty and abominable before God (Ezek 16:49-50). Therefore *they will weep and wail when they see the smoke of her burning.*

10. Although they will gaze on the burning city and mourn deeply, *they will stand far off, in fear of her torment.* They have no real love for her, so during her fall they will keep their distance. *They will say, "Alas, alas, the great city, Babylon, the mighty city! For in one hour your judgement has come".* The worldly spirit of Babylon is *great* and *mighty.* Those who are captivated by it will utter a double woe on it – *"Alas, alas!"* John wants

his Christian readers to recall that worldly greatness is always accompanied by disobedience to God the Holy One (Eph 2:2), and worldly power is ever held in derision by God Almighty (Ps 2:2-4). In verse 8 the suddenness of the great city's destruction is highlighted by the fact that her plagues will come in *a single day*, but now in verse 10 this is further intensified, for her judgement will come in *one hour*. It will be overwhelming.

11. *The merchants of the earth weep and mourn for fallen Babylon.* Like the kings of the earth, they will *weep*: the Greek word *klaiousin* means a loud lament rather than silent weeping. But they will also *mourn for her, because no one buys their cargo any more.* Leon Morris observed that "Financial loss, not esteem for the city, prompts their distress". It is a sad truth that even the good things that we do are sometimes done for motives that are mixed, if not utterly selfish.

12. John now gives a list of the cargoes which will no longer be deemed desirable. It is comparable to the lists of articles that the merchant nations traded with Tyre (Ezek 27:12-24). Even the rich will no longer purchase *gold* and *silver, jewels* and *pearls*. What would be the use of lavish richness when the city was suffering judgement? The same goes for clothing made of *fine linen* and *purple*, or *silk* and *scarlet* cloth. Fine linen was then purchased in Egypt, and silk was imported from China. Purple and scarlet were the clothing of the great whore (17:4). Next come *articles made* of *scented wood* (like cedar), *ivory*, and *costly wood* (perhaps from the olive tree). Woods that were fragrant or had variegated colour and deep veining were highly esteemed, both by cabinet makers and by the wealthy citizens of Rome and elsewhere. Then come objects made of *bronze* or *iron* (which may have included cutlery and mirrors) and *marble* (for making floors and walls, and for sculptures). There would be no more demand for any of these, so merchants who supplied them would no longer be required.

13. The list continues with prized spices and aromatic plants, then various special drinks and foods, before ending with animals and slaves. *Cinnamon* was imported from south China, and the Greek word *amomon* which is translated as *spice* was a fragrant plant from India used for making costly hair unguent. *Incense, myrrh* and *frankincense* were purchased for their therapeutic aromas. *Wine* and *olive oil* were

much sought after and, as is the case today, could be purchased for different prices depending on their purity and quality. *Choice flour and wheat* were used to bake exotic breads and cakes. Imported *cattle and sheep* were valued for their special flavour. *Horses and chariots* were joined together to produce state-of-the-art military armaments. The Greek word *somata*, here translated *slaves*, literally means *bodies*, and provides a vivid illustration of the social conditions that were common in antiquity. Henry Mounce wrote, "Slave traders regarded their human cargo as so much merchandise to be auctioned off to the highest bidder". The final item on the list, *psychai anthropon*, means *souls of men*, translated as *human lives*. It is a Hebrew phrase which means little more than human livestock. Some slaves were used as mules. They were made to carry heavy loads until they died.

We who live in a day when slavery is condemned should pause and think about the ways in which modern churches in affluent countries enslave and manipulate their flocks in ways that result in some Christians losing their faith (Lk 17:1-2).

14. The fallen city is informed in plain language that her luxuries are now a thing of the past. *"The fruit for which your soul longed has gone from you, and all your dainties and your splendour are lost to you, never to be found again"*. The loss of exotica would mean nothing to most of the slaves and the poor, for they had never enjoyed them, but it would constitute a major disaster for those who were addicted to them. The wealth of first-century Rome was proverbial. In the Hebrew Talmud we read that "Ten portions of wealth descended on the world: nine were taken by the Romans and one by the rest of the world".

15. As in verse 11, *the merchants of these wares, who gained wealth from her, will stand far off, in fear of her torment, weeping and mourning aloud*. They will not approach the fallen city to help its people and offer comfort to them. Instead, out of sheer self-interest, they will distance themselves for fear of getting caught up in her torment. This time we are told that they will weep and mourn *aloud*.

16. Their lamentation will be similar to that of the kings in verse 10. They begin with the same invocation, *Alas, alas, the great city*, but instead of focusing on her might that she has lost, they bewail the destruction of the clothing and jewellery that they had sold to her, which had made

them prosperous: *clothed in fine linen, in purple and scarlet, adorned with gold, with jewels and with pearls.*

17. The kings say that the fallen city's judgement has come *in one hour,* but for the merchants the tragedy is that *in one hour all this wealth has been laid waste.* After the kings and merchants, it is the turn of *all the shipmasters and seafarers, sailors and all whose trade is on the sea* to have their say. *They also stand far off.* Nobody really loves the rich. The tears that are shed are not for them, but for the loss of influence or revenue or trading that will result from their overthrow.

18. The men who work on the sea *cry out when they see the smoke of her burning.* To see the source of their prosperity go up in flames will be a terrible blow to their morale: they will then look ahead only to poverty and loss, for there is nothing that can compare to her. They will cry, *"What city was like the great city?"* This entire section is reminiscent of the ancient laments over the fall of Tyre: "Who was ever destroyed like Tyre?" (Ezek 26:17-21, 27:25-36).

19. The men of the sea will carry their mourning further than the wealthier kings and merchants. *They throw dust on their heads, as they weep and mourn* (Ezek 27:30). Kings and merchants are wealthy and have savings to tide them over for a while, but for sailors the fall of the great city means loss of security. For a third time we hear the repeated cries of *alas,* and for the third time the suddenness of the tragedy is conveyed by the phrase *in one hour.* The sailors wail, *"Alas, alas, the great city, where all who had ships at sea grew rich by her wealth! For in one hour she has been laid waste".* As with the merchants, what will cause this third group of men such distress is the loss of their income and security.

Meditation: The Curse of abundant Possessions

One day, in the context of a family dispute, Christ warned the crowd around him, "Take care! Be on your guard against all kinds of greed; for one's life does not consist in the abundance of possessions". Then he told them a story of judgement, which we know as the Parable of the Rich Fool. "The land of a rich man produced abundantly. And he thought to himself, 'What should I do, for I have no place to store my crops?' Then he said, 'I will do this; I will pull down my barns and build larger ones, and there I will store all my grain and my goods. And I will say to my soul, Soul, you have ample goods laid up for many years; relax, eat, drink, be merry. But God said to him, 'You fool! This very night your life is demanded of you. And the things you have prepared, whose will they be?' So it is with those who store up treasures for themselves but are not rich towards God" (Lk 12:13-21). Christ warned people about the dangers of greed, and told them what a deadly sin it was, because our life does not consist in the abundance of our possessions. Greed, covetousness, and materialism are all contrary to authentic human living. Of course we all need some material blessings, but by themselves our possessions cannot satisfy us nor will they bring us fulfilment. There is more to life than the *abundance* of our possessions. The kings, merchants and seamen of Revelation 18:9-19 got this wrong, for their lives were all about materialism.

There was a farmer who had a problem. There had been a bumper harvest, and his storage facilities were inadequate. It was a good problem to have. He decided to pull down his barns and build larger ones, and at this point God inconveniently interrupted the farmer's plans with death. Moreover God, who does not observe all the customs and courtesies of our polite society, went on to call him a fool. Because God said "You fool!" this man has gone down not as the rich farmer but as the rich fool. Was this fair? We might say that what he opted for was not folly but good business practice. If you enjoy a bumper harvest, it makes sense to build some big barns. We turn, therefore, to examine the farmer's thoughts.

He thought to himself, "What should I do?" This question is usually asked by people in anguish or pain. If their harvest has failed and they don't know where their next meal is coming from, it is a fair question, but the rich farmer asked the question when he was faced by the dilemma of success. He moaned about it: "Oh dear, what should I do?" His problem was not destitution but affluence, and his solution was selfish. "What should *I* do? *I* have no place to store *my* crops. *I* will do this. *I* will pull down *my* barns. *I* will build larger ones. There *I* will store all *my* grain and *my* goods. And *I* will say to *my* soul, relax, eat, drink and be merry". I, I, I, I, I, I, I, seven times. My, my, my, my, my, five times. He did not thank God for having blessed him, nor did he think of the poor and needy. He was very selfish and thought of himself. Furthermore, he was the prey of three obsessions:

First, he was obsessed with storage. Only one solution occurred to him for the problem of his bumper harvest – better storage facilities. That way he could hoard his little fortune. But there were better solutions. The alternative to storage is distribution, and the alternative to hoarding is sharing. Of course he had to keep part of the harvest to feed himself and his family, to sell and get some money, and to provide seed for the next year's harvest. But what about his enormous surplus? He could have distributed it. He could have partially filled some of the barns of his neighbours who had been less fortunate than he. Such generous provision is enjoined in the Old Testament (e.g. Deut 15:7-8). Ambrose, who was the Bishop of Milan in the fourth century, imagined himself speaking to the rich farmer: "But you already *have* more barns. You have the bellies of the poor and needy, the larders of widows, the mouths of hungry orphans and infants. You could store some of the grain there". But our rich farmer did not even consider the possibility of sharing his bonanza, so God said to him, "You fool! This very night your life is demanded of you. And the things you have prepared, whose will they be?" If we have an instinct to hoard, this parable teaches that we shall not go on hoarding forever. One day death will bring all our proprietary rights to an end.

Secondly, he was obsessed with financial security. He was looking forward to building and filling his barns, because then he could say to his soul, "Soul, you have ample goods laid up for many years: relax, eat, drink, be merry". Again, it is easy at first sight to sympathise with this man. So many people think like him. Is it not the case that the purpose of our working life is to lay up a nest-egg that will see us through future years when we are no longer wage-earners? Of course it is right to make adequate provision for the future if we can, although God would have us remember those who cannot do this. But the Bible often reflects upon the uncertainty of riches. In his Sermon on the Mount Jesus said, "Do not store up for yourselves treasures on earth, where moth and rust consume and where thieves break in and steal; but store up for yourselves treasures in heaven, where neither moth nor rust consumes and where thieves do not break in and steal" (Mt 6:19-20). And elsewhere in the New Testament we read that "There is great gain in godliness combined with contentment. If we have food and clothing, we will be content with these. But those who want to be rich fall into temptation and are trapped by many senseless and harmful desires that plunge people into ruin and destruction. For the love of money is a root of all kinds of evil" (1 Tim 6:6-10). We are not to boast about tomorrow. We do not know what tomorrow will bring.

Thirdly, he was obsessed with self-indulgence. Storage can bring a false sense of security, which in turn can lead to self-indulgence. Thanks to his bumper harvest, the farmer would be able to put his feet up and be happy because he had ample goods laid up for many years. He would relax, eat, drink and be merry. All would be well – except that he had left God completely out of his calculations. And God spoke to him. "You fool! This very night your life is demanded of you". The word "fool" in the Bible has a special meaning. It almost means "atheist", but not quite. It means someone who believes in God but nevertheless behaves as if God did not exist. Twice in the psalms we read, "Fools say in their hearts, there is no God" (Ps 14:1, 53:1).

Oh, these fools know perfectly well that God exists. Many fools are fully aware that God has revealed himself in the Bible, supremely in the person of his Son Jesus Christ. But in everyday life they shrug their shoulders and say to themselves, "There is no God". They are very foolish, because the essence of godliness is to know God and his Son Jesus Christ, and to share our life with them. But the essence of godlessness is to live for the moment and completely ignore God, like wealthy kings, merchants and seamen. It is to forget that a day is coming when each of us will have to render an account of ourselves to God.

What could the powerful kings, wealthy merchants and prosperous sailors in our passage have learnt from this parable? It would certainly have challenged their sinful desires to be hoarders, to aim for financial security and autonomy, and to indulge all their desires and whims – but these are not the main thrust of the parable. The Parable of the Rich Fool is ultimately about what is involved in being human. What does it mean for anyone to be an authentic human being, made in the image of God?

The answer is both negative and positive. Negatively, our life does not consist in the abundance of possessions. Positively, the life that is truly life is to live in close and loving relationship with God who is our Creator, Saviour and Fortifier. Negatively, it is not to store up treasures for ourselves on earth. Positively, it is to be rich towards our God. Negatively, it is not to rely on our little fortunes. Positively, it is to trust in our great God. Negatively, it is not to want a bit more than what we already have. Positively, it is to live in contentment. If people fall for the charms of the whore, they will mourn when time is called and she is overthrown. But if they do not, they will be untouched by the terrible fire of God's judgement that is coming to consume the covetous and worldly.

XLIV

18:20-19:10 Babylon is judged and Heaven rejoices

John now tells us about Babylon's overthrow and her subsequent desolation. She who was guilty of slaughtering prophets and saints has become a dark, solitary and silent place. The reaction to her judgement is rejoicing in heaven. Indeed, the word "Hallelujah!" rings loudly. George Frederic Handel based the "Hallelujah Chorus" of his famous oratorio "Messiah" on the song of joy in 19:1-8.

20. John calls heaven to be glad on account of the destruction of Babylon. *Rejoice over her, O heaven, you saints and apostles and prophets!* This is not a vindictive outcry, but a proper delight in the perfect justice and retribution of God (Isa 26:9). John and the other members of the witnessing church had opted to be faithful to Christ, and they were despised and persecuted for their stand. But their ultimate vindication was sure, for God is faithful, and John prophesied that in the end they would sing, *God has given judgement in our favour against the worldly city.* This would be a passionate and heartfelt cry that justice must win in the end, and that they would delight in her victory. The cry is addressed to heaven itself (which includes the angels that appear so often in this book), and to the godly people who live there – holy saints, commissioned apostles, and prophets who had spoken the word of God. They had been wronged, and these wrongs would be put right.

21. At this moment there was a vivid demonstration of the power of the forces of good. *Then a mighty angel took up a stone like a great millstone and threw it into the sea.* In a book that has power as one of its themes, we are left in no doubt that some angels have great power. Leon Morris wrote, "The throwing of a great stone into the sea is a symbolic action like many recorded in the prophets. It recalls Jeremiah's action in having a stone attached to a book and cast into the Euphrates, thus symbolising the destruction of Babylon (Jer 51:63-64)". Here the meaning is made clear by the angel: "*With such violence Babylon the great city will be thrown down, and will be found no more*". The city will be destroyed under the most terrible circumstances, and no trace of its evil past will remain (Ezek 26:21).

22. The mighty angel continues the explanation of his symbolic deed, addressing himself to the great city. *"The sound of harpists and minstrels and of flautists and trumpeters will be heard in you no more"*. The worldly mindset takes kindly to music, both classical and contemporary, but Babylon will fall silent, and melodies and harmonies will no longer sound there. *"An artisan of any trade will be found in you no more"*. Arts and crafts will cease in Babylon. Gifted men and women will no longer create anything there. *"The sound of the millstone will be heard in you no more"*. Normal daily life, including the production of food, will stop.

23. *"The light of a lamp will shine in you no more"*, for Babylon will be a dark place. *"The voice of bridegroom and bride will be heard in you no more"*, for all good human relationships, including marriage, will cease to be (Jer 25:10). Why? Because the worldly city got it all wrong. She was intent on her own greatness instead of God's: *"Your merchants were the magnates of the earth"*. And what they lived for, their profit making, was accompanied by bewitching activities and manipulative guile: *"All the nations were deceived by your sorcery"* (Nah 3:4).

24. Above all their other evils, the worldly city hated God's people and put them to death. *"In you was found the blood of prophets and of saints, and of all who have been slaughtered on earth"*. Every city, town, village and hamlet on earth has the spirit of Babylon in it, the spirit that abhors and kills the people of God. Even Jerusalem! Indeed, the strongest words of condemnation Jesus Christ ever spoke were against Jerusalem, and they make for terrible reading (Mt 23:29-39).

19:1. What will our reaction be after the future destruction of the worldly city? It will be to sing loud praises to God for his perfect holiness and justice. John writes, *After this I heard what seemed to be the loud voice of a great multitude in heaven*. This multitude may include not only angels (as in 5:11) but also the redeemed, whose understanding of God's salvation would be greater. They sing together, and begin by urging each other to "praise God". This is what the word *Hallelujah* means. It occurs often in the psalms, but only four times in the New Testament, all of them in this chapter (v 1, 3, 4, 6). The singers go on, *"Salvation and glory and power to our God"*. God has worked salvation, manifested his glory and revealed his power. Already here on earth, but ever more so in heaven, we may respond to him with gratitude, reverence and trust.

2. Now comes the reason for this outburst of praise: *"For his judgements are true and just"*. There is something deeper than doom or mere punishment here. Justice is done. On earth we are accustomed to might being right, but on judgement day right will be mighty. All the wrongs perpetrated on earth will be put right when *he judges the great whore who corrupted the earth with her fornication*. But we in our turn are often happy to be corrupted. Thomas Torrance put it like this: "The world likes a complacent, reasonable religion, so it is always ready to revere some pale Galilean image of Jesus, some meagre anaemic Messiah, and to give him a moderate rational homage. The truth is that we have often committed adultery with alien ideologies, confounded the gospel with the religions of nature, and imbibed the wine of pagan doctrines and false principles and deceitful practices. We have sought to bend the will of God to serve the ends of man, to alter the gospel and to shape the church to conform to the fashions of the times". There will be just retribution, for *God will avenge on her the blood of his servants*. Evil powers will not be allowed to get away with evil. They will be called to account.

3. The second *Hallelujah* of the four now rings out, for *the smoke goes up from the evil city forever and ever*. After the whore and those who were devoted to her are consumed, all that remains is rising smoke. We are told that the after-effects of the destruction of evil will continue to be seen forever, perhaps as a reminder to all the redeemed of what they have been saved *from*. But they have also been saved *for* something. As Leon Morris put it, "The destruction of the great whore is but the prelude to the new era". Martin Kiddle wrote that "Their hallelujah rings out the old, but it also rings in the new". Phil Moore echoed this: "The eradication of the old is the price which always has to be paid for the advent of the new".

4. *The twenty-four elders and the four living creatures fell down and worshipped God who is seated on the throne*. The senior beings in heaven join in the praise, and prostrate themselves in humble adoration before God in his majesty, saying, *"Amen, Hallelujah!"* Their "Amen" indicates their assent to what has been said, and their "Hallelujah" is the third occurrence of this call to praise in this passage.

5. *Then from the throne came a voice*, perhaps that of an angel, *saying, "Praise our God, all you his servants, and all who fear him, small and great"*.

All those who engage in divine service are lowly before their God, for they are his *servants*, and they rightly *fear* him (Ps 111:10, 128:1-4). Some of them may have a higher rank and greater responsibility, hence the classification into both small and great.

6. Then *John heard another voice*. He describes it diffidently, for it is heavenly: *It seemed to be the voice of a great multitude, like the sound of many waters and like the sound of mighty thunderpeals*. It was a voice like that of a crowd talking in unison. It was trustworthy, like the waves of sea-water that broke on the cliffs of Patmos (1:15). It was powerful, like thunderclaps that are very close by (14:2). *It cried out, "Hallelujah! For the Lord our God the Almighty reigns"*. For a fourth and last time in the book, a "Hallelujah" rings out. The reason given is different this time. It is not because the worldly city has been overthrown, but because the Lord, who is again described as *our* God, reigns supreme, for he is the Almighty one. Those who have chosen to be his followers and servants have chosen well. They are on the winning side.

7. Therefore the voice says, *"Let us rejoice and exult"* (Mt 5:12). It adds, *"Give him the glory"*, this time not because of his justice or power but because his grace is about to be lavished on his people, *"for the marriage of the Lamb has come, and his bride has made herself ready"*. Israel was thought of as the bride of God (Isa 54:5-6, Ezek 16:8-14, Hos 2:14-17). The symbolism of marriage was used by Christ during his ministry (Mt 25:1-13, Mk 2:19, Jn 3:29). Paul also used it (2 Cor 11:2, Eph 5:25-33). In Revelation it also comes in 19:9; 21:2, 9; and 22:17.

8. The voice concludes its song, saying, *"To the bride of the Lamb it has been granted to be clothed with fine linen, bright and pure"*. What does the fine linen symbolise? John himself informs us: *The fine linen is the righteous deeds of the saints*. Leon Morris suggests that the Greek word *dikaioma* does not refer to deeds anywhere else, and it should here be translated as "the (imputed) righteousness" or "the sentence of justification". The white robes of the multitude in 7:9, 14 were not made white by the good deeds of those who wore them, but by their washing themselves "in the blood of the Lamb".

9. Then *the angel*, perhaps referring back to the speaker in verse 5, *commanded John* to put quill to parchment once again. *"Write this: Blessed are those who are invited to the marriage supper of the Lamb"*.

This is the fourth of seven beatitudes in the book of Revelation. According to Christ's saying, "Many are called but few are chosen" (Mt 22:14), but those who are both called and chosen will receive an invitation to the marriage supper. And what an invitation! They will be there at the marriage of the Lamb. The church is described not only as the bride (v 7) but also as the wedding guests (Mt 22:1-13). The angel declares that *these words* of benediction *are true words of God* (21:5, 22:6). In times of persecution it needs to be underlined that it is the persecuted who are blessed.

10. *Then John fell down at the angel's feet to worship him.* He may have thought mistakenly that the angel was Christ. He himself would not have worshipped a creature in preference to the Creator, though some early Christians were tempted to do this (Col 2:18). *The angel firmly corrected him,* saying, *"You must not do that! I am a fellow servant with you and your comrades who hold the testimony of Jesus. Worship God!"* (Mt 4:10). *"For the testimony of Jesus is the spirit of prophecy".* We may learn that angels and redeemed people are fellow servants of God. They both hold "the testimony of Jesus, which is the spirit of prophecy". This could mean either "the testimony that Jesus bore on earth, which is at the heart of true prophecy", or "the testimony borne to Jesus by his servants, where the true spirit of prophecy always manifests itself". Both are equally true.

Meditation: A Time for Lamentation and a Time for Celebration

This passage is bittersweet. It is sad, calling for a thoughtful consideration of the ills of this world, but also joyful, calling for heartfelt hallelujahs.

(a) *The themes of chapter 18.* Richard Bewes picked out the following:

(i) There is **certainty** (v 1-3). The prophetic past tense is used. So certain is the fall of the worldly city that it is described as having happened already.

(ii) There is **warning** (v 4-5). God's people are told to keep their distance, in case they become entangled in Babylon's sins and thus also in her downfall.

(iii) There is **retribution** (v 6-8). No tears should be shed when the harlot's demise is announced. The God of justice is putting right all the wrongs.

(iv) There is disillusionment (v 9-19). Three different groups of people – kings, merchants, sailors of cargo ships – are tied up with the worldly city, whose money means everything to them. One day they will lose it all. This is inevitable.

(v) There is justice (v 20). When Babylon falls the reaction will not be a vindictive glee, but the satisfying of that timeless longing that justice should be done and seen to be done, and that the scales should be set right.

(vi) There is *finality* (v 21-24). The destruction of the harlot spells the end of her civilisation – including its music, technology, relationships and economics.

(b) A juxtaposition of opposites. Chapter 18 finishes with a pair of paradoxical opposites, first a celebration and then a lament. Verse 20 urges heaven, together with the saints, apostles and prophets, to rejoice because of God's judgement and condemnation of Babylon for the way in which she has treated them. There will be a celebration of the perfect justice and righteous judgement of God, who is perfectly holy and loving.

But there will also be a lament. Babylon will be destroyed with irresistible power, as if a giant millstone had been flung violently at her. Even what was good about the worldly city's life will disappear with her – the sound of music, the skill of master craftsmen, the everyday domestic routine of preparing food, the light of lamps and the happy conversation of bride and groom. As John Stott put it, "Never again would these innocent sounds and sights of human culture gladden the life of the city. Why not? Answer: because of the pride of Babylon's people, who boasted of their greatness; because of Babylon's resort to sorcery in order to deceive the nations; and because Babylon had shed the blood of martyrs. Because of these sins Babylon will be no more, and with her disappearance all in her that is good, beautiful and true will disappear as well". Then 19:1-8 returns to the celebration, which is exuberantly joyful.

(c) What was so very wrong with Babylon? John Stott wrote a particularly helpful summary. He pointed out that in the first century AD Babylon was Rome. But Babylon has flourished throughout history and throughout the world. Babylon is Vanity Fair, wherever it exists. Its profile can be drawn with ease from chapters 17 and 18 of the book of Revelation. It seems to have six components:

(i) *Idolatry*, meaning spiritual unfaithfulness or promiscuity (18:4, 19:2).

(ii) *Immorality* in the literal sense as well as the symbolical (17:2, 4; 18:3).

(iii) *Extravagance* and completely unacceptable luxury (18:3, 7-9, 12-13).

(iv) *Sorcery* or magic used for manipulating people (18:23, also Isa 47:12-13).

(v) *Tyranny* and oppression which lead inexorably to the martyrdom of God's people (17:6, 18:24, 19:2, also Isa 14:4-6).

(vi) *Spiritual pride* or arrogance, which can sometimes turn into self-deification (18:7, also Isa 14:12-17, 47:7-9, Jer 50:31-32, Ezek 28:2).

The urgent call is still made to come out of her, in order to avoid contamination. **(d) *The Hallelujah chorus*.** Revelation 19:1-8 gave rise to the Hallelujah chorus in Handel's oratorio "Messiah". We know what Handel experienced as he wrote the music for the "Messiah". In his book *Singing with the Angels*, Robert Coleman relates the story brilliantly. In 1741 Charles Jenners wrote the libretto "A Sacred Oratorio" and sent it to George Frederic Handel, together with a note saying that "The Lord gave the word". At that time Handel had been rejected by the English nobility and his business affairs were in a bad way. As he began to read through the manuscript, Handel was deeply struck by the words "He was despised and rejected of men . . . God did not leave his soul in hell . . . He will give you rest". The words completely captured his imagination, "I know that my Redeemer lives . . . King of kings! Lord of Lords! Forever and ever . . . Hallelujah!" He picked up his pen and began to write. He was excited – more than that, thrilled.

The music for the words began to flow through his mind so swiftly that he could scarcely write the notes fast enough. For 24 days Handel did not leave his London flat. His manservant brought him food, but it was often untouched. Occasionally he would jump up and run to his harpsichord, waving his arms up in the air and singing loudly, "Hallelujah! Hallelujah! Hallelujah!" He later said, "I think I did see all heaven before me, and the great God himself". He was caught up in another world. Never before had he experienced such profound religious exhilaration, nor would he ever know the same intensity of feeling again. But in the few days when his mind was absorbed in the wonder and praise of God, this rather ordinary man gave to the world a musical composition that still lifts the soul towards heaven whenever it is sung. Its words are divinely inspired, and the music is celestial.

XLV

19:11-16 The Rider on the white Horse

The most important key to interpreting the book of Revelation is to realise that it is a revelation of *Jesus Christ* (1:1). When we do so, our interest is aroused, our attention is arrested and our imagination is captured. We love to see Jesus as the Lord who watches over the seven churches, as the one who sits with God on his throne, as the Lamb who was slain, as the Lion who is more majestic than Aslan, as he breaks the seven seals of the book of destiny, and as he receives the worship of heaven and directs affairs on earth. We look forward to seeing him returning in glory to judge the world, and coming as a bridegroom to claim his bride. There are many spectacular depictions of Jesus Christ in different forms and guises, and in this section we shall see him as the rider on the white horse. It is good to study the book of Revelation, and to find in it the one whom our soul loves (Song 3:4).

11. In the previous section we read about Christ as our heavenly bridegroom, but John, always full of surprises, first presents him to us as a heavenly warrior. Once again, as in 4:1, *he saw heaven opened*. Once again, as in 6:1-2, *there was a white horse*. This is startling, perhaps even more so than before. White is the colour of victory, and our hearts begin to beat faster as we wonder who is riding this horse. And – yes, it is Jesus Christ, who is riding swiftly towards his final triumph.

    John proceeds to tell us that *the rider is called Faithful and True*. Since in 3:14 Christ referred to himself as "the faithful and true witness", the identity of the rider is now firmly established. He is the one and only completely reliable person, wholly trustworthy in his testimony about the truth. *In righteousness he judges and makes war*. There are some warriors who are neither vindictive nor lusting for conquest, and Christ is certainly one such. He judges and conducts warfare in righteousness (Isa 11:4). Those who suffer injustice for Christ long for wrongs to be put right, and need a strong warrior on their side. Here he is – here he comes!

12. *The rider's eyes are like a flame of fire* (1:14) for he searches out all things, and nothing can be hidden from his gaze (Heb 4:13). He comes in royal majesty, for *on his head are many diadems*, many more than on the dragon (12:3) or on the beast (13:1). They represent the universal allegiance that he receives. When it comes to crowning Christ with many crowns we might think of the Lamb upon his throne, but John suggests that he is thus crowned in his guise as a mounted warrior.

    He has a name inscribed that no one knows but himself. Now here is a mystery that still waits to be revealed. There are certain aspects about the being and the work of Christ that we do not yet know. Indeed, there are hidden depths about his person that we shall never fully fathom, although we may try to do so during the numberless years of eternity. Only God knows his Son's full name (Mt 11:27), but Christ reveals more of himself to everyone who conquers (2:17). Leon Morris suggested an additional insight: "Those who practised magic in the first century believed that to know a name gave power over the one whose name it was. John may well be saying that no one has power over Christ. He is supreme".

13. *He is clothed in a robe dipped in blood.* The blood here is almost certainly a reference to the cross. Some commentators think that the blood may be that of his impenitent foes whom he has destroyed, but verse 15 will make it clear that the rider has not yet destroyed them, although he is on his way to doing so. Christ overcame evil by shedding his own blood. We are now told another of his names: this time *his name is called The Word of God* (with a strong link to Jn 1:1). The expression "the Word" was pregnant with meaning for many educated people in the first century. Some Greek philosophers (including Heraclitus) taught that it was the rational principle that pervaded the universe, and the Jews used "the Word of God" as an indirect alternative for the divine name. To both Greeks and Jews the phrase suggested something that was important or supremely significant.

14. *The armies of heaven, wearing fine linen, white and pure, were following him on white horses.* The armies may be saints or angels. John does not say, but most commentators opt for the latter. This is perhaps because of the repeated references in the New Testament to Christ being accompanied by angels when he returns (Mt 16:27 = Mk 8:38 = Lk 9:26, Mt 25:31, 2 Thess 1:7). The saints are also said to be clad in bright and pure clothes, but they are the bride of Christ rather than his army (v 8). We notice that it does not say that those who make up the armies of heaven have garments dipped in blood, for it was Christ alone who shed his blood for our sins. Nor are they said to hold weapons; it is the lone rider at the front who will consummate on his own the victory that he has already won.

15. There is a holy and stern side to Christ's nature, and John turns to it. *From his mouth comes a sharp sword with which to strike down the nations* (1:16), and this points to the power of his speech. He will strike down the nations not with armies but with words (Isa 11:4, 49:2). Then *he will*

rule them with a rod of iron (2:27, 12:5), for he has absolute authority over them and he cannot be resisted. And woe to the persistently impenitent. They will be cast into the divine winepress, which we have read about in 14:19-20. And then *Christ will tread the wine press of the fury of the wrath of God Almighty.* It will be indescribably awful for those who persistently spurned Christ to have to look into the face of holy love and to be the recipients not just of his wrath, but of its fury.

They will be utterly destroyed. This was prophesied over 500 years before Christ, in a bittersweet poem about a man who was returning from the wine press after trampling down certain people in his anger, so that his garments were stained crimson with *their* blood (Isa 63:1-6). In the verse we are studying, it is clear that the rider on the white horse has not yet trodden the wine press, so the blood on the robe he was wearing (v 13) must have been *his own.* It is by the blood of the Lamb that we may conquer Satan (12:11).

16. We have read of three names of the rider on the white horse (v 11, 12, 13) and now we have a fourth, written on him. *On his robe and on his thigh he has a name inscribed, "King of kings and Lord of lords".* It is written on his robe, so that all may see it, but what of his thigh? Most commentators are perplexed by this, but F.F. Bruce suggests that the Aramaic *regel* ("leg") has inadvertently replaced an original *degel* ("banner"). John may have intended "on his robe and his banner", and if so, these are good places to advertise that Christ is the Sovereign Lord of the universe, far above every name that is named, now and always (Eph 1:20-23).

Meditation: The Man with four Names

Certain liberal scholars hold that the portrayal of Christ in this passage contradicts the depiction of the gracious and merciful Christ found elsewhere in the New Testament, but this is not so. Throughout the New Testament, the achievement of victory through judgement is an essential and inescapable aspect of Christ's total work. He is full of grace and mercy, but he always respects the decisions of those who have chosen to reject him, and who persist in their impenitence. Christ has won a great victory over evil, and on his return he will finally destroy it. Without this final consummation, our redemption would remain forever incomplete.

Having studied the picture of the rider on the white horse, we have seen various details of what he looks like. The images of the one who returns to be our judge are striking, but what is his name? Of course we know that he is Jesus Christ, but what is he called in this passage? It is very noticeable that he has four names. Three of them are clearly given to us, but one is mysterious and unknown.

(a) He is called Faithful and True (v 11). In the Bible, faithfulness on God's part or on Christ's usually refers to his covenant or to his promises and warnings. He – God or Christ – is faithful to the covenant he has made with his people, and also to his promises and warnings. They are true and they will all be fulfilled. In Christ God's new covenant has been established, and through Christ all of the promises and warnings of God will be proved true. The Son of God, Jesus Christ, was not 'Yes and No', but in him it is always 'Yes'. In him every one of God's promises is a 'Yes'. For this reason we say 'Amen' to the glory of God (2 Cor 1:19-20).

The Bible is marvellously replete with promises of salvation and warnings of judgement. Some are yet to be fulfilled, so the saints of God cry out, "How long?" (6:10). How long before the promises are fulfilled? Where is the God of justice? And God replies, "Be patient for a while. Wait for me. The day of fulfilment *will come*". Perfect justice is going to put right every wrong. All of the promises and warnings in the Bible will be fulfilled in Christ, for he is rightly called *Faithful and True*. Jesus Christ always was, is, and will be absolutely reliable and true.

(b) He has a name inscribed that no one knows but himself (v 12). How can this be? Our name stands for our identity, who we are. Likewise, the known names of Christ point to the sort of person he has been revealed to be. Therefore the fact that he has an unknown name means that he has not yet been fully revealed to us. Those who know Christ deeply are the first to admit that there are aspects of his divine-human person and depths in the finality of his work that they have neither plumbed nor understood. Only on the last day, when he returns to wind up this present age, shall we see him as he is. Then, and only then, shall we know him as he knows us (1 Cor 13:12, 1 Jn 3:2). It is then that his secret name will be made known to those who love him. Those who are God's people are the bride of the Lamb and, as Phil Moore pointed out, "A bride adopts the name of her husband, and Jesus promises in 3:12 that he will put his name on us". The marriage name may be his secret name, which is also mentioned in 2:17.

Christians need to remember that Jesus Christ has a name that nobody knows yet except for himself. Humility is a quality greatly pleasing to God. Therefore it is particularly fitting for God's people to be humble, especially when they marvel together at Christ's great and worthy name. He remains a partial enigma to us all. He knows us perfectly because his eyes are like a flame of fire, but we do not know him perfectly. It should come as no surprise to us if we discover mysteries about his person and work that we just cannot understand. He is far too majestic to fit into our puny brains, for he has many diadems on his head. What we do not know about him may be summed up in the name that no one knows but himself.

(c) His name is called The Word of God (v 13). In the prologue to John's Gospel, Christ is called the Word that was with God and was God. At the turning point in history, the Word became flesh and dwelt among us, full of grace and truth. But what does it mean, to call him the Word of God? Just as we reveal ourselves through the words we speak, so God makes himself known to people through his word. We read his word when we read the Bible, but God has revealed himself supremely through his incarnate Word, Jesus Christ. "No one has ever seen God. It is God the only Son, who is close to the Father's heart, who has made him known" (Jn 1:18). To say that Jesus Christ is the Word of God is to say that he is the final revelation of God. Not that everything about him has yet been revealed; we have seen that Christ has an unknown name. But all that God has chosen to reveal to us so far has come to its climax and fullness in Jesus Christ.

In particular, we are told that he who is the Word of God is wearing a blood-stained robe. It is on the cross, where his blood was shed for sinners like us, that he revealed both the holiness and the love of God. God's holiness and justice are revealed in his settled determination to judge sinners like us, who deserve to be the objects of his wrath. His love and mercy are revealed in his settled purpose to bear in our place, as our substitute, the judgement we deserve. Christ is the Word of God, so if we wish to know what God is like, all we need to do is to listen to Christ and to look at him, especially as we see him on the cross. There is no fuller revelation of what God is like than the one we observe in Christ crucified.

(d) He has a name inscribed "King of kings and Lord of lords" (v 16). This is the most spectacular of all Christ's names, and it reminds us, together with the Hallelujah chorus, of the climax of Handel's oratorio "Messiah". King of kings and Lord of lords, forever and ever, Hallelujah! Earthly kings and lords become intoxicated and are corrupted by their power and fame. Only Jesus Christ can cut them down to size. Emperors, kings, presidents and dictators are allowed to amass territory, they may subjugate people, and they sometimes insist on the absolute allegiance of their subjects. They forget that there is someone who is enthroned in heaven as King of kings and Lord of lords (17:14, Deut 10:17), and that God in heaven laughs at their pathetic pretensions, scoffs at their childish ambitions, rebukes them in his wrath, and says to them, "I have established my king, King Jesus the Messiah, on Zion, my holy hill" (Ps 2:4-6). He goes on, "Now therefore, O kings, be wise; be warned, O rulers of the earth. Serve the Lord with fear, with trembling kiss his feet, or he will be angry, and you will perish in the way; for his wrath is quickly kindled" (Ps 2:10-11).

We may read how the apostles quoted Psalm 2 soon after Pentecost, when Peter and John were forbidden by the Jewish authorities to preach or teach in the name of Jesus. After they were released by the court, the first thing they did was to convene a prayer meeting with their fellow Christians, to pray for boldness. They prayed, "Sovereign Lord", King of kings and Lord of lords, "you said by the Holy Spirit through our ancestor David, your servant, 'Why did the Gentiles rage, and the peoples imagine vain things? The kings of the earth took their stand, and the rulers have gathered together against the Lord and against his Messiah'" (Ps 2:1-2). They then applied this to recent events, remembering how Herod and Pontius Pilate, with the Romans and the Jews, "gathered together against your holy servant Jesus, whom you anointed, to do whatever your hand and your plan had predestined to take place. And now, Lord, look at their threats, and grant to your servants to speak your word with all boldness" (Acts 4:23-31).

They had a vision of the Lord of human lords and the King of human kings, and they allowed him to transform their guilty silence into holy and loving boldness. This vision of Jesus Christ, enthroned by God the Father at his right hand, is only discerned by the eye of faith. It is by faith that we see heaven opened, and that we look through the open door in heaven and see the rider on the white horse as he rides through the skies. Out of his mouth comes a sharp sword with which to strike down the nations, and he will rule them with a rod of iron (Ps 2:9). It is not some mighty angel who will tread the wine press of the fury of the wrath of God the Almighty – it is Christ, the rider on the white horse. These great truths are not apparent to our earthly eyes, but they are nevertheless realities which we may discern with the eyes of our faith. The same

Jesus who was born in Bethlehem and was laid in a manger is the glorified Christ who is now exalted and sovereign at the right hand of God. One day he will be acknowledged and acclaimed by all people as King of kings and Lord of lords.

It is good to remember his names. *Jesus* means "Saviour" and *Christ* means "God's Anointed One". He is also *the Lamb*, but he has many other names, of which we have picked up four in this study. He is *Faithful and True*, because in him all the promises and warnings of God are fulfilled. He has *a name inscribed that no one knows* but himself, because there are many things about him which are too marvellous for us to know now. He is *the Word of God*, because he is the pinnacle of the revelation of God about himself. And he is *King of kings and Lord of lords* because all authority in heaven and on earth has been given to him. There can be no doubt that God has rightly exalted him and given him "the name that is above every name, so that at the name of Jesus every knee should bend, in heaven and on earth and under the earth, and every tongue should confess that Jesus Christ is Lord, to the glory of God the Father" (Phil 2:9-11).

XLVI

19:17-20:6 Four Features of the End of Time

Before presenting us with details about Satan's doom and an ultimate vision of the Final Judgement, John intrigues us with four pictures of the end of time. He has told us about the marriage supper of the Lamb, and now he depicts for us an alternative banquet which he refers to by the epithet "the great supper of God" (19:17-18). Secondly, he gives us an initial glimpse of Armageddon, which is to be the last battle (19:19-21). Thirdly, he briefly summarises the period between Christ's first and second comings, and informs us that there will be difficult times before the end arrives (20:1-3). Fourthly, he tells us about the resurrection of the witnesses of Christ who died before Christ's return (20:4-6). After these insights we shall be ready for the revelation of the final judgements of God and of Christ.

17. *Then John saw an angel standing in the sun.* This vision was strikingly vivid and left a deep impression in John's mind. For sheer horror it takes some beating. *With a loud voice the angel cried to all the birds that* *fly in mid-heaven*, a term which means "up in the air" (8:13, 14:6). He said to the birds, *"Come, gather for the great supper of God"*. We now realise that at this supper those who feast will not be people but birds. In this respect it will be an altogether different occasion from the marriage supper of the Lamb (19:7, 9; see also Ezek 39:17-20).

18. What would be on the menu for these birds? They were to gather *"to eat the flesh of kings, the flesh of captains, the flesh of the mighty, the flesh of horses and their riders – the flesh of all, both free and slave, both small and great"*. All has become clear, and the vision is gruesome. The angel is inviting the birds of the air to come and feast on the corpses of many people from all classes of society: kings and captains, the powerful and the heroic, the free and the enslaved, the unimportant and the celebrities. This is the company of the impenitent, of those who have done what is evil in the sight of God and then persistently rejected his salvation. None of them will be excluded from this alternative supper party. They would remain unburied for the pleasure of the birds. In ancient times this would have constituted the ultimate dishonour, a fate worse than death. Of course this is a revolting picture that is not to be taken literally, but it is clear that the resolute enemies of God are greatly to be pitied because they will be utterly destroyed.

19. The battle lines are ready. Armageddon is about to begin. *Then John saw the beast and the kings of the earth with their armies gathered to make war against the rider on the horse and against his army.* The forces of evil are drawn up in battle array for the final conflict against the forces of good, led by the rider on the white horse. Before the battle his robe is dipped in his own blood (19:13), but afterwards it will be red with the blood of those he has trampled on (Isa 63:1-6).

20. John says nothing about the battle. The implication is that although the forces of evil may seem mighty, they will be utterly helpless when they confront the rider on the white horse. The rider, who is Jesus Christ, will win a devastating victory, unaided by anyone else (20:7-9, Isa 59:15b-17, 63:3a, 5). John proceeds to inform us that *the beast was captured, and with it the false prophet who had performed in its presence the signs by which he deceived those who had received the mark of the beast and those who worshipped its image.* For the beast, see section XXXII on pages 168-175 and for the false prophet, see section XXXIII on pages

175-181. The beast will use his power to gather his troops together for the final battle, and the false prophet will still be characterised by the false signs by which he deceives all who have the mark of the beast on their foreheads. But when the day of Armageddon comes, they will both be utterly helpless.

They will be forcibly captured and *then they will both be thrown alive into the lake of fire that burns with sulphur.* This lake of fire will be mentioned again in 20:10, 14, 15 and 21:8. Leon Morris explains its symbolism succinctly: "Being cast into the lake of fire signifies utter destruction. All that the beast stood for is no more". Likewise the false prophet, with his devious insincerity, will also be no more, and the godly will suffer no further deceitful spiritual abuse or betrayal of their trust.

21. What of the impenitent who fought with the beast and the false prophet? They, *the rest, were killed by the sword of the rider on the horse, the sword that came from his mouth.* It was his word that destroyed them (19:15, Isa 11:4). Christ did his strange deed and worked his alien work (Isa 28:21b). How he would have preferred to do his natural work of salvation! But they refused (Isa 30:15). The picture of destruction ends with the sequel to verses 17-18. *The birds* enjoyed the great supper of God, and *gorged themselves with the flesh of the wicked.*

This is a thought-provoking text. George Eldon Ladd noted that "Some scholars find elements of universalism in the New Testament. This, however, can be done only when certain verses are taken out of their biblical context. The New Testament expects masses of people to remain unrepentant and obdurate in heart, and they can anticipate nothing but the judgement and the wrath of the Lamb".

20:1. *John now sees another angel coming down from heaven, holding in his hand the key to the bottomless pit and a great chain.* Because he holds the key to the bottomless pit, he may be the same as the star-angel mentioned in 9:1-2. Perhaps John is highlighting the unimportance of Satan by implying that it is neither God the Father nor Christ who is dealing with him here, but an unnamed angel. He has authority over Satan, to restrain him with a symbolic chain and imprison him.

2. *The angel seized the evil one,* who is called by all four of the names by which he is referred to in this book: *the dragon, that ancient serpent, who is the Devil and Satan.* Then *he bound him for a thousand years.* As we shall see in the meditation that follows, there are three main interpretations of the 1,000 years. The one that fits most comfortably with the rest of scripture is that this period symbolises the Christian age, which extends from the resurrection of Christ to his return in glory. 1,000 is the cube of ten, and ten is a number that often symbolises completeness in the Bible. Satan has been bound and restrained for nearly all of this age, although he will be released shortly before the end (see the next verse). But by whose power was he forced to accept his binding? It was Jesus Christ's power, when he triumphed over Satan on the cross (Mk 3:27, Col 2:13-15).

3. *The angel threw Satan into the pit, and locked and sealed it over him.* He is held under divine control (Isa 24:22) awaiting his final punishment (which John will spell out in 20:10). His activities are curtailed. But how can this be reconciled with the fact that he seems to be so active in our time (12:12)? The answer is that both are true. Satan is hard at work, for he knows that his time is short. But Christ has won a decisive victory over him and, with the help of his people, is proceeding to spread his kingdom throughout the earth. All the evil on earth comes from the hyperactivity of Satan. But it is also true that Satan does not have a free hand, and John often speaks of the forces of evil being given authority to afflict people.

Here he tells us that Satan is locked up *so that he would deceive the nations no more, until the thousand years are ended.* As Leon Morris put it, "The end of the world is in God's control, not Satan's. John may also mean that although Satan is busy, he is restrained from doing his worst. He cannot destroy the church. He cannot even destroy the martyrs, for they reign with Christ". But the period of restraint will end, and *after that he must be let out for a little while.* We shall learn soon what will happen then (20:7-10). Dark times lie ahead – but only briefly.

4. John now turns his attention to those who have suffered for Christ's sake. First of all *he saw thrones, and those seated on them were given authority to judge.* He then describes those who were enthroned, saying, *I also saw the souls of those who had been beheaded for their testimony to Jesus and for the word of God. They had not worshipped the beast or its image and had not received its mark on their foreheads or their hands.* On the thrones John saw people sitting, and they were given authority

to judge. Who exactly were they? They would have included apostles (Mt 19:28), saints (1 Cor 6:2-3), and all those who conquer (3:21, 12:11). John here specifies "the beheaded", a noble company that includes all the godly who remain true to Jesus when others disdain him, and who are unashamed of God's word when others reject it. They refuse to worship the beast or even to think like the beast. It is they who now sit on thrones and have been given the authority to judge.

One of the recurring themes in the book of Revelation is that in the end perfect justice must and will be served. It is therefore appropriate that *the beheaded came to life and reigned with Christ a thousand years*. Even though they had been ignominiously put to death, they would immediately begin to live again with Christ. John earlier wrote that he saw their *souls*, so it is possible that in the intermediate state, until the bodily resurrection, they lead a disembodied existence. It is, however, a superlatively happy one which involves reigning with Christ, and it is even better than serving him here on earth (Phil 1:23). Moreover, this blissful state of affairs will extend until the end of the Christian era.

5. *The rest of the dead*, that is to say those who have not trusted in Christ and do not belong to God's people, *will not come to life until the 1,000 years are ended*, in other words until Christ returns to wind up this present age. John then reflects about *the first resurrection*. What is he talking about? He refers to the coming to life of the Christian dead, and to the event that led directly to it. By "the first resurrection" John means the moment of conversion, when the new Christian is born again or born from above (Jn 3:3, 5, 7). The second resurrection is the later coming to life of the dead. It takes place immediately after death for those who die in Christ, and at the end of time for everybody else.

6. *Those who share in the first resurrection*, because they have been born again, *are blessed and holy*. Here we have the fifth of the seven benedictions in the book of Revelation (the first was in 1:3). Not only do they receive great blessing from God, they are also holy like he is. Initially the holiness is imputed by God as a free undeserved gift, but as time passes they become what they are, as the Holy Spirit infuses holiness into their lives. *Over such people the second death has no power*, for their names are written in the book of life (20:15). Instead *they will be priests*

of God and of Christ (5:10, Isa 61:6, 1 Pet 2:5). And John repeats what he said in 20:4, namely that *they will reign with Christ 1,000 years*. As Leon Morris wrote, "The supreme joy of the blessed ones is that they are associated with Christ in priesthood and in royalty".

Meditation: The Millennium

(a) The period of 1,000 years mentioned on six occasions in 20:2, 3, 4, 5, 6 and 7 is usually called the millennium, and Christians who regard the Bible as being the word of God are divided on how they interpret it. As Leon Morris wisely wrote, "It is important to approach the chapter with humility and charity". The present author happily admits that he may be wrong in the view he has adopted, but he is entitled to outline the reasons why he has opted for that view.

(b) Premillennialists believe that when Christ returns, the Christian dead will be raised, and any believers who are still alive on Earth will be caught up with them in the clouds to meet him in the air (1 Thess 4:17). *Then* they will reign on earth with Christ for 1,000 years. After this Satan will be released for a short time, and then the impenitent and the unbelievers will be raised from the dead. Last of all, the Final Judgement will take place. Premillennialists believe in two physical resurrections, the first one for the blessed and second one for the cursed.

(c) Postmillennialists disagree with premillennialists and believe that the return of Christ will take place *after* the 1,000 years. Some of them envisage that the 1,000 years will be a time when the gospel message will triumph in this present age, perhaps as a literal period of 1,000 years at the end of time. They interpret "the first resurrection" in the same way as amillennialists.

(d) Amillennialists do not believe in a literal period of 1,000 years. They take it as a symbolic period that extends from the first coming of Jesus Christ to his return in glory. In their view, the 1,000 years is the same as the three and a half years ("time, times and half a time") of 12:14, as the 42 months of 11:2 and 13:5, and as the 1,260 days of 11:3 and 12:6. They divide time into two equal halves, "before Christ" and "after Christ", and since 7 is the number of completeness, 7 years is symbolic of the totality of time. Our present age, after Christ, is half of this, namely three and a half years = 42 months = 1,260 days, reckoning 30 days for every month. Amillenialists also interpret "the first resurrection" (20:5) as the moment of conversion or new birth of the believer, who has risen from the death of sin. The early church highlighted the insight that baptism has an element of resurrection about it (Rom 6:2-3, Col 2:12).

(e) The present commentary is written assuming an amillennial point of view, which in the opinion of the present writer helps to interpret the book of Revelation in line with the rest of the Bible. Revelation seems to many a weird book, different from all the other books of the Bible. It would be weird indeed if it was the only book in the Bible that taught that a certain period of a thousand years would have great importance in connection with the end times. But everywhere in Revelation there are terms that are used symbolically, so why not the 1,000 years as well? The present writer is certain that Revelation was not written to be a weird book, and that it loses its weird appearance if you interpret it in the light of the rest of scripture. John was forced to use symbolism because of the subversive nature of his message at a time of great tribulation. He was writing to Christians who were undergoing severe persecution at the hands of the imperial power, and his book was an extraordinary blessing for them – but it had to be a visionary book.

(f) It is most important to realise that the differences between pre-, post- and a-millennialists are of *secondary* importance. We who know and love Christ and his word are to welcome each other and have fellowship with each other, "but not for the purpose of quarrelling over opinions" (Rom 14:1). In his commentary on Romans, John Stott wrote that "We must not elevate non-essentials, especially issues of custom and ceremony, to the level of the essential and make them tests of orthodoxy and conditions of fellowship. Nor must we marginalise fundamental theological or moral questions as if they were only cultural and of no great importance". He also listed some contentious "matters of indifference" on which scripture does not clearly pronounce: practices such as the mode of baptism (by immersion or affusion), episcopal confirmation (whether it is a legitimate part of Christian initiation), the giving and receiving of a wedding ring (controversial in England in the 17th century), the use of cosmetics, jewellery and alcohol; and beliefs such as which charismata are available or important, how frequently we should expect signs and wonders, how and when Old Testament prophecy has been or is being fulfilled, when and how the millennium was or will be established, the relation of history to eschatology, and the precise nature of heaven and hell.

(g) Leon Morris suggests that in this section, which mentions the millennium on a handful of occasions, "John is simply taking us behind the scenes, as he has done so often before. Despite the persecution of believers, Christ is not defeated, nor are those who have died for his sake. Our peep behind the scenes shows us

martyrs reigning and Satan bound. The martyrs only appear to have died. They are alive thanks to their first resurrection. Later in the chapter John speaks of the release of Satan as the way in which the nations are gathered for the final battle. But here he is surely concerned with present realities – the apparent release of the martyrs and their real triumph". Even in such a controversial chapter, the central theme of the book of Revelation predominates: *Christ is the victor.*

XLVII

20:7-15 The Final Judgement

Satan is doomed. He has been doomed ever since he was utterly defeated by Jesus Christ on the cross. John will now briefly describe his final fate to us. After doing so, he will give us an awe-inspiring but equally brief vision of the final judgement of humankind. In the end, the triumph of good over evil will be clear to everyone. If anyone wilfully spurns the undeserved grace of God and rejects his offer of free forgiveness, they must and will be destroyed. There will be no place in the new Earth for those who remain impenitent and harden their hearts. Perfect justice will be seen to have been done. Even death and Hades will be overthrown.

7. *When the 1,000 years are ended, Satan will be released from his prison.* This repeats the prophecy at the end of verse 3. Most Christians agree that this event will take place shortly before the winding up of this present age.

8. After his release, *Satan will come out to deceive the nations.* He will resume his deceitful activities on an international basis, *at the four corners of the earth, Gog and Magog.* Like the unclean spirits that resemble frogs in 16:13-16, he will gather the nations for the final battle. It is difficult to interpret the place names Gog and Magog. From their use in this verse, it would seem that they symbolise all people. In the Bible, the name *Gog* is mentioned in a genealogy (1 Chron 5:4), in a prophecy (Ezek chapters 38, 39), and here. As for *Magog*, it appears in two genealogies, the first of which is very old (Gen 10:2, 1 Chron 1:5), and the Ezekiel chapters, and here. Magog is the land from which Gog came (Ezek 38:2). Leon Morris has pointed out that in later Judaism Gog and Magog were thought of as two leaders who symbolised the forces of

evil. John here uses the names to refer to the armies of the wicked, deceived and *gathered together by Satan for battle*. There will be a final great attack on God and his people. *The attackers will be as numerous as the sands of the sea* (Gen 22:17). This will be the final battle.

9. John builds up the suspense. *They marched up over the breadth of the earth and surrounded the camp of the saints and the beloved city*. The odds seem to be heavily stacked against God's people. This may be a widespread attack, over the entire breadth of the earth. Wherever the godly are to be found, i.e. *their camp*, they will be attacked. *The beloved city* is the opposite of "the great city", where people live in organised community and in opposition to God. By contrast, in "the beloved city" live the godly, who seek to live in obedience to God's word. And so we are now all set to read about the ultimate battle, which may feature horrible treachery by the wicked and wonderful heroism by the Lamb and his followers.

But John says nothing about the ultimate war. Why? Because no battle happens. The forces of good sustain no casualties. It is all over in an instant. As before in 19:19-21, where the forces of evil are killed by the sword of the rider on the white horse, the people of God just wait for God to win. They know that they are not to fear or be dismayed, for the battle is not theirs but God's (2 Chron 20:15). This battle is not for them to fight: their part is simply to trust in God. All they have to do is take their position (on their knees), remain still, and see the victory of God on their behalf (2 Chron 20:17). It will all be over in an instant. *Fire will come down from heaven and consume the forces of evil* (Ezek 38:21-23). Leon Morris wrote that "John consistently thinks of the power of God as so overwhelming that there cannot even be the appearance of a battle when he wills to destroy evil".

10. But what about Satan, who summoned the wicked and gathered them together for the final battle? *The devil who had deceived them was thrown into the lake of fire and sulphur. There he will join* his chief henchmen, *the beast and the false prophet* (19:20). *There all three of them will be tormented day and night, forever and ever*. If we take this at its face value, it suggests that Satan, the beast and the false prophet will be made to suffer without intermission and without end. In the meditation we shall consider a different interpretation.

11. John now moves on to the last of his discussions about God's judgement. He invites us to accompany him behind the scenes and witness the final judgement of men and women. The setting is majestic and overpowering. *John saw a great white throne and the one who sat on it.* Is the enthroned one God the Father or is it his Son? It seems likely that it is Christ, whom God has appointed to preside at the final judgement (Mt 25:31-46; Jn 5:22; Acts 10:42, 17:30-31; 2 Tim 4:1). Although God is the judge of all, he judges all through the Son. On that great and final day (Isa 2:10-21), only one person will capture everyone's attention. Only one being will be lit up by the spotlights of glory. The radiance of all the universe will light up his majesty. He alone will be exalted on that day. Leon Morris wrote that, "John invests the scene with the greatest solemnity". In the demeanour of the one sitting on the throne there will be something altogether terrifying, and so *the earth and the heaven will flee from his presence.* The present universe, tainted by the fall (Rom 8:20-22), is not fit for the presence of the Holy One. It must be renewed by fire (2 Pet 3:7, 10). For it *no place will be found.* In its present form it will cease to be (Mk 13:31), but in the next life it will be recreated (21:1).

12. *John then saw the dead, great and small, standing before the throne.* Every person who ever lived will be there. No one will be excluded on the grounds of their self-perceived importance or unimportance. Then, with absolutely everyone present, a momentous event will take place: *books are opened* (Dan 7:9-10). How easily we forget about these books, which record people's lives. And there is a special book that is set apart from the others. *Also another book is opened, the book of life.* The book of life has an Old Testament pedigree (Ex 32:32-33, Isa 4:3, Mal 3:16) as well as one in the New (Lk 10:20, Phil 4:3). It has already received three mentions in Revelation (3:5, 13:8, 17:8) and there are two more to come (20:15, 21:27). Those whose names are inscribed in the book are assured of eternal life. They are clothed with garments of salvation and covered with a robe of righteousness (Isa 61:10). *And the dead were judged according to their works, as recorded in the books.* Throughout the Bible it is made clear that God judges people according to their works. It is a fair measuring-stick, and God by his very nature will judge everyone justly (Gen 18:25).

13. *The sea gave up the dead that were in it, and Death and Hades gave up the dead that were in them.* This is John's way of underlining the fact that absolutely everyone will be included in the final judgement, irrespective of where and how they met their death, even if they met it in "the sea". The sea here represents chaos and destruction, which explains its absence in the new heaven and the new earth (21:1). Death is common to all of us. Hades is our universal destination, although it seems to consist of two quite separate sections, one for the godly and one for the wicked (Lk 16:23, 26). All three, the sea, Death and Hades, will surrender the people who are in them, so that they may attend the final judgement. And then *all will be judged according to what they have done.* John repeats what he has just said in the previous verse. To be judged according to our works is the same as to be judged according to what we have done (Ps 28:4, Jn 5:28-29). God's judgment is impartial and just. It is neither arbitrary nor biased. Since it is based on what we have done, it will be in perfect harmony with what is factual and true. No one will wish to question its correctness.

14. *Then Death and Hades will be thrown into the lake of fire.* In the great Welsh hymn "Guide me, O thou great Jehovah" Christ is proclaimed as "Death of death and hell's destruction". We are told that the beast and the false prophet (19:20) and the devil (20:10) will be thrown into the lake of fire, but there are other forces associated with evil that will suffer the same fate. Death is the last enemy, so it must be overthrown (1 Cor 15:26, 2 Tim 1:10). Hades is the realm of the dead, so it too must be destroyed. At this point, when Death and Hades are cast into the lake of fire, the end of history has finally arrived.

John adds a significant insight: *this is the second death, the lake of fire.* God had warned Adam and Eve that if they ate of the forbidden fruit, they would die (Gen 2:17). And when they did so, they were immediately separated from God (Gen 3:8). Like them, we too have all sinned (Rom 3:23) and are likewise cut off from God. We are therefore due to receive the wages of sin, which is death, but God has offered us the free gift of eternal life thanks to Christ's death for our sins on the cross (Rom 6:23). If we accept God's free gift of salvation, our names will be written in the book of life. But if we obstinately refuse the gift and persist in impenitence, our rebellion will be sealed by death twice over. The first death is our physical decease, which terminates our lives in this world. Later, at the end of the present age, will follow the general resurrection and the final judgement. Any people whose names are not found in the book of life will then undergo the second death, which is final destruction in the lake of fire.

15. John reiterates the ultimate perdition that awaits the lost. *Anyone whose name was not found written in the book of life will be thrown into the lake of fire.* After the second death of the impenitent, death will be no more. Along with the pain and sorrow that it brings, it will not form part of the new creation (21:4). The promise of Isaiah 25:8 will then become a reality, and God will swallow up death forever. What will follow next will be altogether good, and John will attempt to describe it to us in the last two chapters of Revelation.

Meditation: Seven important Facts about the final Judgement

(a) The judgement of Satan will have everlasting consequences. Satan and his henchmen, the beast and the false prophet, are fallen and utterly evil spirits who, by persistently provoking men and women to sin, have lost everything that was good in their personality. F.F. Bruce suggested that the beast and the false prophet might be code words for impersonal systems rather than for personal spirits, and this is possible. Satan, on the other hand, is such a perverted spirit that he must be destroyed. Verse 10 speaks of a lake of fire, but it is difficult to conceive how physical fire could bring eternal torment to spiritual beings. George Eldon Ladd suggested a different interpretation: "This is picturesque language describing a real fact in the spiritual world: the final and everlasting destruction of the forces of evil which have plagued people since the Garden of Eden". Verse 10 teaches the end of the malevolent influence of the two beasts and their utterly devious leader. Satan will never lead anyone astray again. For the time being "the whole world lies under the power of the evil one" (1 Jn 5:19), but "the ruler of this world has been condemned" (Jn 16:11).

(b) The final judgement will be an answer to prayer. It will finally take place as a consequence of the prayers of many martyrs: "How long, Sovereign Lord, until you judge the inhabitants of the earth and avenge our blood?" They were told to wait a little longer until their number was complete (6:9-11). Their prayers were backed up by the prayers of all the saints (8:3-5), and after years and

lifetimes of patient waiting, the great Day of the Lord – the Day of Judgement – will arrive at last. It is part of the hope of every Christian. Perfect justice will finally prevail.

(c) The contents of the books will be disclosed. They contain a perfect record of our works. Augustine thought of them as part of the divine memory. Our deeds, including our spoken words (Mt 12:36-37) and even our thoughts and intentions (Heb 4:12-13) have been recorded and will be disclosed on the Day of the Lord. All the wrongs we have perpetrated, all our selfish schemes including those that we thought had succeeded, all our tricks, lies, and manipulative tactics – all are recorded for exposure on the final day. Most of them are undiscovered and maybe forgotten by us. But they did happen. On the final day the books will be opened, and their contents will be seen by all.

If we have ears to hear, we should hear Christ's words: "Nothing is covered up that will not be uncovered, and nothing is secret that will not become known. Therefore whatever you have said in the dark will be heard in the light, and what you have whispered behind closed doors will be proclaimed from the housetops" (Lk 12:2-3). Richard Bewes wrote that when these books are opened, "the assessment will be entirely accurate. No one is going to question God's justice. Ultimately the future verdict of God's assessment is simply the under-lining of decisions and attitudes that we have adopted over a lifetime. It would be quite illogical for someone to expect to have everything to do with God in the next life, after having had nothing to do with him in this one".

(d) The final judgement will be according to what we have done. This is clearly affirmed in the Bible, both in the Old Testament and the New (Ps 62:12; Prov 24:12; Jer 17:10, 32:19; Mt 16:27; Rom 2:6; 1 Pet 1:17; Rev 2:23, 22:12, etc). Those whose names are in the book of life are there because their good works prove that they have truly repented of evil and trusted in God or in Christ. In the Bible works are never the basis or means of our salvation, but they are the evidence that we have been saved, and because of this they constitute an excellent criterion for judgement. There will be nothing impersonal about the Day of Judgement. Each one of us will be judged individually, personally and fairly. Our good works are not the reason why we shall be found in the book of life, but they provide the vital evidence that we belong to God.

In the Old Testament we read that those whose names are written in the book will be delivered on the last day and raised to everlasting life, but those who are evildoers will face shame and everlasting contempt (Dan 12:1–2). As John Stott observed, "When John says, 'the dead were judged according to their works, as recorded in the books', he is not saying that sinners are justified by their good works. No, we sinners are justified by God's grace alone through faith in Christ alone. At the same time, we will be judged by our good works. The reason for this is that the Judgement Day will be a public occasion, and that our good works will be the only public and visible evidence which can be produced to attest the authenticity of our faith. Faith without works is dead" (Jas 2:17, 26).

(e) Christ promised that his people will not come under judgement. This is a wonderful and little known promise: "Very truly, I tell you, anyone who hears my word and believes him who sent me has eternal life, and does not come under judgement, but has passed from death to life" (Jn 5:24). For those who have obeyed God and trusted in Christ, being under judgement is a thing of the past. They will need to attend the Day of Judgement. Their book must be opened. This will reveal that their lives were imperfect, "since all have sinned and fall short of the glory of God" (Rom 3:23). But it will also be evident that the overall trend of their lives was that they acknowledged their sins and had faith in God. Therefore they will not come under judgement, because when the book of life is opened it will be seen that their name is written in it.

(f) The quality of what God's people have done will be put to the test. There is no escaping this. If we trust and obey Christ, we have our names written in the book of life. So we are building our lives on the only reliable foundation, which is Christ (1 Cor 3:10-11). But what materials are we using for building the house of our lives? If we use gold, silver and precious stones, our house will survive the fire on the Day of the Lord, and we will be rewarded for the way we built it. But if we build using wood, hay and stubble, our work will be burned up. We will suffer loss, even though we ourselves will be saved, but only as through fire (1 Cor 3:12-15).

(g) The coming judgement will affect us in this life. It will be a comfort and a challenge. It will comfort us because we are saved by God's amazing grace, and because one day true justice will be established. And it will challenge us to live a life that is worthy of Christ and whose worth will one day be revealed.

XLVIII

21:1-8 The new Heaven and the new Earth

From the lake of fire and the terrible fate of the lost, John turns to the wonderful destiny of those who are saved. We are coming to the end of this visionary book, but before John signs off he shares with us the glimpses he has been given of the final state of redeemed humanity in the life to come. There is a magnificent future in store for those who love God. The beauty and value of the new Earth will make all the seductive splendours of Babylon pale by comparison, and will help us to recognise the transitory nature and the seductive pull of the whore's allurements for what they are. In his hymn "Glorious things of thee are spoken", John Newton included the following memorable lines, which sum up our glorious future:

> Fading is the worldling's pleasure, all his boasted pomp and show;
> Solid joys and lasting treasure none but Zion's members know.

1. *John saw a new heaven and a new earth.* This is the heart of our Christian hope (2 Pet 3:13), as well as being what the saints of the Old Testament looked forward to (Isa 65:17, 66:22). The Greek word for "new" used here is *kainos*, which means "fresh". It emphasises the quality of what is new rather than its recent creation. There is to be a complete and radical transformation of all things for the better, and this is necessary *because the first heaven and the first earth had passed away.* That the first earth must pass away is understandable (Rom 8:20-22), but why should the first heaven also be marked for dissolution? Leon Morris suggests that at present its description contains "symbols of God's separateness, like a 'sea of glass' (4:6). But the final state of affairs will be characterised by God's nearness".

   John also tells us that *the sea was no more.* The sea is always restless and is a symbol of chaos and insubordination. It was considered to be a source of evil, for the beast came up from there (13:1). The wicked were compared to "a tossing sea that cannot keep still; its waters toss up mire and mud" (Isa 57:20). In antiquity many lives were lost at sea because of dangerous storms. But in the next life this seething cauldron of trouble will no longer exist. As he nears the end of his book John mentions seven evils that will be *no more*: the sea (v 1), death, mourning, crying and pain (v 4), anything accursed (22:3) and the night (22:5). Can this be the last of John's heptads? They have certainly animated the book of Revelation!

2. *John also saw the holy city, the New Jerusalem.* It was not a city that we could find on this earth, for it was *holy* and *new*. But its name, Jerusalem, suggests some continuity with this earth. This city was *coming down out of heaven from God.* It was descending to the new earth. Would this "coming down to earth" deprive it of its heavenly qualities? Leon Morris made some pertinent points: "[John] is not thinking of the new earth as the place of men's felicity, in distinction from the new heaven as God's dwelling place, for God 'will dwell with them' (v 3). In fact after the New Jerusalem has descended, there will be no clear difference between heaven and earth. Perhaps John has in mind that there is already a sense in which God's people experience the heavenly city. It is this which is their bliss in the presence of a multitude of earthly distractions and difficulties. And this of which they now experience a foretaste (and which is expressed in the idea of *Jerusalem*) will be perfectly realised hereafter. Heaven will come down to earth". John saw the city *prepared as a bride adorned for her husband* (Isa 62:4). We who are part of the bride of Christ will be preparing ourselves carefully for the wedding day.

3. Once again *John heard a loud voice from the throne.* Both the volume and the source of the voice point to the importance of its announcement: "*See, the home of God is among mortals. He will dwell with them; they will be his peoples, and God himself will be with them*". The word used for God's home is "tabernacle", and refers to his Shekinah glory travelling with them (Lev 26:11). Leon Morris notes, "This term denotes the glory of God's presence among his people. John is conveying two thoughts, those of God's presence and God's glory". In this verse John says three times that God will come and live with the redeemed. Those who are saved will be his *peoples*, which suggests that people of every race and nation will be found in the holy city (7:9). Christ had said to his followers, "I have other sheep that do not belong to this fold" (Jn 10:16), and his great commission was that his followers should go and make disciples of all nations (Mt 28:19-20).

4. It is remarkable how the three promises in Isaiah 25:8 are all repeated in this verse. *God will wipe every tear from their eyes* echoes "the Lord

God will wipe away the tears from all faces". Like a mother who attends to her child after a fall, God will tenderly console those who have been broken. *Death will be no more* is the same as "[God] will swallow up death forever": it is the final reversal of the curse of Genesis 2:16-17 and 3:19. Death will have been swallowed up in victory (1 Cor 15:54). *Mourning and crying and pain will be no more* is a reworking of "the disgrace of his people he will take away from all the earth". Because there is no more disgrace, there need be no more tears of humiliation and lamentation. This is all a direct consequence of the fact that *the first things will have passed away*. Life as we know it will be replaced by a completely new order of things.

5. *God himself now speaks from the throne*. In this case, it is not just a loud voice being heard from the throne (as e.g. v 3), but it is made clear that the speaker is God. His words are a reassurance to the suffering and witnessing church, to whom he says, *"See, I am making all things new"*. Of course, God is renewing us daily in this life (2 Cor 3:18, 4:16-18, 5:16-17; Col 3:1-4), but we may all find solace in the knowledge that in the next life *all things* will be made new. So overawed was John at this that he forgot his duty as the recorder of heavenly revelation, and God proceeded to say, *"Write this, for these words are trustworthy and true"*. All scripture is trustworthy and true, and it has all been recorded for our benefit.

6. God continues his declaration, *"It is done! I am the Alpha and the Omega, the beginning and the end"*. All the events that will bring the present age to its final consummation will one day have happened. Everything connected with the past will be over and done with. God is *the Alpha and the Omega*, the first and the last letters of the Greek alphabet. He himself originated history, and at the end he will have completed it (1:8, 17; 22:13). He makes a wonderful promise: *"To the thirsty I will give water as a gift from the spring of the water of life"*. He had made the same promise through the prophets of old (Isa 12:3, 55:1), and had repeated it and amplified it through his Son Jesus Christ (Jn 4:10, 13-14; 7:37-39). It is valid in the heat of the day in this life, as well as in the bliss and joy of the next.

7. God continues speaking in the same vein as his Son: *"Those who conquer will inherit these things"* (2:7, 11, 17, 28; 3:5, 12, 21). All his promises

and all those made by his Son will come to pass; not one will fail (Josh 23:14). Those who are faithful and overcome Satan (12:11) will inherit all things. Furthermore, God says *"I will be their God and they will be my children"*. This is the reassuring ancient covenant formula (Gen 17:7; Ex 6:7; 29:45; Lev 26:12; Num 15:41; Deut 29:13; 2 Sam 7:14; Jer 7:23,11:4, 24:7, 30:22, 32:38; Ezek 11:20, 14:11, 34:24, 36:28, 37:23 and 27; Zech 8:8; 2 Cor 6:16; Heb 8:10). It has been an encouragement to God's people down the ages, and is a good promise to meditate on when we die.

8. But not all will conquer Satan. There are also those who will be content to keep on being deceived by him. They are *the cowardly, the faithless, the polluted, the murderers, the fornicators, the sorcerers, the idolaters and all liars*. Leon Morris points out the aptness of *the cowardly* being placed at the head of this list: "In the circumstances in which John's readers found themselves, courage was a prime virtue. All the more is this the case in that John is speaking now of final realities. To be cowardly before the enemies of God means to lose the things of God at the last. John is speaking not of natural timidity and fear, but of that cowardice which in the last resort will choose self and safety before Christ".

The *faithless* are the untrustworthy who give way during testing times. The *polluted* are those who are made unclean by their participation in heathen practices. The *murderers* are those who mercilessly persecute the people of God. The *fornicators* are those who are impure as a result of sexual sin. The *sorcerers* are those who manipulate others through magical rites, good luck charms and false miracles, such as making an image speak (13:15). The *idolaters* are those who put a living person or a dead idol in the place of the one true God. Last in the list are *all liars*, who exchange the truth about God for a lie (Rom 1:20-23), and end up living a lie. In Revelation truth is commended and falsehood is condemned (2:2, 3:9, 14:5, 21:27, 22:15). It is sad that in our own day numerous church leaders are liars, especially in affluent countries in Europe and North America. Indeed, as Robert Mounce observed, "all eight classes of people mentioned in the verse may refer to professing believers who have apostatised". They are all guilty before God of serious sins. *Their place will be in the lake that burns with fire and sulphur, which is the second death* (it was also mentioned in 20:14).

Even now, as he tries to describe the indescribable glories of the life to come, John cannot forget that there are many who will miss out on them, and who will instead be destroyed in hell.

Meditation: What will not be there in the next Life

The next life will not be an ethereal out-of-body experience. Instead it will be down to earth. We who are God's people will have new bodies (1 Cor 15:35-58), and we shall live in a new earth. As George Eldon Ladd put it, "Biblical thought always places people on a redeemed earth, not in a heavenly realm removed from earthly existence". We should therefore discard the false image of spectral saints sitting on cotton-wool clouds and playing harps. The next life will not be like this. Before John shares with us the vision of what it will be like, he lets us know what will not be there, and he begins with a rather surprising item.

(a) The sea. The news that the sea will be no more (v 1) saddens all those who love the seaside: the consistency of the waves, the cleanness and refreshment of the salty water, the feel of wet sand under their feet, the vastness of it – the sea is such a wonderful part of God's creation. Here is good news for lovers of the sea: there is no reason why it should not exist in the new earth. This is because John is using "the sea" as a symbol. For the ancients the sea was a dangerous place, and some people drowned there. A storm at sea could be a terrifying experience (Ps 107:23-32). Even at its calmest, it was seen as a threatening and restless place. One Bible author compared the sea to nervous and hyperactive troublemakers by writing of "wild waves of the sea, casting up the foam of their own shame" (Jude 13). John is using symbolic language to teach us that there will be no people like that in the life to come. But there may well be a literal sea. If so, its waters will be safe, and it will be great fun. We shall not need to apply sun cream (22:5).

(b) Tears. John goes on to tell us that there will be no more tears. "He will wipe every tear from their eyes" (v 4). At first there will be some tears when we get to the new earth: tears of sadness that some whom we loved are not there, tears as we realise how deep and harrowing were some of the hurts in this life, and tears of disappointment because of the selfishness and pride that marred so much of our lives even as Christians. But God will take his spotlessly clean handkerchief out of his pocket and wipe away all our tears, and then tears will be a thing of the past. John Skinner commented that "Perhaps no words have ever been written that have sunk deeper into the aching heart of humanity than this exquisite image of the divine tenderness".

(c) Death. The last enemy to be destroyed is death (1 Cor 15:26), but destroyed it will be and then "death will be no more" (v 4). In this life, the reality is that one out of one die. Death opens its mouth and swallows people up, one by one. There is a relentlessness about death that depresses us all. Death is the terror of kings and the king of terrors. On the final day, however, it will be God's turn to open his mouth, and "he will swallow up death forever" (Isa 25:8). This promise will be wonderfully fulfilled when God brings about death's destruction. It is a clear expression of the believer's hope of eternal life (Jn 3:16, 5:24, 10:28, 17:3).

(d) Mourning and crying and pain. These three will be no more (v 4). We who are the people of God are privileged to suffer disgrace for the name of Jesus Christ here in this life. We are hindered in our mission by circumstances and by sins – sins of worldly people, and also our own sins. We may be unable to live according to our true dignity, which is as sons and daughters of God (Jn 1:12-13). Instead of delighting in God, at times we will mourn. Instead of worshipping Christ, at times we will cry. Instead of rejoicing in the Holy Spirit, at times we will suffer pain. These sad moments will not recur in the life to come. Our new nature will be fulfilled in a perfect environment once the body of our humiliation has been transformed by Christ so as to conform to his glorious body (Phil 3:20-21).

(e) Cowardice, faithlessness, pollution, murder, fornication, sorcery, idolatry and all lying. These sins are exceedingly serious, especially when committed by professing Christians (v 8). Cowardice may lead believers to be ashamed of Christ and his words (Mk 8:38). Loss of faith may lead them to apostasy (Heb 10:23-25). Giving way to peer pressure may prompt some to participate in activities that will make them unclean in the eyes of God (Eph 5:6-7). It may even prompt them to persecute and murder those who love God (13:6-7). Fornication is strictly out of bounds for those who hold to Christ's name (Eph 5:3-5). Sorcery or witchcraft are likewise deadly for Christian faith, as is the manipulative approach which is associated with them (Isa 47:8-9). Idolatry is an altogether absurd activity, since idolaters become like their idols (Ps 115:3-8). Lying involves aligning oneself with falsehood rather than truth, even though the living God is the God of truth (1 Jn 5:20). Each of these eight sins will lead to the destruction in hell of those who impenitently persist in them. When they are cast into the lake that burns with fire and sulphur which is the second death, red-hot lava will consume every sinner who has obstinately persisted in pride and rebellion.

It is wonderful to think about what we have been saved *for*. We shall enjoy God and worship him forever. We shall spend the numberless years of eternity trying to grasp fully the unfathomable depths of God's love, the self-giving deeds of Christ the Lamb, and the beauty of the endowments given to us by God's Spirit.

Equally, it is wonderful to think about what we will be saved *from*. A future in which restless and selfish individuals behave like a stormy sea, a future marked by tears of grief and shame, a future in which death goes on destroying, a future full of frustration resulting in mourning, crying and pain, and a future in which everyone including ourselves is scarred by selfishness and pride – why, this is not a future that God's people could look forward to. It would be hell.

XLIX

21:9-21 The radiantly holy City

The emphasis now turns from what will not be there in the life to come, to what will. John uses a series of vivid images involving precious jewels and gemstones to impress upon his readers the perfection and purity of the New Jerusalem.

9. *One of the seven angels who had the seven bowls full of the seven last plagues* reappeared. *He went to John and said to him, "Come, I will show you the bride, the wife of the Lamb".* The description of this summons and its wording are very similar to those in 17:1, where John was asked to see the judgement of the great whore, Babylon. George Eldon Ladd wrote, "This can hardly be accidental. John intends a deliberate contrast between the harlot city of the beast and the heavenly city of God's dwelling". Having summoned John to see the bride of the Lamb, the angel will now proceed to show him not the redeemed people of God, but the new holy city of Jerusalem. Because the marriage has now taken place, to see the dwelling of God's holy people is tantamount to seeing them in their glory.

10. *The angel carried John away in the spirit.* John was caught up in a trance. He described it as being *in the Spirit.* This had already happened to him three times (1:10, 4:2, 17:3), and it was invariably accompanied by visions or words granted to him by God. In his vision *he was taken to a great, high mountain* (Ezek 40:2). Perhaps the heavenly city can only be seen from a high vantage point, and Leon Morris suggests that this is the high point of faith. From there, *John saw the holy city Jerusalem coming down out of heaven from God* (v 2). George Caird thought that "Jerusalem can never appear other than 'coming down out of heaven', for it owes its excellence to the condescension of God and not to the building of men".

11. *The city has the glory of God.* Although nothing could be more striking than this wonderful fulfilment of God's promise to his people of old (Isa 60:1-2, 19), John now proceeds to elaborate on it. *The city had a radiance like a very precious jewel, like jasper, clear as crystal.* Its radiant light was like a transparent precious stone. Jasper is opaque, so maybe John was thinking of a diamond. Leon Morris pointed out that "there is often uncertainty on the identification of precious stones in antiquity, as in 4:3" – and, indeed, as in verses 19 and 20 in this passage.

12. *The city has a great, high wall* that makes it completely secure and inviolable. This wall *has twelve gates, and on each gate is an angel.* These twelve angels are celestial gatekeepers, following the prophetic picture of sentinels on the walls of Jerusalem (Isa 62:6-7). Angelic gatekeepers are a mark of dignity. They control who may enter or leave. Entrance into God's holy city is not open to anyone who wishes to enter, but only to those whom God chooses. *On the gates are inscribed the names of the twelve tribes of the Israelites* (Ezek 48:30-34). As Leon Morris pointed out, "the heavenly city is the true fulfilment of Israel's high calling. The ancient people of God are not forgotten in the final disposition of things". The twelve apostles will also feature in the architecture of the city (v 14).

13. *On each of the sides of the city, the east, the north, the south and the west, there are three gates.* The total number of gates is twelve (v 12). The order of the points of the compass is unusual, and it does not quite coincide with the one used by Ezekiel to describe the gates in his vision of the holy city (Ezek 48:30-34).

14. *The wall of the city has twelve foundations.* They presumably hold the twelve parts of the wall that rise in between each adjacent pair of gates. *On the twelve foundations are the twelve names of the twelve apostles of the Lamb.* Leon Morris put it like this: "The combination of the twelve tribes in verse 12 and the twelve apostles is a way of saying that Israel of old and the Christian church are united in God's final

scheme of things. This truth has been brought out in various places in Revelation and it is emphasised once more in the concluding scenes". Christ is here called the Lamb to remind us of the way in which God won our salvation.

15. *The angel who was talking to John had a measuring rod of gold to measure the city and its gates and its walls.* As we have seen previously in 11:1, measuring implies assessing (Ezek 40:3-4, Zech 2:1-2), so the angel will now measure the city and its gates and walls to verify that they match up to God's standards. They will pass the assessment, for this is a holy city (Eph 2:19-22, 1 Pet 2:4-6).

16. The city is a square, and yet it is more than that, for it is a cube. *The city lies foursquare, its length the same as its width; and the angel measured the city with his rod, fifteen hundred miles; its length and width and height are equal.* It is not easy to visualise such a city, for it is both two-dimensional and three-dimensional. Although it constitutes a mathematician's dilemma, the message is clear. In the Old Testament temple, the Holy of Holies where God dwelt was a perfect cube (1 Ki 6:19-20). In the next life all of God's people will live in the Holy of Holies. More than that, we themselves are the holy city, so we shall collectively form the dwelling place of the one true God, together with his Son Jesus Christ and the Holy Spirit of God. We shall be with God and he will live alongside and within us. All of us will be in perfect fellowship with God and with each other.

The dimensions of the city are all fifteen hundred miles, which is 12,000 stadia in the original Greek. The number 12,000 is twelve times the cube of ten. Twelve is the number of God's people both in the Old Testament and the New, a thousand is ten cubed, and ten is the number of completeness. It represents the perfect total of the people of God. In his massive commentary on Revelation, Isbon Beckwith commented that the seer was "struggling to express by symbols the vastness, the perfect symmetry, and the splendour of the New Jerusalem".

17. *The angel also measured the wall of the city, one hundred and forty-four cubits by human measurement, which the angel was using.* 144 cubits is about 70 metres. If this is the height of the wall, it does not fit easily with the height of the city, which is 1,500 miles. If it is its width, it would be over ten times wider than the Great Wall of China, and about three times wider than the impregnable walls of Nebuchadnezzar's Babylon. It is clear that these measurements are symbolical, and maybe the idea John wants to put across is that those who live in the New Jerusalem will be perfectly safe, even though there is obviously no need for any defensive walls once every enemy has been defeated (Isa 54:14).

18. *The wall is built of jasper, while the city is pure gold, clear as glass.* The word for jasper has been used to describe God (4:3), so the wall proceeds from him and tells us something of what he is like. He is a defensive wall around his people, protecting and delivering us from all the evils of this life. This is a most helpful message for Christians who are being sidelined or persecuted. The city itself will be of pure gold. It will shine brightly like crystal-clear glass, which was extremely precious in antiquity. Leon Morris wrote that "John is speaking of the heavenly city as built of the most costly materials" (1 Cor 2:9).

19. *The foundations of the wall of the city are adorned with every jewel,* as in the afflicted city that God loves (Isa 54:11-12). At this stage it would be natural to ask why such lavish decoration is provided for the foundations of a city. After all, the foundations are underground and out of sight. We shall think about this in the meditation that follows. John proceeds to list twelve jewels that decorate the foundations. *The first was jasper, the second sapphire, the third agate, the fourth emerald.* Jasper could well be diamond (see the comment on v 11). Sapphire is either the deep blue stone we call by this name, or possibly lapis lazuli. Likewise agate could also be chalcedony, which is found near Chalcedon in Asia Minor. Emerald is a green stone, highly valued in every age.

20. *The fifth onyx, the sixth carnelian, the seventh chrysolite, the eighth beryl, the ninth topaz, the tenth chrysoprase, the eleventh jacinth, the twelfth amethyst.* Onyx is a layered stone of red and white, used for making cameos. Carnelian is blood-red, used for engraving. Chrysolite is a yellowish topaz. Beryl is sea-green. Topaz is a yellow rock crystal, sometimes the colour of gold. Chrysoprase is an apple-green variety of quartz. Jacinth is a shadowy blue. Amethyst is purple and transparent, and was used in powdered form as an antidote to drunkenness.

The twelve stones may be the same as the ones on the high priest's breastplate (Ex 28:17-21), although a few of the names differ. This may be because John has translated them from Hebrew to Greek. According to Philo and Josephus, these particular stones may have been linked with the twelve signs of the zodiac. If this was so, the sequence of the signs is reversed in John's list, as if to imply that the purposes of God overturn and confound the findings of pagan astrology.

In his book "When Jesus Returns", David Pawson suggested that John's twelve gemstones provide remarkable evidence for the divine inspiration of Revelation. Now that we can produce purer light (polarised and laser), a hitherto unknown quality of precious stones has been revealed. When thin sections are exposed to cross-polarised light (as when two lenses from sun-glasses are superimposed at right angles), they fall into two very distinct categories. The so-called "isotropic" stones (e.g. rubies and garnets) lose all their colour, for they depend on random rays for their brilliance. But "anisotropic" stones produce all the colours of the rainbow in dazzling patterns, whatever their original colour. Remarkably, all the stones in John's list belong to this latter category. Maybe the light will be much purer in the next life. If so, then John's choice of stones was inspired, for at the end of the first century AD nobody knew that different forms of light existed.

21. *The twelve gates are twelve pearls, and each of the gates is a single pearl.* In the background to this was the thought that the heavenly city would contain giant pearls. In a rabbinic writing, the *Baba Bathra*, we read, "The Holy One, blessed be he, will in time to come bring precious stones and pearls which are thirty cubits by thirty, and will cut out from them openings ten cubits by twenty, and will set them up in the gates of Jerusalem". Our minds would boggle if we tried to imagine the size of the giant oysters in which the pearly gates are to be formed, but this is not necessary because the language is symbolic and visionary. *The street of the city is pure gold, transparent as glass.* In antiquity most of the glass produced contained flaws that marred its transparency, but the gold used to build the city is compared to perfect glass. It is absolutely pure gold, and altogether flawless.

Meditation: A Tale of two Cities

(a) A great contrast. In his commentary on Revelation, George Beasley Murray noted that "Revelation as a whole may be characterised as *A Tale of Two*

Cities, with the sub-title, *The Whore and the Bride*". There is a marked contrast between Babylon, the worldly city, which is depicted as a whore, and the New Jerusalem, the heavenly city, which is depicted as a bride. One is of this world and represents the unbridled passion and evil of human beings. The other descends from heaven to the new earth and is the epitome of all that is pure and beautiful. John Stott likewise wrote, "An angel invited John, 'Come, and I will show you the bride', just as another angel had invited him earlier, 'Come, and I will show you the great whore' (17:1). The bride and the prostitute, Jerusalem and Babylon, are set in antithesis to one another throughout the book". It is impossible to belong to both.

(b) An interesting identification. Each city is closely identified with the people who dwell in it. In verse 2 John saw the holy city, New Jerusalem, coming down beautifully dressed like a bride, then in verses 9 and 10 he was invited to see the bride but was shown the city. Robert Mounce put it like this: "The New Jerusalem descends from heaven adorned as a bride for her husband. The adornment is given in detail in verses 11-21. In 19:7 the people of God were presented as the bride; here the same figure is used of the place of their abode, the heavenly Jerusalem". F.F. Bruce likewise wrote, "With a sovereign disregard of rules against mixing metaphors, the beloved community is portrayed as both bride (19:7-8) and city (21:10-27)". Revelation is the story of two women, the whore and the bride of the Lamb. Equally it is a tale of two cities, Babylon and the New Jerusalem. The whore is equated with Babylon, God's people with the holy city.

(c) An angel for all seasons. This section begins with John being approached by an angel who was to "show him the bride". Leon Morris believed the angel might be the same as the one who showed him the judgement of the whore (17:1). John would like us to see that God's servants do not select their tasks. God may send us for judgement or for blessing or for both, one after the other. Either way, we are to go where we are sent, and speak whatever God tells us to speak. John may also have in mind that there is a single divine purpose. It issues in the appearance of the bride of the Lamb, but it necessarily involves the judgement of the whore. It is therefore impossible to reside in both Babylon and New Jerusalem. The way into the latter can only be discerned when we renounce the former. The judgement on sin is the indispensable prelude to the establishment of the city of God. The 19th century poet Christina Rossetti put it as follows: "Hourly, momentarily, there come to me mercies or chastisements. The chastisements are veiled mercies, as it were veiled angels.

The mercies that I name chastisements are no less merciful than those which at once I recognise as mercies". In Revelation, judgement and mercy are inextricably interwoven.

(d) A perfect city. As Richard Bewes observed, "The company of the redeemed people of God is portrayed as a beautiful bride and as a shining city. The bride is united to her husband, Christ, and the city demonstrates perfect unity and union. The images that feature here convey the ideas of perfect purity (v 11), perfect security (v 12), perfect government (v 12), perfect structure (v 13-14), perfect access (v 12, 21), perfect fellowship (v 16, for the cube, like the Holy of Holies, stands for the dwelling place of God), perfect beauty (v 18-21), perfect worship (v 22), perfect vision (v 23-25) and perfect culture (v 26)".

(e) God's treasures. We ourselves may be counted among the trophies of grace that form part of God's personal collection of priceless treasures. These treasures were worth dying for, so God considers them beyond price. The most important event in our life is our entry into God's kingdom, which is here signified by the pearly gates. Blessed be that moment when we first put our trust in Christ! The most important decisions that we make in our lives are those whereby we lay foundations for Christian living, which are here signified by the gemstones on the foundations. Blessed are all those deep roots that we laid down in our aim to walk in purity of life as befits the dwelling place of God! (1 Cor 3:16, 2 Cor 6:16). Like the roots of a tree or the foundations of a building, they are largely invisible. Our giving to the poor and needy is unknown to others, but it is noticed and rewarded by God (Mt 6:2-4). Our prayers are unseen and unheard by others, but they rise up to God who will reward them (Mt 6:5-6). Our self-discipline and self-control are not apparent to others, but they are seen in secret by God, who will reward them (Mt 6:16-18). If a building has foundations made of costly jewels, they will be invisible to all, except to God. He knows and sees what is done in secret. The holy city will retain the pearly gates and the jewelled foundations from this life.

(f) The supreme glory of the next life. We might well ask if there will be anything completely new and special in the next life that we have not come across before in this life. We shall have new bodies, yes, but they will be in continuity with our present bodies. We shall live in a new earth, yes, but it will be familiar and similar to this one, with a heightening of what is good and a complete absence of what is evil. The pearly gates and the jewelled foundations will speak to us of our best decisions in this life, to follow Christ and make use of the means of grace given to us by the Holy Spirit. Will anything be completely new? Oh yes. Just wait and see. Watch this space. John is about to reveal to us the full glory of the next life.

L

21:22-22:5 All Light and no Darkness at all

John describes the glory of the New Jerusalem by affirming that it is full of light. There is no night there. Elsewhere in the Johannine writings we read that "God is light and in him is no darkness at all" (1 Jn 1:5). John is putting across in his own way the truth that in the next life God will move in and live with us. What awaits us in the new earth is so marvellous and so incredible that it is better if we learn about it symbolically. Then we shall be in a position to think laterally and work out for ourselves the full implications of the love and the sheer grace of God.

22. John continues his description of the New Jerusalem with the statement that *he saw no temple in the city*. This is a surprise. It is clear from 3:12, 7:15, 11:19, 14:17, 15:5-8, 16:17 that there is a temple in heaven in which God is enthroned. It is a high and holy place, but there are hints even in the Old Testament that God also has a second home which is more modest (Isa 57:15). One could well think that if God is going to dwell with his people, there would be a temple for him in the midst of the holy city. But John says categorically that this is not the case. In a city that is a perfect cube, modelled on the Holy of Holies, there is no need for a temple: all is holy and God is always served and worshipped. Symbol has given way to reality, and the temple is replaced by God and the Lamb in person.

So John adds an amazing gloss about the city: *its temple is the Lord God the Almighty and the Lamb*. Leon Morris wrote, "The heaping up of the titles, *Lord, God* and *Almighty* is impressive. Each has been used before, but the cumulative effect adds splendour. In the last state of things it is God's presence alone which counts, and that is not confined to any one part of the city. It is characteristic that John adds *and the Lamb*. The Lamb is at the centre of everything throughout this book". It is clear that God is no longer to be set apart from people in a temple.

As the presence of God and the Lamb fills the city, they do not need special housing.

23. Just as there is no need for a temple for God to dwell in, nor is there any need for light if he is present. *The city has no need of sun or moon to shine on it, for the glory of God is its light, and its lamp is the Lamb.* God's glory will be the light of his people (Isa 60:19-20), so luminaries like the sun and moon will be obsolete and unnecessary. Once again the Lamb is on a level with God, this time when it comes to the question of light for God's people (Jn 9:5).

24. *The nations will walk by this light.* This stresses the universality of the city. In the Bible *the nations* is another way of saying "the Gentiles". It is not only the Jews who will be there in the next life, but non-Jews also. We shall find people who belonged to all the countries, tribes, peoples and languages of the world (5:9, 7:9, 11:9, 13:7, 14:6). *The kings of the earth will bring their glory into the city* (Isa 60:3-11). This highlights the pre-eminence of the New Jerusalem. All that is glorious will be there, including whatever is wholesome and beautiful in this life.

25. In the city *the gates will never be shut by day – and there will be no night there.* This city is different from all the cities we have visited in this life. Here and now the gates are open when there is light, but at night they are shut. But in the holy city there is no night, for God is always present and he is the source of perpetual light. It follows that its gates will never shut (Isa 60:11). Anyone who loves God and his Christ will have permanent access to the city where they dwell, and any intrepid explorers who desire to visit the sights of the new earth will be allowed to leave the city and return to it as they please.

26. *People will bring to the holy city the glory and the honour of the nations.* This means that people of every country will bring their homage to God and to Christ, but it may mean more than this. Commenting on verses 24 and 26, John Stott wrote that "We should not hesitate to affirm that the cultural treasures of the world will enrich the New Jerusalem. Nature is what God gives us; culture is what we human beings make of it. Since human beings are ambiguous, so is our culture. Some of it is evil and even demonic, but some of it is also beautiful, good and true. It is this that will adorn the holy city". This bringing of glory and honour by the nations will be the fulfilment of a strand of Old

Testament prophecy (e.g. Isa 60:11, "the nations shall bring you their wealth", and Hag 2:7, "the treasure of all nations shall come"). As F.F. Bruce likewise wrote, "The glory of the church is incompatible with a dead-level uniformity; the variety of national contributions helps to make up her many-splendoured life".

27. It is hardly surprising that after pointing out the perfect dimensions and the variegated magnificence of the New Jerusalem, John returned to a consideration of what will *not* be there. There will be no temple (v 22), no need for sun or moon (v 23), no night and so no locking of the gates (v 25), and finally, in this verse, there will be nothing that is impure or unworthy. *Nothing unclean will enter it, nor anyone who practises abomination or falsehood.* All those objects associated with abuse or sexual impurity or false worship will find no place in the holy city. Nor will certain people, and here John repeats two of the categories he mentioned in verse 8. Those who practice abomination are idolaters, and those who indulge in falsehood are liars. In this life it is important that people worship the Lord their God and serve only him (Mt 4:10, Lk 4:8), and that they speak and live the truth rather than a lie (Jn 17:17). This is because *the only people* that will enter the New Jerusalem are *those who are written in the Lamb's book of life.*

22:1. *Then the angel*, who had spoken to John back in 17:1 and then again in 21:9, *showed John the river of the water of life, clear as crystal, flowing from the throne of God and of the Lamb.* The spring of the water of life is mentioned back in 7:17 and 21:6. It bubbled up from the divine throne and soon became a flowing river. Its water is mentioned again later in 22:17. We shall trace its ancestry in the Old Testament and its fulfilment in the New in the meditation that follows. Its water is clear as crystal, sparkling and brilliant. It is the water of life, and it originates from the throne of God and of the Lamb. Leon Morris noticed that "For the third time in this section John adds *and of the Lamb* to his references to God. He will not let us miss the supreme significance of the Lamb in the final state of things". And John continues by describing the course of the river.

2. The river flows *through the middle of the street of the city*. The redeemed live in the city, beside the source of the life-giving stream that proceeds from the very presence of God, so for them it is convenient to have the

river of the water of life close to their home. *On either side of the river is the tree of life.* This is a reference to the special tree that grew in the Garden of Eden (Gen 2:9, 3:22-24), whose fruit our earliest ancestors were unable to procure because they had eaten the forbidden fruit of the tree of knowledge. But now the tree of life is freely accessible at last, *with its twelve kinds of fruit, producing its fruit each month.* It seems to be a plural tree. John Stott wrote, "Perhaps there is only one tree on each side, but I prefer the view of some commentators, already prophesied by Ezekiel (Ezek 47:7, 12), that many trees of life line both riverbanks along its full length so that, like the water, their fruit will be readily available to all".

Like the fruit of the Holy Spirit which is nine-fold in its nature (Gal 5:22-23), the fruit of the tree of life appears to be twelve-fold. This may relate to the variety and the different character of each of the twelve months of the year in our present life. Something like this variety will be replicated by the fruit of the tree of life. Moreover, *the leaves of the tree are for the healing of the nations.* In this context, *healing* may mean health-giving, so that in some unexplained way the leaves of the tree of life will promote the enjoyment of a full life in the New Jerusalem.

All their past sins forgiven and their hurts healed, people from every nation will join together and delight in life in all its wonderful abundance (Jn 10:10). In this connection it may be significant that the Greek word used for "tree" here is *xylos*, which the apostles Peter and Paul both use when referring to the cross (Acts 5:30, 10:39, 13:29; Gal 3:13; 1 Pet 2:24). This ties in well with John's repeated mention of the Lamb in close conjunction with God in this section (21:22, 23; 22:1, 3).

3. All this is so because *nothing accursed will be found there any more.* The curse of Genesis 3:17-18 is cancelled, because it cannot survive in the presence of God. Also, Jerusalem of old may have been under a ban or curse, which doomed it to destruction by the hands of their enemies, but in fulfilment of an ancient prophecy this would never happen again. It would abide in security (Zech 14:11). Instead, *the throne of God and of the Lamb will be in the holy city, and his servants will worship him.* Where the one true and living God and his Christ rule, there can be nothing accursed. On the contrary, God's servants will worship him.

In fact the verb for "worship" used here is *latreuo*, which means to serve someone you adore and revere. It will be profoundly wholehearted and enriching. As Leon Morris put it, "Heaven is not a place of indolent leisure, but a place where service is rendered, centring on God". But this is not all; there will be more to worship even than this.

4. *They will see his face.* In this life, even Moses was not allowed to see the face of God (Ex 33:17-23). Indeed, no one can see God's face and live. But in the life to come it will be different. God's people will be transformed so that they become completely pure in heart, and in fulfilment of Christ's promise *they will see God* (Mt 5:8). This vision of God will consummate their bliss. There will be nothing between them and him. Furthermore, *his name will be on their foreheads* (14:1). All of their thoughts will concern the One whom they love with all their being.

5. Once again we are told that *there will be no more night* (21:25). This will fulfil the prophecy of Zechariah that there will not be days and nights in the future life, but instead we will enjoy one continuous day (Zech 14:7). We end this section as we began it, with the reassurance that in the New Jerusalem *they need no light of lamp or sun, for the Lord God will be their light* (21:23). Our vision will be both beatific and radiant, with perfect light. John adds the beautiful promise that *they will reign forever and ever.* Leon Morris commented that "It is not said that they will reign *over* anyone, and, indeed, it is difficult to see who their subjects could be. The term indicates a blessed and exalted state. They share in royalty".

Meditation: Pure Light; living Water; the Tree of Life; seeing God

In the New Jerusalem all the good things of this life will be heightened in quality, but in addition there will be some aspects that will be completely new.

(a) The light of life. The light in the next life will be radiant and pure. It will be wonderful to see everything perfectly clearly. Sometimes, when we first put on a new pair of glasses, we experience a foretaste of this. Everything looks sharp, and the colours are vivid. This is what it is going to be like. It will be a double treat to look and see, because everything will be clear and beautiful. The grass will be greener, and when the breeze causes the leaves on the trees to rustle, the sight and sound will be utterly captivating. Similarly, in the holy city our *spiritual* vision will also be perfectly clear. It will be natural for us to see issues

with a right sense of judgement, and to be able to work out which is the best out of various available options. We begin to think rightly in this life, because Christ is the light of the world, and if we follow him we need never walk in darkness, for we will have the light of life (Jn 8:12). Christ is the true light, and he enlightens everyone (Jn 1:9).

(b) The water of life. The flow of living water is plentiful, for it is described as a river through the middle of the street of the city (22:1-2). This utterly refreshing flow was anticipated in the Old Testament (e.g. Ps 46:4, Isa 12:3). Leon Morris thought that John may have had two prophecies in mind: "Zechariah saw 'living waters' going out from Jerusalem (Zech 14:8), and Ezekiel a river which flowed out from the Temple and went down to the Dead Sea, growing deeper as it went and bringing life everywhere (Ezek 47:1-12). All that was foreshadowed in such visions John sees fulfilled". Christ came to bring this vision to fulfilment, starting in this life. He said that anyone who drank from the water that the world gives would thirst again, but that if we drink of the water that he gives us, our spiritual thirst will be quenched, and the water that he gives us will become in us a spring of water gushing out (Jn 4:10, 13-14). What a lovely promise this is! We may be channels of his living water to those around us who are spiritually thirsty. When we feel thirsty ourselves, all we need do is come to Christ and drink deeply from his wells of salvation. We shall be drinking of the Holy Spirit (Jn 7:37-39). This can begin to be true now, in this life, but in the life to come it will happen always.

(c) The tree of life. There it is, at last. Men and women chose the way of death, and so the way to the tree of life was barred to them at a very early stage, in the third chapter of the Bible. It would have been everlasting hell if they had eaten of its fruit after sinning, before Christ had borne away our sins in his body on the tree (1 Pet 2:24). Now, in the very last chapter of the Bible, the tree of life is once more available to people in the holy city, and they may eat from it any time they want, and then they will live forever in the bliss of eternal life (Jn 17:3). In the great drama of the Bible, there is no mention of the tree after Act 1, Scene 3 – until it reappears like a jack-in-the-box in the final and everlasting Scene of the last Act. What a find it will be! We have spent years looking for it, and have longed for the moment when we may reach out and take its fruit for ourselves. It is by God's grace that we shall eat from it, and we shall do so by faith.

(d) The beatific vision that fulfils. In this life we cannot see God face to face. We may see his glory (Ex 33:18, 22), which has been defined as "the outward shining of his inward being". In our mind's eye we may have seen God in the

person and work of his incarnate Son (Jn 1:14, 18; 2:11; 14:9) and glimpsed him in the love with which his people love one another (1 Jn 4:12). But this is to see God dimly, as in a metallic mirror, and to know him only in part. In the next life we shall see him face to face and then we shall know him fully (1 Cor 13:12).

From time immemorial the people of God have looked forward to seeing God as part of their future hope (Ps 17:15). At present there is a shroud over us which prevents us from seeing the beatific vision (Isa 25:7), but when Christ returns the shroud will be lifted and we shall see him as he is (1 Jn 3:2). Only then shall we fulfil the purpose for which we were made, which is to glorify God and enjoy him forever. John Stott had no doubt about the importance of this: he wrote that "This beatific vision is an indispensable part of God's ultimate purpose for his people".

As F.F. Bruce put it, "Here and now the sanctification of believers consists in their being progressively conformed to the likeness of God by the power of the Spirit, as they reflect the divine glory revealed to them in the face of Christ (see 2 Cor 3:18-4:6). John describes the climax of that process, for the beatific vision involves the perfect glorification of those who receive it: 'I will write on you the name of my God, and the name of the city of my God, the New Jerusalem that comes down from my God out of heaven, and my own new name' (3:12)".

We should not be troubled in our hearts. Christ is taking his time as he prepares a place for us. But it is so wonderful that it will prove to be well worth the wait. And if he goes to prepare a place for us, he will come again and take us to himself, so that where he is, we may be also. And we know which way to take to get there. Christ himself is the way (Jn 14:1-6).

LI

22:6-13 The Angel and John testify

The Revelation ends with a triple attestation, first by the angel (v 6, 10), then John (v 8), and later by Christ himself (v 16, 20). These are interspersed with several brief interjections spoken either by Christ or John. Two matters are being stressed in these last sixteen verses: the importance of the whole book and the imminence of Christ's return. We are to study and keep the words of this book of Revelation, for the Lord's long awaited second coming will happen soon.

6. The angel who has been speaking to John and who showed him the river of life now testifies to the reliability of the Revelation. *He said to John, "These words are trustworthy and true"*. These two adjectives, *trustworthy* and *true*, have been used by Christ to describe himself (3:14), and they form one of his names as the victorious rider on a white horse (19:11). Here, towards the end, they probably refer to Revelation in its entirety. Leon Morris suggested that "The whole book, then, is to be relied on". The angel continued his attestation: *"The Lord, the God of the spirits of the prophets, has sent his angel to show his servants what must soon take place"*. This description of God as the God of the spirits of the prophets is unusual. It seems to be related to the phrase "the testimony of Jesus is the spirit of prophecy" in 19:10. There is a definite link between God and true prophets, but to which true prophets does the angel refer?

If it is those of the Old Testament, then no true prophecy ever came by human will alone, "but men and women moved by the Holy Spirit spoke from God" (2 Pet 1:21), and this is the sense in which he is the God of the spirits of the prophets. But Leon Morris thought that it was likely that the prophets of the New Testament were in John's mind. Although "the spirits of prophets are subject to the prophets" (1 Cor 14:32), their inspiration comes from God, and it is this that enables them to declare divine truth. They were being oppressed, and this was a reminder to them that God is not ashamed to be called their God. In their trouble he "sent his angel to show his servants what must soon take place" (1:1). The same God who had inspired all these prophets old and new had given the visions of Revelation to John, and so the entire book is itself a prophecy (v 7).

By reading it, we who are his readers are able to visualise in our minds certain imminent events. This verse does not teach that every event in the vision would happen "soon", but that certain events that had previously been veiled were now unveiled. Resting our faith in the God of the spirits of the prophets, we may pray for Christ's second coming (v 20), and this will help to expedite its arrival.

7. As if to confirm the imminence of his return, Christ now speaks, unannounced: *"See, I am coming soon!"* He then promises a blessing: *"Blessed is the one who keeps the words of the prophecy of this book"*. This is the sixth of seven blessings in Revelation, and the seventh will follow soon in verse 14, probably sooner than Christ's return! We should notice that the book is described as a prophecy. The prophecies in it were not written to satisfy our intellectual curiosity regarding the future, but in order that Christians should *keep the words* of them. To keep the words of the prophecies of this book is not only to retain them in our memory and believe that the events that are symbolised by them will come to pass, but also to regulate our lives by them, to think, speak and act in accordance with them, and to maintain our Christian profession without any compromise. This needs to be said. There are many who are prepared to read the book from beginning to end, but not all are willing to treat Revelation as the word of God. Those who disdain it and fail to appreciate its divine origin will miss out on Christ's blessing.

8. John now adds his own attestation to that of the angel. *I, John, am the one who heard and saw these things.* Leon Morris wrote that "There is an emphasis about the words *I, John*. The previous verses have assured us of the divine attestation. This one assures us that the human instrument vouches for what he has written. He saw certain things and heard certain things. He is not writing at second hand".

   When John had heard and seen these things, he fell down to worship at the feet of the angel who had shown them to him. This second attempt at angel-worship is extraordinary, following as it does on the heels of a previous one which had earned him a rap on the knuckles (19:9-10). In the light of Colossians 2:18 Leon Morris surmised that "It is likely that among the recipients of Revelation there were some who were tempted to this kind of worship. John wants to make it clear that he sees its attractiveness, but it is forbidden. So he repeats the prohibition".

9. Most of the prohibition is couched in words that are identical to those in 19:10. *The angel said to John, "You must not do that! I am a fellow servant with you and your comrades the prophets, and with those who keep the words of this book. Worship God!"* The angel places himself on a similar level to John, the prophets and any readers of Revelation who choose to keep its words. They are all *fellow servants* of God (the word *sundoulos* means "a fellow slave"). Angels tell forth the word of God like prophets, and keep the words of the divine prophecies just as

John's readers seek to keep his words. This means that prophets and those who read them and keep their words rank with the angels as servants of God. But even the great servants of God are not worthy of worship (Acts 14:11-15). As Christ said, "Worship the Lord your God, and serve only him" (Mt 4:10, Lk 4:8).

The fact that John worshipped an angel, not just once but on two occasions, is a salutary reminder that even the beloved disciple who heard and saw all these visions could go astray. We are to "keep awake and pray that [we] may not come into the time of trial; the spirit indeed is willing, but the flesh is weak" (Mk 14:38).

10. The angel added two further commands. First *he said to John, "Do not seal up the words of the prophecy of this book, for the time is near"*. Sometimes when prophets received revelations that did not concern their own contemporaries but some future generation, they were told to seal up the book of their prophecy (e.g. Isa 8:16; Dan 8:26, 12:4 and 9). But John's prophecy was not for some distant generation but for the entire Christian church, including people of his own time. So he was not to put a seal on the Revelation. He was not to keep its prophecies hidden. They were intended for immediate publication. The words that John heard from "the seven thunders" were of a different nature; he was told to seal them up and not to write them down (10:3-4). But the rest of what he saw and heard he did write down. It was to be read by posterity. John reiterates that it is *prophecy*, and that the fulfilment of what he wrote was imminent, for *the time is near*.

11. Secondly, the angel stressed the verifiable fact that when times of crisis come, most people will show forth their true colours and position themselves resolutely either on God's side or on Satan's. *"Let the evildoer still do evil, and the filthy still be filthy, and the righteous still do right, and the holy still be holy"*. As F.F. Bruce commented, "Because the time is short, there will be but little opportunity for repentance and change: the wicked are confirmed in their wickedness (Dan 12:10), the righteous in their righteousness". The angel declares that if evildoers wilfully persist in their evil course, they cannot be diverted. Conversely, when the righteous and the holy persevere in their godly path in spite of the hostility of the ungodly, this is proof that they are what they profess to be. Moreover the return of Christ is certain and it is near, and he will have the last word. He will assess people justly and rightly. There is still time for repentance, but because he is coming soon, the occasion must be seized. This very day, today, if anyone listens to his voice, they should heed it and not harden their hearts (Ps 95:7-8).

12. Christ repeats what he said in verse 7: *"See, I am coming soon"*. He said so back in 3:11, and will say it again in verse 20. There is an urgency about all these repetitions. His return will be unexpected, and this will catch some people out (16:15). Moreover, when he returns there will be an exact requital. *"My reward is with me, to repay according to everyone's work"*. Christ will bring rewards for his servants, and he will give to each of them what is their due, but he will also punish those who persist in impenitent unbelief and disobedience. Everyone will be affected. As we have seen, judgement will be according to works done (2:23, 18:5-6, 20:12, etc. and see also Jer 17:10, 1 Cor 4:5, Eph 6:8, Col 3:23-25).

13. In 1:8 and 21:6, God had declared, *"I am the Alpha and the Omega"*. Christ repeats this and adds that he is also *"the first and the last"*. Then, just as God did in 21:6, Christ likewise adds, *"I am the beginning and the end"*. The three phrases say the same thing. Christ is eternal, just as God is. God and Christ are set apart from every created being. Only Christ is fully like the invisible God.

Meditation: Concerning a Book, a Return and the present Urgency

There are similarities between the prologue and epilogue of Revelation. The book is a true prophecy (1:3; 22:6, 9-10, 18-19) written by a properly commissioned prophet (1:1, 9-10; 22:8-10) in order to be read in the churches (1:3, 11; 22:18) so as to encourage the faithful (1:3; 22:7, 12, 14). As the book nears its end, John wants to remind us of some important truths that he wants us to take for granted.

(a) The book carries a guaranteed authority. The book of Revelation is attested by a divine angelic messenger, by John who wrote it, and by Christ himself. This amounts to an extremely powerful testimony, which it would be folly to ignore. As Richard Bewes clearly put it, the prophecy is to remain unsealed in view of the impending return of Christ, and this will determine our attitude to it. We are not to disobey it (v 7), nor are we to hide it (v 10), nor are we to add to it or subtract from it (v 18-19). The reason is the same in each case: Jesus Christ has said, 'I am

coming soon'. The prophecy is complete and important. It is not a work of fiction. It is not just a collection of dreams and visions. It is a true account of the absolute victory of Christ, who has triumphed over evil, selfishness, and death. It is written for all to read, but perhaps especially for Christians who are being persecuted in the world or sidelined in the church because they trust in him.

(b) The imminence of Christ's return. Three times he said "I am coming soon" (v 7, 12, 20), but almost 2,000 years have gone by since this prophecy was written. Nor is this problem peculiar to Revelation. Paul wrote that the time was short and so people should adjust their lifestyle accordingly (1 Cor 7:29-31). In one of his early letters he seemed to include himself with the people who would still be alive when Christ returned (1 Thess 4:15). As Robert Mounce commented, "One way to solve the problem of this as-yet-unfulfilled expectation is to hold that God is more concerned with the fulfilment of his redemptive purposes than he is with satisfying our ideas of appropriate timing. All the issues which will find their fulfilment at that point in time yet future when history will verge into eternity, are also being fulfilled in the ever advancing present. The end and the beginning are only two of the perspectives on the same great adventure. The final overthrow of evil was determined from the beginning and has been in force since the defeat of Satan by the sacrificial death of Christ and his triumphant resurrection".

This prompts the important question, how then should we interpret the adverb 'soon' in Christ's words, 'I am coming soon'? John Stott proposed the following answer: "We need to remember that, with the great events of Christ's birth, death, resurrection, exaltation, and sending of the Holy Spirit, the new age has dawned (e.g. Lk 11:20, Acts 2:17, 1 Cor 10:11, 2 Tim 3:1, Heb 1:2, 1 Pet 1:20, 2 Pet 3:3, 1 Jn 2:18), and that there is now nothing on God's eschatological calendar before the *Parousia*. The *Parousia* is the very next event on his timetable. 'It was, and still is, true to say', wrote Charles Cranfield, 'that the *Parousia* is at hand'. Thus Christian disciples are characterised by faith, hope and love. Faith apprehends the *already* of Christ's achievement. Hope looks ahead to the *not yet* of his salvation. And love characterises our life *now* in the meanwhile. Therefore 'soon' may be chronologically inexact; but it is theologically correct".

F.F. Bruce wrote, "In the Christian doctrine of the last things, the imminence of the end is moral rather than chronological. Each successive Christian generation, for aught that is known to the contrary, may be the last. In that sense the time is always near (1:3). It is therefore the path of wisdom for believers to be ready to meet their Lord. When he comes and institutes the final judgement, the verdict will be the one which people by their attitude to God and their way of life have already incurred for themselves (Jn 3:18). Until then the 'water of life' remains available to anyone who wishes to take it as a gift (22:17)".

(c) *The need for urgency about eternal issues.* John appeals to people and warns them against the background of the final judgement that draws near. When Christ returns, he will "repay according to everyone's work" (v 12). In the beginning he initiated all things as the agent of creation, but at the end he will consummate all things as the Judge. For he is the Alpha and the Omega, the first and the last, the beginning and the end (v 13). Christ repeats what he said about himself in 1:17. This claim is so tremendous that only God could make it, and indeed has made it (1:8, 21:6). With such an extraordinary claim repeated by Christ, John begins and ends his book. For Christ is the living one, who was dead but is now alive forever and ever, and he has the keys of Death and of Hades (1:18).

From Christ's perspective the end is so near that time is quickly running out to change the character and habits of people. Evildoers will continue to do evil, and the filthy-minded will go on thinking their filthy fantasies. But on the other hand, the righteous will continue to do what is right, and the holy will go on living holy lives (v 11). Now of course this does not mean that Christians are not to continue their task of making disciples of all nations. Although time is not on their side, there is still the opportunity for the impenitent to turn to Christ in repentance and faith. John's point is that because the end is at hand, people will have to reap the consequences of what they have done and of how they have lived. The overall trend of their lives will speak either for or against them on the fateful day when Christ comes to be their judge. A time will arrive in every person's life when any radical change will be impossible because his or her character has already been determined by a lifetime of habitual action. Either death or the return of Christ, whichever comes first, will foreclose any possibility of alteration. The deliberate choice of every person will define and fix their unalterable fate. May God give all those who know him the courage and the love to reach out to those who do not yet know him, and to reason with them until they repent and believe, before the sands of time finally run out.

LII

22:14-21 Two severe Warnings and two final Attestations

This final section of Revelation contains two severe warnings (in verses 15 and 18-19), and two attestations by Christ himself (in verses 16 and 20). There is also an invitation in verse 17 addressed to the thirsty, to come and take the water of life as a gift, and a farewell in verse 21 by John, who asks for the grace of the Lord Jesus to be with all the saints, meaning those who are leading holy lives.

14. After Christ's words in verses 12-13, there is a change of speaker, and John pronounces the last of the seven benedictions in the book: *Blessed are those who wash their robes.* Here the verb *wash* is in the present tense, and this suggests a repeated and ongoing washing. There is also an initial washing, once and for all (7:14), but Christians face daily pressures to conform to this world, and in practice they find regular cleansing from sin almost essential (1 Jn 1:7, 9; Jn 13:9-10). All cleansing from sin, whether it be the initial once and for all justification or the subsequent regular cleansing when they confess their sins, is accomplished only by the blood of Christ. But why is God's blessing said to depend on them washing their robes? *Because then they will have the right to the tree of life and may enter the city by the gates.* From the tree of life they may take and eat its fruit, and then they will enjoy everlasting life (v 2). When they arrive at the pearly gates, they may enter the holy city through them (21:25, 27). This is a great double blessing – to be given eternal life, and to have unhindered access into the presence of God. Both are given to Christians freely through Christ's atoning work on the cross.

15. Another stern warning now follows, which all readers should take careful note of, for the contrast could not be greater with those whose way into the city is barred: *Outside are the dogs and sorcerers and fornicators and murderers and idolaters, and everyone who loves and practices falsehood.* The *dogs* are those who do evil deeds (Ps 22:16, Phil 3:2), though what these deeds are is not made clear. Perhaps they are false church members who are out to discredit godly people. The other categories in this list also appear in 21:8 – the *sorcerers* are those who manipulate and control others through magical rites, the *fornicators* are impure as a result of sexual sin, the *murderers* are the ones who persecute the people of God, and the *idolaters* worship a living person or a dead idol instead of the one true God. At this point Leon Morris noticed that "the separate mention of *loving falsehood* and *practising it* makes up a total of seven types of sinner, quite in John's manner". In other words, we have another heptad – and this one really is the final one! On a serious note, we may heed Robert Mounce's words: those who love and practise falsehood will become like their leader who is "Satan, the deceiver of the whole world" (12:9, 13:13-15, 16:14 and John 8:44).

16. Once again Christ speaks, and this is emphasised by the opening four words, *"It is I, Jesus, who sent my angel to you with this testimony for the churches"*. The angel who guided John through the various visions of the book of Revelation is now authenticated by Christ himself. It was at his behest and on his authority that the angel spoke (1:1). The angel was sent to give testimony to the churches. The word *you* is plural; John heard the words first, but they were not only for him. The message was not a private one, which is why it was not to be sealed (v 10). It was for all Christians in the Christian era. As in chapters 2 and 3, the Spirit is speaking to the churches through it. *Jesus then describes himself* once again *as the root and the descendant of David* (5:5) and as *the bright morning star* (2:28). Here, towards the end of Revelation, are two further echoes of the letters to the seven churches.

The expression *the root and the descendant of David* is peculiar to this book. King David is being compared to a tree, and Christ would then be the root and shoot of David, both his originator and his descendant (Isa 11:1, 10). F.F. Bruce wrote, "His eternal being (verse 13) and his Davidic descent are set in paradoxical juxtaposition (see Mk 12:35-37, Rom 1:3-4)". Moreover, since Christ is *the bright morning star*, his presence heralds a new day for his hard-pressed readers, and he will remain forever with every believer who has persevered to the end (2 Pet 1:19). The ultimate reward of all his true followers is to be with their Lord always (Mt 28:20). Nothing could be better than that.

17. At this stage the Holy Spirit, everywhere present in Revelation as the one who inspired John's words and who illuminates them to his readers, makes one of his rare explicit appearances. He joins together

with the true church. *The Spirit and the bride say, "Come"*. Austin Farrer commented that "The Spirit and the bride are one voice – what inspiration prompts, the body utters". But to whom are they speaking? It must be to unbelievers. But what of the next line? *And let everyone who hears say, "Come"*. This is an invitation to new believers to join together in the outreach, so that all of God's people will be one as they present Christ. John then fills out the gospel invitation: *And let everyone who is thirsty come* (Jn 6:35). *Let anyone who wishes take the water of life as a gift* (Jn 7:37-39). Leon Morris suggested that "the deepest needs of people will be met, though those needs must be felt". The word for *as a gift* is an adverb meaning "freely" or "without charge". The invitation is an urgent one. When Christ returns, it will be too late to respond.

George Eldon Ladd pointed out that "There will come a time when repentance is no longer possible. But that hour has not yet come; and until that day, the Spirit issues the invitation through the prophets for people everywhere to come, and the church re-echoes the invitation, saying, *Come*". The invitation is then echoed by those who hear and heed it, and at the end John himself adds his own words to invite those who read his prophecy to come and drink of the water of life. As F.F. Bruce wisely commented, "In a book so full of judgement, it is exhilarating to find the gospel invitation extended so plainly and freely at the end. No assessment of the Christian quality of Revelation is adequate which does not give full weight to these words. The blindest idolater, the fiercest persecutor, were he Nero himself or, we might add, the most abject apostate, may come if he wishes, and accept the full and free benefits which the gospel provides".

18. Now comes the final warning of the book, and it is a very necessary one. The words of the Revelation are divinely inspired. They are not to be tampered with. So John decisively pronounces a curse: *"I warn everyone who hears the words of the prophecy of this book"*. Leon Morris encouraged us to "notice that it is called *the prophecy*. This is more than a product of human genius. It comes from God". Furthermore, John addresses *everyone who hears the words of the prophecy*. He makes it perfectly plain that he is warning them. This book is not to be modified in any way (Deut 4:2, 12:32; Prov 30:6; Jer 26:2). So *if anyone adds to the words of Revelation, God will add to that person the plagues described in this book*.

John is not concerned about possible scribal errors of transmission, nor with minor errors of judgement in interpreting his message. What is preoccupying him is deliberate distortions and perversions of what he says. These falsities may arise when additions are made which downplay the overall thrust of his prophecy. Life will not be happy for those church leaders who teach their flock to treat writings other than the Bible in the same way that they treat the Bible itself. To do this is to add to the words that God has inspired, and very possibly to contradict them. Such leaders will be held responsible if their flock roams astray as a direct result of their unhelpful additions to God's word (Ezek 33:7-9).

19. There is also the opposite error. Not only should people not add to the words of this book, they should also not subtract from them: *if anyone takes away from the words of the book of this prophecy, God will take away that person's share in the tree of life and in the holy city, which are described in this book.* Leon Morris has noted that "the same verb is used of the person's taking away from the words of the prophecy as of God's taking away *their share*. There is a fitness about this. The punishment fits the crime". In our own day, in numerous churches in affluent countries, there is a great deal of taking away from the word of God. The present author was once invited to tea with a kind hostess and a retired Anglican bishop. Amidst all the pleasantries the bishop advised him, in so many words and in a serious tone, never to read the book of Revelation because "it contains so much that clearly runs contrary to Christian teaching". This was not a matter of taking away a few words; it was a premeditated attempt to expunge the whole book!

20. Christ now speaks for the last time. He is *the one who testifies to these things.* The idea of testimony is important in Revelation, but also in the other Johannine writings (John 1:7-8, 3:11, 3:32-33, 5:31-40, 8:13-14, 15:26, 19:35, 21:24; 1 Jn 5:6-13, 3 Jn 3, 12). As in verse 16, Christ again claims that the testimony for the churches that can be found in this book is from him. Then he says, *"Surely I am coming soon!"* His words are greeted with the heartfelt prayer that he will do just this: *Amen. Come, Lord Jesus.* The word *Amen* is a Hebrew participle which may mean "So be it" and indicates agreement with what the previous speaker has said. The prayer that follows is equivalent to the Aramaic expression *maranatha* which is translated as "Our Lord, come!" in 1 Corinthians 16:22.

The last note struck in the book of Revelation is the longing for the return of the Lord. John's ultimate confidence is not in human efforts for the betterment of mankind, but in God who is alive and active. His love and his wrath are revealed in the events of human history, and he played a decisive part in that history when he sent Jesus Christ to be one of us and to be stricken for our transgressions. One day God will send him back to us, this time not in great weakness but as a warrior who will finally defeat death and evil, and wind up this present age. It is only by holding fast to our faith in him that we retain our true hope in this present world.

21. The final words are *the grace of the Lord Jesus be with all the saints. Amen.* This would be a typical ending to a first century Christian letter. Maybe John felt that his apocalypse was akin to a letter. After all, it contained the letters to seven churches in Asia Minor. He salutes his readers with the longing that the grace of the Lord Jesus Christ might remain with all holy people. He puts the emphasis on universality. He reminds us that *all* Christians, not just a few, depend on God's grace. Every good thing finds its origin in the vast and undeserved grace of God.

Meditation: Why is there a Curse near the end of Revelation?

The persecuted and sidelined people of God have enjoyed many passages in this book that tell of some of the blessings which God has already given to them, as well as other blessings which he will lavish on them in the life to come. But there have also been many sombre passages that tell of the judgement of God on those who oppose God and his people. Persecuted Christians are not to seek revenge on their enemies who oppose, abuse and oppress them. It is hurtful to be despised in these ways for being a follower of the one true God. He has revealed himself first of all in scripture, and supremely in his Messiah and servant Jesus Christ. Our first reaction on encountering these enemies may be to seek revenge for such great outrage, but this would be wrong. Our second reaction may be to curse those who have spiritually abused us. Jesus Christ left matters in the good hands of God.

Perhaps a proper Christian reaction is to realise that the enemies of God and of Christ have placed themselves under a curse. This means that the abused have no need to curse back, since their abusers are already under a curse because of their hatred of God and his word. When we finally take this to heart, our desire for revenge and vindication will gradually turn to pity. Those who are under God's curse are the most pitiable people in the world. We shall want to pray for them to come to Christ and take the water of life as a gift (v 17). If we pray in this way, we shall be obeying Christ's injunction, "Love your enemies and pray for those who persecute you, so that you may be children of your Father in heaven: for he makes the sun rise on the evil and on the good, and sends rain on the righteous and the unrighteous" (Mt 5:44-45).

What curses have the enemies of God and of Christ placed themselves under? If we point them to the curses that may be found in the Old Testament, they might argue that the Old Covenant curses no longer apply to those who have placed themselves under the terms of the New Covenant. So they show no interest in Old Testament curses (e.g. Deut 28:15-68, and the imprecatory psalms such as Psalms 69:22-28, 109:6-20, and 139:19-22). We might turn to the New Testament, where we could point to the curses on those who do not love Jesus as Lord (1 Cor 16:22), those who preach a different gospel than the one which is based on God's grace (Gal 1:8-9), those who rely on their own works to be right with God (Gal 3:10), and those who presume to add to or subtract from scripture (verses 18-19).

But nowadays many enemies of God also have serious problems accepting the Book of Revelation and the letters of the Apostle Paul, and they declare that we should not quote from these writings, just as we should not quote from the Old Testament. In their view such curses cannot be the word of God for sophisticated believers in the 21st century. So we shall inevitably end up by pointing them to curses pronounced by Jesus Christ: on those whose religion is just an act or show put on to impress others (Mt 6:2-6, 16-18; 23:13-36); or those whose unscriptural teaching causes young disciples to sin (Lk 17:1-2); or those who show no care or love for the poor and needy (Mt 25:41-46, Lk 6:24-25); or those of whom all speak well (Lk 6:26); or those evildoers who profess to follow Jesus Christ but whom Christ never knew (Mt 7:21-23). We might also point out that half of Jesus Christ's thirty recorded parables either have the judgement of God as their main theme or else assume its inevitability. We might remind them that the most severe statements about hell in the whole Bible were pronounced by Jesus Christ, and that to be damned means to be under the curse of God. At this stage these enemies of God will raise their hands in despair rather than lose face, and they will usually refuse to continue their dialogue with us because of our "intransigence".

When God's enemies curse us, our first and foremost duty must be to pray for them (Lk 6:27-28, Rom 12:14). Perhaps their curse will rebound on them or turn into a blessing for us (Gen 12:3, Deut 23:4-5, Neh 13:2, Ps 109:28, Prov 26:2). But the curses of our Lord have eternal consequences (Mt 25:41), so occasions may arise when it is both right and loving to point out to these enemies the curses that they have placed themselves under (Lk 17:3).

The curses in verses 18-19 are not aimed at those outside the church, who have not studied God's word and have never been faced with the good news of Christ. For them the message is "Let everyone who is thirsty come". They are aimed at those in the church who refuse to meet God's demands and Christ's challenge to be his obedient disciples, even though they insist on bearing the name of Christ. As a result, these nominal Christians feel obliged to manipulate and twist God's word. They add to it numerous permissions that enable evil-doers to do what it forbids, and they subtract from it anything that might cause them – or any outsider – any offence. Their theology is flawed because they consider that since God is loving, he is bound to tolerate actions that he has said are evil. To believe this is to disregard his holiness altogether. God is, indeed, love, and he does indeed love us. But God is also holy, and the love with which he loves us is holy love.

It is therefore appropriate that the very last thought from the book of Revelation concerns God's blessing on those who live holy lives. It is set forth beautifully and concisely in the last verse. "The grace of the Lord Jesus be with all the saints. Amen". Richard Bewes wrote, "This final sentence is a prayer for strength and grace on behalf of God's people, in the trial of today's arenas, of whatever form. Wherever we are called to be, and whatever adversity we may be called to face, the Lamb is still in the midst of the throne and the past is atoned for. The rider on the white horse is in control and inspires our pilgrimage. The bright morning star is there before our gaze. And tomorrow belongs to us!"

APPENDIX 1

The Heptads of Revelation

One of the most noticeable traits of the book of Revelation is the predilection of its author, John, for arranging his material in sevens. Four of the heptads are very obvious and well known: the seven churches of chapters 2 and 3, the seven seals of chapters 6 and 8:1-5, the seven trumpets of chapters 8:6-9:21 and 11:15-19, and the seven bowls of chapter 16. But there are several other heptads in the book. Some are difficult to spot because they involve the sevenfold appearance of the same word or theme in different sections. Here is a list of 36 heptads noted by the present author during the course of writing this commentary.

Heptad 1. The Son of God is called *Jesus* 14 times in Revelation. This is a heptad twice over, for $7 \times 2 = 14$. The first such reference comes in 1:1.

Heptad 2. The Son of God is called *Christ* seven times in Revelation. The seven references come in 1:1, 2, 5; 11:15; 12:10 and 20:4, 6.

Heptad 3. The *seven blessings* in Revelation. They come in 1:3, 14:13, 16:15, 19:9, 20:6, 22:7 and 22:14.

Heptad 4. The *seven churches* in Revelation. The first mention of them comes in 1:4, and they are dealt with in detail in chapters 2 and 3.

Heptad 5. The *seven spirits*. This is John's way of referring to the Holy Spirit. He does so in 1:4, 3:1, 4:5 and 5:6. John is referring to the sevenfold endowment of the Spirit of God mentioned in Isaiah 11:2 (see the Meditation for section VIII).

Heptad 6. The *throne of God* is mentioned 42 times in Revelation. This is a heptad six times over, for $7 \times 6 = 42$. The first mention of it is in 1:4. Also the word *throne* appears a total of 49 times in Revelation, and $49 = 7 \times 7$, which is a heptad of heptads or a "squared heptad".

Heptad 7. The *seven golden lampstands.* John sees the glorified Christ patrolling them (1:12), and Christ informs us that they represent the seven churches (1:20).

Heptad 8. The *seven stars* in Christ's right hand (1:16). They are explained by Christ as representing the "angels" or essential natures of the seven churches (1:20).

Heptad 9. A group of *seven angels* is mentioned seven times in Revelation. This is a heptad of heptads (1:20, 8:2, 8:6, 15:1, 15:6-8, 16:1 and 21:9).

Heptad 10. There are seven mentions of *white clothing* in Revelation. They come in 3:4-5, 18; 4:4; 6:11; 7:9, 13 and 19:14.

Heptad 11. *Four living creatures*, resembling a lion, an ox, a man and an eagle, appear seven times in Revelation (4:6-8, 5:6, 6:1, 7:11, 14:3, 15:7 and 19:4).

Heptad 12. The scroll (or scrolls, see comment on 5:1 on p. 66-67), sealed with *seven seals*, which were opened by the Lamb one by one in chapter 6 and in 8:1-5.

Heptad 13. The Son of God is called *the Lamb* twenty-eight times in the book of Revelation. This is a quadruple heptad. The first such reference comes in 5:6.

Heptad 14. The Lamb has *seven horns* (5:6). A horn is a symbol of power and the number seven denotes completeness, so the Lamb is completely powerful.

Heptad 15. The Lamb has *seven eyes* (5:6). His vision is all-encompassing, and there is nothing that can escape his searching gaze. He can see into our thoughts and intentions as if he had X-ray eyes.

Heptad 16. The extent of Christian mission is to include *every tribe and language and people and nation* (5:9, 7:9, 10:11, 11:9, 13:7, 14:6 and 17:15). The four words vary and so does their order, but John uses a phrase like this seven times.

Heptad 17. The glorified Lamb of God is worthy to receive *seven rewards*: power, wealth, wisdom, might, honour, glory and blessing (5:12).

Heptad 18. *The altar in heaven* is mentioned seven times in Revelation, namely in 6:9; 8:3, 5; 9:13; 11:1; 14:18 and 16:7.

Heptad 19. There are *seven classes of people*, six of which are great or powerful, who must face God and Christ on the Day of Judgement (6:15).

Heptad 20. Angels ascribe *seven qualities* to God, each preceded by the definite article in Greek: the blessing, the glory, the wisdom, the thanksgiving, the honour, the power and the might (7:12). This list is very similar to the one in Heptad 17.

Heptad 21. *Seven trumpets* are blown, one after the other, by angels who herald the temporal judgements of God (8:6-9:21, 11:15-19).

Heptad 22. *The bottomless pit* is mentioned seven times in Revelation, namely in 9:1, 2, 11; 11:7; 17:8; and 20:1, 3.

Heptad 23. The *seven thunders* sound out their message, but John is forbidden from writing it down (10:3-4). This is a mysterious heptad. We do not know what these seven thunders are, nor what their message was, nor why John was not permitted to include it in Revelation.

Heptad 24. The Son of God is called *Lord* seven times in the book of Revelation. The references are 11:8, 14:13, 15:4, 17:14, 19:16, 22:20 and 21. God the Father is called *Lord* fourteen times. The word *Lord* appears a total of twenty-one times. There are several heptads here, since 7 = 1 x 7, 14 = 2 x 7 and 21 = 3 x 7.

Heptad 25. There are *seven significant signs* in Revelation chapters 12-14. In one sense, they form the heart of the book. See section XXVIII, p. 146-151.

Heptad 26. The dragon, who is Satan, has *seven heads*. He is aspiring to be like God, for seven is God's number (12:3).

Heptad 27. The dragon also wears *seven diadems*, one on each head, signifying the great power he has been given over all the nations (12:3).

Heptad 28. The beast, like the dragon, has *seven heads*, for he likewise aspires to be like God (13:1).

Heptad 29. *Seven visions or calls* that relate to the coming judgement in 14:6-20 (in verses 6-7, 8, 9-11, 12, 13, 14-16 and 17-20).

Heptad 30. *Seven different angels* who either proclaim judgement or play a part in bringing it about in 14:6-20 (in verses 6, 8, 9, 14 & 16, 15, 17 & 19, and 18).

Heptad 31. John sees the angels bearing *the seven plagues* (15:1, 6).

Heptad 32. These angels are given *seven golden bowls* full of the wrath of God, who lives forever and ever (15:7).

Heptad 33. The seven heads of the beast are *seven mountains*, i.e. the Seven Hills of Rome (17:9). In John's time the beast was identified with Rome.

Heptad 34. The seven heads of the beast are also *seven kings* (17:9). If the kings stand for emperors, they could well be Augustus, Tiberius, Caligula, Claudius, Nero, Vespasian and Titus. But they may equally represent *seven empires*, for example those styled as the Old Babylonian, Assyrian, New Babylonian, Medo-Persian, Greco-Macedonian, Roman, and the seventh one which stands for all the anti-Christian governments after the fall of Rome.

Heptad 35. John lists *seven evils that will be no more* in the life to come: the sea (21:1), death, mourning, crying and pain (21:4), anything accursed (22:3) and the night (22:5).

Heptad 36. John lists *seven types of people who are barred from entry* into the holy city: dogs, sorcerers, fornicators, murderers, idolaters, lovers of falsehood, and those who practice falsehood. (22:15).

APPENDIX 2

The Trinity in Revelation

In heaven God is worshipped without ceasing as one who is *"Holy, holy, holy"* (4:4-8). This trisagion suggests that God is three in one, and there are strong hints that John holds on to firm Trinitarian beliefs throughout the book of Revelation.

(a) God the Father. The first thing we learn about him is that he is eternal, for *he is, he was and he is to come* (1:4). He is therefore *the Alpha and the Omega*, and what is more, *the Almighty* (1:8). God the Almighty can be heard but not seen. It is true that John discerned a form seated on the divine throne, but he appeared to be *like jasper and carnelian* (4:2-3). His dazzling radiance makes a more detailed description impossible. The throne on which he sits and reigns is a throne of grace surrounded by a rainbow. Around it we see 24 other thrones for exalted heavenly beings called "elders". There are also four living creatures resembling a lion, an ox, a man and an eagle (4:4-10). The elders and the four living creatures reappear, and the latter will usher in the judgements of God, both temporal and final.

God the Father is the great Creator and Sustainer of the universe who is *worthy to receive all glory, honour and power* (4:11), and even more besides (7:12). He created heaven and what is in it, the earth and what is on it, and the sea and what is in it (10:6). He is addressed as *the sovereign Lord, holy and true*, and is invoked as the avenger of blood (6:10). On the great final day he will reward his servants, the prophets and saints and all who fear his name, both small and great, and he will destroy those who destroy the earth (11:18). He is worthy of praise because of the greatness of his deeds and the justice of his ways, so it is perfectly right and proper for us to fear him and glorify his name, for he alone is holy (15:3-4).

God the Father is the Holy One who is perfectly just in all his judgements, for he gives to those who shed the blood of saints and prophets exactly what they deserve (16:6). He remembers the iniquities of the impenitent and worldly (18:5). The whole of Revelation deals with his judgements, both temporal and final. The opening of the seven seals reveal temporal judgements allowed by God to help us to apprehend reality (6 and 8:1-5), the blowing of the seven trumpets announce more serious temporal judgements sent by him as warnings to lead us to repent (8:6-9:21 and 11:15-19), and the pouring of the seven bowls result in widespread final judgements ordained by God as just retribution for the unrepentant (16).

(b) God the Son. It is he who is being manifested in the book of Revelation. He is Jesus Christ, the faithful witness, the firstborn of the dead and the ruler of the kings of the earth, who loved us and freed us from our sins by his blood (1:5). He walks among the seven churches, which glow with his light (1:12-13, 20). He is dressed in priestly garments, his wise head and hair are white as snow, and his eyes are penetrating like a flame of fire. His feet carry him where he wills, for he is inescapable, and his voice is deep and dependable. He holds his churches, with their failings and encouragements, in his hand. His words are as sharp as a sword, and his face is like the sun shining with full force (1:13-16). It is no wonder that when John saw him, he fell at his feet as though dead (1:17), but Christ promptly reassured him by proclaiming himself to be the living one who was dead, but is now alive forever and ever, and who has the keys of Death and Hades (1:18).

Later on Christ is described as both *the Lion of the tribe of Judah and the root of David* (5:5), and then makes his appearance – not as the Lion but as *the Lamb* (5:6), which is by a long way John's favourite title for him. Just as God the Father is worthy to receive worship, so is the Lamb. He has seven horns and seven eyes, meaning that both his power and his vision are perfect. He is worthy to take the book of destiny and open up its seven seals, and he is also worthy to receive every honour and reward, because by his blood he ransomed for God saints from every part of the world (5:9-12). The Lamb does proceed to open the book of destiny (6:1-17, 8:1-5), and when he breaks the sixth seal, we learn, paradoxically, that one of his attributes is wrath (6:16). On the last day those who have rejected God will be terrified by the sight of God's face and by the wrath of the Lamb.

Salvation belongs to the Lamb just as much as it does to God (7:10). It is the Lamb who will be the shepherd of God's people, and who will guide them to springs of the water of life (7:17), both in this world and the next (21:6, 22:1-2).

Christ will return. He has promised that he will come *soon* (3:11; 22:7, 12, 20) and that his return will be unexpected, like a thief who comes in the night (16:15). In a vision of Christ's militant and victorious return, John describes him by means of four names: *Faithful and True, the name that no one knows but himself, the Word of God* and *King of kings and Lord of lords.* His appearance is fearsome: his eyes are like flames of fire, and on his head are many diadems; he is clothed in a robe dipped in blood; and from his mouth comes a sharp sword with which he will strike down the nations. He will judge and make war in righteousness; he will rule the nations with a rod of iron; and he will tread the wine press of the fury of the wrath of God the Almighty (19:11-16).

God has entrusted all judgement to his Son, and it is he who will be the judge of all people at the Final Judgement. Those who know him and love him may be confident that their names will be found written in the book of life (20:11-15).

(c) God the Holy Spirit. He is described as *the seven spirits who are before God's throne* (1:4, 3:1, 4:5 and 5:6). Like the Father and the Son he is in the Godhead, and his function is to execute the will of God and to shine the spotlight of glory on Jesus Christ, making him real to his people. He also acts as both our sanctifier and teacher. His ministry on our behalf is all about enabling us to have a perfect vision of the Lamb. In the book of Revelation he makes few explicit interventions (see 2:7, 11, 17, 29; 3:6, 13, 22 and 14:13, 19:10, 22:6), but towards the end we read that the Spirit and the bride say "Come" (22:17).

Tom Wright has written helpfully about the role of the Holy Spirit: "The Spirit has been a mysterious presence throughout John's book: sometimes sevenfold, sometimes 'the Spirit of prophecy'. So much of the focus has been on God and the Lamb. We might have thought, if we weren't careful, that John believed in a Binity rather than a Trinity. How wrong we would have been. It is the Spirit that enables the bride to be the bride. It is the Spirit that enables the martyrs to keep up their courage and bear true witness. It is the Spirit that inspires the great shouts and songs of praise. The Spirit goes out from God's throne and, breathing into and then through the hearts, minds and lives of people of every nation, tribe and tongue, returns in praise to the Father and the Lamb. This is as Trinitarian as it gets, and the bride is caught up in that inner-divine life, so that when she says 'come!' to her beloved we cannot tell whether this is the Spirit speaking or the bride, for the answer is both. The Spirit of the Messiah enables his bride to be who she is, lovely in limbs, and lovely in eyes not his". The Spirit is rarely seen in Revelation because of his humility and the self-effacing nature of his ministry.

John has written elsewhere of the Holy Spirit's desire to guide God's people into all the truth and to glorify Christ (Jn 14:16-17, 15:26, 16:13-15). It is helpful to think of him as the divine spotlight. Amid the darkness he shines the light on all that is true, and particularly on Christ who is the truth (Jn 14:6). A spotlight does not shine on itself, and this is why there are few mentions of the Holy Spirit in Revelation. By this the Holy Spirit exemplifies the humility of God, but in fact he is all over the place. It is he who inspired every word in Revelation, and when God's people study the book, it is he who lights it up for them, illumining their minds with God's truth, and thereby becoming our Sanctifier and Teacher.

Here is a prayer to the Trinity, based on a prayer that John Stott used first thing in the morning during his final years:

**

Almighty and everlasting God,
Creator and Sustainer of the universe,
I fear you, I thank you, I praise you, I worship you, and I love you.
Jesus Christ,
Lamb of God and Lord of lords,
I fear you, I thank you, I praise you, I worship you, and I love you.
Holy Spirit,
Sanctifier and Teacher of the people of God,
I fear you, I thank you, I praise you, I worship you, and I love you.

**

Glory be to the Father for his holy love and his holy word,
And to the Son for his self-giving and his holy intercession,
And to the Holy Spirit for his sevenfold endowment,
As it was in the beginning, is now, and ever shall be,
World without end, Amen.

**

Heavenly Father, I pray that this day
I may live in your presence and please you more and more,
Bearing fruit in every good work. Amen.
Lord Jesus Christ, I pray that this day
I may deny myself,
Take up my cross
And follow you. Amen.
Holy Spirit, I pray that this day your fruit will ripen in my life:
Love, joy, peace,
Patience, kindness, goodness,
Faithfulness, gentleness and self-control. Amen.

**

Holy, blessed and glorious Trinity, three persons in one God,
Have mercy on me the sinner. Amen.

**

APPENDIX 3

The Portrait of the Christian in Revelation

Christians are loved by God. Christ has freed us from our sins by his blood, and made us to be a kingdom of priests serving his God and Father (1:5-6). We share in Jesus the persecution and the kingdom and the patient endurance (1:9).

Like the Ephesian Christians, we are to be known for our service, our endurance and our belief (2:2). However, like them we are liable to lose our first love. When this happens, we are to remember, repent and return (2:4-5). Good as it is to learn and teach sound doctrine, this must always be accompanied by a deep realisation of God's amazing grace to us sinners (2:2, 6).

Like the Christians in Smyrna, we shall learn what true riches are from times of poverty (2:9), and our faith will be refined in times of affliction. We know that we are to be faithful even unto death, if this should be God's will for us (2:10).

Like the Christians in Pergamum, we shall be enabled to hold fast to Christ's name even if we have to live and work where Satan's throne is (2:13). We may encounter all manner of weird and insidious temptations to indulge in idolatrous practices and the misuse of God's good gift of sex (2:14). If we lapse, there is a way back to God from the darkness, but we must repent (2:16).

Like the Thyatiran Christians, we shall find the temptations of the world very alluring. There will even be false prophets in the church calling us to be realistic and adopt some of the standards by which the world rules its people (2:20-22). In order that we may keep close to Christ, we must ask him to search our minds and hearts and guide us in the way of eternal life (2:23, 28).

Like the Christians in Sardis, we shall be tempted to rely on past glories and on our present reputation. But there is a difference between reputation and reality, between what we fondly think of ourselves and what God thinks of us. If we focus on our appearance and reputation, this is bound to lead to hypocrisy, but if we place ourselves under God's searching gaze, he will enable us to be real (3:1-3).

Like the Philadelphian Christians, we shall pray for and make good use of open doors of opportunity for passing on the good news about Christ, and we shall not deny Christ's name (3:8). Instead we shall endeavour to keep his word of patient endurance and to hold fast to what we have already made our own (3:10-11).

Like the Christians in Laodicea, our faith may sometimes become insipid and lukewarm (3:15-16). Material prosperity may make us feel autonomous, with no desire to be helped by God, when the truth is that we are wretched, pitiable, poor, blind and naked (3:17). We need to keep coming to Christ continually for true riches, for God's righteousness and for a proper vision of service (3:18). Nothing can compare with true fellowship with the humble and risen Christ (3:20).

Several Christians are called to join the noble band of martyrs, and God has a special message for them. We hear it when the Lamb opens the fifth seal of the book of destiny (6:9-11). The martyrs naturally and rightly await the moment of vindication when God will avenge their blood. How much longer must they wait? The answer is, until their number is complete, until evil has reached its height and spent itself. Christians are not to seek revenge, since vengeance belongs to God. But because it is his prerogative, God is committed to bring about just retribution and to put right every wrong. He has promised that he will do this, and has left multiple warnings to those who persecute us of the judgement that awaits them. He will keep all his promises and fulfil all his warnings.

Christians are marked with God's seal on their foreheads (7:3-8). We must all face the great ordeal, but we shall come out of it spotless, for we have washed our robes and made them white in the blood of the Lamb (7:14).

Christians are to be men and women of prayer. Our prayers will rise to God like sweet-smelling incense, and will trigger the release of his judgements (8:3-5).

Christians are to read their Bibles. We shall find that this will leave a bittersweet taste. It will be sweet as honey initially, for there is very good news in the Bible for all who know and love God. But later there will also be a bitter taste, because there is also woeful news of judgement to come for those who remain impenitent (10:8-10). In the meantime, God makes his sun rise on the evil and the good, and sends rain on the righteous and the unrighteous. Some of his temporal judgements will affect the whole world because of their ecological nature (8:6-13).

Christians are to measure or assess their church (11:1-2). Our measuring rod for evaluating churches is God's yardstick, which Christ used when he composed his letters to the seven churches (chapters 2 and 3). The divine standard involves the altar and the worshippers, which speak of our consecration.

Christians are to bear witness to Christ. We may speak with God's authority, and our testimony will sometimes result in the overthrow of evil and sometimes in its magnification and exaltation (11:3-10). In either case the final victory will belong to Christ and to his suffering witnesses (11:11-13).

Christians are to engage in the intense spiritual battle against Satan (chapter 12). We shall need to recharge our spiritual batteries regularly, and we may do this by fleeing into the wilderness, to a place prepared for us by God, where we shall be nourished (12:6, 14). We shall overcome the accuser of Christians by the blood of the Lamb and by the word of our testimony, for we shall not cling to life even in the face of death (12:11). The reason why Satan wars against us is that we keep the commandments of God and hold the testimony of Jesus (12:17, 14:12).

Christians have had their names written in the book of life of the Lamb that was slaughtered from the foundation of the world (13:8). We have faith in God, and so we endure (13:10). We have the Lamb's name and his Father's name written on our foreheads, and this reflects the way we think (7:3, 14:1). We will be with God on Mount Zion on the last day, and not a single one of us will be lost (7:4, 14:1). Only we shall be able to sing the new song of the redeemed before the throne, for only we know what it is like to be redeemed (14:3). We are spiritual virgins for we have not indulged in idolatry; we follow the Lamb wherever he goes; we have been redeemed as sacrificial first fruits dedicated to God and the Lamb, and our words have been found to be truthful and wholesome (14:4-5).

Christians will conquer the beast and its image, and will rise above the number of its name. We shall sing the song of Moses and of the Lamb, praising God for the perfection of his deeds and his ways. We shall affirm how proper it is to fear God and glorify his name, for he alone is holy (15:2-4).

Christians long to be ready for Christ's return. Because he will come like a thief, a special blessing is promised to those of us who stay awake and keep wearing our robe of righteousness instead of denuding ourselves and exposing ourselves to shame (16:15). We therefore resolve to shun all unrighteousness.

Christians are preparing to sing the heavenly chorus of worship (19:5-8). We fear God, whether we are small or great, and we worship the One who reigns. This fact leads us to rejoice and to give him all the glory. We are his bride, and because the day of our marriage to Christ is drawing near, we gladly wear the robe of righteousness that he has given us.

Christians are blessed and holy. We share in the first resurrection, which is our rebirth and renewal by the Holy Spirit. The second death will have no power over us, because we are priests of God and of Christ (20:6), and our names will be found written in the book of life (20:15).

Christians heed the warnings of Christ. We do not wish to be left outside (22:15) and we know the danger of adding to or subtracting from God's word (22:18-19). We therefore study it avidly. This is no problem – indeed, studying God's word is one of our greatest delights, and we love to meditate on it day and night. As a result we find that in spite of every affliction we endure, God is prospering us in unimaginable ways. We love God. We have met him in Christ. As we read God's word and do as he says, the Holy Spirit keeps pointing us to Christ, making him wonderfully real. And as we get to know Christ better and better, we also get to know God – and to know God and his Son Jesus Christ *is* eternal life (Jn 17:3).

In conclusion, here are two helpful tips for Christians, for which the present author is indebted to the book *The Best that I can be* by John Oswald Sanders:

First, Christians are to strive and persevere in prayer. Our prayers will help to expedite the end (8:1-9), and this will lead to Satan's final destruction (11:15-19, 20:7-10). The world derides us because of our prayers – prayer is such a feeble activity. But as the Methodist minister Samuel Chadwick wrote, "Satan dreads nothing but prayer. The number one concern of the devil is to keep the saints from praying. He fears nothing from prayerless studies, prayerless work, prayerless religion. He laughs at our toil, mocks our wisdom, but trembles when we pray".

Christ taught us to model our prayers on what we call the Lord's Prayer. This is a *comprehensive prayer*, covering every aspect of life, both from God's point of view and ours. It is a *universal* prayer, appropriate to the needs of people of every tribe and language and people and nation. It is a *simple* prayer, meaningful even to the young, the illiterate and the severely handicapped. It is a *profound* prayer, whose themes range over eternity and plumb the deepest aspirations and thoughts of people. It is a *brief* prayer, its statement in Matthew 6:9-13 totalling a mere 58 words in the New Revised Standard Version.

In the Lord's Prayer we learn the proper spirit in which we should offer prayer to God. We should pray in an *unselfish* spirit, for we are addressing "our Father", and not "my Father". We should pray in a *filial* spirit, for we are the children of God approaching our Father. We should pray in a *reverent* spirit, yearning that his name may be hallowed. We should pray in a *loyal* spirit, desiring the spread of his kingdom. We should pray in a *submissive* spirit, seeking his will and not our own. We should pray in a *dependent* spirit, realising that it is he who supplies our everyday needs. We should pray in a *penitent* spirit, asking him to forgive our sins. We should pray in a *forgiving* spirit, in our turn forgiving those who have wronged us. We should pray in a *humble* spirit, trusting God to help us to resist temptations and tests. We should pray in a *victorious* spirit, for he will deliver us from the evil one.

What is more, the prayer embraces all our relationships: *child and father* ("Our Father"), *worshipper and God* ("Hallowed be your name"), *subject and king* ("your kingdom come"), *servant and lord* ("Your will be done"), *suppliant and benefactor* ("give us"), *sinner and saviour* ("forgive us"), *traveller and guide* ("lead us"), *adventurer and rescuer* ("deliver us"). Praying like this will bring all our relationships into focus. In these and in other ways, Christians are to strive and persevere in prayer.

Secondly, Christians are to be consecrated to God. We are to offer ourselves to him in sacrifice at his altar (6:9, 8:3-4, 11:1). We are to present our bodies to him as a living sacrifice (Rom 12:1). This is a decisive act, but we may need to repeat it. To consecrate ourselves is a conscious decision, and many Christians have been helped by thinking through a form of words about consecration, and then using it as a prayer to devote them-selves afresh to God. Matthew Henry is well known for having written a six volume commentary on the Bible in the first part of the eighteenth century, but not many of his readers are aware that he found it a very great help to consecrate his life to God at a young age. Here is the simple state-ment of personal consecration that his father encouraged him and his siblings to use in their early years:

> *I take God the Father to be my God;*
> *I take God the Son to be my Saviour;*
> *I take the Holy Spirit to be my Sanctifier;*
> *I take the Word of God to be my rule;*
> *I take the people of God to be my people;*
> *And I do hereby dedicate and yield*
> *My whole self to the Lord:*
> *And I do this deliberately, freely, and forever. Amen.*

According to Hebrews 10:5-7, it appears that Jesus Christ may have dedicated himself to God the Father using an even simpler prayer, found in Psalm 40:7.

> *Here I am; in the scroll of the book it is written of me.*
> *I delight to do your will, O my God; your law is within my heart.*

APPENDIX 4

Who exactly were the Nicolaitans?

The answer that most commentaries give to this question is that the *Nicolaitans* were the followers of a man called Nicolaus or Nicholas. Irenaus wrote that they owed their origin to Nicolaus, a proselyte of Antioch, who was one of the seven deacons appointed by the apostles in the primitive church (Acts 6:5). Victorinus of Pettau, who wrote the earliest surviving commentary on Revelation around AD 260, refers to the *Nicolaitans* as "false and troublesome men who, as ministers under the name of Nicolaus, had made for themselves a heresy, to the effect that what had been offered to idols might be exorcised and eaten, and that anyone who had committed fornication might receive peace on the eighth day".

Leon Morris was quite unconvinced by these suggestions, and regarded them as plausible conjectures or speculations. He wrote that, etymologically, the name *Nicolaitans* combines 'victory' and 'people'. Moreover, in Hebrew it is possible to derive a similar meaning from the word *Balaam*, so one might conjecture that the Balaamites (2:14) were similar to the Nicolaitans (2:6, 15). Furthermore, the practices of the Balaamites and the followers of Jezebel (2:20) were much the same, so it appears that this latter group was also akin. Although he admitted that it could not be proved, it was Leon Morris's considered opinion that all three – Nicolaitans, Balaamites, and followers of Jezebel – were connected, while not being identical. So his suggestion was that they were "not the enemy from outside openly seeking to destroy the faith. The false teachers claimed 'not that they were destroying Christianity but that they were presenting a new and modernised version of it' (Barclay). This is the insidious fifth column, destroying from within". In our own day there are many instances of these renewed attacks on the church from within, and the book of Revelation once again proves to be the word of God for the church as it is held in contempt by intruders who have stolen into it (Jude 4), just as was the case back in the first century.

There is a gloss to this interpretation of the etymology of the word Νικολαΐτης, pronounced *Nikolaitēs*. Working independently of Leon Morris, Andrew Miles pointed out to the present author that the first half of the word is derived from the Greek word for victory, *nikos*, which relates to Nike, goddess of victory, who was worshipped in Asia Minor in the first century. The second half is derived from laos, meaning a group of people, and this is reflected in our modern word *laity*. Therefore *Nicolaitans* need not be followers of one Nicholas, but they could instead be followers (the people) of Nike, the pagan goddess of victory. If this was the case, they must also have engaged in the idolatrous feasts and fornication that were associated with her cult. This in its turn receives support from another definition in Thayer's Greek lexicon, where *Nicolaitans* is translated "destroyers of the people". In the context of the appearance of this term in 2:15 this links up satisfactorily with the immediately prior mention of Balaam, who provoked the Israelites to commit idolatry by first alluring them with the temporary bliss that would be theirs when they gave themselves over to sexual relations with pagan Moabite women (Num 25:1-3, 31:8, 15-18).

It is not surprising, and it may be more than a mere coincidence, that in Hebrew *Balaam* means "failure of the people" or "not of the people". When we conjoin the references to Balaam and the Nikolaitans in 2:14-15, it seems that the letter to the church at Pergamum was addressed to a mixed congregation of Christians from both Hebrew and Gentile backgrounds. This might have been a powerful means of uniting those groups in Christ through their shared historical experience, and of promoting cultural and moral humility amongst the faithful.

Andrew Miles did some further research and discovered an article on the internet from 2022, about a significant archaeological discovery made in 1925. Digging in Izmir's Bergama district, archaeologists unearthed a column from the ancient city of Pergamum, with the figure of Nike holding her skirts with her hands. She is shown with wings, a dress and laurel leaf motifs. The marble column is believed to be around 2,000 years old and was one of the first artefacts brought to the Izmir Archaeology Museum. It is now being shown to the public for the first time in nearly a century. Further details and some interesting photographs may be found via the following link: https://www.albawaba.com/editors-choice/greek-cult-nike-makes-it-turkey-1486423

All of this may indicate that the Nicolaitans were literal worshippers of Nike, and participated in services held as part of her cult. But in a book like Revelation, which is so full of symbolism, it may also be a veiled criticism of some Christians who were so obsessed with success in the church that they could be compared to the worshippers of Nike, the goddess of success. If so, this has a contemporary ring in our own day, when the top priority of church leaders is to draw people into the church at all costs. This prompts many in the church to regard success as more important than personal holiness and faithfully following Christ.

But how and why does the modern cult of Nike come about? Church leaders are aware that the Biblical message continues to put many people off (as it always has), with its insistence on repentance and holy living. Therefore worldly church leaders see fit to ditch the good news and to replace it with social welfare. Victory and success are perceived by church members in terms of people coming to the church for various social activities, but not in terms of them coming to serve and worship God out of fear and love for him.

The outcome of this emphasis on the social side of the gospel is that orthodoxy is being abandoned in a wholesale way by certain church leaders, in a misguided attempt to strip the Christian message of anything that might cause anyone any offence. What is being discarded includes the "bad news", which is the truth that everyone has sinned and fallen short of the glory of God, and the corresponding "good news", which is the truth that Jesus Christ died as our substitute in order to propitiate God in his holy anger against sinners. In the affluent west, it is a sad fact that nowadays the bad news is seldom preached, and when a few tentative attempts are made to preach the good news, the message no longer concentrates on presenting us with Christ as our Saviour from the penalty of sin, or with the Holy Spirit as our Saviour from the power of sin. Church leaders even appear to have lost the Christian hope that one day God will completely deliver them from the very presence of sin by giving them new bodies in a new earth.

It is only too clear that in Revelation John does not shirk either the bad news or the good. As a result of his courageous and forthright presentation of Christ as not only the victor over Satan but most especially as the Lamb of God, millions of members of the persecuted and suffering church continue to be comforted by the last book of the Bible, and to find that their hope is renewed by it. And many opponents of the gospel, including the Anglican bishop I mentioned on page 296, feel obliged to continue in their efforts to discourage people from reading it.